COBOL PROGRAMMING

COBOL PROGRAMMING
A STRUCTURED APPROACH

PETER ABEL
British Columbia Institute of Technology

Reston Publishing Company, Inc.
Reston, Virginia
A Prentice-Hall Company

Library of Congress Cataloging in Publication Data

Abel, Peter
  Cobol programming, a structured approach.

  Includes index.
  1. COBOL (Computer program language) I. Title.
QA76.73.C25A23   001.64'24   80-10488
ISBN 0-8359-0833-X

© 1980 by Reston Publishing Company, Inc.
A Prentice-Hall Company
Reston, Virginia 22090

10 9 8 7 6 5

Printed in the United States of America

CONTENTS

v

PART II   BASIC COBOL

PREFACE

Programming in COBOL: A Structured Approach offers a new and better approach to COBOL, the most commonly used business programming language. The most elementary features of COBOL are introduced first with a simple example program. After only one chapter of COBOL (Chapter 2), the student is able to write a simple program by concentrating on only the statements necessary to write such a program and by temporarily using the simple ACCEPT and DISPLAY statements for input/output. The text adds new concepts gradually with program examples, and consequently the student is never overwhelmed by the topic.

Structured programming is introduced early. Even before formally discussing the topic, the text adopts and illustrates structured programming features: indentation of code, meaningful names, and organization into main logic and subsidiary sections. By the time Chapter 7 describes structured programming, the student is already accustomed to its features.

A problem in current COBOL texts is omission of specific topics. Thus, one book omits programming style and strategy, another omits control break logic, and another omits advanced handling of tables or disk files. Ideally, one text should cover all of these essential topics, and *COBOL Programming: A Structured Approach* does just this.

Although COBOL is intended to be a universal language, there are two main reasons for the variety of COBOL versions:

1. Differences in computer design (hardware).
2. Differences in operating systems (software).

How does a textbook handle this situation? Because the IBM system is the most common computer system used in the data processing industry, the programs in this text have been designed with IBM features. However, the text points out features that are unique to IBM and that deviate from ANS standards. Your compiler may have some differences from the examples in this text in the following areas:

1. Debugging aids.
2. SELECT statements that define input and output files.
3. Definition of arithmetic data in Working-Storage.
4. Specifications for page overflow.
5. Disk devices and disk file organization methods.

These areas represent a small portion of a COBOL program; consequently, students should be able to easily adapt the material in this text to their compiler version. Students should also use the manufacturer's COBOL reference manual along with this text.

In the text, a reference to the IBM 370 or 360/370 implies the general IBM computer series based on the 360. This includes the 3000 series released in 1977 and the 4300 series released in 1979.

ORGANIZATION

Chapters 0 and 1 contain elementary material on computers and programming. Those familiar with another language can skip these chapters or use them as a review. Chapters 2 through 5 cover the basics of COBOL, representing 80 percent or more of standard program coding. Chapters 6 and 7 are concerned with programming style and the use of PERFORM in structured programming. From this point on, the chapters can be studied in various sequences. (Chapter 8, Report Design, is independent of COBOL programming and may be referenced at any time.) The following chart indicates the relationships of the chapters. For example, Chapters 9 and 10 in a box means that Chapter 9 should be read before Chapter 10.

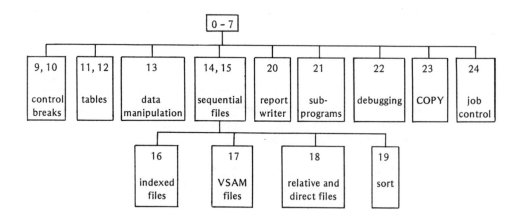

NOTATIONS USED IN THIS TEXT

Some COBOL statements allow a number of options; the text shows their general format according to the following pattern:

Uppercase words	Words in uppercase, such as SPACES and READ, are COBOL reserved words. They must be spelled correctly and used in a program only according to COBOL specifications.
Lowercase words	Words in lowercase are generic terms that represent words or symbols that the programmer supplies.
Brackets [ ]	Brackets indicate that the enclosed entries are optional and may be included or omitted.
Braces { }	Braces enclose two or more vertically stacked items, one of which the programmer is to select.
Ellipses ...	Ellipses immediately following a pair of brackets or braces indicate that the programmer can optionally repeat the enclosed material.

For example:

$$\underset{required}{\text{ADD}} \quad \underset{choice}{\left\{ \begin{matrix} \text{identifier-1} \\ \text{literal-1} \end{matrix} \right\}} \quad \underset{\substack{optional\ and\ choice}}{\left[\left\{ \begin{matrix} \text{identifier-2} \\ \text{literal-2} \end{matrix} \right\} \right]} \quad \underset{\substack{can\ repeat \\ previous\ entry}}{...} \quad \text{identifer-3} \quad \underset{optional}{\text{[ROUNDED]}}.$$

ACKNOWLEDGEMENT

The author is grateful for the assistance from all those who contributed typing, reviews, and suggestions and to IBM for permission to reproduce some of their copyrighted materials. The following materials are printed with permission, and with modifications, from publications copyrighted in 1972, 1973, 1975, and 1978 by International Business Machines Corporation as IBM form numbers GC20-1649, GC20-1684, GC28-6396, and GA33-1515: Figures 0-3, 8-1, 14-1, 14-7, Appendix B, and general formats of COBOL statements.

PETER ABEL

PART I
COMPUTER FUNDAMENTALS

CHAPTER 0

INTRODUCTION TO COMPUTERS

OBJECTIVE: To examine the internal characteristics of the digital computer, its input/output devices, and the function of the stored program.

INTRODUCTION

Computers, like other automated devices, were developed to replace human labor. There are two classes of computers, *analog* and *digital*. The *analog* computer measures physical variables such as rotation speed, water pressure, and electric current. Speedometers, steam pressure gauges, and barometers are good examples of analog computers. The *digital* computer works with digits to perform calculations. Unlike the analog computer that can perform only one function, the digital computer can perform many functions through the use of a *stored program*, which is a set of instructions that the computer executes. Another program can replace the stored program at any time to perform a different function. This text uses the term *computer* to mean the common digital computer.

The modern digital computer using the stored program was developed in the 1940s to provide fast, accurate calculations to solve complex problems. Since that time the computer has made its impact in two main areas: scientific and business. In the scientific area, the computer performs calculations for applications such as bridge and building designs, simulation models of the national economy, and statistical studies of the population. In the business area, the computer processes and controls large volumes of data (data processing). Common business applications include accounting, billing, sales analysis, inventory and production control, and airline reservations. In addition, government agencies make use of computers for income tax, pension, depreciation, and many other reports.

What can a computer do? The computer has the ability to deal with data in the form of numeric values and alphabetic characters. The computer can perform arithmetic and can make comparisons. Assume, for example, that a computer installation maintains data about customers on disk storage in the form of a record for each customer, each record containing customer number, name, address, balance owed, and credit limit. The computer, if programmed accordingly, can read each customer record and compare the balance owed against the credit limit. It can also add all customer balances and print a final total. But remember that the computer can process only data with which it is provided, and only according to the instruction steps with which it is programmed.

Some of the advantages of the computer are as follows:

- It provides solutions and reports that otherwise may be impossible to achieve and can provide both technical innovation and better control over business activity.
- It provides faster answers, which give better return on investment and better control over data.
- It provides more accurate answers and, consequently, a more reliable base for decision making.
- It often provides for lower operating costs, sometimes because there are fewer people performing routine functions, but mostly because of benefits listed in the preceding points.

These advantages are not always achieved. The computer is no panacea for the problems of business and industry. Its success depends on the planning, experience, effort, skill, and cooperation of many people.
—

BINARY NUMBER SYSTEM

The basic numbering system of computers is in binary format. A decimal (base 10) number has ten digits: 0 through 9, but a binary (base 2) number has two: 0 and 1. For any number system, the position of the digit determines its value. Consider the decimal number 1111:

$$\text{decimal } 1111 = (1 \times 10^3) + (1 \times 10^2) + (1 \times 10^1) + (1 \times 10^0)$$
$$= 1000 + 100 + 10 + 1$$

Unlike a base-ten number, a binary number uses the base of two. Consider the same number, 1111, expressed in binary:

$$\text{binary } 1111 = \text{decimal } (1 \times 2^3) + (1 \times 2^2) + (1 \times 2^1) + (1 \times 2^0)$$
$$= 8 + 4 + 2 + 1 = 15 \text{ decimal (or } 2^4 - 1)$$

As another example, the value of the decimal number 1010 is determined by

$$\text{decimal } 1010 = (1 \times 10^3) + (0 \times 10^2) + (1 \times 10^1) + (0 \times 10^0)$$
$$= \quad 1000 \quad + \quad 0 \quad + \quad 10 \quad + \quad 0$$

A decimal digit zero has no value, nor has a binary digit zero. The same number 1010 expressed in binary is

$$\text{binary } 1010 = \text{decimal } (1 \times 2^3) + (0 \times 2^2) + (1 \times 2^1) + (0 \times 2^0)$$
$$= \qquad 8 \quad + \quad 0 \quad + \quad 2 \quad + \quad 0 \quad = 10 \text{ decimal}$$

In this way, a binary number using only digits 0 and 1 can represent any decimal value. The computer represents the digits 0 and 1 as "off" or "on" conditions. It is this simplicity that makes binary the important fundamental numbering system of computers.

BITS

One storage location of a computer is called a *byte* and consists of a specified number of *bits* (an abbreviation for "binary digit"). A bit is similar to a binary digit, since a bit can be "off" (zero) or "on" (one). To illustrate, consider a computer in which each storage location or byte consists of four bits to represent data:

8	4	2	1
0	0	0	0

A storage location (byte)

All bits off (0000) means zero. If only the bit numbered 1 (the rightmost one) is on (0001), the value in the location is 1. If only bit 2 is on (0010), the value is 2. If both bits 1 and 2 are on (0011), the value is 3. Combinations of bits provide values 1 through 9.

Actually, each byte has one extra bit, called a *parity bit,* that is not used to represent data. On the typical computer, each byte must have *odd parity,* which means that the number of bits on must always be an odd number. For example, the value in a byte is 7: bits 4, 2, and 1 are on. Because this is an odd number of bits (3), the computer sets the parity bit off:

Parity bit off

P	8	4	2	1
0	0	1	1	1

Assume that the value in a byte is 9: bits 8 and 1 are on. To force odd parity the computer sets the parity bit on (3 bits again):

Parity bit on

P	8	4	2	1
1	1	0	0	1

It is possible, although rare, that an on bit condition is somehow "lost" and becomes off. When processing the contents of a byte, the computer automatically checks the parity. If the parity is even, the computer signals a warning and stops processing; the computer may require servicing. Setting bits on and off is an entirely automatic process over which the programmer has no control.

A reference to bit capacity does not normally include the parity bit. Thus, the previous example would be a *four-bit* code. Computers use a six-bit code, a seven-bit code, or an eight-bit code. The more bits, the more characters a byte can represent. For example, a seven-bit code can represent 2^7 or 128 different characters, and an eight-bit code can represent 2^8 or 256 characters. Only occasionally do COBOL programmers need to be concerned with the bit format of their computer.

COMPUTER SYSTEM

Computers have evolved radically since the first primitive models, and although there are many manufacturers and types, their basic structure remains the same. Figure 0-1 illustrates the four main components of a computer: input/output, main storage (memory), arithmetic/logic, and control. Arithmetic/logic and control together form what is called the *Central Processing Unit (CPU)*.

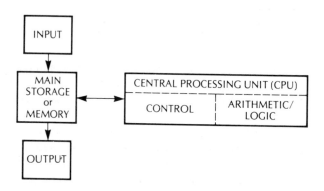

FIGURE 0-1   Basic Computer Components.

Input/Output

The computer must be able to access new data. The computer "reads" data into its storage from input devices such as card readers and disk storage. Also, because the computer must communicate its results to the user, it "writes" data from storage onto devices such as printers and magnetic tape.

Main Storage, or Memory

A computer program is written to solve a specific problem. The program consists of *instructions* (such as read, add, and compare) and *data* (numbers used in calculations, and areas used to develop answers and to read input data). The instructions and data may be on punched cards that are read or *loaded* into the computer storage. These instructions in storage are the stored program that directs the computer to read input data, make calculations, and write output. Figure 0-2 illustrates a possible organization of the stored program in main storage.

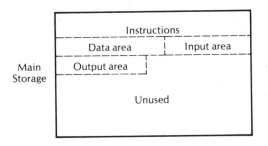

Main Storage

Areas may be anywhere in storage in any sequence.

FIGURE 0-2   Map of Program in Main Storage.

The size of storage varies considerably by computer model, from as little as a few thousand storage locations (bytes), to millions. Storage size in an installation depends on the volume of data and the complexity of the problems. An instruction may require only a few locations, whereas an area for data may require hundreds of locations. Each storage location (byte) has a specific address (numbered consecutively from location 0, the first one) that enables the control unit to locate stored instructions and data as required. The amount of available main storage is expressed in sizes such as 16K, 32K, 64K, and up to sizes as large as 1000K, where K = 1024 bytes. Different computer models provide various storage capacities.

Here is a simple example of the add operation using storage locations, which is to add the number 005 to the number 225. Assume 005 is in locations 2338, 2339, and 2340, and 225 is in locations 2263, 2264, and 2265:

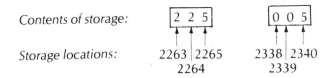

Contents of storage: | 2 2 5 | | 0 0 5 |

Storage locations: 2263 | 2265   2338 | 2340
                            2264   2339

Assume that an add operation is the letter *A*. The instruction to add the *contents* of locations 2338–2340 to the *contents* of locations 2263–2265 would be

| A | 2 2 6 3 | 2 3 3 8 |

(This is similar to the way that most computers work.) Locations 2263–2265 now contain the number 230. Locations 2338–2340 still contain the number 005, unchanged by the add operation. This instruction itself would require nine storage locations consisting of three parts. The letter A is the *operation,* telling the computer what function to perform. The location numbers 2263 and 2338 are *operands* that specify which storage positions to process.

When storage locations are directly referenced by number, it is known as programming at the *machine language* level. But few people today code in machine language. Programming languages like COBOL use statements that are similar to the English language, and a special translator program converts the COBOL statements to machine language.

The Central Processing Unit (CPU)

The CPU consists of two main units: an *arithmetic/logical unit* and a *control unit.* The *arithmetic/logical unit* performs addition, subtraction, multiplication, division, shifting, and moving. Its logic capability enables the programmer to code instructions that can compare one value in storage to another and permits the program to change the sequence of instruction execution. The *control unit* directs and coordinates the computer system. It controls the arithmetic/logic unit, input/output units, transfer of data into and out of main storage, and the location of data and instructions to be executed. The time required to transfer data is known as *access time,* which is measured in thousandths of a second (milliseconds), millionths of a second (microseconds), or even billionths of a second (nanoseconds). The type and number of input/output devices, the type and complexity of arithmetic/logic circuitry, the size of storage, and the access time vary considerably by computer model.

Instruction Execution

A computer program consists of instructions and data areas, all kept temporarily in main storage during execution. An instruction is comprised of at least two parts:

1.   The operation—the function the computer is to perform such as read, add, or move.
2.   The operand(s)—the address of a data area, instruction, or input or output unit.

The computer extracts the instruction to be executed from main storage and delivers it to the CPU. For example, the instruction could be read data (the operation) from a specific disk drive (the operand) into main storage. Many instructions involve two operands, such as add (the operation) the contents of one main storage location (operand-2) to the contents of another location (operand-1) using the arithmetic unit.

The CPU sequentially extracts instructions one at a time from main storage until encountering an instruction that specifies a *branch* operation. This operation directs the sequence of execution to some other instruction in the program that is not in the regular sequence. For example, an instruction is a compare (IF) operation that checks an arithmetic field for its sign, plus or minus, using the logical unit. If the sign is minus, control is to branch to some other instruction in the program, and if it is plus, control is to continue with the next sequential instruction following the compare operation.

Input Units

Input devices are used to enter data into the computer's main storage. The most commonly used input devices are

- Card readers. These read punched cards that were originated from keypunch devices or computer output. Typical reading speeds are 600–1200 cards per minute.
- Magnetic tape drives. Magnetic tape, which is similar to that used in a home music system, can store millions of bytes of data on one reel.
- Disk storage devices. These flat, spinning disks are similar to phonograph records and contain millions of bytes of data stored in circular tracks.

In addition to providing input data to the system, the magnetic tape and disk devices have another important use: storage of large quantities of data. Other input devices with specialized uses include

- Visual display terminals. These are used for input of data or for inquiry about the current status of stored data.
- Optical Character Recognition (OCR) devices. These devices are used for reading computer-printed documents, such as a customer's telephone bill.
- Magnetic Ink Character Recognition (MICR) devices. These are used for reading encoded checks in the banking industry.

Data is entered into an input device through some applicable medium. For example, a card reader reads the holes in punched cards, and a disk drive reads data stored as magnetized spots on a rotating disk.

Output Units

Output devices are used to provide information from the computer's main storage. The computer directs the output device to record and "write" data from main storage; for example, the computer can direct the printer to "write" or print data on printed forms. Common output devices include

- Line printers. There are many different types of line printers, but all have common features. Printing speeds range from a few hundred to several thousand lines per minute. Many line printers can print 60 or more different characters, including the numbers 0 through 9, letters A through Z, and special characters such as $, #, *, and +. Typical line printers can print 10 characters to the inch and 120, 132, or 144 characters on a line.

The paper used for computer printing is called *continuous forms*. These forms are perforated horizontally so that each sheet can be separated after printing. Manufacturers supply these forms in various sizes, usually 11 or 15 inches wide and 11 inches long. At six lines per inch, this length permits up to 60 lines of print per page. The forms are available in single part and in two or more parts with carbon inserts. The forms may be preprinted according to the user's design (e.g. customer bills), or they may contain only horizontal lines or bars (known as *stock tab forms* or *continuous printout*).

- Card punches. These are used for punching cards, such as cards used in customer bills (when bills are paid, the punched cards are reentered as input). Typical punch speeds are quite slow, for example 300–600 cards per minute.
- Magnetic tapes. These are used for recording data files such as customer records and for temporary storage used for intermediary results.
- Disk storage devices. These are used for recording data files such as customer records and for temporary storage. Many computer systems store or *catalog* programs on disk for ready execution.
- Typewriter or visual display terminals. These provide the status of records either at the computer or at remote locations.
- Computer Output Microfilm (COM) devices.

PUNCHED CARDS

Data may originate from many sources and may be entered into the computer system in many ways. The punched card as a means of recording data was originated by Herman Hollerith, a statistician. The U.S. Census of 1880 had taken 7½ years to complete, and because of a 25 percent increase in population and more detailed information, it was probable that the 1890 census would not be finished before the next census began. Hollerith devised a machine to punch holes in a paper card to represent data and machines to sort and process the cards. Although the feeding of 50–80 cards per minute is slow by today's standards, the census was successfully completed in 2½ years.

Despite its early origins, the punched card is still a common source of data input and recording. There are two main card formats: the common 80-column card measuring 7⅜ inches by 3¼ inches and punched with rectangular holes, and the 96-column compact card punched with round holes, which was designed in 1969 for the IBM System/3. This text discusses the more universal 80-column card.

As shown in Figure 0-3, the common punched card contains 80 columns, and each column contains twelve punching positions or *rows*. The rows are divided into two areas: *numeric* rows numbered 1 through 9, and *zone* rows called 12-zone, 11-zone, and 0-zone (the 12-zone is the topmost punch, the 11-zone next, then the 0-zone, and then 1 through 9 to the bottom). The 0 is both numeric and zone, depending on how it is used.

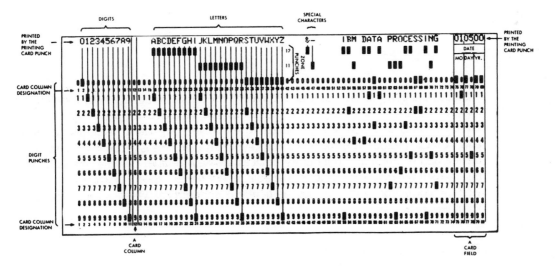

FIGURE 0-3   80-Column Punched Card.

A single punch in a column, 0 through 9, represents the ten digits. A combination of two punches (called a *multipunch*), one a zone and one numeric, represents alphabetic characters. The letters A through I use the 12-zone with numeric 1 through 9 respectively. The letters J through R use the 11-zone with numeric 1 through 9 respectively, and letters S through Z use the zero-zone with numeric 2 through 9 respectively:

Letter	Zone	Digit
A–I	12	1–9
J–R	11	1–9
S–Z	0	2–9

A single punch in the 11-zone represents the minus sign (−), and a single punch in the 12-zone represents the plus sign (+), although the plus sign is not often used. A unique combination of two or three multipunches in a column represents special characters, such as *, $, and %.

Punched cards enter the reading unit of the card reader one at a time. The reading unit senses the presence of the holes either by metal reading brushes or by photoelectric cells. There is one brush or photoelectric cell for each card column. In this way, the reading device reads the card by translating the punched holes into electronic signals, which are sent to the computer. The entire 80 columns, including blank columns if any, are read into an 80-byte area in main storage that the program has designated for the input record. The punched characters are represented in main storage by bytes of specific bit values.

DATA ENTRY DEVICES

Various data entry devices are used to record the initial input data to be used by the computer system. Common transactions that are recorded for data entry include customer sales and payments, changes to employee pay rates, inventory receipts, and COBOL program instructions. The keypunch machine is a common data entry device. Other important data entry devices are key-to-tape, cassette, diskette, and disk, which provide advantages in variable record length, speed, flexible format, and ease of correction and may be particularly economical when processing large volumes of data.

The Keypunch Machine

A keypunch machine is used to punch data in the form of rectangular holes into punched cards. Punched cards are placed into a card hopper, and an operator punches the cards with a keyboard similar to that of a typewriter. The cards are punched from left to right (columns 1 through 80).

The punched card, itself, normally constitutes a *record* of data, such as a payment from a customer. This record is subdivided into related *fields* of data, such as customer number, payment amount, and date paid. A collection of related records comprises a *file* or *data set,* such as a day's customer payment records.

Punched-card processing has some advantages. Operators can easily manipulate the file, rearrange records, and add or delete records. Punched-card processing may still be economical when processing a small to medium volume of data requiring few keypunch devices, and not requiring great speed. But the punched card does have certain inherent drawbacks. The keypunching step is relatively slow, and the punched cards require considerable manual handling, are easily damaged, and cannot be easily reused. Only a few current keypunch devices provide "editing," detect errors, and produce totals. And only some newer models, which physically punch the card after the operator has keyed the entire record, permit error correction without repunching the card.

Key-to-tape

The first data-entry devices to permit an operator to write data directly onto a standard reel of ½-inch magnetic tape were introduced in 1965. An operator can easily transfer a completed tape reel to a computer, which reads the data directly from the tape into main storage for processing.

Key-to-cassette

Operators key data onto a cassette tape, which is usually about 2½ by 4 inches, and small enough to facilitate easy handling and mailing. The cassette tape can store about 200,000 characters and is particularly suited for transmitting transactions from a branch office to a central office. Key-to-cassette is otherwise similar to regular magnetic tape, but is easier to mail and store.

Key-to-diskette

The *diskette* or *floppy disk* is a recordlike disk 8 inches in diameter that can store 240,000 characters of data. It is typically used to transmit data over a transmission line from a branch operation directly into a computer in a central office. When time is not so critical, the branch office can mail the diskette to the central office to be processed directly through a diskette reader into the computer.

Key-to-disk (Multistation Systems)

In *multistation* systems, the keying devices are connected to a single computer processor that writes the data onto disks. Generally the computer processor is small, is separated from the main computer, and is dedicated to handling only the key-to-disk devices. The processor contains a stored program that provides useful "editing" or input data validation, error detection, and statistical summarization. A multistation system can immediately notify an operator of errors, such as a field length that is too long, or a character that is invalid. An operator can periodically copy disk data records onto a tape reel and send it to a central computer for processing.

Direct Data Entry (Interactive Terminals)

Terminal processing is a recent development in data entry and is expanding rapidly. Terminal devices, such as a typewriter or a cash register, are directly connected to the computer system on-line. When an operator keys in an entry or transaction on a terminal, it is read directly into the computer's main storage and processed. The computer receives data from the terminal and transmits information to the terminal.

OPERATING SYSTEM

Most computers in use today come equipped with an *operating system,* which is a set of programs that the manufacturer supplies. The operating system handles the various jobs that need to be run, such as payroll earnings, customer bills, and depreciation accounting. The heart of the operating system is the *Supervisor,* which is a program that resides permanently in main storage, as shown in Figure 0-4.

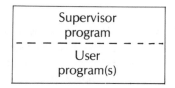

FIGURE 0-4   Supervisor Program in Main Storage.

For example, if a program is executing and has trouble and "bombs out," the Supervisor takes control of the computer and terminates the program. The Supervisor then arranges for the next program to be run.

Some functions of the typical Supervisor are the following:

- Handles the steps between jobs.
- Loads programs into main storage for execution.
- Performs job accounting of the time taken for each program to execute.
- Determines priority for the programs waiting to be executed.
- Checks for requests from users at visual display terminals.

Programmers and operators notify the Supervisor of what job to perform by means of *job control,* punched cards, or entries keyed into a terminal. Typical jobs are to compile a COBOL program, to execute a program, or to sort records on a disk file.

PROBLEMS

0–1.   What is the difference between a digital and an analog computer?

0–2.   What are the advantages of computers?

0–3.   Express the following binary numbers in decimal:
(a) 0101, (b) 1011, (c) 10101, (d) 111010.

0–4.   Express the following decimal numbers in binary:
(a) 5, (b) 8, (c) 17, (d) 25.

0–5.   Distinguish between a bit and a byte.

0–6. What is the purpose of the parity bit?

0–7. What are the four main components of a computer system?

0–8. What is the stored program?

0–9. How many storage locations (bytes) is 16K?

0–10. What is machine language?

0–11. What are the main units of the CPU and their purpose?

0–12. What is a branch instruction?

0–13. Name five input devices and five output devices.

0–14. Indicate the card holes to be punched for the letters C, L, and T.

0–15. Name three devices used for data entry in a data processing system.

0–16. Compare the terms field, record, and file.

0–17. What is an operating system? Describe the role of the Supervisor.

CHAPTER 1

INTRODUCTION TO PROGRAMMING

OBJECTIVE: *To present the basic requirements for writing typical business programs.*

INTRODUCTION

This chapter provides a general background of business system programming requirements, including typical business environment applications. Input data formats, flowcharts, and the basic steps of programming are introduced.

BUSINESS APPLICATIONS

In a business environment, there are certain basic data processing applications that most installations perform. They are the following:

Accounts Receivable and Billing

Most companies sell items on credit and must maintain customer records. Data maintained include customer name, customer address, and current amount owed. Accounting for sales, payments, N.S.F. checks, and interest is a large share of the computer department's programming effort.

Inventory

Many companies maintain a large stock of inventory items that are either sold to customers or issued to manufacturing departments within the company. Data maintained include stock number and name, current quantity on hand, unit cost of item, and selling price. Accounting for stock issues, receipts, returned goods, and out-of-stock items is a major programming application.

Accounts Payable

Most companies purchase goods from other companies: either finished goods for resale or unfinished goods for manufacturing. A company orders goods and sets up an account payable for each supplier; suppliers then send invoices to the firm for payment. The computer system must provide for paying the supplier, including discounts.

Payroll

For companies with thousands of employees, the payroll accounting for wages, labor distribution, and tax and pension deductions can be burdensome. Because payroll is complex and constantly changing, it is difficult to program. Often an economic evaluation will suggest that payroll should not be given high priority among other applications that have a better economic justification.

Sales Analysis and Forecasting

Companies' sales departments require information on sales by category, such as sales area, salesman, and product. A well-planned computer system can provide useful forecasting of expected sales for future periods.

Table 1-1 lists common business transactions showing relevant source documents or input data, and data files affected by these transactions.

INPUT DATA

The function of a data processing system is to accept data, process it, and produce information. Some estimates show that data entry involves one-third of data processing costs. This relatively high cost reflects the importance of having accurate data. Information, to be of any use, must have the following qualities: accuracy, completeness, and timeliness.

TABLE 1-1   Common Sources of Data

TRANSACTION	SOURCE DOCUMENT	DATA FILES AFFECTED
Sale of Items and Collections:		
Customer purchases item for cash	Cash sales slip	Cash Receipts, Inventory, Sales Analysis
Customer purchases item on credit	Credit sales invoice	Customer Accounts, Inventory, Sales Analysis
Credit customer pays on account	Customer payments	Cash Receipts and Customer Accounts
Purchase of Items and Payments:		
Company purchases an item from supplier on credit	Purchase order	Accounts Payable and Inventory
Supplier invoices company; company pays	Accounts Payable voucher	Accounts Payable and Cash payments

The well-known expression "garbage-in, garbage-out" (GIGO) implies that if the *input* data is inaccurate, then the *output* information is inaccurate. But not only must the data be accurate; the processing programs also must be reliable. Given that $1.00 = 100\%$ and that $1.00 \times 1.00 = 1.00$, then

$$\text{Quality of data} \times \text{Quality of processing} = \text{Quality of information}.$$

According to this formula, only 100 percent accurate data and 100 percent accurate processing will yield 100 percent accurate information. Computer programs can be tested and retested for all conceivable conditions, but in a complex system many problems are completely unforeseen. Many programmers have expressed dismay that their program ran error free for six months, and then a "bug" turned up. This rare combination of circumstances confirms Murphy's Law: "If anything can go wrong, it will," and its corollary, "and at the worst possible time."

Data processing involves verifying, combining, calculating, and summarizing. The first step, verifying the data, attempts to ensure that the input data is accurate.

Data Entry of a Source Document

The initial input data is usually on a *source document*. Figure 1-1 shows a typical source document the vendor fills out when making a sale to a customer. The computer system requires the entry of certain data fields, as shown by numbers on the source document—in this example, the sales invoice number (1), date (2), customer number (3), item number (4), quantity sold (5), and unit price (6). An

QUANTZ COMPANY SALES INVOICE

① INVOICE NO.   61742

SOLD   _Midland Supplies_
TO   _427 North Way_   MO   DAY   YR

                          ② DATE | 01 | 28 | xx |

SHIP   _Same_   ③ CUSTOMER NO. ____26841____
TO
                            CUST. ORDER NO.___A–00264_____

                            SALESMAN NO. _____27_____

④ ITEM NO.	DESCRIPTION	⑤ QTY. SOLD	⑥ UNIT PRICE	VALUE
14615	Wrench set–metric	5	12 ¦ 50	62 ¦ 50
15240	Saber saw	2	32 ¦ 50	65 ¦ 00
15315	Router	1	52 ¦ 00	52 ¦ 00
15330	Router bit set	3	11 ¦ 50	34 ¦ 50

FIGURE 1-1   Production of a Data Record from a Source Document.

operator keys these fields into a punched card, magnetic tape, or disk, depending on the data-entry device. In addition, especially for punched cards, the operator may key in a special code (in column 1 in this case) to distinguish the records in one file from the records in other files. When the operator has completed entering the day's data or a specified portion of it, the records are usually entered as a *batch* into the computer system.

Data Records

A *file* contains all the records associated with a particular application, such as inventory. A *record* contains the data associated with one particular item, such as an inventory stock item. The record contains whatever *fields* are necessary to produce the required information regarding each record and the file. Unlike the fixed length of the punched-card record, disk and tape records may be any practical length, such as 25 or 2500 characters.

The punched card is a record of data and may be subdivided into fields. Figure 1-2 illustrates a punched card divided by vertical lines into fields. Some fields may contain *alphabetic* data, such as customer name. Other fields contain *numeric* data, such as the unit price in columns 26–30. (A field such as an address may contain

	①	②	③	④	⑤	⑥	
CODE	INV. NO.	DATE	CUST NO.	ITEM NO.	QTY.	U/PRICE	
x	61742	0128xx	26841	14615	005	01250	Circled numbers show the sequence of fields
Columns: 1	2–6	7–12	13–17	18–22	23–25	26–30	as keyed

FIGURE 1-2   Punched Card Divided into Fields.

alphanumeric data, which is mixed alphabetic and numeric data.) Fields may contain subfields: the date field in Figure 1-2 (columns 7–12) contains the subfields month, day, and year. The entire card (all 80 columns) does not have to be used or divided into fields.

A minus sign indicates that a field has a negative value. In data processing, the minus sign is usually an 11-zone punch over the units position of the amount field. For example, in Figure 1-2, if the quantity field in columns 23–25 is minus, column 25 should contain an 11-zone punch, and the number –345 is punched as 34$\overline{5}$.

Remember, punched cards (and tape and disk) serve two main purposes:

1. To record *programs.*
2. To record *data.* Information for data processing begins as data entry *source documents.* The source document data are punched according to a pre-designed record format. The records then become input to the computer for processing.

The computer reads all 80 card columns including blank spaces into 80 consecutive bytes in main storage. You define the record as an 80-character input area in the program and define each field within the input area with its name and length. If the record is the one defined in Figure 1-2, you code the program so that positions 2 through 6, for example, are reserved for "invoice number."

Data Files

A group of records (card, tape, or disk) that contains related information is called a *file,* or *data set.* There are two main types of files: *master* and *detail* (or *transaction*). A *master file* contains permanent or semipermanent information. For example, an inventory master file would consist of one master record for each inventory item. Each master record would be identified by a code (such as 01) in specified columns. The master record could contain the inventory stock number, unit description, unit cost, quantity on hand, and date. A *detail* or *transaction file* contains temporary data that apply only to a current period. An inventory detail file would consist of one record for each receipt of an inventory item. The detail record would be identified by a code (such as 02) and could contain the inventory stock number, unit cost, quantity received, and date. The detail records are used to *update* the data on the master file as follows: A computer program reads both the master and detail files. For each stock number, the program adds the quantity received to the quantity on hand and produces a new updated master file. These basic principles of file updating also apply to the processing of tape and disk files.

APPROACH TO PROGRAMMING

Programming is more than simply coding instructions for the computer to execute; usually there are four important steps: analysis, design, flowcharting, and coding.

Analysis

The first step, analysis, should consist of interviewing people concerned with a programming problem, studying input data to be processed, and designing the output required. If other existing programs use the same input or make use of the output, then the new program must be integrated with the present system.

Design

In the second step, design, the input and output record formats are designed. The input data may be on source documents. Therefore, a card record would have to be designed in order to be keypunched. Next, the printed report format would be designed, depicting each print position to be used.

Flowcharting

The third step, flowcharting, depicts the solution to a programming problem. A *flowchart* is a pictorial representation of a program's flow of logic, showing each step that the program coding is to take. If a programming problem can be flowcharted, it can be coded. A flowchart serves the following purposes:

- It helps define and clarify the programming problem. Because the flowchart is more general and less technical than the coding, defining and simplifying the logic of the problem is facilitated.
- It acts as useful documentation when the program has to be reviewed or modified.

A later section of this chapter describes flowcharting in detail.

Coding

In the final step, coding, the programming problem is put into code, using the preceding analysis, design, and flowchart. The logic of the flowchart is followed carefully to avoid making logic errors in coding. After coding the program, you should carefully *desk-check* by reviewing the coding and tracing some imaginary data through the program logic. This practice will minimize program errors.

PROGRAM TRANSLATION

Each computer comes equipped with a set of executable instructions that vary by manufacturer and model. Instructions include, for example, read, move, add, subtract, compare, and print.

Machine Language

The computer executes only machine language instructions, which are loaded into storage as the stored program. The Add instruction in Chapter 0 is an example of machine language because the "operands" reference the address of storage locations by number. At one time, programmers wrote programs in machine language, but machine language became far too complex and detailed to be used.

Symbolic Language

Because of the complexity of machine language, programmers code in *symbolic languages,* which are special languages designed by computer manufacturers to facilitate program writing. An instruction in symbolic language is similar to the English language. For example, the Add instruction example in Chapter 0 could be coded symbolically in COBOL as ADD AMT TO ACCUM.

A translator program such as Assembler, COBOL, FORTRAN, or PL/I is used to translate symbolic language to machine language. The five steps of a COBOL program from coding through program testing are as follows:

1. The programmer writes the COBOL program—called the *source program*—on special coding sheets.
2. The source program is then keypunched onto punched cards (or onto disk through a visual display terminal).
3. The COBOL translator *(compiler)* reads the source program and translates it into machine language, which is the *object program.* This translating procedure is known as *compiling.* The compiler performs the following:

- Accounts for the amount of storage required for instructions and data and assigns storage positions to them.
- Supplies messages for programming errors, such as invalid use of an instruction or a spelling error.
- Prints the original symbolic coding on a printer form. This printout is useful in "debugging" the program and in making subsequent changes.
- Writes the machine language object program onto an output device such as a card punch, disk, or tape, for use when the program is to be executed.

4. The programmer corrects any errors signaled by the compiler. In order to execute the corrected program, the object program is loaded into the computer's main storage, replacing any previous storage contents.

5. The programmer tests the program by using input data that will test the arithmetic and logic in the program.

FLOWCHARTING

In order to design a computer system and to code its attendant programs, a programmer should ask the following:

1. *What is the required output?* The designing of output report formats is one of the first steps in programming—the programmer has to know what output is required. As well as printing the results on a report, the program may display them on a visual display terminal or record them on tape or disk.

2. *What is the required input?* Is the input data already stored in some available form, or if not, can it be calculated?

3. *Given the required input, what processing must the program perform to achieve the required output?* This step involves solving *how* to translate the available input data into output information.

These three stages—input, processing, and output—are the essence of the computer program and are usually solved in general terms before coding by means of a *program flowchart*. The flowchart consists of standard symbols that are drawn to trace the logic of a solution to a programming problem. Each symbol represents executable operations that the program is to perform such as test or add. (Symbols are not drawn for nonexecutable statements, such as those that define data areas.)

Many programmers prefer to rough out their initial flowchart solution because they often find errors and oversights once they begin coding. However, the final flowchart should be neat, legible, and preferably in pencil. Most computer manufacturers supply a plastic flowchart template. The most commonly used flowchart symbols and their uses are as follows:

SYMBOL   MEANING

TERMINAL   Represents the initial entry to, or the final exit from, the program (or subroutine).

PROCESS   Represents one or more processing instructions, such as move, add, or subtract.

INPUT/OUTPUT   Represents an input or an output operation, such as read a disk record, or write a printer record.

DECISION   Represents logical decision making. This symbol may have two or three exits (called *branches*). Example: Branch to one instruction if a value is negative, and branch to another instruction if the value is positive.

A   Represents an on-page connector and indicates that the program flow links to a routine on the same page that also has a connector. Both connectors contain the same unique letter. This connector is used if a straight line cannot be drawn easily to the next symbol.

B p.2   Represents an off-page connector and indicates that the program flow links to a routine on a different page that also has an off-page connector. Both connectors have a common unique letter and a page number.

These flowchart symbols provide for all possible computer operations: read input, make logical tests, perform arithmetic, move data, and write results. *The particular advantage of flowcharting is that a knowledge of a programming language is not required; only a knowledge of basic computer operations is necessary.*

All narrative within the flowchart symbols should be simple, clear, and free from any technical terminology. In effect, anyone can read a flowchart, and it is suited to any computer language. It is acceptable to use abbreviations and to combine operations in one symbol when they are related. As a rule, the flow of logic through the symbols is vertically *downward* or horizontally to the *right*. To depict the flow of logic upward or to the left, or to clarify the flow in any direction, arrowheads ▷ are used. Other than the terminal symbol, which denotes the start and the end of the flowchart, every symbol must have a line that provides an entry into the symbol and a line that provides an exit out of the symbol. The flowchart, like the program, should have no dead ends.

Each page of a flowchart should be numbered, and each page or routine should have a heading. It is a good practice to organize a large program into logical sections of separate routines, each of which typically has a heading, one entry, and one exit.

Commonly accepted flowchart notations include the following:

+	Add	=	Equal
−	Subtract	≠	Not Equal
× or *	Multiply	<	Less Than
÷ or /	Divide	>	Greater Than
**	Exponentiation	:	Compare
EOF	End of File	EOJ	End of Job

Flowchart Example I—Read, Process, and Write

As a simple example, assume a file of inventory records for which we have to produce a report of stock value (quantity of stock on hand × unit cost = stock value). For illustration's sake, only one input record is used, containing stock number, description, quantity, and unit cost. The record can be on any format—punched cards, tape, or disk. Note that the program in Figure 1-3 has a beginning point,

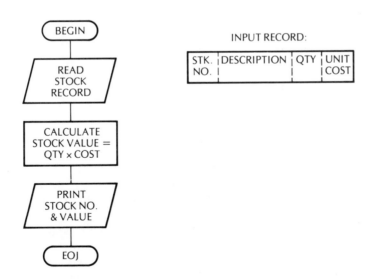

FIGURE 1-3   Read, Process, and Write.

BEGIN, and a termination point, EOJ, to indicate the first and last executable instructions in the program. The program simply reads the input record, multiplies quantity by unit cost, moves the data to the print area (it is not necessary to give a flowchart symbol for the move instruction; it is implied in the next symbol), and prints the required output information.

Flowchart Example II—Repetitive Processing

The program in the preceding example is so simple that it would be easier to perform the calculation manually. An inventory file would normally consist of hundreds or thousands of records and would require many time-consuming calculations that would be subject to errors. Figure 1-4 illustrates *repetitive processing,* or *looping,* in which the program reads, calculates, prints, and then returns (by means of a *branch*) to read the next input record. The program continues in this manner until it has exhausted all the input data.

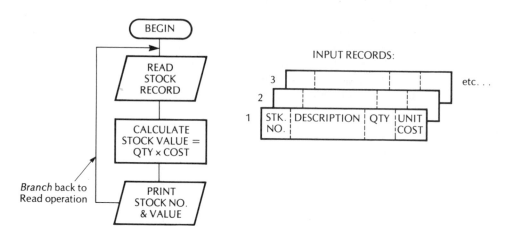

FIGURE 1-4   Repetitive Processing.

The flowchart in Figure 1-4 has one important omission: there is no program exit. There must be some provision for terminating the program when the end of the data is reached. Indeed, for a loop of any kind the program must always have some means of exiting. Without an exit, a program could loop endlessly; this is a common programming error. A computer operator can recognize that a program is looping and can terminate the program. Some computers have a built-in interval timer that automatically cancels a program after it has run a specified time. In Figure 1-4, the program *would* read past the last record in the input file, and the system would signal that there is an error condition.

Flowchart Example III—End-of-file Processing

On a typical computer, input data is followed by a special end-of-file (EOF) indicator, which varies according to the type of input device as follows:

Input Device:	EOF Indication:
Punched Card	A special job control card.
Magnetic Tape	A special system EOF record.
Disk Storage	A record that has a "length" of zero bytes, or an EOF mark.
Terminal	The program is coded to "ask" the user if there is to be no more data, for example, by keying in an account number as all zeros, or to reply Y (Yes) or N (No) to the query: "Any more input data?"

Except for terminals, the computer operating system automatically tests for the EOF record and directly links to a designated end-of-file address, which is defined in the READ statement in COBOL.

As Figure 1-5 shows, you place the end-of-file test immediately after the read operation. The read operation, therefore, has *two* symbols: the first symbol represents the transfer of data from the input device into main storage, and the second symbol represents the logic test for end-of-file (EOF). The flowchart now shows an initial read operation, followed by the loop that calculates, prints, and reads. After the second read is the decision symbol: if not end-of-file, loop back to process the input record, and if end-of-file, terminate the program run.

Flowchart Example IV—Final Totals

Most reports require final control totals at the end of the program run. In Figure 1-5, the appropriate final totals would be for stock values and for the number of input records. In addition to accumulating and printing these totals, the flowchart in Figure 1-6 provides for printing a page heading at the top of the first page.

A program that accumulates totals must define an arithmetic field as an accumulator and initialize it to zero. In COBOL, a field can be defined so that it contains an initial zero, but it should not be defined in the flowchart. The rule is as follows: symbols are drawn to denote all executable instructions, but are not drawn to denote data definition.

It is not absolutely necessary to know the technicalities of a computer language to understand flowcharting. However, an insight into the COBOL language will make program logic clearer.

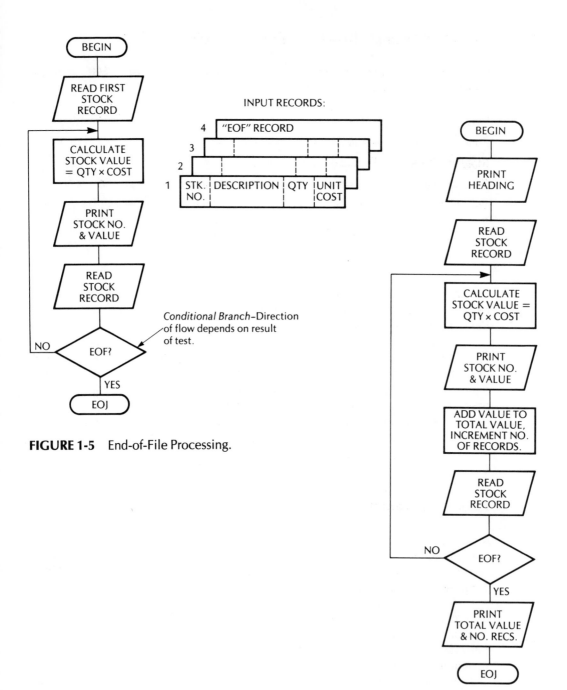

INPUT RECORDS:

4 "EOF" RECORD

STK. NO.	DESCRIPTION	QTY	UNIT COST

Conditional Branch–Direction of flow depends on result of test.

FIGURE 1-5   End-of-File Processing.

FIGURE 1-6   Final Totals.

PROBLEMS

1-1. What are the main applications that your computer installation performs?

1-2. Distinguish between a master file and a transaction file.

1-3. Distinguish between machine language and symbolic language.

1-4. What is a compiler? What is involved in compiling a program? Clarify the role of source program and object program in your explanation.

1-5. What is the purpose of the flowchart?

1-6. A program is needed to process employee wage records. Each record must contain employee number, employee name, hours worked, and rate of pay. The program has to calculate hours × rate = wage for each input record and prints all input fields and the wage. Draw a flowchart for this program using standard flowchart symbols and logic.

1-7. Expand the program in Problem 1-6 to provide for printing a page heading and a final total of employee wages.

PART II
BASIC COBOL

CHAPTER 2

INTRODUCTION TO COBOL

OBJECTIVE: To introduce the basic requirements of COBOL programming, and to enable the reader to code a simple COBOL program.

INTRODUCTION

This chapter introduces the general organization of a COBOL program, the format of its coding sheet, and the components of a simple COBOL program.

The name *COBOL* is an acronym for *Common Business Oriented Language*. COBOL is a common high-level language usable on many computers of various size and manufacture. The COBOL language was developed in 1959 when it was recognized that a common standard language would be preferable to the proliferation of languages being used at that time. Many computer manufacturers and users contributed to help make COBOL a business data processing language that is similar to English and to a large degree self-documenting. A Conference on Data Systems Languages (CODASYL) periodically meets to revise COBOL specifications according to current developments in the field. Consequently, today's COBOL is much improved over early versions. The American National Standards Institute (ANSI) is concerned with language standards and, since the U.S. Federal Government requires ANSI standards when ordering computers, most COBOL versions are ANS COBOL.

The first ANS version of COBOL appeared in 1968 (known in this text as ANS-68 COBOL), and a revised version appeared in 1974 (ANS-74 COBOL). Despite the intentions of its designers, COBOL is not identical in all its versions. Computer manufacturers have made "language extensions" to suit the particular needs of their computer hardware and operating systems. As a result, COBOL versions vary, and a program written for one computer usually requires minor revisions to compile correctly on another computer. For convenience, this text uses the IBM DOS and OS 370 versions of ANS COBOL and emphasizes the ANS-74 requirements.

COBOL programs consist of four *Divisions* that divide the program logically in the following sequence: *Identification, Environment, Data,* and *Procedure.* Briefly, the Identification Division specifies the name of the program; the Environment Division defines the input/output devices and records; the Data Division defines required fields, constants, and work areas; and the Procedure Division includes the executable statements that read input records, perform logic and calculations, and write output records.

COBOL is organized as a hierarchy: within a Division are optional Sections; within a Section are Paragraphs; and within a Paragraph are Sentences.

COBOL CODING SHEET

Figure 2-1 illustrates a COBOL coding sheet that contains a simple program. The COBOL statements listed are coded and keyed according to specified columns. (If a program is entered into a terminal, the columns are usually the same as those shown.) These specified columns and their explanations are as follows:

COLUMN   EXPLANATION

1-3   Reserved for an optional 3-digit page number.

4-6   Reserved for an optional line or statement number. These are sometimes prenumbered 010, 020, 030, etc. An entry on page 1, line 3 would contain 001030 in columns 1-6. These columns act as a sequence number, and the compiler checks that the numbers are in ascending sequence; if they are not in sequence, the compiler prints an error message. The use of sequence numbers helps to locate program statements that may have been accidentally misfiled, but in order to intentionally change the card sequence, you must repunch the sequence numbers. Consequently, many programmers avoid using these columns,

7   Reserved for continuation and comments. Sometimes a statement will exceed the width of the coding sheet. To indicate that a statement continues from the preceding iine, enter a hyphen (-) in this column. Try to use only one statement per line to avoid errors. Also, an asterisk (*) in column 7 indicates a *comment line*.

8-72   Reserved for regular COBOL statements, and consists of two distinct areas. Columns 8-11 are *Area-A,* and columns 12-72 are *Area-B.* COBOL statements begin in one of these two areas depending on the type of statement.

Area-A: Certain coding must begin in columns 8, 9, 10, or 11.

COBOL CODING FORM

PROGRAM NAME Listrun
PROGRAMMER F. Martini
DATE Dec. 18, 19XX
SPECIAL PUNCHING INSTRUCTIONS
PAGE 1 OF 1

SEQUENCE (PAGE) (SERIAL) | CONT. | A | B | COBOL STATEMENT | IDENTIFICATION

```
       IDENTIFICATION DIVISION.
       PROGRAM-ID. LISTRUN.
       AUTHOR. F. MARTINI.
       REMARKS. PROGRAM READS & PRINTS A CARD RECORD.

       ENVIRONMENT DIVISION.
       CONFIGURATION SECTION.
       SOURCE-COMPUTER. IBM-370.
       OBJECT-COMPUTER. IBM-370.

       DATA DIVISION.
       WORKING-STORAGE SECTION.
       01  CARD-RECORD                 PIC X(80).

       PROCEDURE DIVISION.
           ACCEPT CARD-RECORD.
           DISPLAY CARD-RECORD.
           STOP RUN.
```

FIGURE 2-1 COBOL Coding Sheet.

The following commonly begins in column 8 *(Margin-A)*:

- Division names
- Section names
- Paragraph names
- File descriptions (FD)
- Record definitions (01 entries)

Area-B: All other COBOL statements must begin in column 12 or higher. The common convention is to begin in column 12 *(Margin-B)*, or to indent to a column that is a multiple of four, such as column 16, 20, or 24. Later sections of this book cover the specific requirements for each type of statement.

73–80   Reserved for an optional program identification, such as PAYROLL.

SPECIAL COBOL FEATURES

Reserved Words

There are over 300 *reserved words* that are meaningful to and restricted by the COBOL compiler. Although many reserved words are common English words, COBOL limits their use by certain requirements. Reserved words include, for example, ACCEPT, ADD, ADDRESS, ALL, AND, AREA, BLOCK, CHARACTER, CONTROL, and DATA. (Some manufacturers, for example Burroughs, Digital Equipment, Honeywell, and IBM, have reserved words that are unique to their own particular COBOL versions.) You can use any variation of a reserved word that you want; thus, ADD is reserved, ADDER is not. But note that ZERO, ZEROS, and ZEROES are all reserved words.

Every COBOL statement contains at least one reserved word. In the following COBOL statements, the reserved words are underlined. The other words are names that are supplied by and meaningful to the programmer:

```
ACCEPT CUST-RECORD.
MOVE NAME-IN TO NAME-PRINT.
```

Appendix B provides a complete list of reserved words for IBM OS COBOL. Refer to such a list regularly because the mistaken use of a reserved word will cause an error message during program compilation.

Punctuation and Formatting

A period immediately follows names of all Divisions, Sections, Paragraphs, and Sentences. At least one blank follows the period, as follows:

PROCEDURE DIVISION.   *period, followed by blank(s)*

ACCEPT CUST-RECORD.

Commas and semicolons may be placed within sentences to clarify the meaning to the programmer, but COBOL ignores them. There also must be at least one blank following a comma or semicolon.

Spacing

Since the COBOL compiler prints the original source program (with any error diagnostics) on compilation, it is often desirable to insert one or more blank lines between logical sections of coding. You can direct IBM compilers to space lines at any point in the listing with SKIP1, SKIP2, or SKIP3. The statement to direct the compiler to begin printing at the top of the next page is EJECT. These statements may begin anywhere in Area-B and have no punctuation.

The following are the IBM features for line spacing:

```
AREA B:
        SKIP1           SPACE 1 LINE
        SKIP2           SPACE 2 LINES
        SKIP3           SPACE 3 LINES
        EJECT           EJECT TO TOP OF NEXT PAGE
```

Other compiler versions may require the use of blank cards or a *comment card* (asterisk in column 7) with no comment. ANS COBOL specifies ejecting to a new page by a slash (/) in column 7.

Character Set

ANS COBOL allows for 51 different characters, although some small COBOL versions may accept fewer characters. The characters include the following:

NUMERIC DIGITS 0–9   ALPHABETIC LETTERS A–Z

	blank	+	plus sign	/	slash
.	period or decimal	−	minus or hyphen	$	dollar sign
,	comma	=	equal sign	''	or ' quote
;	semicolon	<	less than	(	left parenthesis
*	asterisk	>	greater than	)	right parenthesis

Even if COBOL compiler supports a particular special character, the character may not be available on the printer. Some programmers try to avoid using special characters for this reason.

Comments

An asterisk (*) in column 7 tells COBOL that the information on this line is a comment only. Comments may contain any word or number, including reserved words. For example:

```
COL. 7
     *       THIS ROUTINE CALCULATES HOURS X RATE
```

Comments are often used to clarify a particular calculation or logic test to make a program more understandable.

NOTE Statement

The NOTE statement is another method of providing for comments. In simple terms, this statement begins with the reserved word NOTE, and the character string that follows is the comment. NOTE is no longer an ANS COBOL standard, although most compilers still accept it. The use of NOTE is not recommended because it is now obsolete and has no advantage over the asterisk comment.

IDENTIFICATION DIVISION

The first division of a COBOL program is the *Identification Division,* which identifies the program and its origin. There is one required Paragraph name—PROGRAM-ID—and several optional names. For example:

AREA: A   B

```
        IDENTIFICATION DIVISION.
        PROGRAM-ID. program name.◄――――――――――    up to 8 characters

        AUTHOR.   Name of programmer(s).
        DATE-WRITTEN.   June 17, 19xx.
        DATE-COMPILED.
        REMARKS.   Any relevant program description may appear here. If it ex-
                   ceeds more than one line, no continuation in column 7
                   need be indicated.
```

Identification Division entries may appear in any sequence, and the compiler does not check the contents of any entry. PROGRAM-ID provides the name of the program. The precise rule for the program name length and the validity of its characters varies by computer system. For example, the maximum program name length for IBM is eight characters and for CDC is seven characters. The ANS-74 standard requires an alphabetic letter (A–Z) as the first character. As a general practice, code a program name that is acceptable to the operating system because the system may have to change the name to suit its requirements. Most examples in this text include the required PROGRAM-ID, but omit the other optional entries.

DATE-WRITTEN and DATE-COMPILED must contain a hyphen as shown. If the DATE-COMPILED entry is left blank (as in the example), some compilers will insert the actual date of compilation in the program listing.

The REMARKS entry provides for general comments about a program, and although it is no longer part of the ANS-74 standards, most compilers still accept it. The revised comment method is to code an asterisk in column 7.

ENVIRONMENT DIVISION

The second division, the *Environment Division,* defines the input/output devices and records, and contains the *Configuration Section,* which defines the computer involved in the processing. The Environment Division is generally unique to the COBOL version and computer used. The program in Figure 2-1 contains only a Configuration Section (since the program uses ACCEPT and DISPLAY, the Input-Output Section is not required; it is covered later with the READ and WRITE statements).

```
AREA:  A    B
       ENVIRONMENT DIVISION.
       CONFIGURATION SECTION.
       SOURCE-COMPUTER. IBM-370. )    Items within the
       OBJECT-COMPUTER. IBM-370. (    Configuration Section
```

Within the Configuration Section, SOURCE-COMPUTER specifies the computer that is to compile the program (convert COBOL source statements into executable object code). OBJECT-COMPUTER identifies the computer that is to *execute* the compiled object code. Usually a computer both compiles and executes the same program (in the example: IBM-370).

On the CDC-6000 series, the SOURCE and OBJECT entries would be

```
SOURCE-COMPUTER. 6600.
OBJECT-COMPUTER. 6600.
```

The Configuration Section, itself, and all its entries are optional.

DATA DIVISION

The third division, the Data Division, contains Sections concerned with defining data, and areas that the program references. The example program in Figure 2-1 requires only the *Working-Storage Section* (note the hyphen in Working-Storage).

```
AREA:  A    B
       DATA DIVISION.
       WORKING-STORAGE SECTION.
       01  CUST-RECORD           PIC X(80).
```

The digits 01 are a *level number* beginning in Area-A and define the name of a *record,* which in this program is called CUST-RECORD. The name of the record begins in Area-B and may be any unique name that follows the COBOL rules of names (a descriptive name is best). This entry contains a PICTURE (or PIC) clause, PIC X(80), that defines the input record as follows:

- PIC—Reserved word, abbreviation for PICTURE.
- X—Alphanumeric (the defined data item may contain alphabetic data, numeric data, blanks, or special characters).
- (80)—The data item is 80 positions long. The (80) is a *repetition factor* that indicates the length of the field.

The program reads *(Accepts)* the 80-character record into this area (CUST-RECORD) in storage. A later section of this text will show how to define fields within a record and also various constants and work areas that most programs require.

Other Sections that the Data Division provides are as follows:

- *File Section:* A section that you define when using the READ and WRITE statements for input/output.
- *Communication Section:* A section concerned with the handling of telecommunication messages.
- *Linkage Section:* A section to provide information that is to pass between two programs.
- *Report Section:* A section that defines reports that the "Report Writer" feature is to generate.

You may also initialize constant values in the Working-Storage Section using the VALUE clause as follows:

```
01    PRINT-RECORD    PIC X(120)  VALUE SPACES.
                                  VALUE clause
```

The VALUE clause sets the entire 120 bytes of PRINT-RECORD to *blanks*. In COBOL, the reserved word SPACES represents a field of blanks, and in this case it is the same length (120) as the PICTURE definition.

Data Division Names

COBOL recognizes certain reserved words as unique to the language and having special meaning. All other names in the Data Division are supplied by, and have special meaning to, the programmer. The important rules governing COBOL names are as follows:

1. Names may be up to 30 characters in length.
2. The first character must be a letter (A–Z) or number (some COBOL versions permit only a letter).
3. Other characters may be letters, numbers, or hyphens, but no embedded blanks, and no special characters.
4. The last character must not be a hyphen.

The following printout lists some valid and invalid names:

```
VALID:          INVALID:            EXPLANATION:

SAM             SAM'S               ILLEGAL CHARACTER  (')
MEAT-BALL       MEATBALL-           TRAILING HYPHEN    (-)
MEATBALL        MEAT BALL           EMBEDDED BLANK
TOTAL-1         TOTAL.1             ILLEGAL CHARACTER  (.)
DATA-FLAG       DATA-VALIDATION-INDICATOR-SETTING
                                    MORE THAN 30 CHARACTERS LONG
FIFTY           50                  NOT VALID AS A DATA NAME, BUT VALID AS A
                                        PROCEDURE NAME AND AS A NUMERIC LITERAL
OUTER-SPACE     SPACE               RESERVED WORD, CAN BE REFERENCED BUT NOT
                                        DEFINED
```

SPACE and 50 are reserved words; you cannot define them in the Data Division, but can reference them in the Procedure Division as

IF LINE-COUNT = 50 MOVE SPACES TO PRINT-LINE.

Each name in a COBOL program should be unique. For example, if you were to give the name WAGE to two different fields in a program, COBOL would not know which one to reference in a statement such as

MOVE ZEROS TO WAGE.

PROCEDURE DIVISION

The last division, the *Procedure Division,* contains the program's executable statements, using the data items defined in the Data Division. The statements in the Procedure Division represent the processing and logic of the flowchart and are coded in the sequence in which they are to execute, such as, in simple terms:

1. Accept (Read) an input record.
2. Calculate results.
3. Move results to the output record area.
4. Print the output results.

Most statements in the Procedure Division begin with *verbs,* such as DISPLAY, ACCEPT, MOVE, and ADD.

Figure 2-2 shows the compilation of the program coded in Figure 2-1. Note the line numbers to the left that the compiler generates and prints.

The Procedure Division in Figure 2-2 contains the following:

```
        AREA:
        A    B
   15   PROCEDURE DIVISION.
   16       ACCEPT CUST-RECORD.
   17       DISPLAY CUST-RECORD.
   18       STOP RUN.
```

This program simply reads and prints one card record. Later programs are more realistic and process any number of input records.

The Procedure Division statements in Figure 2-2 and their explanations are as follows:

Statement   Explanation

16   ACCEPT causes the computer to read an input record into CUST-RECORD, as defined in the Data Division. The 80-character input record is read into CUST-RECORD character-for-character and erases any previous contents in the input area. Since unused blank areas of the card record are also read into this storage area, you must define CUST-RECORD as the full 80 characters. Note that COBOL verbs such as DISPLAY, ACCEPT, and STOP begin in Area-B. The following indicates an 80-column input record and the input area in the Data Division:

Input record:

Input Area (CUST-RECORD) in Data Division:

```
00001          IDENTIFICATION DIVISION.
C0002          PROGRAM-ID. LISTRUN.
00003          AUTHOR. F. MARTINI.
00004          REMARKS. PROGRAM READS AND PRINTS AN INPUT RECORD.

00006          ENVIRCNMENT DIVISION.
00007          CONFIGURATICN SECTION.
00008          SOURCE-COMPUTER. IBM-37C.
00009          OBJECT-COMPUTER. IBM-370.

00011          DATA DIVISION.
00012          WORKING-STORAGE SECTION.
00013          01  CUST-RECORD          PIC X(80).

00015          PROCEDURE DIVISION.
00016              ACCEPT CUST-RECORD.
00017              DISPLAY CUST-RECORD.
00018              STOP RUN.
```

line numbers generated
    by compiler

FIGURE 2-2 Compiled Program.

ACCEPT as used here causes the compiler to assume that the input is on the normal system reader device. (Under other situations, ACCEPT is also used for input through a terminal.)

17   DISPLAY causes the contents of the defined field (**CUST-RECORD**) to print on the normal system output device, in this case a printer.   The statement is also used to display information on a visual display terminal.)

18   STOP RUN terminates program execution and returns program control to the Supervisor (to determine the next program to run). All COBOL programs require this statement, although it is not necessarily the last statement in the program.

DEFINING FIELDS

As a rule, an input record contains various fields, each of which requires special processing. Some fields are alphanumeric and others are numeric. Figure 2-3 is similar to Figure 2-2, but the input record now contains three fields: customer number (5 characters), customer name (20 characters), and customer address (20 characters). The remainder of the 80-character record is unused and may or may not be blank. The input and output records appear as follows:

INPUT-RECORD:	1–5	6–25	26–45	46–80
	Customer#	Name	Address	

OUTPUT-RECORD:	1–24	25–29	30–32	33–52	53–55	56–75	76–120
		Customer#		Name		Address	

In the Data Division, INPUT-RECORD is subdivided into customer number, name, and address. Whereas 01 denotes record level number, numbers 02–49 may be used to denote fields *within* the record. This example uses (arbitrarily) level number 03 (it could be 02, but it is a common practice to skip numbers to allow space for inserting other levels later if necessary; some installations use a standard of 01, 05, 10, 15, etc). In this same way, the reserved word FILLER defines *unused* areas and, consequently, the entire record is fully defined, including unused areas. Therefore, the input is defined for 80 characters—the length of one card record. Fields within INPUT-RECORD are not initialized with a VALUE because each input record that the program reads erases any previous data in this area.

OUTPUT-RECORD defines the 120 print positions and spaces between customer number, name, and address for better readability. The maximum length for DISPLAY in many COBOL versions is 120 print positions. The FILLER entries in OUTPUT-RECORD require initializing to blank (VALUE ' ' or VALUE SPACES) because they may contain "garbage." The customer number, name, and address fields need not be initialized to blank because the program moves data into them.

When subdividing a record, code a PICTURE specification for each individual (elementary) field, and not for the 01 (group) record level. Technically, you may code the 03 in Area-A, but indenting to Area-B makes the record definition clearer. Each field is in alphanumeric format (not used for arithmetic) and is PIC X(n).

Because the program has to move each input field to a different position for printing, a separate output area is required. Three MOVE statements transfer the contents of CUSTOMER-IN, NAME-IN, and ADDRESS-IN to three output fields (CUSTOMER-OUT, NAME-OUT, and ADDRESS-OUT). In effect, MOVE *copies* the contents of the input fields, leaving the sending fields unchanged, and erasing any previous contents in the receiving fields. Note that in each case the receiving field is the same length as the sending field.

You may assign any unique name to a record or field in the Data Division. Large programs with many names may become difficult to understand unless the names are meaningful. Thus, many programmers adopt a convention that assigns a prefix or a suffix to distinguish fields in the input and the output areas. Figure 2-3 uses the suffix -IN to identify input fields and the suffix -OUT to identify output fields. As a result, the statement

MOVE NAME-IN TO NAME-OUT

clearly indicates that the name from the input record is being moved to the name position in the output record.

```
00002          IDENTIFICATION DIVISION.
00003          PROGRAM-ID. CUSTREC.
00004          REMARKS.   READ A CUSTOMER RECORD AND PRINT   CUSTOMER
00005               NUMBER, NAME, AND ADDRESS.

00007          ENVIRONMENT DIVISION.
00008          CONFIGURATION SECTION.
00009          SOURCE-COMPUTER. IBM-370.
00010          OBJECT-COMPUTER. IBM-370.

00012          DATA DIVISION.
00013          WORKING-STORAGE SECTION.
00014          01   INPUT-RECORD.
00015               03   CUSTOMER-IN      PIC X(5).
00016               03   NAME-IN          PIC X(20).
00017               03   ADDRESS-IN       PIC X(20).
00018               03   FILLER           PIC X(35).

00020          01   OUTPUT-RECORD.
00021               03   FILLER           PIC X(4)      VALUE ' '.
00022               03   CUSTOMER-OUT     PIC X(5).
00023               03   FILLER           PIC X(3)      VALUE ' '.
00024               03   NAME-OUT         PIC X(20).
00025               03   FILLER           PIC X(3)      VALUE ' '.
00026               03   ADDRESS-OUT      PIC X(20).
00027               03   FILLER           PIC X(65)     VALUE ' '.

00029          PROCEDURE DIVISION.
00030               DISPLAY 'CUSTOMER LIST'.
00031               ACCEPT INPUT-RECORD.
00032               MOVE CUSTOMER-IN TO CUSTOMER-OUT.
00033               MOVE NAME-IN TO NAME-OUT.
00034               MOVE ADDRESS-IN TO ADDRESS-OUT.
00035               DISPLAY OUTPUT-RECORD.
00036               DISPLAY 'END OF CUSTOMER LIST'.
00037               STOP RUN.
```

```
Sample output:

CUSTOMER LIST
     12345   J. MCDOAKS                    423 EAST SECOND ST
END OF CUSTOMER LIST
```

FIGURE 2-3   Processing Defined Fields.

The DISPLAY Statement

Under DISPLAY, the output record can be any length up to 120 (on some COBOL versions including IBM OS, the maximum is 132 characters). If the defined length exceeds this maximum, each DISPLAY executed will cause the excess data to print on a second line, even if the excess data is all blank.

The program in Figure 2-3 illustrates another feature of DISPLAY. At the beginning of the Procedure Division, the program prints a heading:

DISPLAY 'CUSTOMER LIST'.

The item displayed is a *"literal,"* an alphanumeric constant contained within quotes. The message prints beginning at the leftmost column of the printer forms. You can also cause the program to space blank lines on the page by "printing" blank lines using

DISPLAY ' ' or DISPLAY SPACES.

SPACES is a reserved word used to reference blank areas. You may also use SPACES to clear areas to blanks:

MOVE SPACES TO PRINT-AREA.

CROSS-REFERENCE TABLE

The COBOL compiler produces various optional information, and one of its more useful options is a *Cross-Reference Table* that provides the statement number of each defined data name and the number of each statement that references the data name. Figure 2-4 shows the table that the program in Figure 2-3 produced following the compiled program listing. In the table, DATA NAMES are those defined in the Data Division. For example, the table shows that INPUT-RECORD is defined in 000014 and referenced in 000031. PROCEDURE NAMES are all Paragraph and Section names in the Procedure Division. This program contains no Procedure names.

```
                                        CROSS-REFERENCE DICTIONARY


    DATA NAMES                    DEFN        REFERENCE

    ADDRESS-IN                    000017      000034
    ADDRESS-OUT                   000026      000034
    CUSTOMER-IN                   000015      000032
    CUSTOMER-OUT                  000022      000032
    INPUT-RECORD                  000014      000031
    NAME-IN                       000016      000033
    NAME-OUT                      000024      000033
    OUTPUT-RECORD                 000020      000035

    END OF COMPILATION
```

FIGURE 2-4   Cross-reference Table.

For small programs such as in Figure 2-3, the Cross-Reference Table is of minimal value, but for large programs with many names and references, it is a useful adjunct to program maintenance.

COBOL ORGANIZATION

The following is a summary of the grammatical construction of a COBOL program.

Organization:	Example:
IDENTIFICATION DIVISION.	IDENTIFICATION DIVISION.
Paragraphs.	PROGRAM-ID.
Entries.	SALESO5.
ENVIRONMENT DIVISION.	ENVIRONMENT DIVISION.
SECTIONs.	INPUT-OUTPUT SECTION.
Paragraphs.	FILE-CONTROL.
Entries.	SELECT PAY-FILE,
Clauses.	ASSIGN TO SYS018 . . .
DATA DIVISION.	DATA DIVISION.
SECTIONs.	WORKING-STORAGE SECTION.
Entries.	01 IN-RECORD.
Clauses.	03 IN-CODE
	PIC XX.
PROCEDURE DIVISION.	PROCEDURE DIVISION.
SECTIONs.	C000-CALC SECTION.
Paragraphs.	C100-PARA.
Sentences.	IF COUNT NOT = ZERO,
Statements.	DIVIDE TOTAL BY COUNT
Phrases.	GIVING AVERAGE.

Note that Sections are not defined in the Identification Division and are not required in the Procedure Division. A *Sentence* in the Procedure Division consists of one or more *statements* containing various *phrases* and terminates with a period.

The names of Divisions, Sections, Paragraphs, and the level 01 number must begin in Area-A (columns 8–11). Data Division level numbers higher than 01 may begin in Area-A, but usually begin in Area-B (columns 12–72). Entries in the Identification and Environment Divisions, and Sentences in the Procedure Division must begin in Area-B.

Except for the foregoing restrictions, COBOL is "free format", and technically you can begin coding almost anywhere on a line, insert any number of blanks where at least one is required, and code more than one Sentence on a line. But although COBOL is free form, most installations have established standards regarding indenting to make programs easier to keypunch and to read.

WRITING A COBOL PROGRAM

Writing a program for the first time is often an overwhelming experience, particularly regarding where to begin. Therefore, the following steps in writing a COBOL program may be helpful:

1. With the programming problem clearly in mind and input record layout available, design the output report, carefully indicating all data fields and headings.
2. Draw a flowchart of the programming problem. The first flowchart will probably be rough and may have to be revised if the problem is complex.
3. Code the Identification Division and the Environment Division. These are the easiest Divisions to code and contain the fewest variations. Since the contents of these Divisions vary little between programs, refer to a sample program for the format.
4. Use separate coding sheets for both the Data Division and the Procedure Division. Complete as much as possible of the Data Division—including names of input and output fields—before coding any of the Procedure Division.
5. Now code the Procedure Division, referencing both flowchart and Data Division names. Recheck the coding carefully.
6. Design input test data and determine the expected test results in advance. The program should test every possible calculation and decision. Simple programs like the ones in this chapter may require very little testing, but complicated programs often involve considerable time and effort to test.
7. Determine the job control statements required to compile and execute the program.
8. Organize job control statements, source program deck, and test data, and run the job on the computer.
9. Examine the computer printout for job control and compiler error diagnostics. Often these errors are serious and the job must be rerun.
10. Examine the program report output (if any!). Do not be surprised if the first few runs do not compile or execute cleanly (blame these errors on the computer or the keypunch operator!). Correct all indicated bugs and rerun the job. Carefully check all printed output. All headings and fields should print in the correct locations, and all results should be accurate.

DEBUGGING

Even a simple program can contain program errors or *bugs,* and one of the programmer's most exacting and challenging tasks is *debugging.* Most program errors are quite self-evident, although in a large program an obscure bug may require days to locate and correct. Bugs may appear at any step in the programming process—during compilation, so that the program cannot execute; during execution, so that it "bombs out"—or the program may execute successfully but produce invalid data.

Compilation Errors

A program's syntax must make sense to enable the COBOL compiler to convert the source code to machine-executable code. For example, find the bugs in the following segment of code:

```
DATA DIVISION.
WORKING STORAGE.
    01   INPUT-AREA        PIC X80.
```

There are five bugs altogether, so if you have not found them all, keep trying. The answers are at the end of this section.

The compiler assigns a statement number to each line of code, and on finding a syntactical error, the compiler generates an error message indicating the line number and the *probable* cause of the error. Sometimes coding is so confusing that the compiler prints an error message that does not make much sense, but, nevertheless, an error exists and must be corrected.

There are four levels of compiler messages, depending on the seriousness of the error. The diagnostics may vary somewhat by COBOL version, but the typical forms are as follows:

1. *W—Warning.* An error in the source code, but not serious enough to prevent compilation and execution. Examples: a level 01 starting in Area-B, or the word SECTION or DIVISION missing. Correct the error even if the program compiles correctly.
2. *C—Conditional.* An error in the source code that the compiler has attempted to remedy. Its correction may or may not be valid. Example: a continuation of a literal from one line to a second line beginning in Area-A (instead of Area-B).
3. *E—Error.* A serious error in the source code. The compiler cannot attempt a correction and deletes the statement. A common example is a spelling error:

```
DATA DIVISION.
01   RECORD-IN.
    03   SUPPLIER-NO-IN   PIC X(6).
    .
    .
PROCEDURE DIVISION.
    MOVE SUPPLIER-NO TO SUPPLIER-NO-OUT.
```

In the MOVE statement, SUPPLIER-NO should be SUPPLIER-NO-IN. Assuming no definition of SUPPLIER-NO is elsewhere in the Data Division, the compiler cannot determine what field to reference.

4. *D—Disaster.* A very serious error in the source code. The compiler is unable to continue processing. This type of error is fortunately quite rare; if it occurs, check the source program—perhaps it is written in the wrong language!

It is a good practice to correct all diagnostics—even the warnings—if possible. Some errors generate error messages in other statements that are themselves actually correct. For example, the compiler finds an error in a statement that defines a name:

01 RECORD-IN   PITURE X(80).

The word PITURE should be PICTURE or PIC, and the compiler does not make wild guesses as to spellings. As a result, the compiler rejects this statement, and any other statement that references RECORD-IN also generates an error message.

The five bugs in the earlier statements, as you may have detected, are as follows: DATA DIVISION does not end with a period, WORKING-STORAGE is missing the hyphen and the word SECTION, 01 should begin in Area-A, and PIC X(80) is missing the parentheses.

Compilation Error Examples.   The compiler provides error diagnostics by "CARD" number. The program in Figure 2-5 contains the following program errors:

CARD NUMBER	ERROR
00007	The CONFIGURATION SECTION entry is missing. In this case, the compiler has assumed an entry and has issued only a warning (W) message.
00008	IBM is incorrectly spelled as BMI in OBJECT-COMPUTER. The compiler ignores this entry, treats it only as a comment, and therefore no diagnostic is printed.
00016	The entry PIC X(35) is incorrectly stated as (15), but there is no error message because the compiler does not know that the level 01 group is supposed to define an 80-character input area.
00022	The level entry 03 is incorrectly stated as 02. The compiler treats the 03 entries that follow as subfields defined within NAME-OUT and does not permit the "group item" to have a PICTURE clause.
00029	INPUT-RECORD is incorrectly spelled IN-RECORD.
00030	The compiler did not report a logic error on this line; can you find it?
00032	MOVE is incorrectly spelled MVOE.

```
00002          IDENTIFICATION DIVISION.
00003          PROGRAM-ID. CUSTREC.
00004          REMARKS. EXAMPLES OF COMPILE ERRORS.
00005
00006          ENVIRONMENT DIVISION.    ←
00007          SOURCE-COMPUTER. IBM-370.
00008          OBJECT-COMPUTER. BMI-370.
00009
00010          DATA DIVISION.
00011          WORKING-STORAGE SECTION.
00012          01   INPUT-RECORD.
00013               03   CUSTOMER-IN      PIC X(5).
00014               03   NAME-IN          PIC X(20).
00015               03   ADDRESS-IN       PIC X(20).
00016               03   FILLER           PIC X(15).
00017
00018          01   OUTPUT-RECORD.
00019               03   FILLER           PIC X(4)      VALUE ' '.
00020               03   CUSTOMER-OUT     PIC X(5).
00021               03   FILLER           PIC X(3)      VALUE ' '.
00022               02   NAME-OUT         PIC X(20).
00023               03   FILLER           PIC X(3)      VALUE ' '.
00024               03   ADDRESS-OUT      PIC X(20).
00025               03   FILLER           PIC X(65)     VALUE ' '.

00027          PROCEDURE DIVISION.
00028               DISPLAY 'CUSTOMER LIST'.
00029               ACCEPT IN-RECORD.
00030               MOVE CUSTOMER-OUT TO CUSTOMER-IN.
00031               MOVE NAME-IN TO NAME-OUT.
00032               MVOE ADDRESS-IN TO ADDRESS-OUT.
00033               DISPLAY OUTPUT-RECORD.
00034               DISPLAY 'END OF CUSTOMER LIST.
00035               STOP RUN.
```

```
CARD    ERROR MESSAGE

00007   ILA1002I-W   CONFIGURATION SECTION HEADER MISSING. ASSUMED PRESENT.
00022   ILA2034I-E   GROUP ITEM HAS PICTURE CLAUSE. CLAUSE DELETED.
00029   ILA3001I-E   IN-RECORD NOT DEFINED. DISCARDED.
00031   ILA3001I-E   MVOE NOT DEFINED. DELETING TILL LEGAL ELEMENT FOUND.
00034   ILA1098I-C   NONNUMERIC LIT NOT CONTINUED WITH HYPHEN AND QUOTE.
                     END LITERAL ON LAST CARD.
00035   ILA1007I-W   STOP NOT PRECEDED BY A SPACE. ASSUME SPACE.


ILA0004I- OUTPUT OPTIONS SUPPRESSED DUE TO ERROR SEVERITY LEVEL

END OF COMPILATION
```

FIGURE 2-5   Compilation Errors.

00034   The literal 'END OF CUSTOMER LIST' is missing the ending quote.
00035   The compiler expected the literal in the preceding statement to continue on this line because of the missing quote. The error message is incorrect and is an example of an error that generates error messages in other statements.

The serious error messages (E) have cancelled the compilation. Figure 2-3 contains the correct code for this program.

Execution Errors

If the compiler can make some sense of a program, it generates machine-executable code. There is a good chance, however, that the first run or two will "blow up" or "bomb out," a common outcome for both new and experienced programmers. Two examples that cause such a disaster are attempting to divide a field by a zero value, and performing arithmetic on a field containing blanks. In these examples the computer Supervisor (not the COBOL compiler, for during execution it is gone from the scene) would take control, print a diagnostic (which may or may not be clear), and terminate the run.

Logic Errors

Usually several runs are required to eliminate compilation and execution errors. Eventually a program will compile and execute cleanly, but the program output may still be incorrect because of logic errors. For example, a statement in the Procedure Division may reference the wrong data area, as in the following:

```
MOVE NAME-IN TO CUST-NO-OUT.
MOVE CUST-NO-IN TO NAME-OUT.
```

Logic errors often occur because the definition of the input record in the Data Division does not match the actual input record. This is the first area to check when there is a logic error because the program may be otherwise perfect, and hours spent checking code in the Procedure Division will not locate the error.

There are many other errors that can occur, especially as programs become more complicated. Although you may never entirely eliminate coding errors, you can certainly minimize them. Before coding, think the problem through carefully and design the print layout and flowchart accordingly. After coding, take the time to desk-check: review every statement in the program—especially definitions in the Data Division and punctuation in the Procedure Division; and finally, double-check the logic of all IF statements.

PROBLEMS

2–1. What is the ANS COBOL version?

2–2. What are the four COBOL Divisions?

2–3. Explain the purpose of the COBOL coding sheet fields: columns 1–3, 4–6, 7, 8–72, 73–80.

2–4. What is a COBOL reserved word? Give three examples.

2–5. In COBOL, what is the purpose of (a) the period? (b) the comma and semicolon?

2–6. What method does your installation's COBOL compiler use to space lines and eject forms to the top of a page?

2–7. How does your installation's compiler provide for a comment line?

2–8. Check the validity of the following names defined in a COBOL program:

(a) HAM, (b) STAN'S, (c) ZEROS, (d) COUNT-20, (e) TOTAL-CURRENT-PAY.

2–9. What are the rules concerning the name of a COBOL program (PROGRAM-ID)?

2–10. What are the *required* statements in the (a) Identification Division; (b) Environment Division; (c) Data Division; (d) Procedure Division?

2–11. On a coding sheet, define an item in Working-Storage called INPUT-RECORD that is 80 characters long.

2–12. On a coding sheet, define a print line in Working-Storage called PRINT-LINE, 120 characters long, and initialized to blanks.

In the following problems, use the ACCEPT verb for input and the DISPLAY verb for output.

2–13. Code an input statement to read INPUT-RECORD defined in Problem 2-11.

2–14. Code a statement to print the contents of PRINT-LINE defined in Problem 2-12.

2–15. Code a statement that prints the message (literal) 'LIST of AUTOMOTIVE PARTS'.

2–16. Code the statement that terminates program execution.

2–17. Now use the preceding six COBOL statements in a program that reads and prints a record containing a description of automotive parts. Devise an input record containing imaginary data. Include the required job control cards for your installation, compile and execute the program, and examine the printout for any COBOL diagnostics.

2–18. Define an input record using any valid descriptive names that contains the following fields:

COLUMNS

1–6	Part number
7–28	Part description
29–80	Unused

2–19. Define a print record using any valid descriptive names for the following fields:

COLUMNS

1–20	Unused
21–26	Part number
27–29	Unused
30–51	Part description
52–120	Unused

2–20. Use the preceding input and output records in the Working-Storage Section of a program that reads and prints the records according to their defined formats. Devise an input record using an imaginary part number and description. Code, compile, and test the program. Check for compiler diagnostics.

Suggestion: Insert some intentional errors to see how the compiler handles them. Examples are a spelling error in a name, a statement in the wrong Area, and the omission of a required Division or Section name.

CHAPTER 3

ELEMENTS OF COBOL

*OBJECTIVE: To present the COBOL coding to handle repetitive processing
and to handle different types of data, including arithmetic data.*

INTRODUCTION

The previous chapter introduced the general organization of COBOL programs
and the coding for simple programs that read only one input record and process
only alphanumeric (descriptive) data. This chapter covers the processing of a variable
number of input records and the use of the PERFORM statement for repetitive
processing. Later sections are concerned with simple arithmetic processing: defining
numeric input fields and the printing of edited numeric values (for commas and
decimal point).

REPETITIVE PROCESSING

Preceding example programs simply read and processed a single input record. To be
really useful, the program should be able to process any number of input records.
Such a program reads and processes the first record and then must "loop" back to
read and process additional records. A special "end-of-file" or "trailer" record is
required to indicate that there is no more input data.

Figure 1-6 earlier provided a standard approach to repetitive processing. The
flowchart shows an initial read, a processing of the record, print, and another read.
After this second read, the program tests whether the record is the end-of-file. The

55

special record could contain, for example, all nines in the control field (stock number in the example). If the stock number does not contain nines, the program loops back to process the record that was just read. If the stock number does contain nines, the program processes the end-of-job instructions (in that case, final totals) and terminates processing. Use of a trailer record with nines is adequate for the first few programs, but later, using the READ statement, a special job control card normally handles the end-of-file condition.

The COBOL statement used for repetitive processing is PERFORM UNTIL. The flowchart approach as indicated in Figure 3-1 uses a *subroutine* for the PERFORM statement and is an improvement on the program in the previous chapter that provided for reading only one input record.

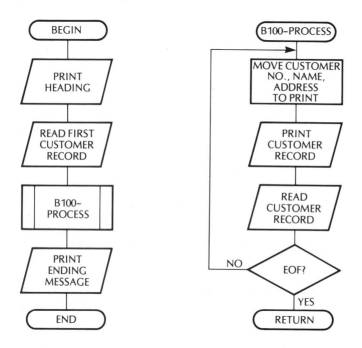

FIGURE 3-1   Use of a Subroutine for Repetitive Processing.

The part of the program in Figure 3-1 that *repeats* is in the subroutine, as an isolated section of coding. By definition, any point in a program can perform a subroutine only through use of a PERFORM statement. (In fact, a subroutine can perform another subroutine, but should not attempt to execute itself.) Note the flowchart symbol that indicates a subroutine. (There are other symbols in use as well.)

| | Section Name | |

The subroutine symbol indicates that at this point, the program has a PERFORM statement that leaves the main flow of execution, executes a Paragraph or Section, and returns to the statement immediately following the PERFORM. The subroutine itself is depicted separately, with its own entry and exit points.

The flowchart in Figure 3-1 consists of a "main logic" routine and a subroutine that the program executes repetitively. The main logic routine indicates subroutine processing by means of a special symbol with vertical lines in it indicating that at this point the program exits to the separate subroutine, processes the subroutine one or more times, and eventually returns.

Figure 3-2 provides the coding for a program based on the one in the previous chapter. Remember that other divisions have Sections, such as the Working-Storage Section in the Data Division. The subroutine, called B100-PROCESS, is in a separate Section in the Procedure Division and is fully separated from the main processing routine.

The PERFORM UNTIL Statement

In the example program, the PERFORM links to the Section specified, B100-PROCESS. The program executes the statements in the Section through to the EXIT statement. The program continues executing the Section repetitively (MOVE, DISPLAY, ACCEPT) as long as no input record contains nines. Once an ACCEPT reads a record with nines in the Stock number, the program returns control to the statement immediately following the PERFORM. There must be a proper trailer record with nines to enable the PERFORM to terminate, otherwise the program will continue reading input records following the data for this program, with unpredictable results.

Note that the PERFORM UNTIL *implies* a logic test—whether to loop again through the Section or to return—at the end of the Section. The PERFORM UNTIL tests using a *literal* coded as '99999', which indicates an alphanumeric value; STOCK-NO-IN is also alphanumeric because it is defined as PIC X(5).

What if there is only one input record, containing nines? If the initial ACCEPT in the main logic has read a record containing nines, the PERFORM recognizes the condition immediately, and instead of executing the subroutine, it continues with the main logic. If the first record does not contain nines, the program executes the statements in the subroutine. The ACCEPT reads the next record. The PERFORM then has to determine whether to repeat the subroutine (not nines) or to return to the main logic (STOCK-NO-IN = '99999'). The PERFORM therefore automatically tests the UNTIL condition on entering the subroutine and on reaching the end of the subroutine. (At least, it is simpler to think of it this way.) A later chapter covers in detail other uses of the PERFORM.

The paragraph name, B999-RETURN, is the last statement in the subroutine. Its purpose is in effect only documentation, a convention to indicate clearly to the programmer and others that the Section is to end at this point. The EXIT statement within the paragraph B999-RETURN is also a COBOL convention to indicate that the

```
00002              IDENTIFICATION DIVISION.
00003              PROGRAM-ID. CHAPT3A.

00005              ENVIRONMENT DIVISION.
00006              DATA DIVISION.
00007              WORKING-STORAGE SECTION.
00008              01   INPUT-RECORD.
00009                    03   CUSTOMER-IN      PIC X(5).
00010                    03   NAME-IN          PIC X(20).
00011                    03   ADDRESS-IN       PIC X(20).
00012                    03   FILLER           PIC X(35).

00014              01   OUTPUT-RECORD.
00015                    03   FILLER           PIC X(4)     VALUE ' '.
00016                    03   CUSTOMER-OUT     PIC X(5).
00017                    03   FILLER           PIC X(3)     VALUE ' '.
00018                    03   NAME-OUT         PIC X(20).
00019                    03   FILLER           PIC X(3)     VALUE ' '.
00020                    03   ADDRESS-OUT      PIC X(20).
00021                    03   FILLER           PIC X(65)    VALUE ' '.

00023              PROCEDURE DIVISION.
00024                    DISPLAY 'CUSTOMER LIST'.
00025                    ACCEPT INPUT-RECORD.
00026                    PERFORM B100-PROCESS UNTIL CUSTOMER-IN = '99999'.
00027                    DISPLAY 'END OF CUSTOMER LIST'.
00028                    STOP RUN.

00030              B100-PROCESS SECTION.
00031                    MOVE CUSTOMER-IN TO CUSTOMER-OUT.
00032                    MOVE NAME-IN TO NAME-OUT.
00033                    MOVE ADDRESS-IN TO ADDRESS-OUT.
00034                    DISPLAY OUTPUT-RECORD.
00035                    ACCEPT INPUT-RECORD.
00036              B999-RETURN.   EXIT.
```

Printed report:

```
CUSTOMER LIST
     12345    J. MCDOAKS          423 EAST SECOND ST
     25534    A. SMITH            1205 SPRINGDALE AVE.
     32287    J. BROWN            4721 W. 22ND STREET
     56338    R. NEILSEN          4321 ALEXANDER ST.
END OF CUSTOMER LIST
```

FIGURE 3-2   Repetitive Processing.

Section is to return here. Note, however, that the EXIT does not generate any executable code, but on many compilers is only a form of documentation.

The technique for handling a subroutine is to enter at the top and to exit at the bottom. The program should enter the subroutine only by means of a PERFORM, and not by preceding statements dropping into it. In this program, the preceding statement is STOP RUN.

Paragraph names and Section names begin in Area-A and may be up to 30 characters in length.

NUMERIC INPUT DATA

Computer programs generally involve data upon which arithmetic must be performed. Because the computer internally represents arithmetic data differently from alphanumeric data, you must define arithmetic fields uniquely so that the compiler can generate special executable code. Therefore, you designate a numeric input field with PICTURE 9s, for example:

05 QUANTITY-IN   PIC 9999.

Each 9 represents one digit in the input field. In order to represent a decimal point, you use the letter *V*, which tells the compiler the position of an assumed decimal point (although none actually exists in the field). Consequently, QUANTITY-IN could also be coded as 9999V. A PICTURE clause for an amount such as 1234.56 is coded as follows:

05 AMOUNT-IN   PIC 9999V99.

Assumed decimal point

Negative Values

Many arithmetic fields contain a negative value. To represent a negative value, input fields are commonly punched with an 11 (or X) punch in the units position of the negative field:

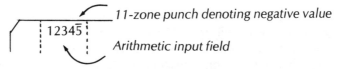

11-zone punch denoting negative value

12345

Arithmetic input field

The absence of the 11-zone punch indicates a positive value (a 12-zone punch also indicates a positive value, but is seldom used). A PICTURE format such as 9999V99 indicates an *unsigned* value, and in effect "strips" a zone so that the input amount will always be positive, even if punched as negative. To indicate a *signed* input value, simply precede the 9s with the letter *S*:

05 AMOUNT-IN   PIC S9999V99.   *Signed input field*

Such a format tells the compiler that the input field is numeric and signed and prevents the compiler from stripping the zone from the field.

Note: When in doubt, allow for a signed value. Many arithmetic fields in business programming provide for *reversing* and *correcting entries:* customers can overpay their balances, payments can be NSF, and fields such as hours worked and stock quantity can validly be negative.

Repetition Factor

Alphanumeric fields are usually defined with a *repetition factor* to indicate the number of characters that the compiler is to generate. For example, the repetition factor in PIC X(3) is 3, and this clause could also be coded as PIC XXX. Numeric data may also use repetition factors. In the preceding example, QUANTITY-IN, defined as PIC 9999, could also be defined as PIC 9(4). Similarly, AMOUNT-IN, defined as PIC 9999V99, could be coded as 9(4)V99 or even as 9(4)V9(2).

PRINTED ARITHMETIC FIELDS

PICTURE 9s can also be used for printing. Assume the following print field contains the value 000123:

> 05 AMOUNT-OUT   PIC 9999V99.   *Unedited print field*

The amount 000123 prints as 000123. Desirably, this amount should print with the leftmost zeros suppressed, and with a comma and a decimal point. This can be accomplished by *editing,* using the PICTURE characters Z, comma (,), and decimal point (.), as follows:

> 05 AMOUNT-OUT   PIC Z,ZZZ.99.   *Edited print field*

With this edited format, the amount 000123 prints as 1.23 (leading zeros and the comma are suppressed), and 123456 would print as 1,234.56. The letter Z (like the 9) represents a digit but also provides for zero suppression. The comma and decimal point each require one print position. Note: These special editing characters must not be used for input definition or arithmetic calculations.

Negative Printed Values

If a negative value is printed with the format PIC Z,ZZZ.99, it prints with no minus sign; consequently, the value appears to be positive. You can generate a minus sign or a CR credit symbol to the right of an amount as in the following example:

05 AMOUNT-OUT PIC Z,ZZZ.99 −. or PIC Z,ZZZ.99CR.	*Edited, signed* *print fields*

The minus sign requires one print position and the CR symbol requires two positions. If the printed value is positive, the minus sign or CR symbol does not print.

These are the basic editing features. Many less common but useful editing features are covered later in the text.

PROGRAM EXAMPLE

Figure 3-3 depicts an inventory program that reads records containing stock number, quantity, unit-cost, and description, calculates quantity times unit-cost, and prints the results. The input/output formats are as follows:

Input:

	Stock	Qty	U/Cost	Descr'n	
1–4	5–9	10–12	13–16	17–36	37———80
blank	xxxxx	999	9999	x———x	blank

assumed decimal point

Output:

Stock		Descr'n		Qty		U/Cost		Value
6–10	11–15	16–35	36–39	40–43	44–48	49–53	54–58	59———69
xxxxx		x———x		ZZ9 −		ZZ.99		ZZ,ZZZ.99CR

LEVEL NUMBERS

COBOL level numbers in the Data Division have special meaning to the compiler:

- 01 indicates an individual record, which may contain fields within it.
- 02–49 define fields within the level 01 record.
- 66 is used in conjunction with the RENAMES clause.
- 77 defines independent data items.
- 88 defines condition names.

Subfields

Just as a record may be divided into fields, a field may be divided into *subfields,* and subfields may be further divided. Fields at the same level must each have the same level number (between 02 and 49). Subfields within a field must each have the same

```
00002          IDENTIFICATION DIVISION.
00003          PROGRAM-ID. CHAPT3B.
00004          REMARKS. INPUT IS STOCK RECORDS.  PROGRAM CALCULATES
00005               STOCK-VALUE (QTY X UNIT-COST).

00007          ENVIRONMENT DIVISION.
00008          CONFIGURATION SECTION.
00009          SOURCE-COMPUTER. IBM-370.
00010          OBJECT-COMPUTER. IBM-370.

00012          DATA DIVISION.
00013          WORKING-STORAGE SECTION.
00014          01  STOCK-RECORD-IN.
00015              03  FILLER          PIC X(4).
00016              03  STOCK-NO-IN     PIC X(5).
00017              03  QTY-IN          PIC S999.
00018              03  UNCOST-IN       PIC S99V99.
00019              03  DESCRIP-IN      PIC X(20).
00020              03  FILLER          PIC X(44).

00022          01  STOCK-RECORD-OUT.
00023              03  FILLER          PIC X(5)    VALUE ' '.
00024              03  STOCK-NO-OUT    PIC X(5).
00025              03  FILLER          PIC X(5)    VALUE ' '.
00026              03  DESCRIP-OUT     PIC X(24).
00027              03  QTY-OUT         PIC ZZ9-.
00028              03  FILLER          PIC X(5)    VALUE ' '.
00029              03  UNCOST-OUT      PIC ZZ.99.
00030              03  FILLER          PIC X(5)    VALUE ' '.
00031              03  VALUE-OUT       PIC ZZ.ZZZ.99CR.
00032              03  FILLER          PIC X(42)   VALUE ' '.

00034          PROCEDURE DIVISION.
00035              DISPLAY 'STOCK CALCULATION REPORT'.
00036              DISPLAY SPACES.
00037              ACCEPT STOCK-RECORD-IN.
00038              PERFORM B100-PROCESS UNTIL STOCK-NO-IN = '99999'.
00039              DISPLAY SPACES.
00040              DISPLAY 'END OF STOCK VALUE RUN'.
00041              STOP RUN.

00043          B100-PROCESS SECTION.
00044              MOVE STOCK-NO-IN TO STOCK-NO-OUT.
00045              MOVE DESCRIP-IN TO DESCRIP-OUT.
00046              MOVE QTY-IN TO QTY-OUT.
00047              MOVE UNCOST-IN TO UNCOST-OUT.
00048              MULTIPLY QTY-IN BY UNCOST-IN GIVING VALUE-OUT.
00049              DISPLAY STOCK-RECORD-OUT.
00050              ACCEPT STOCK-RECORD-IN.
00051          B900-RETURN.  EXIT.
```

Input Data:

```
                         Unit
              Stock Qty cost
         12   00230 001 0100 RIVETTERS
         12   00236 015 0035 ASSEMBLERS
         12   00245 100 1525 RE-INFORCERS
         12   00277 525 0375 CO-ORDINATORS
              99999
```

Printed Report:

```
     STOCK CALCULATION REPORT

         00230     RIVETTERS              1      1.00         1.00
         00236     ASSEMBLERS            15       .35         5.25
         00245     RE-INFORCERS         100     15.25     1,525.00
         00277     CO-ORDINATORS        525      3.75     1,968.75

     END OF STOCK VALUE RUN
```

FIGURE 3-3 Calculation of Stock Value.

level number, but a higher number (up to 49) than that of the *field* in which they are defined. The following shows the subfields day, month, and year defined within a date field:

```
01   RECORD-IN.                          1 - 5 6 -  11
     05   ACCOUNT-NO-IN    PIC X(5).     |XXXXX|XX XX XX|
     05   DATE-IN.                       |ACC'T|  DATE  |
          10   DAY-IN      PIC XX.       |      |DA MO YR|
          10   MONTH-IN    PIC XX.
          10   YEAR-IN     PIC XX.
```

Items at any one level must have the same level number; therefore, ACCOUNT-NO-IN and DATE-IN are at the same level: 05; DAY-IN, MONTH-IN, and YEAR-IN are at the same level: 10. For any item, the PICTURE definition must be at the lowest level number. If a field is defined with subfields, then the subfields must contain the PICTURE specification. Technically, *group items,* such as RECORD-IN and DATE-IN, contain lower level items within them, but *elementary items,* such as ACCOUNT-NO-IN, DAY-IN, MONTH-IN, and YEAR-IN, are at the lowest levels within their groups and must contain PICTURE clauses.

INDEPENDENT DATA ITEMS—LEVEL 77

You have seen that there are two major types of COBOL data statements: PICTURE X for defining alphanumeric data used for descriptive information, and PICTURE 9 for defining numeric data used for arithmetic calculations. You also have seen that level 01 defines records, with or without related subdivided fields, numbered 02, 03, etc. But most programs also require accumulators, constants, and work areas. These are *independent items* that have no subdivisions or direct relationships to any other item. The level number for these independent items is 77, and they must be coded before level 01 entries in the Working-Storage Section are coded.

Actually, three basic data symbols are used to define PICTURE: A for alphabetic, X for alphanumeric (mixed alphabetic and numeric), and 9 for arithmetic data. Neither PICTURE A nor PICTURE X can be used to define arithmetic data.

ALPHABETIC DATA—PICTURE A

PICTURE-A format defines fields that are to contain only blanks and the letters *A* through *Z*. Attempting to define or move a number or any other character in such a field causes an error. One serious limitation of PICTURE-A format is that it does not accept names with an apostrophe, such as O'HARA. An example of PICTURE-A format is as follows:

```
77  TITLE    PIC A(19)   VALUE 'SYSTEMS CORPORATION'.
```

Because it is easy to make a mistake with PICTURE-A format, many programmers never use it. Instead, like this text, they always use PICTURE X to define alphabetic fields.

ALPHANUMERIC DATA—PICTURE X

PICTURE X defines fields that are not to be used for arithmetic processing. This format accepts letters and blanks (like PICTURE A), numbers, and any other type of valid character. Figure 3-4 gives examples of PICTURE-X format that define alphanumeric items initialized with literal values.

```
       AREA A:    B:
              77  PREV-CUSTOMER         PIC X(5)      VALUE SPACES.
              77  ERROR-MESSAGE         PIC X(15)     VALUE 'OUT OF SEQUENCE'.
              77  COMPANY-NAME-1        PIC X(9)      VALUE 'BUG CO.'.
              77  COMPANY-NAME-2        PIC X(5)      VALUE 'BUG CO.'.
              77  ASTERS                PIC X(5)      VALUE ALL '*'.
              77  TITLE-2               PIC X(44)     VALUE 'QUARTERLY REPORT OF SA
                  'LES TOTALS BY DISTRICT'.
Continuation
```

FIGURE 3-4   Example of Alphanumeric Data.

Explanations of the statements in Figure 3-4 are as follows:

- PREV-CUSTOMER is a 5-character field initialized to SPACES, or blanks. SPACES (a figurative constant) is a reserved word that can be initialized in, or moved to, an alphanumeric field and is used in compares.
- ERROR-MESSAGE is a 15-character field containing the value 'OUT OF SEQUENCE'.
- COMPANY-NAME-1, although defined as nine characters long, contains a 7-character constant. The compiler left-adjusts the constant and inserts two blanks on the right.
- COMPANY-NAME-2 attempts to define a 7-character value in a 5-byte field; the compiler truncates two characters from the right, as in 'BUG C'. Most compilers would print a warning message about the truncated characters.
- ASTERS uses the figurative constant ALL to generate the same character in every position of the field. (VALUE '*****' would provide the same result.)
- TITLE-2 contains a constant that exceeds column 72. Note the continuation character (−) in column 7 of the next line, and another apostrophe in Area-B.

QUOTE

An apostrophe or quotation mark (depending on the compiler) normally terminates an alphanumeric constant. But to place or indicate an apostrophe within a constant, the figurative constant QUOTE must be used. Assume that a constant to be represented is 'SAM'S'. Some compilers indicate this embedded QUOTE in the constant as follows:

```
77   TITLE            PIC X(5)    VALUE 'SAM' QUOTE 'S'.
```

Other compilers (including IBM FCOBOL) allow QUOTE only in a separate PICTURE, and therefore the required 5-character constant must appear in the following awkward fashion:

```
01   SAM-TITLE.
     03   FILLER       PIC X(3)    VALUE 'SAM'.
     03   FILLER       PIC X       VALUE QUOTE.
     03   FILLER       PIC X       VALUE 'S'.
```

Usage

There are three classes of character data:

1. *Alphabetic (PICTURE A)*—for defining fields containing exclusively alphabetic characters (and rarely used).
2. *Numeric character (PICTURE 9)*—for defining arithmetic input/output fields with one digit per storage position.
3. *Alphanumeric character (PICTURE X)*—for defining fields with mixed alphabetic and numeric data.

All three data classes permit the DISPLAY usage, which you may explicitly define as

```
   77  FIELDA  PIC X(8)  VALUE SPACES  USAGE IS DISPLAY.
OR 77  FIELDA  PIC X(8)  VALUE SPACES  DISPLAY.
```

Omission of the USAGE clause (as in the examples in this text) causes the compiler to assume (default to) DISPLAY. The importance of this feature becomes clear in the section on arithmetic data when assigning usage as COMPUTATIONAL to arithmetic work fields generates more efficient code.

Alphanumeric Literals

You can also assign literals to an alphanumeric field. Such literals must be within quotes and may contain any character except an apostrophe. The maximum length is 120 characters. Examples:

```
MOVE 'INVALID RECORD' TO ERROR-MESSAGE.
MOVE ' ' TO PRINT-LINE.
```

These same rules apply to literals of unequal lengths; if a literal is too long, the compiler truncates on the right, and if a literal is too short, the compiler inserts blanks on the right. By using literals you do not have to define fields in the Working-Storage Section, but some programmers feel that by minimizing the use of literals programs are easier to maintain.

ARITHMETIC DATA IN WORKING-STORAGE

Any field that is to be used for arithmetic processing must be defined as PICTURE 9. The maximum length of an arithmetic field for input, output, Working-Storage, or a literal is 18 digits. The following define arithmetic fields in Working-Storage:

```
                                              CONTENTS:
77   AMT-STORE     PIC 99999.                 UNKNOWN
77   LINE-CTR      PIC 999      VALUE 1.         001
77   FACTOR        PIC 9        VALUE 5.           5
77   TOTAL-SALES   PIC 9999V99  VALUE 2.50.     000250
77   HUNDRED       PIC 99       VALUE 100.       (1)00
```

invalid

- AMT-STORE defines a 5-digit field.
- LINE-CTR defines a 3-digit field, initialized to 001; the compiler right-adjusts the constant and inserts zeros to the left. If the program is to add to LINE-CTR, then it should be initialized to some value, since its contents may otherwise contain "garbage." Note that, unlike alphanumeric values, arithmetic values are not enclosed in quotes.
- FACTOR defines a constant value 5. The program could, for example, add the contents of FACTOR to LINE-CTR as follows:

ADD FACTOR TO LINE-CTR.

- TOTAL-SALES is defined as PICTURE 9999V99. The V indicates an *implied* decimal point; none actually exists. V is a pointer that shows the compiler where to align the decimal point for data transfer and arithmetic. Note: Any arithmetic PICTURE without a V implies a V on the right; thus, 999 is the same as 999V.

- HUNDRED is a 2-digit field defined as a 3-digit constant, 100. This is called a SIZE error, for which the compiler generates an error message.

Signs

COBOL always treats the contents of a field defined as PICTURE 999 as positive, but because of corrections and reversing entries, many amount fields may be validly negative—for example, quantity, value, sales amount, hours worked, and customer balance. (Some fields, however, may be defined as always positive; these are usually *rates*, such as rate-of-pay or stock selling price.) The letter S in the PICTURE clause (as in PIC S999) stipulates a signed amount for an input field or a level-77 work field. To minimize incorrect results, always code arithmetic values (level 77 and input items) with a leftmost S.

```
77   AMOUNT-SOLD      PIC S9999V99 VALUE +0.      0000 0C+
77   ROUND-POS        PIC S9       VALUE +5.           5+
77   ROUND-NEG        PIC S9       VALUE -5.           5-
77   COUNT            PIC S999     VALUE +1.         001+
```

- AMOUNT-SOLD allows for a positive or a negative amount. Some COBOL versions require that when PICTURE contains an S, the value must be preceded by a plus (+) or minus (−) sign, in this case VALUE +0.
- ROUND-POS and ROUND-NEG show constant amounts set to +5 and −5 respectively.
- COUNT is defined as three digits, and the amount +1 is stored on the right as 001+.

    To improve compiler efficiency (generate less machine code and execute faster), you should define level-77 arithmetic items as COMPUTATIONAL (abbreviated COMP), or on the 360/370 as COMPUTATIONAL-3 (COMP-3).* For example:

```
77   AMOUNT-SOLD2      PIC S9999V99 COMP-3 VALUE +0.
```

Note: Do not define card input or print fields as COMP or COMP-3. Omission of any COMP usage causes the compiler to assume DISPLAY usage, which is correct for input/output data, but not recommended for normal arithmetic work fields.

*For the 360/370, COMP-3 tells the compiler that the data is to be *packed* in storage, two digits per byte, plus a sign. Other formats: COMP for binary data, and COMP-1 and COMP-2 for floating-point data. CDC-6000 COBOL provides COMP-3 to permit processing of data generated by an IBM system.

Arithmetic Literals

You can also use literals to process arithmetic data. An arithmetic literal is not enclosed in quotes, contains digits 0-9, and may contain a decimal point and, on the left, a sign (+ or −). The maximum length of an arithmetic literal is 18 digits. Examples:

```
VALID:      MOVE  C  TO AMOUNT-SOLD.
            ADD   5  TO LINE-COUNTER.
            MOVE -25.5 TO FACTOR.

INVALID:    ADD 1/2 TO FACTOR.                SLASH (/) IS INVALID
            MOVE $25.00 TO AMOUNT-SOLD.       DOLLAR ($) IS INVALID
            MOVE 25. TO FACTOR.               DECIMAL PT. AT END OF
                                              LITERAL INVALID - USE 25.0
```

MOVE STATEMENT

MOVE is one of the most commonly used COBOL verbs. Its purpose is to transfer the contents of one field to another field. For example, a program may move descriptive fields from the input record to the print area or move calculated arithmetic values to the print area.

MOVE duplicates the data from one storage area into another storage area. The previous contents of the receiving field are entirely replaced; the contents of the sending field are unchanged. As a rule, you should restrict moves between areas of similar data—alphanumeric moves to alphanumeric, and numeric moves to numeric. The only problem that may arise is when the length of the receiving field differs from the length of the sending field. The effect is the same as when a VALUE constant does not agree with the length of its PICTURE. You may also use literals, SPACES, and ZEROS as the sending field.

Alphanumeric MOVE Examples

```
        WORKING-STORAGE SECTION.
        77  ERROR-MESSAGE        PIC X(13).
                                          RESULT IN ERROR-MESSAGE:
        PROCEDURE DIVISION.
1.          MOVE 'END' TO ERROR-MESSAGE.           |END          |
2.          MOVE 'OUT OF SEQUENCE' TO ERROR-MESSAGE.  |OUT OF SEQUEN|
3.          MOVE SPACES TO ERROR-MESSAGE.           |             |
```

Example 1 moves an alphanumeric literal, 'END', which is shorter than the receiving field; the compiler left-adjusts the literal and fills blanks to the right in the receiving field. In example 2, the literal is too long, and two characters are truncated from the right. Example 3 uses the reserved word SPACES to move blanks to ERROR-MESSAGE.

Numeric MOVE Examples

```
WORKING-STORAGE SECTION.
77  AMOUNT                  PIC S999V99.
                                           RESULT IN AMOUNT:

    PROCEDURE DIVISION.
4.        MOVE 12.5       TO AMOUNT.             012.50
5.        MOVE 12345.678  TO AMOUNT.             345.67
6.        MOVE ZEROS      TO AMOUNT.             000.00
7.        MOVE ZEROS      TO DEPT-TOTAL, SALES-TOTAL.
```

Example 4 moves a numeric literal that is shorter than the receiving field. The literal is aligned according to the decimal points—one zero is filled to the left and one zero is filled to the right—correctly. In example 5, the literal 12345.678 is too long on both the left and the right. Therefore, two digits are truncated from the left (an error!), and one digit is truncated from the right (a common truncation of an unwanted decimal place). Leftmost truncation is called a SIZE error. Example 6 uses the reserved word ZEROS to clear AMOUNT to zeros. Example 7 moves a value (ZEROS) to more than one field (DEPT-TOTAL and SALES-TOTAL) using only one MOVE statement. Note that you cannot move SPACES to a numeric field.

PROGRAM EXAMPLE

The program in Figure 3-5 is similar to the program in Figure 3-2, but now includes a final total of stock value. COBOL does not permit accumulating arithmetic amounts in input or output areas. Therefore, this program defines two level-77 items in Working-Storage: STOCK-VALUE for storing the calculated amount, and TOTAL-VALUE for accumulating the final total.

In the Procedure Division, MULTIPLY moves the calculated amount to STOCK-VALUE, and it is then moved to VALUE-OUT. (In Figure 3-2 the multiply moved the result directly to VALUE-OUT.) This example adds the result to TOTAL-VALUE, but COBOL does not permit adding an edited field (with commas, decimals, etc.); it has therefore defined STOCK-VALUE as a temporary work field.

The following shows the print record format for Figure 3-5:

	Stock		Descr'n		Qty		U/Cost		Value
Detail line:	16–20	21–25	26–45	46–49	50–53		59–63	64–68	69——79
	XXXXX		X——X		ZZ9 –		ZZ.99		ZZ,ZZZ.99CR
Total line:						TOTAL VALUE =			ZZZZ,ZZZ.99CR

```
00002              IDENTIFICATION DIVISION.
00003              PROGRAM-ID. CHAPT3C.
00004              REMARKS. PROGRAM CALCULATES AND PRINTS STOCK-VALUE,
00005                        AND PRINTS FINAL TOTAL OF VALUE.

00007              ENVIRONMENT DIVISION.
00008              CONFIGURATION SECTION.
00009              SOURCE-COMPUTER. IBM-370.
00010              OBJECT-COMPUTER. IBM-370.

00012              DATA DIVISION.
00013              WORKING-STORAGE SECTION.
00014              77   STOCK-VALUE          PIC S9(5)V99     VALUE +0   COMP-3.
00015              77   TOTAL-VALUE          PIC S9(7)V99     VALUE +0   COMP-3.

00017              01   STOCK-RECORD-IN.
00018                   03   FILLER          PIC X(4).
00019                   03   STOCK-NO-IN     PIC X(5).
00020                   03   QTY-IN          PIC S999.
00021                   03   UNCOST-IN       PIC S99V99.
00022                   03   DESCRIP-IN      PIC X(20).
00023                   03   FILLER          PIC X(44).

00025              01   STOCK-RECORD-OUT.
00026                   03   FILLER          PIC X(5)     VALUE ' '.
00027                   03   STOCK-NO-OUT    PIC X(5).
00028                   03   FILLER          PIC X(5)     VALUE ' '.
00029                   03   DESCRIP-OUT     PIC X(24).
00030                   03   QTY-OUT         PIC ZZ9-.
00031                   03   FILLER          PIC X(5)     VALUE ' '.
00032                   03   UNCOST-OUT      PIC ZZ.99.
00033                   03   FILLER          PIC X(5)     VALUE ' '.
00034                   03   VALUE-OUT       PIC ZZ,ZZZ.99CR.
00035                   03   FILLER          PIC X(42)    VALUE ' '.

00037              01   TOTAL-RECORD-OUT.
00038                   03   FILLER          PIC X(42)    VALUE ' '.
00039                   03   FILLER          PIC X(14)    VALUE 'TOTAL VALUE ='.
00040                   03   TOTAL-VALUE-OUT PIC ZZZZ,ZZZ.99CR.
00041                   03   FILLER          PIC X        VALUE '*'.
00042                   03   FILLER          PIC X(50)    VALUE ' '.

00044              PROCEDURE DIVISION.
00045                  DISPLAY 'STOCK CALCULATION REPORT'.
00046                  DISPLAY SPACES.
00047                  ACCEPT STOCK-RECORD-IN.
00048                  PERFORM B100-PROCESS UNTIL STOCK-NO-IN = '99999'.
00049                  MOVE TOTAL-VALUE TO TOTAL-VALUE-OUT.
00050                  DISPLAY SPACES.
00051                  DISPLAY TOTAL-RECORD-OUT.
00052                  STOP RUN.

00054              B100-PROCESS SECTION.
00055                  MOVE STOCK-NO-IN TO STOCK-NO-OUT.
00056                  MOVE DESCRIP-IN TO DESCRIP-OUT.
00057                  MOVE QTY-IN TO QTY-OUT.
00058                  MOVE UNCOST-IN TO UNCOST-OUT.
00059                  MULTIPLY QTY-IN BY UNCOST-IN GIVING STOCK-VALUE.
00060                  MOVE STOCK-VALUE TO VALUE-OUT.
00061                  ADD STOCK-VALUE TO TOTAL-VALUE.
00062                  DISPLAY STOCK-RECORD-OUT.
00063                  ACCEPT STOCK-RECORD-IN.
00064              B900-RETURN.  EXIT.
```

FIGURE 3-5 Final Totals.

```
Printed report:

STOCK CALCULATION REPORT

      00230      RIVETTERS            1          1.00              1.00
      00236      ASSEMBLERS          15           .35              5.25
      00245      RE-INFORCERS       100         15.25          1,525.00
      00277      CO-ORDINATORS      525          3.75          1,968.75

                                         TOTAL VALUE =          3,500.00   *
```

FIGURE 3-5   (Cont.)

DEBUGGING

Once you start using arithmetic data in programs, the possibility of errors increases considerably. The following are some common error situations involving arithmetic data.

1.   *Input record definition differs from actual input record.* This is a common error. Consider the following definitions:

	1–2	3–6	7——30	31–34	35–38	39——80
Input record	code	Emp#	Employee name	Rate	Hours	Unused

```
                  01   RECORD-IN.                              COLS:
                       03   CODE-IN         PIC XX.            1-2
                       03   EMPNO-IN        PIC X(4).          3-6
                       03   NAME-IN         PIC X(25).         7-31
      Record           03   RATE-IN         PIC S99V99.        32-35
      definition       03   HOURS-IN        PIC S999V9.        36-39
                       03   FILLER          PIC X(41).         40-80
```

On the input record, name is 24 characters, but in the record definition it is 25 characters. Multiplying hours by rate either will "bomb out" or will result in a very strange answer.

2.   *Arithmetic field is defined as alphanumeric.* The compiler will generate an error message for any statement that uses an alphanumeric field for an arithmetic field.

Input field: 03 RATE-IN   PIC X(4).   *Defined as alphanumeric*
Procedure Division: MULTIPLY HOURS-IN BY RATE-IN GIVING WAGE, ROUNDED.

3.   *Accumulator is not initialized to zero.* This is a common error in any programming language.

Working-Storage: 77 TOTAL-WAGE   PIC S9(6)V99.
Procedure Division: ADD WAGE TO TOTAL-WAGE.

Because TOTAL-WAGE is not initialized with a value (such as VALUE ZEROS), its contents will be "garbage," and the ADD statement will probably fail during execution (a *data exception* error on the 360/370). It is a good practice to initialize all level-77 arithmetic fields.

4. *PICTURE is not defined as signed.* In this case, the program cannot handle correcting and reversing entries. For the following, the compiler generates code that "strips" the minus sign from any input hours field, and all hours are treated as positive.

03 HOURS-IN   PIC 999V9.

5. *Decimal point specifier (V) is improperly placed.* If HOURS-IN, above, is defined as S99V99 instead of S999V9, the program will treat the input of 010.0 as 01.00 hours.

6. *Field length is too short for calculated length (SIZE error).* Be sure to allow sufficient space for receiving calculated values. The following is a simplified example:

Working-Storage: 03   WAGE-PR   PIC ZZZ.99CR.
Procedure Division: MOVE 1234.56 TO WAGE-PR.

The arithmetic literal 1234.56 does not fit into WAGE-PR as defined, and the leftmost 1 is truncated. The PICTURE for WAGE-PR should be Z,ZZZ.99CR.

7. *Alphanumeric literal is incorrectly used.* In the following, the alphanumeric literal 12.50 may generate some unexpected value, and some compilers may produce code that causes all compares to be high.

MOVE '12.50' TO TOTAL-WAGE.

Because TOTAL-WAGE is an arithmetic field, the literal should also be coded as arithmetic, without the apostrophes.

8. *Incorrect end-of-file.* For repetitive processing, be sure that the program provides a valid means to terminate, and that a correct end-of-file record exists.

Many coding errors generate inefficient results rather than incorrect results. Be especially careful to code all arithmetic fields in Working-Storage as computational. On the 360/370, the recommended format for ordinary (decimal) arithmetic fields is COMP-3, and for binary data is COMP. Many other computers require COMP for arithmetic fields.

PROBLEMS

3–1. Define an input record with the following fields using descriptive names:

Cols.
1–6   Part number
7–28 Description

29–32 Quantity on hand
33–37 Price
38–80 Unused

Quantity on hand is numeric format with no decimal places, and Price has two decimal places. Quantity on hand may be negative.

3–2. Define a print record with the following fields using descriptive names:

Cols.
21–26 Part number
30–51 Description
54–58 Quantity (as xxxx −)
62–67 Price (as xxx.xx)
70–79 Sales amount (as x,xxx.xxCR)

3–3. Code a program combining the preceding input and output formats in Working-Storage. The program calculates quantity × price = sales amount.

3–4. Consider the following incomplete record structure:

```
01   EMPLOYEE-RECORD-IN.
     03   CODE-IN
     03   EMPLOYEE-NO-IN
     03   EMPLOYEE-NAME-IN
     03   DATE-IN
          05   MONTH-IN
          05   YEAR-IN
     03   WAGE-IN
     03   FILLER
```

(a) Which are group items and which are elementary items?

(b) Complete the punctuation and PICTURE clauses. CODE-IN is two characters, EMPLOYEE-NO-IN is five characters, EMPLOYEE-NAME-IN is 25 characters, DATE-IN is mmyy, and WAGE-IN provides for amounts such as $1,234.56. The entire record is 80 characters long.

3–5. Code the following alphanumeric items in Working-Storage:

(a) A 5-character field named SAVE-FIELD, and uninitialized.

(b) A field containing the value 'INVALID RECORD'.

(c) A 50-character field named UNDER-LINE containing a string of dashes.

(d) A definition of the word CAT'Y (abbreviation for category).

3–6. Code the following numeric items in Working-Storage as signed and computational according to the requirements of your compiler:

(a) An accumulator named TOTAL-SALES providing for totals up to $5,000,000.

(b) A numeric field named APPLE-PI containing the constant 3.1416.

(c) A numeric field named NEG-AMT containing the constant −235.87.

3–7. Expand the program in Problem 3-3 to permit any number of input records. Provide also for a final sales total at the end of the run and for an end-of-file stopper.

CHAPTER 4

ARITHMETIC AND LOGIC

OBJECTIVE: To cover more advanced COBOL processing involved with arithmetic, editing, and program logic.

INTRODUCTION

This chapter continues the elements of COBOL with more advanced features: arithmetic operations, COMPUTE, editing, and IF statement logic. An understanding of this material enables the coding of quite complex programs.

ARITHMETIC

COBOL arithmetic is quite simple. The basic arithmetic verbs are ADD, SUBTRACT, MULTIPLY, and DIVIDE (another, COMPUTE, is in a later section). These verbs reference numeric data items defined in the Data Division and numeric literals. COBOL provides automatic decimal alignment according to the PICTURE clauses of the referenced fields. For example, the following two values, if added together, align correctly on the decimal point:

$$123.456 + .5 = 123.956$$

Be sure that the fields are defined correctly and the *receiving* field is large enough for the generated result. This practice is vital, because if the receiving field is too short, the operation may cause the loss of the leftmost significant digits (a SIZE error).

ROUNDED Option

The ROUNDED option provides for the rounding of answers. If the number of decimal places in a calculated result exceeds the number of decimal places in a receiving field, ROUNDED causes a program to automatically add +5 or −5, according to the sign, to the first unwanted digit position.

In the following simple arithmetic statements, the receiving field is underlined and is the only field that the operation changes.

```
ADD 2 TO LINE-CTR.
SUBTRACT PAYMENT FROM CUSTOMER-BALANCE.
MULTIPLY SALES-TAX-RATE BY AMOUNT-SOLD, ROUNDED.
DIVIDE TOTAL INTO AMOUNT, ROUNDED.
```

Assume that the fields the MULTIPLY statement references are defined as follows:

```
77   AMOUNT-SOLD         PIC S9(4)V99 COMP-3 VALUE +1234.55.
77   SALES-TAX-RATE      PIC SV99     COMP-3 VALUE +.05.
```

COBOL generates the product in a concealed work area: 00061.7275. ROUNDED causes +5 (or +50 in this case) to add:

$$
\begin{array}{rl}
00061.7275 & \textit{Initial calculated value} \\
+ \qquad .0050 & \textit{Addition of rounding factor} \\
\hline
00061.7325 & \textit{Rounded value}
\end{array}
$$

Because AMOUNT-SOLD is defined as two decimal places, the amount moved into it is 00061.73 (without ROUNDED the result would be 00061.72). Note carefully in MULTIPLY which field is the receiving field.

GIVING Option

The GIVING option moves an arithmetic result to a third field that is not involved in the calculation. The receiving field is the only one that is changed:

```
ADD TAX, PENSION GIVING DEDUCTIONS.
SUBTRACT DEDUCTIONS FROM GROSS-PAY GIVING NET-PAY.
MULTIPLY HOURS BY RATE GIVING GROSS-PAY, ROUNDED.
DIVIDE 26 INTO ANNUAL-TAX GIVING TAX, ROUNDED.
```

Arithmetic Options

There are a variety of ways to perform arithmetic operations, some of which you may never use. The following section lists these operations and should be a useful reference. Some options are not available on all compilers. Assume that all fields are defined correctly as arithmetic declaratives, and names are simplified as A, B, C, etc. for clarity, although such meaningless names are not recommended in a real program. Any of these statements may use the ROUNDED option.

ADD.   The two general formats for the ADD statement are as follows:

```
r---------------------------------------------------------------------¬
|                              Format 1                               |
+---------------------------------------------------------------------+
|        ⌡identifier-1⌡   ⌈identifier-2⌉                              |
| ADD    ⌡literal-1   ⌡   ⌊literal-2   ⌋ ... TO identifier-m [ROUNDED] |
|                                                                     |
|    [identifier-n [ROUNDED]] ... [ON SIZE ERROR imperative-statement] |
L---------------------------------------------------------------------J
```

```
r---------------------------------------------------------------------¬
|                              Format 2                               |
+---------------------------------------------------------------------+
|      ⌡identifier-1⌡  ⌡identifier-2⌡  ⌈identifier-3⌉                 |
| ADD  ⌡literal-1   ⌡  ⌡literal-2   ⌡  ⌊literal-3   ⌋  ...            |
|                                                                     |
|    GIVING identifier-m [ROUNDED] [ON SIZE ERROR imperative-statement]|
L---------------------------------------------------------------------J
```

Examples:

ADDITION: EXPLANATION:

1. ADD A TO X.   ADD CONTENTS OF A TO X.
2. ADD A, B, C TO X.   ADD THREE ITEMS TO X.
3. ADD A, B, C GIVING X.   STORE SUM OF THREE ITEMS IN X.

SUBTRACT.   The two general formats for the SUBTRACT statement are as follows:

```
r---------------------------------------------------------------------¬
|                              Format 1                               |
+---------------------------------------------------------------------+
|           ⌡identifier-1⌡   ⌈identifier-2⌉                          |
| SUBTRACT  ⌡literal-1   ⌡   ⌊literal-2   ⌋   ...                    |
|                                                                     |
|    FROM identifier-m   [ROUNDED]                                    |
|                                                                     |
|    [identifier-n [ROUNDED]] ... [ON SIZE ERROR imperative-statement] |
L---------------------------------------------------------------------J
```

```
---------------------------------------------------------------
|                          Format 2                           |
|-------------------------------------------------------------|
|                                                             |
|              (identifier-1)  [identifier-2]                 |
|   SUBTRACT   {           }   [          ]    ...            |
|              (literal-1  )   [literal-2  ]                  |
|                                                             |
|              (identifier-m)                                 |
|   FROM       {           }   GIVING identifier-n            |
|              (literal-m  )                                  |
|                                                             |
|   [ROUNDED]    [ON SIZE ERROR imperative-statement]         |
|                                                             |
---------------------------------------------------------------
```

Examples:

```
SUBTRACTION:

1. SUBTRACT A FROM X.                    SUBTRACT CONTENT OF A FROM X.
2. SUBTRACT A, B, C FROM X.              SUBTRACT THREE ITEMS FROM X.
3. SUBTRACT A FROM X GIVING Y.           SUBTRACT A FROM X, STORE IN Y.
4. SUBTRACT A, B, C FROM X GIVING Y.     SUBTRACT ITEMS FROM X, STORE IN Y.
```

MULTIPLY. The two general formats for the MULTIPLY statement are as follows:

```
---------------------------------------------------------------
|                          Format 1                           |
|-------------------------------------------------------------|
|                                                             |
|              (identifier-1)                                 |
|   MULTIPLY   {           }   BY identifier-2  [ROUNDED]     |
|              (literal-1  )                                  |
|                                                             |
|        [ON SIZE ERROR imperative-statement]                 |
|                                                             |
---------------------------------------------------------------
```

```
---------------------------------------------------------------
|                          Format 2                           |
|-------------------------------------------------------------|
|                                                             |
|            (identifier-1)     (identifier-2)                |
|   MULTIPLY {           }  BY  {           } GIVING identifier-3 |
|            (literal-1  )     (literal-2  )                  |
|                                                             |
|     [ROUNDED]    [ON SIZE ERROR imperative-statement]       |
|                                                             |
---------------------------------------------------------------
```

Examples:

```
MULTIPLICATION:

1. MULTIPLY A BY X.                 MULTIPLY A AND X, STORE IN X.
2. MULTIPLY A BY B GIVING X.        MULTIPLY A AND B, STORE IN X.
```

DIVIDE.   The two general formats for the DIVIDE statement are as follows:

```
----------------------------------------------------------------------
|                              Format 1                              |
|--------------------------------------------------------------------|
|                                                                    |
|            {identifier-1}                                          |
|    DIVIDE  {          }   INTO identifier-2  [ROUNDED]             |
|            {literal-1  }                                           |
|                                                                    |
|        [ON SIZE ERROR imperative-statement]                       |
|                                                                    |
----------------------------------------------------------------------
```

```
----------------------------------------------------------------------
|                              Format 2                              |
|--------------------------------------------------------------------|
|                                                                    |
|            {identifier-1} {INTO} {identifier-2}                    |
|    DIVIDE  {          }   {    } {          }   GIVING identifier-3 |
|            {literal-1  }  {BY  } {literal-2  }                     |
|                                                                    |
|        [ROUNDED] [REMAINDER identifier-4]                          |
|        [ON SIZE ERROR imperative-statement]                       |
|                                                                    |
----------------------------------------------------------------------
```

Examples:

```
DIVISION:

1. DIVIDE A INTO X.                DIVIDE A INTO X, STORE IN X.
2. DIVIDE A INTO X GIVING Y.       DIVIDE A INTO X, STORE IN Y.
3. DIVIDE X BY A GIVING Y.         DIVIDE X BY A, STORE IN Y.
```

Note that DIVIDE item 3 has the same effect as item 2. Some compilers allow for a REMAINDER option for DIVIDE because there are occasional uses for a remainder. For example, an interest calculation requires that a program allow for a leap year. The program can divide the year by 4; if the remainder contains zero, it is a leap year. (There is an exception: although the year 2000 is a leap year, the end of centuries 1800, 1900, and 2100 are not.) Also, some disk addressing techniques use remainders to generate disk addresses.

REMAINDER must be coded following the ROUNDED option if both are coded and may be used only with a GIVING clause. Some compilers permit use of REMAINDER only if the quotient contains no decimal places. The following example stores the remainder in a field named REMAIN-AMT:

DIVIDE 26 INTO ANNUAL-TAX GIVING TAX ROUNDED, REMAINDER REMAIN-AMT.

The ANS standard provides for a GIVING clause with more than one item, as

MULTIPLY A BY B GIVING X, Y.

This example stores the product in both X and Y. Not all compilers permit this feature.

SIZE ERRORS

A SIZE error occurs when an arithmetic calculation generates a value that exceeds the size of a receiving field. One common example is an attempt to divide by a zero value. A SIZE error can cause the loss of leftmost significant digits, as shown in the following example:

```
WORKING-STORAGE SECTION.
77  HOURS              PIC S99V99  COMP-3.
77  RATE-OF-PAY        PIC 99V99   COMP-3.
77  WAGE               PIC S999V99 COMP-3.

PROCEDURE DIVISION.
    MULTIPLY HOURS BY RATE-OF-PAY GIVING WAGE, ROUNDED.
```

Assume that HOURS contains 90.00, and RATE-OF-PAY contains 12.00. The result of the MULTIPLY statement as generated in the COBOL work area is 1080.00. But WAGE as defined can accommodate values only as large as 999.99. When attempting to move the product into WAGE, the MULTIPLY statement delivers an unpredictable result in WAGE and signals no error condition. There is, however, an ON SIZE ERROR option that can test for such an error:

```
MULTIPLY HOURS BY RATE-OF-PAY GIVING WAGE, ROUNDED,
    ON SIZE ERROR DISPLAY 'INVALID WAGE'.
```

If a SIZE error occurs for this statement during execution, the program goes to the error routine specified without changing the contents of WAGE. The error routine can also print a warning message. If there is no SIZE error, the program stores the correct value in WAGE and continues with normal processing.

When coding, try to avoid causing SIZE errors as much as possible. Thus, check for a zero divisor before dividing, and define a product field to accept the largest possible result. In the example, HOURS and RATE-OF-PAY are both defined as 99V99; consequently, after rounding, the product WAGE could be as large as 9999V99. SIZE errors may also occur with ADD, SUBTRACT, and COMPUTE. By carefully defining data fields, you will need to use ON SIZE ERROR only occasionally.

COMPUTE STATEMENT

The COMPUTE verb is used for arithmetic expressions that are too complicated for the usual ADD, SUBTRACT, MULTIPLY, and DIVIDE. Its general format is as follows:

COMPUTE result [ROUNDED] = expression [ON SIZE ERROR statement]

GIVING is not used with COMPUTE, and the arithmetic operators of COMPUTE are as follows:

+ Addition	− Subtraction	* Multiplication
/ Division	** Exponentiation	

You may also use parentheses with COMPUTE. COMPUTE processes an expression within parentheses first, and their use can often make the expression clearer. The following examples illustrate the use of COMPUTE with complicated calculations:

1. To calculate depreciation based on the diminishing balance, multiply the undepreciated asset cost (original cost less accumulated depreciation to date) by the depreciation rate:

```
COMPUTE DEPRECIATION ROUNDED
    = (ORIGINAL-COST - ACCUM-DEPRECN) * DEPREC-RATE.
```

Note the space before and after the arithmetic operators (− and *). ANS COBOL permits a space after the left parenthesis and before the right parenthesis, as in (A * B), but this is not allowed under IBM/370 COBOL. Without parentheses, the program would first multiply ACCUM-DEPRECN by DEPREC-RATE, and then subtract this product from ORIGINAL-COST

2. To calculate the Economic Order Quantity of inventory stock, the following formula is used:

$$EOQ = \sqrt{\frac{2 \times AR \times AC}{i}}$$

where AR = annual requirement of stock, AC = acquisition cost, and i = possession cost as a percentage. To calculate the square root, use an exponent of .5:

```
COMPUTE ECON-ORDER-QTY
    = ((2 * ANN-REQT * ACQUIS-COST) / POSS-COST) ** .5.
```

The following rules pertain to COMPUTE:

1. At least one space must precede and follow each arithmetic operator.
2. COMPUTE first performs the contents of parentheses. The next priority is exponentiation, then multiplication and division (from left to right in the expression), and then addition and subtraction (from left to right). When parentheses are within parentheses, the contents of the innermost pair are evaluated first. In the EOQ example, COBOL first performs the calculation within parentheses:

```
(2 * ANN-REQT * ACQUIS-COST)
```

The program first multiplies 2 by ANN-REQT, and then multiplies the product by ACQUIS-COST. The result is then divided by POSS-COST, and finally the square root is calculated.

EDITING ARITHMETIC DATA

Arithmetic data defined as input or as level-77 work areas use 9 for a digit, V for an implied decimal point, and S for a sign. Be sure to distinguish these items from arithmetic fields defined for printing. The PICTURE characters 9 and V are both available for print definitions, but not S. The normal practice is to provide for leftmost zero suppression, comma, decimal point, and minus sign or CR symbol to the right of an edited amount. The common edit "insert character" symbols include the following:

INSERT CHARACTER	EFFECT
. Decimal point	Aligns on decimal point position and inserts period.
, Comma	Inserts a comma if there are nonzero digits to the left.
B Blank	Inserts a blank character.
$ Dollar sign	Inserts a dollar sign ($ must be coded on the left).
+ Plus sign or ⎫	Inserts correct plus or minus sign (+ or –), usually
– Minus sign ⎭	on the right.
CR Credit or ⎫	Inserts CR or DB (two characters). These should be
DB Debit ⎭	coded on the right.
/ Slash	Inserts slash (/), often used for printing the date.

Also, you can use the following "replacement characters" in place of leftmost 9s in the PICTURE statement:

REPLACEMENT CHARACTER	EFFECT
Z Zero suppress	Replaces leftmost zeros with blanks.
* Asterisk	Replaces leftmost zeros with asterisks (usually for check protection).
$ Dollar sign	Floating dollar.
+ or –sign	Floating sign.

Decimal Point

The PICTURE letter *V* is an indication to the compiler of the position of the implied decimal point for input and work areas. Most reports require the printing of a decimal point, and for this purpose you use an actual decimal point (.) instead of a V. PICTURE does not permit both V and decimal point (.) in the same definition. Note that a MOVE statement aligns the arithmetic fields according to the PICTURE V and the decimal point in the field definitions:

```
WORKING-STORAGE SECTION.
77   AMOUNT              PIC S9999V999 COMP-3.
01   PRINT-AREA.
     05   FILLER         PIC X(25).
     05   AMOUNT-OUT     PIC 9,999.99CR.

PROCEDURE DIVISION.
     MOVE AMOUNT TO AMOUNT-OUT.
```

If AMOUNT contains 1234.567 (three decimal places), then according to the definitions, the contents of AMOUNT-OUT after the MOVE is 1,234.56 (two decimal places). Remember also that the USAGE for AMOUNT is COMP-3 (COMP on some systems) because it is a field in which arithmetic is performed. The USAGE for AMOUNT-OUT is (understood to be) DISPLAY and is not used for arithmetic.

Zero Suppression

In AMOUNT-OUT defined previously, the PICTURE does not provide for leftmost zero suppression, and a value will print, for example, as 0,000.01. In the following definition of AMOUNT-OUT, the coding of PICTURE Zs to the left causes zero suppression, and such a value will print as 0.01:

```
05 AMOUNT-OUT     PIC Z,ZZ9.99CR.
```

Either blanks (Z) or asterisks (*) may replace leftmost zeros in the suppressed positions, but both may not be used in the same PICTURE.

Comma, Blank, and Zero

PICTURE editing permits insertion of commas (,), blanks (B), and zeros (0), each requiring one print position. This example shows the use of the blank insert character (B):

```
05 AMOUNT-OUT     PIC Z,ZZ9.99BCR.
```

If the edited amount contains 1234.56 −, it will print as 1,234.56 CR (a blank between the rightmost digit and the CR, as defined).

Negative Values

Because of correcting and reversing entries, most amount fields may contain negative values. Thus, even such entries as hours worked can occasionally be negative, although it is not possible to actually work minus hours. Some fields such as rate-of-pay may be defined as always positive, but they are unique. It requires little additional programming effort to ensure that a report is accurate; therefore, to be safe, always code arithmetic input fields and work areas with a leading S, as S999V99, and arithmetic print fields with a minus sign (–), CR, or, in some cases, DB. The symbol DB (for debit) is sometimes used to denote a negative value.

CR and DB are always placed to the right of a value. The minus sign (–) is typically placed to the right in a business report and to the left in a mathematical report. PICTURE editing also places the plus sign (+) to the left or right; the amount prints with a plus sign (+) if positive and a minus sign (–) if negative.

Dollar Sign

The dollar sign ($) is placed to the left of the PICTURE and requires one print position. Many programmers omit the dollar sign because it tends to clutter the appearance of a report. The following PICTURE definition provides for a fixed dollar sign; the value 0000.25 will print as $ 0.25:

05 AMOUNT-OUT   PIC $Z,ZZ9.99CR.

Floating Signs ($, +, and −)

Floating signs are useful for check protection to ensure that no one can insert a number to the left of a printed amount. For example, it would be relatively easy to alter $ 0.25 to become $1,230.25.

Floating dollar signs can be used in place of 9s:

05 AMOUNT-OUT   PIC $,$$9.99CR.

In this case, the amount 0000.25 will print as $0.25. It is also possible to float the minus (−) and plus (+) signs. Floating minus signs cause blanks if positive and a single minus sign (−) if negative; −0000.25 prints as −0.25. Floating a plus sign causes a single plus sign (+) if positive and a single minus sign (−) if negative.

In Table 4-1, the data in the sending PICTURE is moved to the receiving PICTURE. The Edited Result shows the contents after the MOVE statement performs the edit.

Slash

ANS-74 COBOL uses the slash (/) as an editing character, although IBM has not implemented it at the time of this writing. If the slash is not available on your compiler, you have a number of options. You can move slashes as literals directly to the print area. Also, the EXAMINE or INSPECT statements (depending on the compiler version) can insert slashes by replacing blanks in the edited field, as follows:

```
77  DATE-FIELD          PIC 9(6).     (MMDDYY)
77  DATE-OUT            PIC 99B99B99.
      .
      .
      .
MOVE DATE-FIELD TO DATE-OUT.
EXAMINE DATE-OUT REPLACING ALL SPACES BY '/'.
```

TABLE 4-1

SENDING PICTURE	DATA	RECEIVING PICTURE	EDITED RESULT	COMMENT
99999	12345	99999	12345	No editing specified.
999V99	12345	ZZZ.99	123.45	Inserts decimal point.
999V99	000^05	ZZZ.99	bbb.05	Zero suppresses 3 digits.
9999V99	1234^56	Z,ZZZ.99	1,234.56	Inserts comma and decimal point.
9999V99	0001^25	Z,ZZZ.99	bbbb1.25	Zero suppresses.
9999V99	0000^05	Z,ZZZ.99	bbbbb.05	Zero suppresses.
9999V99	0000^00	Z,ZZZ.ZZ	blank	Suppresses all characters.
9999V99	0005^00	$Z,ZZZ.99	$bbbb5.00	Dollar sign.
9999V99	0005^00	$$,$$$.99	bbbb$5.00	Floating dollar sign.
S9999V99	0006^50	Z,ZZZ.99CR	bbbb6.50	Positive value—deletes CR.
S9999V99	-0006^50	Z,ZZZ.99CR	bbbb6.50CR	Negative value—inserts CR.
S9999V99	-0006^50	Z,ZZZ.99 −	bbbb6.50 −	Negative value—inserts minus sign.
S9999V99	0006^50	*,***.99CR	****6.50	Leading asterisks.
S9999V99	0006^50	−,−−−.99	bbbb6.50	Floating minus sign, + value.
S9999V99	-0006^50	−,−−−.99	bbb −6.50	Floating minus sign, − value.
999999	110381	99/99/99	11/03/81	Inserts slashes in date.

BLANK WHEN ZERO

The BLANK WHEN ZERO clause will cause a field containing all zeros to print as blank, regardless of PICTURE editing. For example:

```
05 AMOUNT-OUT    PIC ZZ,ZZZ.99CR  BLANK WHEN ZERO.
```

If the edited amount contains 0000025, the result is .25, but if the amount is 0000000, the result is all blanks. However, a blank field on a report often looks like a program or printer error. Therefore, for most purposes, it is preferable to print .00 and not to use the BLANK WHEN ZERO clause.

THE IF STATEMENT

A typical business program must test for various conditions, such as: Is a code valid? or is an amount zero? Depending on the result of a test, the program must perform some specific action. The COBOL IF statement is used for this purpose. IF compares alphanumeric fields to each other and numeric fields to each other. IF may also use the figurative constants SPACES and ZEROS. The *relational operators* that IF may use are as follows:

IS GREATER THAN	or >	IS NOT GREATER THAN	or NOT >
IS LESS THAN	or <	IS NOT LESS THAN	or NOT <
IS EQUAL TO	or =	IS NOT EQUAL TO	or NOT =

As a word, IS has no function, but some programmers use it for readability.

Alphanumeric Comparisons

IF compares alphanumeric (nonarithmetic) data fields from left to right. Normally the two alphanumeric fields being compared are the same length, as in the next two examples. If the two fields are of different length, the compiler extends the shorter one with rightmost blanks. The following examples use the defined code:

```
77   PREV-CUSTOMER        PIC X(7).
01   CUSTOMER-RECORD.
     03   RECORD-CODE-IN   PIC XX.
     03   CUSTOMER-IN      PIC X(7).
```

1.   *Test for Valid Record Code:*

```
IF RECORD-CODE-IN IS NOT EQUAL TO '21'
   MOVE 'INVALID.RECORD' TO REC-MESS-OUT.
```

If RECORD-CODE-IN contains the value 21, the program bypasses the MOVE and continues with the statement that follows. If not 21, it moves the message and continues with the statement that follows. The indentation of the MOVE is a common convention to indicate to the reader that the MOVE is subject to the IF and has no meaning to the compiler. The same result would occur if the MOVE were on the same line as the IF or directly under the IF. The IF may also be coded with the following shorthand method on many compilers:

```
IF RECORD-CODE-IN NOT = '21'
```

2.   *Test for Valid Customer Sequence.* The following executes two statements if the result of the test is true:

```
IF CUSTOMER-IN NOT > PREV-CUSTOMER
   MOVE 'OUT OF SEQUENCE' TO SEQ-MESS-OUT
   DISPLAY ERROR-RECORD.
```

If CUSTOMER-IN (the current input customer number) is higher than the previously read customer number, bypass the MOVE and the DISPLAY statements. If CUSTOMER-IN is not higher, MOVE the message and DISPLAY the record. Note the importance here of accurate punctuation: the MOVE statement is followed by a *blank* instead of a period. (A comma acts the same as a blank.) If there were a *period* following the MOVE statement, the DISPLAY statement would not be part of the IF logic and would always be executed for CUSTOMER-IN both higher and not higher. The period at the end of the DISPLAY statement terminates the IF logic.

3.   *Test for Alphabetic Data.* You can test whether an alphanumeric field contains only characters A through Z and blanks by using the reserved word ALPHA-BETIC:

```
IF CUSTOMER-NAME IS NOT ALPHABETIC ...
```

4.   *Test for Blanks:* The following statement tests if an alphanumeric record contains blanks:

```
IF CUSTOMER-RECORD = ' '  ...     (OR = SPACES ...)
```

Numeric Comparisons

When using the IF statement for numeric comparisons, both fields being compared must be numeric (PICTURE 9s), but need not be the same length. COBOL makes an *algebraic* comparison; consequently, +1.25 is greater than 0, and 0 is greater than −123.45.

The following are examples of numeric comparisons.

1.   Test if Customer Balance Exceeds Credit Limit:

```
77  CUSTOMER-BALANCE      PIC S9(5)V99.
77  CREDIT-LIMIT          PIC S9(5)V99.

    IF CUSTOMER-BALANCE > CREDIT-LIMIT
       MOVE 'OVERLIMIT' TO LIMIT-MESS-OUT.
```

2.   Test for Zero Divisor: If not zero, calculate price and move to output:

```
77  QTY                   PIC S9(5).

    IF QTY NOT = 0
       DIVIDE QTY INTO VALUE-ON-HAND GIVING STOCK-PRICE
       MOVE STOCK-PRICE TO PRICE-OUT.
```

3. Test for Signs: Numeric tests can also use the reserved words POSITIVE, ZERO, and NEGATIVE:

```
IF AMOUNT IS POSITIVE . . .   same as IF AMOUNT > 0 . . .
IF QTY IS NOT ZERO . . .      same as IF QTY NOT = 0 . . .
IF TOTAL IS NEGATIVE . . .    same as IF TOTAL < 0 . . .
```

4. Test for Numeric Data: You can test if a numeric field contains only the valid digits 0 through 9 by using the reserved word NUMERIC:

```
IF QTY-IN IS NOT NUMERIC ...
```

ELSE

The preceding IF examples were relatively simple; if the result of a comparison is true, then execute one (or more) statements. Some IF conditions are complex, involving special action for both *true* and *not true* conditions. For example, suppose a program has to calculate sales commissions based on total sales for a period. If a salesman has sales exceeding $5,000.00, he receives a commission of $100.00 plus a bonus of 12% of sales over $2,500.00; if not, he receives a commission of only 8% of sales:

```
IF AMOUNT-SOLD > 5000.00
      COMPUTE BONUS, ROUNDED = (AMOUNT-SOLD - 2500.00) * .12
      COMPUTE COMMISSION = BONUS + 100.00
ELSE MOVE ZERO TO BONUS
      COMPUTE COMMISSION = SALES * .08.
```

If the comparison is *true* (sales greater than $5000), the program executes the next two statements and bypasses the ELSE (not true) and its two statements. (The true condition continues until it finds a period or an ELSE.) If the comparison is *not true* (sales not greater than $5000), the program bypasses the true statements and goes to the ELSE in order to execute the not true statements.

PROGRAM EXAMPLE

Figures 4-1 and 4-2 show the flowchart and coding to illustrate a new programming feature—sequence checking.

Sequence Check

Business programs typically require that data records in a file be in ascending sequence according to a *control word* (e.g., account, customer, stock number). In this way, the recipient of a report can easily locate a particular item. In the example, there is a level-77 item called PREV-STOCK. The program checks if the stock number in the input record is higher than the previous stock number:

```
IF STOCK-NO-IN NOT > PREV-STOCK ...
```

For a not-high sequence, the program moves an error message to the print area and by-passes storing the stock number. For records in sequence, the program saves the stock number in a special field in Working-Storage—PREV-STOCK:

```
MOVE STOCK-NO-IN TO PREV-STOCK.
```

In this way, the next test for sequence compares the currently read stock number to the previously processed one.

LOW-VALUES

The *first* compare of STOCK-NO-IN to PREV-STOCK must be validly high. If PREV-STOCK were initialized with VALUE SPACES, and the first input stock number happened to be blank, the two fields would compare as equal. To avoid such a possibility, the program initializes PREV-STOCK with the figurative constant LOW-VALUES, which generates the lowest possible value for the computer, binary zeros (all zero bits). A field containing LOW-VALUES is lower in value than one containing blanks, which on many computers is a unique combination of 0-bits and 1-bits.

Some compilers do not permit initializing with VALUE LOW-VALUES. The solution in such cases is to code

```
MOVE LOW-VALUES TO PREV-STOCK
```

at the start of the Procedure Division. The low value that PREV-STOCK now contains is unlikely ever to occur in the input record. The receiving field for LOW-VALUES must be alphanumeric: PIC X(n). In the first input record, STOCK-IN could possibly contain blanks or character zeros (not binary zeros), but it will never be equal to or lower than PREV-STOCK. There will now never be a false equal or low test condition on the first input record.

Clearing the Print Area

When the program prints an error message, the message remains in the print area because printing does not automatically clear the print area. The next line printed, even if valid, will still contain and print the same message. Similarly, an error line

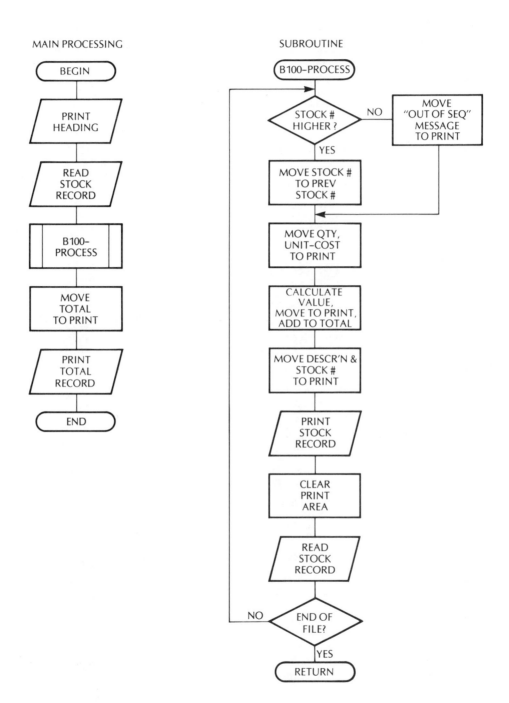

FIGURE 4-1   Test for Sequence.

```
00002              IDENTIFICATION DIVISION.
00003              PROGRAM-ID. CHAPT04.

00005              ENVIRONMENT DIVISION.
00006              CONFIGURATION SECTION.
00007              SOURCE-COMPUTER. IBM-370.
00008              OBJECT-COMPUTER. IBM-370.

00010              DATA DIVISION.
00011              WORKING-STORAGE SECTION.
00012              77  PREV-STOCK          PIC X(5)        VALUE LOW-VALUES.
00013              77  STOCK-VALUE         PIC S9(5)V99    VALUE +0   COMP-3.
00014              77  TOTAL-VALUE         PIC S9(7)V99    VALUE +0   COMP-3.

00016              01  STOCK-RECORD-IN.
00017                  03  CODE-IN         PIC XX.
00018                  03  FILLER          PIC XX.
00019                  03  STOCK-NO-IN     PIC X(5).
00020                  03  QTY-IN          PIC S999.
00021                  03  UNCOST-IN       PIC S99V99.
00022                  03  DESCRIP-IN      PIC X(20).
00023                  03  FILLER          PIC X(44).

00025              01  HEADING-RECORD-OUT.
00026                  03  FILLER          PIC X(15)   VALUE ' '.
00027                  03  FILLER          PIC X(34)   VALUE 'STOCK'.
00028                  03  FILLER          PIC X(23)   VALUE 'QTY      UN-COST'.
00029                  03  FILLER          PIC X(48)   VALUE 'VALUE'.

00031              01  STOCK-RECORD-OUT.
00032                  03  FILLER          PIC X(15)   VALUE ' '.
00033                  03  STOCK-NO-OUT    PIC X(5).
00034                  03  FILLER          PIC X(5)    VALUE ' '.
00035                  03  DESCRIP-OUT     PIC X(24).
00036                  03  QTY-OUT         PIC ZZ9-.
00037                  03  FILLER          PIC X(5)    VALUE ' '.
00038                  03  UNCOST-OUT      PIC ZZ.99.
00039                  03  FILLER          PIC X(5)    VALUE ' '.
00040                  03  VALUE-OUT       PIC ZZ,ZZZ.99CR.
00041                  03  ERR-MESS-OUT    PIC X(41)   VALUE ' '.

00043              01  TOTAL-RECORD-OUT.
00044                  03  FILLER          PIC X(52)   VALUE ' '.
00045                  03  FILLER          PIC X(14)   VALUE 'TOTAL VALUE ='.
00046                  03  TOTAL-VALUE-OUT PIC ZZZZ,ZZZ.99CR.
00047                  03  FILLER          PIC X       VALUE '*'.
00048                  03  FILLER          PIC X(40)   VALUE ' '.
```

FIGURE 4-2   Test for Sequence.

will contain the value calculated for a previous line. In order to prevent this, the program clears each line after printing to ensure that there is no "garbage" from the previous output record:

```
MOVE SPACES TO STOCK-RECORD-OUT.
```

```
00050              PROCEDURE DIVISION.
00051                  DISPLAY HEADING-RECORD-OUT.
00052                  DISPLAY SPACES.
00053                  ACCEPT STOCK-RECORD-IN.
00054                  PERFORM B100-PROCESS UNTIL STOCK-NO-IN = '99999'.
00055                  DISPLAY SPACES.
00056                  MOVE TOTAL-VALUE TO TOTAL-VALUE-OUT.
00057                  DISPLAY TOTAL-RECORD-OUT.
00058                  STOP RUN.

00060              B100-PROCESS SECTION.
00061                  IF STOCK-NO-IN NOT > PREV-STOCK
00062                      MOVE 'EQUAL OR LOW SEQUENCE' TO ERR-MESS-OUT
00063                  ELSE
00064                      MOVE STOCK-NO-IN TO PREV-STOCK.
00065                  MOVE QTY-IN TO QTY-OUT.
00066                  MOVE UNCOST-IN TO UNCOST-OUT.
00067                  COMPUTE STOCK-VALUE = QTY-IN * UNCOST-IN.
00068                  ADD STOCK-VALUE TO TOTAL-VALUE.
00069                  MOVE STOCK-VALUE TO VALUE-OUT.
00070                  MOVE DESCRIP-IN TO DESCRIP-OUT.
00071                  MOVE STOCK-NO-IN TO STOCK-NO-OUT.
00072                  DISPLAY STOCK-RECORD-OUT.
00073                  MOVE SPACES TO STOCK-RECORD-OUT.
00074                  ACCEPT STOCK-RECORD-IN.
00075              B999-RETURN.  EXIT.
```

```
Printed report:

STOCK                  QTY    UN-COST        VALUE

00230   RIVETTERS        1      1.00          1.00
00245   RE-INFORCERS   100     15.25      1,525.00
00236   ASSEMBLERS      15       .35          5.25     EQUAL OR LOW SEQUENCE
00277   CO-ORDINATORS  525      3.75      1,968.75

                         TOTAL VALUE =    3,500.00   *
```

FIGURE 4-2   (Cont.)

FIGURATIVE CONSTANTS

COBOL contains a number of *figurative constants* that you can reference as values. You may assign the following figurative constant to either numeric or alphanumeric fields:

ZERO/ZEROS/ZEROES

The following may be assigned only to alphanumeric fields:

SPACE/SPACES	To clear an alphanumeric field to blanks.
ALL 'char'	To reproduce a string of identical characters.
HIGH-VALUES	To generate the computer's highest value (binary ones).
LOW-VALUES	To generate the computer's lowest value (binary zeros).

All the figurative constants except HIGH-VALUES have been used in this text. HIGH-VALUES is useful in advanced programming to handle end-of-file conditions when a program is reading more than one input file.

ERROR PREVENTION

The following points regarding error prevention were introduced in this chapter.

1. Use ON SIZE ERROR in the program testing stage, but not in a regular production program.
2. Use COMPUTE to make any complicated arithmetic expression clearer.
3. Design edit pictures to agree in size with the actual arithmetic field being edited and to allow for negative values.
4. Initialize a "previous" control word to LOW-VALUES to ensure that a first sequence test will always be high.
5. Clear the print area after printing each line to ensure that there is no "garbage" included in the line that follows.
6. Initialize all arithmetic accumulators to zero.
7. Double-check all IF logic coding. IF logic is critical; improper comparison can cause totally unexpected results. The following code is supposed to check whether the customer balance is greater than the credit limit:

```
IF CREDIT-LIMIT-IN > CUSTOMER-BALANCE-IN
   MOVE 'OVER LIMIT' TO MESSAGE-OUT.
```

This IF statement has incorrectly reversed the two fields being compared, and MESSAGE-OUT will print for customers whose balance is less than their credit limit. Consider the punctuation error in the following:

```
IF CUSTOMER-BALANCE-IN > CREDIT-LIMIT-IN
   MOVE 'OVER LIMIT' TO MESSAGE-OUT.     Period coded
   DISPLAY ERROR-MESSAGE.                in error
```

The period following the MOVE statement should be a comma or a blank. With a period coded, the program will DISPLAY the message when the balance exceeds the credit limit (correctly) and when it does not exceed the credit limit (incorrectly).

Another IF statement error can occur when a required period is missing:

```
IF CODE-IN NOT = '21'
      MOVE 'INVALID CODE' TO ERROR-MESS-OUT,            Comma coded
COMPUTE WAGE ROUNDED = HOURS X RATE.                    in error
```

In the example, the MOVE statement is not followed by a period; as a result, the compiler treats the COMPUTE statement as part of the IF logic that executes only if the statement is true.

8.   Test for blank amount fields. An arithmetic input field, such as an employee's year-to-date gross pay, could be blank on the record. The intention is usually to treat the amount as a zero value. But on IBM computers, an attempt to perform arithmetic on a blank field causes an abnormal termination (a "data exception"). The program could test first if the field is blank:

```
03   GROSS-YD          PIC S9(5)V99.
     .
     .
     .
IF GROSS-YD = SPACES
   MOVE ZEROS TO GROSS-YD.
```

But because GROSS-YD is defined as PIC 9s, the compiler does not permit comparing it against the figurative constant SPACES. And if GROSS-YD is defined as PIC Xs, you can compare it to SPACES but cannot perform arithmetic on it. A simple solution is to define the amount field as follows:

```
03   GROSS-YD-CHAR.
     05   GROSS-YD-AMT          PIC S9(5)V99.
     .
     .
IF GROSS-YD-CHAR = SPACES
   MOVE ZEROS TO GROSS-YD-AMT.
```

The field is now, in effect, defined with two names. GROSS-YD-CHAR assumes the DISPLAY usage (alphanumeric). Because it is a "group item," it contains no PIC clause, but has the same length (seven) as GROSS-YD-AMT. GROSS-YD-AMT redefines GROSS-YD-CHAR with an arithmetic picture. You can now reference the same field as either alphanumeric or as arithmetic, depending on which name you use. The COBOL compiler permits a comparison of GROSS-YD-CHAR to SPACES because they are both alphanumeric, and permits arithmetic processing on GROSS-YD-AMT because it is defined as an arithmetic value and once cleared to ZEROS contains valid data.

PROBLEMS

4-1. Code the arithmetic statements for each of the following, using ADD, SUB-TRACT, MULTIPLY, or DIVIDE. Assume that AMTA, AMTB, AMTC, and AMTD are suitably defined as numeric items.

(a) Add the contents of AMTA to AMTB.

(b) Add the contents of AMTA and AMTB to AMTC.

(c) Add AMTA, AMTB, and AMTC, and store the result in AMTD.

(d) Subtract AMTA and AMTB from AMTC.

(e) Subtract AMTA and AMTB from AMTC and store the result in AMTD.

(f) Multiply AMTA by AMTB, and store the product in AMTA.

(g) Multiply AMTA by AMTB, and store the rounded product in AMTD.

(h) Divide AMTA into AMTB, and store the quotient in AMTB.

(i) Divide AMTA into AMTB, and store the rounded quotient in AMTC and the remainder in AMTD.

4-2. A field defined as PIC S999 contains the value 995. A program adds 5 to the field. What is the effect on the field and program execution?

4-3. What is the purpose of the ON SIZE ERROR clause?

4-4. What is the effect of dividing by a zero value?

4-5. Provide the COMPUTE statements for the following. Use any valid descriptive names.

(a) $y = mn + b$ (straight line)

(b) $D = \frac{1}{2}at^2$ (distance of falling object)

(c) $V = 4/3\,\pi r^3$ (volume of a sphere)

4-6. Indicate the edited result for each of the following:

	SENDING PICTURE	DATA	RECEIVING PICTURE	EDITED RESULTS
(a)	9(5)	12345	9(5)	
(b)	9(5)	12345	9(7)	
(c)	9(5)V99	02345V67	9(5).99	
(d)	9(5)V99	02345V67	9(5)	
(e)	S9(5)V99	00345V67	ZZZZZ.99CR	
(f)	S9(5)V99	−02345V67	ZZ,ZZ9.99CR	
(g)	S9(5)V99	00345V67	$ZZ,ZZ9.99CR	
(h)	S9(5)V99	00045V67	$$$,$$$.99CR	
(i)	S9(5)V99	−00045V67	***,**9.99CR	
(j)	S9(5)V99	00000V00	ZZ,ZZZ.99CR	BLANK WHEN ZERO

4–7. Provide IF statement logic for the following situations. Define any necessary declaratives with descriptive names.

(a) If a customer record field named DISCO contains discount code D, move a value of 0.12 to discount rate (DISCRAT).

(b) If a current customer number is higher than the previously processed number, move the new number (CUSTIN) to the previous number (CUSTPREV).

(c) If a field named DAYS contains an amount greater than 30, move "AMOUNT OVERDUE" to MESSAGE-OUT, otherwise move "CURRENT DUE" to MESSAGE-OUT.

4–8. Code the following program that processes Accounts Receivable records.

Col.
1–2 Record code (23)
6–10 Customer number
11–30 Customer name
31–32 Current month
41–46 Balance owing (two decimals)
57–50 Credit limit (no decimals)
51–80 Unused

Records are in ascending sequence by customer number, one per customer. Compare customer balances to their credit limit. If the balance exceeds the limit, move a message "OVER LIMIT" to the print area. If the record is not in ascending sequence, move an error message to the print area. Print all data from every record except record code. Balance owing may be negative, because of overpayments.

At the end of the run, print the total of Balance Owing.

Provide test data that checks both regular data as well as over limit, out of sequence, and credit balances.

CHAPTER 5

FULL INPUT/OUTPUT

OBJECTIVE: *To cover the requirements for writing COBOL programs using the full input/output features of READ and WRITE.*

INTRODUCTION

ACCEPT and DISPLAY are adequate for programs with a low volume of input and output. Although these statements generate inefficient machine code, their simplicity makes them convenient for introducing COBOL to beginners. The normal input/output statements for card, printer, tape, and disk files are READ and WRITE. These statements involve additional coding requirements in the Environment and Data Divisions. Most systems require programs to open the files before reading or writing the first record, and to close the files after processing the last record.

The program example in Figure 5-1 is more realistic and representative of business COBOL programming. The program is similar to Figure 4-2 in the previous chapter that calculates stock value, but now includes the requirements for the READ and WRITE statements.

The sections following the example program introduce the new features in the Environment Division (the Input-Output Section), the Data Division (the File Section), and the Procedure Division (the OPEN, CLOSE, READ, and WRITE statements).

```
00002            IDENTIFICATION DIVISION.
00003            PROGRAM-ID. CHAPT5.

00005            ENVIRONMENT DIVISION.
00006            INPUT-OUTPUT SECTION.
00007            FILE-CONTROL.
00008                SELECT STOCK-FILE. ASSIGN TO SYS015-UR-2501-S.
00009                SELECT PRINT-FILE. ASSIGN TO SYS014-UR-1403-S.

00011            DATA DIVISION.
00012            FILE SECTION.
00013            FD   STOCK-FILE
00014                 LABEL RECORDS ARE OMITTED
00015                 RECORDING MODE IS F
00016                 DATA RECORD IS STOCK-RECORD.
00017            01   STOCK-RECORD.
00018                 03   CODE-IN        PIC XX.
00019                 03   FILLER         PIC XX.
00020                 03   STOCK-IN       PIC X(5).
00021                 03   QTY-IN         PIC S999.
00022                 03   UNCOST-IN      PIC S99V99.
00023                 03   DESCRIP-IN     PIC X(20).
00024                 03   FILLER         PIC X(44).

00026            FD   PRINT-FILE
00027                 LABEL RECORDS ARE OMITTED
00028                 RECORDING MODE IS F
00029                 DATA RECORD IS PRINT-RECORD.
00030            01   PRINT-RECORD        PIC X(133).

00032            WORKING-STORAGE SECTION.
00033            77   EOF-FLAG            PIC X(3)       VALUE SPACES.
00034            77   PREV-STOCK          PIC X(5)       VALUE LOW-VALUES.
00035            77   STOCK-VALUE         PIC S9(5)V99   VALUE +0   COMP-3.
00036            77   TOTAL-VALUE         PIC S9(7)V99   VALUE +0   COMP-3.

00038            01   HEADING-LINE.
00039                 03   FILLER         PIC X(15)      VALUE ' '.
00040                 03   FILLER         PIC X(10)      VALUE 'STOCK'.
00041                 03   FILLER         PIC X(24)      VALUE 'DESCRIPTION'.
00042                 03   FILLER         PIC X(23)      VALUE 'QTY        UNCOST'.
00043                 03   FILLER         PIC X(61)      VALUE 'VALUE'.

00045            01   DETAIL-LINE.
00046                 03   FILLER         PIC X(15)      VALUE ' '.
00047                 03   STOCK-PR       PIC X(5).
00048                 03   FILLER         PIC X(5)       VALUE ' '.
00049                 03   DESCRIP-PR     PIC X(24).
00050                 03   QTY-PR         PIC ZZ9-.
00051                 03   FILLER         PIC X(5)       VALUE ' '.
00052                 03   UNCOST-PR      PIC ZZ.99.
00053                 03   FILLER         PIC X(5)       VALUE ' '.
00054                 03   VALUE-PR       PIC ZZ,ZZZ.99CR.
00055                 03   ERR-MESS-PR    PIC X(54)      VALUE ' '.
```

FIGURE 5-1   Full Input/output

```
00057          01   TOTAL-LINE.
00058          03   FILLER          PIC X(52)    VALUE ' '.
00059          03   FILLER          PIC X(14)    VALUE 'TOTAL VALUE ='.
00060          03   TOTAL-VALUE-PR  PIC ZZZZ,ZZZ.99CR.
00061          03   FILLER          PIC X        VALUE '*'.

00063      PROCEDURE DIVISION.
00064          OPEN INPUT  STOCK-FILE
00065               OUTPUT PRINT-FILE.
00066          MOVE HEADING-LINE TO PRINT-RECORD.
00067          WRITE PRINT-RECORD AFTER ADVANCING 3 LINES.
00068          MOVE SPACES TO PRINT-RECORD.
00069          WRITE PRINT-RECORD AFTER ADVANCING 1 LINES.
00070          READ STOCK-FILE,
00071              AT END MOVE 'EOF' TO EOF-FLAG.
00072          PERFORM B100-PROCESS UNTIL EOF-FLAG = 'EOF'.
00073          MOVE TOTAL-VALUE TO TOTAL-VALUE-PR.
00074          MOVE TOTAL-LINE TO PRINT-RECORD.
00075          WRITE PRINT-RECORD AFTER ADVANCING 2 LINES.
00076          CLOSE STOCK-FILE, PRINT-FILE.
00077          STOP RUN.

00079      B100-PROCESS SECTION.
00080          IF STOCK-IN NOT > PREV-STOCK
00081              MOVE 'EQUAL OR LOW SEQ' TO ERR-MESS-PR
00082          ELSE
00083              MOVE STOCK-IN TO PREV-STOCK.
00084          MOVE QTY-IN TO QTY-PR.
00085          MOVE UNCOST-IN TO UNCOST-PR.
00086          COMPUTE STOCK-VALUE = QTY-IN * UNCOST-IN.
00087          MOVE STOCK-VALUE TO VALUE-PR.
00088          ADD STOCK-VALUE TO TOTAL-VALUE.
00089          MOVE DESCRIP-IN TO DESCRIP-PR.
00090          MOVE STOCK-IN TO STOCK-PR.
00091          MOVE DETAIL-LINE TO PRINT-RECORD.
00092          WRITE PRINT-RECORD AFTER ADVANCING 1 LINES.
00093          MOVE SPACES TO DETAIL-LINE.
00094          READ STOCK-FILE,
00095              AT END MOVE 'EOF' TO EOF-FLAG.
00096      B900-RETURN.  EXIT.
```

Printed report:

STOCK	DESCRIPTION	QTY	UNCOST	VALUE	
00230	RIVETTERS	1	1.00	1.00	
00236	ASSEMBLERS	15	.35	5.25	
00245	RE-INFORCERS	100	15.25	1,525.00	
00277	CO-ORDINATORS	525	3.75	1,968.75	
00416	COMBINERS	256	2.77	709.12	
00524	BINARIES	9	25.33	227.97	
00584	BAILING UNITS	36	3.68	132.48	
00845	CONTROLLERS	362	.35	126.70	
00933	DIRECTORS	124	.25	31.00	
01238	LIFTERS	632	5.22	3,299.04	
01326	COMPILERS	947	82.61	78,231.67	
01397	RESISTORS	2	25.25	50.50	
02164	ACCESSORS	25-	10.52	263.00CR	
00957	MAXIMIZERS	36	9.22	331.92	EQUAL OR LOW SEQ
02247	OPTIMIZERS	633	.75	474.75	

```
                                 TOTAL VALUE =    86,852.15   *
```

FIGURE 5-1 *(Cont.)*

INPUT-OUTPUT SECTION

The Input-Output Section varies considerably according to COBOL version (this section illustrates the IBM DOS version). The Input-Output Section contains a File-Control paragraph that provides the file names (in Figure 5-2, STOCK-FILE and PRINT-FILE, although any unique names are allowed). There is one SELECT statement for each file that the program uses. For STOCK-FILE, the ASSIGN clause in Figure 5-2 appears as follows:

ASSIGN TO SYS015-UR-2501-S.

- SYS015. This clause assigns STOCK-FILE to a specific system number, in this case SYS015 (the number varies by installation).
- UR-2501-S. This indicates that the input device is a unit record 2501 card reader. UR is a *class indicator;* other classes are UT (utility class for tape and disk sequential processing), and DA (direct access class, for direct processing of disk). The letter S represents the *organization character,* in this case sequential (another is I for indexed sequential).

In the program in Figure 5-2, the printer is named PRINT-FILE and is assigned to a specific system number (SYS014) using an IBM 1403 printer device.

```
00005          ENVIRONMENT DIVISION.     system number     IBM 2501 reader
00006          INPUT-OUTPUT SECTION.                  unit record
00007          FILE-CONTROL.                                       sequential
00008              SELECT STOCK-FILE. ASSIGN TO SYS015-UR-2501-S.
00009              SELECT PRINT-FILE. ASSIGN TO SYS014-UR-1403-S.

00011          DATA DIVISION.
00012          FILE SECTION.
00013          FD  STOCK-FILE
00014              LABEL RECORDS ARE OMITTED          File description
00015              RECORDING MODE IS F                 describes STOCK-FILE
00016              DATA RECORD IS STOCK-RECORD.
00017          01  STOCK-RECORD.
00018              03  CODE-IN          PIC XX.
00019              03  FILLER           PIC XX.
00020              03  STOCK-IN         PIC X(5).       Definition of record
00021              03  QTY-IN           PIC S999.        associated with STOCK-FILE
00022              03  UNCOST-IN        PIC S99V99.
00023              03  DESCRIP-IN       PIC X(20).
00024              03  FILLER           PIC X(44).

00026          FD  PRINT-FILE
00027              LABEL RECORDS ARE OMITTED
00028              RECORDING MODE IS F
00029              DATA RECORD IS PRINT-RECORD.
00030          01  PRINT-RECORD         PIC X(133).
```

FIGURE 5-2   Input/output Specifications.

Under IBM OS, the SELECT statements may appear as follows:

```
SELECT STOCK-FILE. ASSIGN TO UR-2501-S-CDINFILE,
SELECT PRINT-FILE. ASSIGN TO UR-1403-S-PROUT,
```
*Names used in
job control*

Under CDC-6000 COBOL, the SELECT statements may simply appear as follows:

```
SELECT STOCK-FILE. ASSIGN TO INPUT.
SELECT PRINT-FILE. ASSIGN TO OUTPUT.
```

FILE SECTION

The Data Division now contains a File Section. This Section has an FD (File Description) paragraph for each file in the Input-Output Section. The FD contains the same file names as in the SELECT, and these file names are used in the Procedure Division also, thus:

```
ENVIRONMENT DIVISICN.
INPUT-OUTPUT SECTICN.
FILE-CCNTROL.
     SELECT CUST-FILE ...        DEFINES THE FILE NAME

DATA DIVISION.
FILE SECTION.
FD  CUST-FILE ...               DESCRIBES ThE FILE

PROCEDURE DIVISION.
     OPEN INPUT CUST-FILE ...   PROCESSES THE FILE
     READ CUST-FILE ...
```

The FD contains these three descriptions of the file:

1. LABEL RECORDS ARE OMITTED. Tape and disk files contain labels with descriptive information, but card and printer files do not. This clause tells the compiler that the file does not contain labels.
2. RECORDING MODE IS F. This clause tells the compiler that the records are *fixed* in length (not variable as tape and disk records may be). Some COBOL versions permit this clause to be omitted and default to fixed length (most examples in this text omit this clause).
3. DATA RECORD IS STOCK-RECORD. This clause provides the name of the input record(s), in Figure 5-1, STOCK-RECORD. It is only documentation for the programmer and is treated as a comment by the compiler. Following this statement is the actual definition of the input or output record(s), which is identical to the earlier examples using ACCEPT.

After the FD for STOCK-FILE and its record definition is the FD for the printer file. The Data Record for this file is PRINT-RECORD:

```
DATA RECORD IS PRINT-RECORD.
01  PRINT-RECORD       PIC X(133).
```

The actual definitions of the heading line, detail line, and final total line are still in the Working-Storage Section because you can define a VALUE clause in Working-Storage but not in the File Section. (The only entry in the File Section that may contain a VALUE clause is level-88, which technically does not generate a true constant.) In order to print the heading record, you have two options:

1.   Move the record to PRINT-RECORD for printing:

```
MOVE HEADING-LINE TO PRINT-RECORD.
WRITE PRINT-RECORD ...
```

2.   Use the FROM option to write the record directly:

```
WRITE PRINT-RECORD FROM HEADING-LINE ...
```

OPEN STATEMENT

An OPEN statement is required prior to the first READ or WRITE of any file. OPEN makes a file available to a program. (In a multiprogramming system, another program may be using the same file.) Also, OPEN performs checking of tape and disk files. The OPEN must specify whether the file is INPUT or OUTPUT. For example:

1.   One reader, one printer:

```
OPEN INPUT CUST-FILE, OUTPUT PRINTER.
```

2.   Two disk input files, one printer, one disk output file:

```
OPEN INPUT TRANS-FILE, MASTER-FILE,
     OUTPUT PRINT-FILE, NEW-MAST-FILE.
```

Because COBOL is a free-form language, this example may also be coded with one file per line. It is also possible to code a separate OPEN statement for each file. Although less efficient, separate OPEN statements are easier to debug and change.

CLOSE STATEMENT

After a file has been processed, many systems require that you CLOSE the file because the computer system usually must perform additional processing at the end of tape and disk files. Also, CLOSE makes a file available to other programs in the system. You need not specify INPUT or OUTPUT in the CLOSE statement. For example:

1.   One reader, one printer:

```
CLOSE CUST-FILE, PRINTER.
```

2.   Two disk input files, one printer, one disk output file:

```
CLOSE TRANS-FILE, MASTER-FILE,
      PRINT-FILE, NEW-MAST-FILE.
```

You may also use a separate statement to CLOSE each file. Once a file has been closed during a program's execution, it can be referenced again only if it is reopened. Be sure to close all files before executing the STOP RUN statement.

READ STATEMENT

READ causes the computer to read a record into the input area defined in the associated FD paragraph. READ erases any previous contents. You specify in the READ statement the action to take on end-of-file, but you do *not* normally insert a trailer card containing blanks or 9s at the end of the data. The standard practice with IBM DOS systems is to insert a special job control card containing /* in columns one and two:

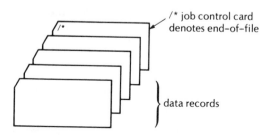

/* job control card
denotes end-of-file

data records

The *system,* not the program, checks for this record, and when found directs the program to the AT END clause in the READ statement. (Under IBM OS, the /* is accepted, but optional. Under any system, disk and tape files have their own special end-of-file indications for which the system also automatically checks.) For example:

```
READ CUST-FILE, AT END MOVE 'EOF' TO EOF-SIGNAL.
```

After the program reads the end-of-file, it must not attempt to perform another READ—it may start reading the next program!
    Note: It is also possible to define the input record in Working-Storage and to

use the READ INTO option. Assume CUST-RECORD is defined in Working-Storage as follows:

```
WORKING-STORAGE SECTION.
01  CUST-RECORD.
    03 ...
    03 ...
    03 ...

PROCEDURE DIVISION.
    READ CUST-FILE INTO CUST-RECORD, AT END ...
```

WRITE STATEMENT

WRITE references a record in the defined output area of the associated FD paragraph and causes the record to be printed. Note that in COBOL the READ statement references the *file name*, but the WRITE statement references the *record name*. WRITE does not erase the previous contents of the print area. There are several variations of WRITE. A common format is as follows:

```
WRITE PRINT-RECORD AFTER ADVANCING XXX LINES.
```

Name of print record in FD

Actual digits or a Working-Storage item containing a numeric value

For example, you may also move a record to the print area and WRITE as follows:

```
MOVE TOTAL-LINE TO PRINT-RECORD.
WRITE PRINT-RECORD AFTER ADVANCING 3 LINES.
```

After Advancing

AFTER ADVANCING is optional; its omission causes COBOL to assume (default to) one line. The following two statements have the same effect:

```
WRITE PRINT-RECORD AFTER ADVANCING 1 LINES.
WRITE PRINT-RECORD.
```

It is possible, and common, to WRITE directly *from* an area outside the FD print area. The WRITE FROM option causes the data record to move to the print area, and you get the same result as in the previous example:

```
WRITE PRINT-RECORD FROM TOTAL-LINE AFTER ADVANCING 3 LINES.
```

Name in FD   *Name in Working-Storage*

In Figure 5-1, the print record is 133 characters, a common maximum printer width. The first (leftmost) character for IBM printers is not printed. WRITE AFTER ADVANCING causes a special character to be inserted in this position to control printer spacing.

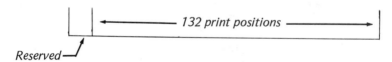

AFTER ADVANCING causes the printer to space first and then print. Another variation of WRITE causes the opposite (print first, then space) using the reserved word BEFORE:

```
WRITE PRINT-RECORD BEFORE ADVANCING XXX LINES.
```

Skipping to the top of a new page involves SPECIAL-NAMES in the Environment Division, and is covered in the next chapter.

After Positioning

IBM 370 COBOL provides for an AFTER POSITIONING clause in the WRITE statement (the clause is not an ANS standard, and perhaps an installation should avoid using features that are not universally implemented). If you use AFTER POSITIONING at all in a program, you will have to use it for every WRITE for a file. AFTER POSITIONING uses either an alphanumeric or a numeric value.

Alphanumeric Value.   This is a one-character PIC X data item containing one of the following (these are the most common):

' '	(blank)	Space one line, then print.
'0'	(zero)	Space two lines, then print.
'−'	(minus)	Space three lines, then print.
'1'	(one)	Skip to top of next page, then print.

For example, space two lines and print:

```
WRITE PRINT-LINE FROM TOTAL-LINE AFTER POSITIONING '0'.
```

Numeric Value.   This is an unsigned numeric value from 0 through 3 and works as follows:

0	Skip to a new page, then print.
1	Space one line, then print.
2	Space two lines, then print.
3	Space three lines, then print.

For example, space two lines and print:

```
WRITE PRINT-LINE FROM TOTAL-LINE AFTER POSITIONING 2.
```

The alphanumeric value is particularly inferior because it is not self-documenting. The numeric value, other than for skip to a new page, is much clearer.

DISPLAY, EXHIBIT, WRITE AFTER ADVANCING, and WRITE AFTER POSITIONING all cause first a space and then the print. Both WRITE with no options and WRITE BEFORE cause print and then space. Mixing these types of statements in the same program may cause *overprinting* (two lines of data printed on the same line).

BUFFERS

A *buffer* is an area in main storage reserved for an input or output record. The use of buffers makes READ and WRITE more efficient than ACCEPT and DISPLAY. Unless you specify otherwise, most compilers assume two buffers for each file.

Input Buffers

Assume, for example, an input area named RECORD-IN and two buffers: buffer-1 and buffer-2. When a program reads the first input record, the system delivers it from the input device into buffer-1 in main storage. It then transfers the record from buffer-1 into the program's input area, RECORD-IN. Then, while the program is processing the first input record, the system reads ahead, delivering the second input record into buffer-2:

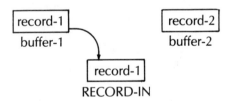

Now, when the program reads the second record, it is already in main storage (buffer-2), and the system transfers the record to RECORD-IN. Once again, while the program is processing record-2, the system reads ahead, delivering the third input record from the input device into buffer-1:

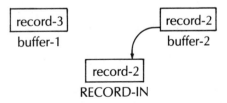

In this way, buffers facilitate the overlapping of reading and processing.

Output Buffers

In a parallel fashion, writing can also overlap with processing. A program moves an output record to an output buffer, and the program continues processing without waiting for the actual writing to occur. At the end of program execution, the CLOSE statement writes the contents of the last record stored in the buffer.

Be careful when using DISPLAY and WRITE on the same printer. If a program WRITES a final total and then DISPLAYS "END OF REPORT," the DISPLAY message will probably print on the form before the final total prints. The reason? DISPLAY does not use a second buffer; it prints immediately, but the system delays printing the WRITE record. A solution is to CLOSE the printer file first, and then DISPLAY the message.

ERROR PREVENTION

The following error prevention points pertain to full input/output.

1. Ensure that your SELECT statements are correct for your system.
2. Double-check the coding in the FILE-CONTROL Section and the FILE Section to ensure that both reference the same name. The coding in each Section is critical. It is simple, for example, to mistakenly code a file as input instead of output, or to spell a file name differently in one Section than the other.
3. Remember to OPEN and CLOSE all files. The names must match those in the SELECT entry.
4. Remember that the READ statement references the file name, but the WRITE statement references the output record name.
5. Some compilers do not allow an IF statement to contain a READ statement. The solution is to place the READ in a separate Section and to PERFORM it:
   IF (condition) PERFORM R100-READ.

PROBLEMS

5–1. For normal input/output, why are READ and WRITE preferable to ACCEPT and DISPLAY?

5–2. What is a buffer? What is the advantage of using two buffers instead of one?

5–3. A file is named SALES-FILE, and the input record named SALES-RECORD contains the following:

COLUMN

1–4	salesman number
5–24	name
25–31	amount sold (xxxx.xx)
32–80	unused.

Code the complete FILE-CONTROL Section, FILE Section, OPEN Statement, and READ statement for this file.

5–4. A print file is named PRINT-FILE, and the output record named PRINT-RECORD contains the following:

COLUMN

11–14	salesman number
17–36	name
39–47	amount sold (xx,xxx.xx)

Code the complete FILE-CONTROL Section, FILE Section, OPEN statement, and WRITE statement (spacing one line) for this file.

5–5. Refer to Problem 3-3. Revise this program so that it uses OPEN, READ, WRITE, and CLOSE. Be sure to code the INPUT-OUTPUT Section and the FILE Section. Compile and test the program. Remember that a job control statement is required to indicate end-of-file.

5–6. Code the following program that calculates Sales Commissions. Records are in sequence by salesman number.

COLUMN

1–2   Record code (56)
5–7   Salesman number
8–10 Category code (type of sale, as TV, furniture, appliance)
11–13Commission rate (e.g., .175 = 17.5%)
14–27 Category description
28–33 Amount of sale (two decimals)
34–39 Cost of sale (two decimals)

For each record, calculate and print gross profit and commission:

$$\text{Gross profit} = \text{Amount of sale} - \text{Cost of sale}$$

$$\text{Commission} = \text{Gross profit} \times \text{Commission rate}$$

Include all other data on the printed line except record code. Check sequence of input records. At the end of the run, print totals of amount of sale, cost of sale, gross profit, and commission.

Provide test data with a variety of rates, and at least one record in which cost is greater than amount sold.

PART III

PROGRAM CONTROL AND LOGIC

CHAPTER 6

LOGIC TESTS AND PERFORM

*OBJECTIVE: To provide the COBOL advanced logic for condition names,
PERFORM statements, and compound IF statements.*

INTRODUCTION

Most complex programs involve logical tests and repetitive processing. This
chapter covers the COBOL PERFORM statement that enables you to control repetitive processing and to organize a program into logical sections. The use of
condition names provides program clarity, and advanced IF logic enables you to
test complex conditions. This chapter is an important lead-in to the next chapter
on structured programming.

CONDITION NAMES—LEVEL 88

A major concern in programming is maintenance, which can be expensive in an
established installation. As a result, programmers adopt standards, use meaningful
names, and keep programs clear and simple. One useful device that makes programs
more self-documenting is the *condition name*. A condition name is a level 88 entry
immediately following the data field with which it is associated. For example, a
program checks the input record for the code '12'; the program may also check for a
condition name instead of the code, as in the following example:

111

Example using conventional test: Example using condition names:

```
01   STOCK-RECORD.                        01   STOCK-RECORD.
     03   CODE-IN           PIC XX.            03   CODE-IN           PIC XX.
     03   FILLER ...                                88   VALID-CODE             VALUE '12'.
     •                                           03   FILLER ...
     •                                           •
IF CODE-IN NOT = '12' ...                      •
                                               •
                                          IF NOT VALID-CODE ...
```

Level 88 has a VALUE clause that contains the code that you want to check. The entry has no PICTURE, nor does it generate a constant. Level 88 is the only entry in the File Section that can have a VALUE clause. But you can now directly reference the condition name in the IF statement:

IF NOT VALID-CODE . . .

means exactly the same as

IF CODE-IN NOT = '12' . . .

You can enter more than one condition name following a data item. For example, assume that a sales record contains codes 1, 2, 3, and 4 to represent sales areas north, east, west, and south respectively. The record can be defined as follows:

```
77   SALES-AREA        PIC X.
     88   NORTH-AREA             VALUE '1'.
     88   EAST-AREA              VALUE '2'.
     88   WEST-AREA              VALUE '3'.
     88   SOUTH-AREA             VALUE '4'.
```

The program can check for the west sales area in two different ways:

1. IF SALES-AREA = '3' . . .   *Conventional test using a literal.*
2. IF WEST-AREA . . . .   *Test using condition name.*

The second method, using a condition name, provides better self-documentation. Also, if the area numbering system were to change, you need only correct the condition name value clause—not every literal in the program that references SALES-AREA.

You can enlarge the condition VALUE clause to allow for a range of values. For example, assume that course grades are based on the following:

80–100%	First class
65–79.9	Second class
50–64.9	Pass
Below 50	Fail

You can arrange condition names for these categories as follows:

```
77    COURSE-GRADE         PIC  999V9.
      88   FIRST-CLASS      VALUE 80.0 THRU 100.0.
      88   SECOND-CLASS     VALUE 65.0 THRU  79.9.
      88   PASS             VALUE 50.0 THRU  64.9.
      88   FAIL             VALUE 00.0 THRU  49.9.
```

And you can easily test for each grade category with statements such as the following:

```
IF FIRST-CLASS PERFORM D000-FIRST-ROUTINE.
```

(i.e. IF grade between 80 and 100)

Condition names are useful in COBOL because they provide IF logic with clearer statements. They should be used carefully, however, because they can cause more confusion than help. Be sure to assign a condition name and its value with a meaningful name, and use a condition name for one purpose only, so that a reader can easily understand the intent of the test.

THE PERFORM STATEMENT

A program, unless very simple, consists of various routines, such as Initialize, Calculate, Format the print line, and Page headings. In large programs, these routines may be substantial, each up to a page or two in size. Therefore, it is usually desirable to organize the program with the routines clearly distinguishable. As was shown earlier, you can remove a routine to a separate section of the program where only a special instruction, PERFORM, can execute it. The routine becomes, in effect, a "closed subroutine." The advantage of such routines is that it is clear to anyone what their purpose is. Using PERFORM, any part of the program can execute the routine.
    The two basic types of PERFORM are:

1.   PERFORM paragraph-name.
2.   PERFORM paragraph-name-1 THRU paragraph-name-2.

Unlike PERFORM UNTIL, introduced earlier, these PERFORM statements execute the designated routine only once before returning to the statement immediately following the PERFORM. The first type of PERFORM executes an entire Paragraph, beginning with the given Paragraph name through to the next Paragraph name, Section name, or end of the program. The second type of PERFORM executes beginning with the first given Paragraph name through to the second given Paragraph name and its associated paragraph. You could, for example, organize a program to make the page heading routine a closed subroutine, and remove it to the end of the program. You may then use two PERFORM statements to process the new page heading Paragraph, B100-HEAD:

```
OPEN ...
PERFORM B100-HEAD.
READ ...
...
WRITE PRINT-LINE ...
ADD 1 TO LINE-CTR.
IF LINE-CTR > 55 PERFORM B100-HEAD.
    .
    .
    .
B100-HEAD.
    MOVE PAGE-CTR TO PAGE-PR.
    WRITE HEADING-LINE ...
    MOVE 3 TO LINE-CTR.
    ADD 1 TO PAGE-CTR.
```

At the end of the paragraph (and coincidentally end of the program), processing returns automatically to the statement immediately following the PERFORM that invoked the subroutine. The problem with this type of PERFORM is that another programmer may later insert more statements in the subroutine, including IF statements and paragraph names. The PERFORM will execute the added statements only until it finds another paragraph name. The programmer would have to trace all the PERFORMs that execute the subroutine to ensure that the correct paragraph is executed. A method that clarifies what is to be executed is the PERFORM THRU statement. The preceding program can be recoded as follows:

```
OPEN ...
PERFORM B100-HEAD THRU B199-EXIT.
READ ...
...
WRITE PRINT-LINE ...
ADD 1 TO LINE-CTR.
IF LINE-CTR > 55 PERFORM B100-HEAD THRU B199-EXIT.
    .
    .
    .
B100-HEAD.
    MOVE PAGE-CTR TO PAGE-PR.
    WRITE HEADING-LINE ...
    MOVE 3 TO LINE-CTR.
    ADD 1 TO PAGE-CTR.
B199-EXIT. EXIT.
```

The last statement, B199-EXIT, is a paragraph name with only one verb: EXIT. EXIT generates no machine code, but is useful to indicate to the programmer that this is the last statement of the performed subroutine—the exit point. Therefore, more than one paragraph may be executed by the PERFORM statement. EXIT, if used, must be the only word in its paragraph.

Section Names

Another, and better, way to organize a program is according to Sections. The Divisions have had Sections such as Input-Output, File Section, and Working-Storage Section. A Section is usually a group of one or more paragraphs (although both a paragraph and a Section may contain no statements at all!). Let's now convert the heading routine to a Section in the Procedure Division, and execute it with PERFORM B100-HEAD. Since the PERFORM knows that it is executing a Section name, it processes automatically through to the end of the Section, regardless of any encountered paragraph names. Technically, the PERFORM executes from a Section name to the next encountered Section name, or if none, to the end of the program.

```
        OPEN ...
        PERFORM B100-HEAD.
        READ ...

        ...
        WRITE PRINT-LINE ...
        ADD 1 TO LINE-CTR.
        IF LINE-CTR > 55 PERFORM B100-HEAD.
        .
        .
        .
B100-HEAD SECTION.
        MOVE PAGE-CTR TO PAGE-PR.
        WRITE HEADING-LINE ...
        MOVE 3 TO LINE-CTR.
        ADD  1 TO PAGE-CTR.
B199-EXIT. EXIT.
```

PERFORM Sections is a common coding standard, and facilitates clear and coherent organization of a program (especially large programs). Such use of PERFORM is fundamental to structured programming, as you will see in Chapter 7.

Iterative Processing

Sometimes it is necessary to execute a routine a number of times over and over again until some specific condition is reached. The variations on PERFORM that permit such iterative processing are as follows:

PERFORM name-1 [THRU name-2] n TIMES.
PERFORM name-1 [THRU name-2] UNTIL condition.

Name-1 and name-2 may be Paragraph or Section names. The THRU clause in brackets is optional—you may code THRU or omit it. The following example is a simplified calculation of interest on an outstanding balance. Beginning with a current balance, it calculates interest (balance times interest rate). To calculate the new balance, the routine adds the computed interest to the balance and subtracts the periodic payment from the balance. The PERFORM executes C000-CALC Section as many times as necessary to reduce the balance to zero. Consequently, the balance could reduce to a negative value without actually becoming zero, and the PERFORM would continue processing indefinitely. But the Section has a check: if it calculates a negative balance, it forces the balance to zero, and the program terminates executing the Section.

```
        PERFORM C000-CALC UNTIL BALANCE = ZERO.
                 .
                 .
                 .
    C000-CALC SECTION.
        COMPUTE INTEREST ROUNDED = BALANCE * RATE.
        ADD INTEREST TO BALANCE.
        SUBTRACT PAYMENT FROM BALANCE.
        MOVE INTEREST TO INTEREST-OUT.
        MOVE BALANCE TO BALANCE-OUT.
        WRITE PRINT-RECORD.
        IF BALANCE IS NEGATIVE MOVE ZEROS TO BALANCE.
    C199-RETURN. EXIT.
```

If the condition is true before the PERFORM executes (that is, the balance is already zero), the UNTIL condition is immediately met, and the subroutine is not executed at all. This program could be coded so that it executes a Paragraph or Section a specified number of times as follows:

```
            PERFORM C000-CALC 20 TIMES.
```

Perform Varying

Another PERFORM option provides for incrementing or decrementing the content of an item until some condition is reached:

PERFORM procedure VARYING item FROM start BY increment UNTIL condition.

A program may need to count the number of times it performs a procedure (Paragraph or Section). (Later chapters on table processing cover this use of PERFORM.)

PROGRAM EXAMPLE

Figure 6-1 is a revision of the program in Chapter 5 and illustrates the new features discussed in this chapter:

1. *Main Logic.* A main logic routine is at the start of the Procedure Division, organized as follows:
   - OPEN files
   - PERFORM page headings
   - PERFORM an initial READ (there may be any number of records, or none, in error)
   - PERFORM the Processing Section until there are no more records (the Section processes each record and reads the next one)
   - PERFORM final totals
   - CLOSE files and terminate

2. *Subsidiary Sections.*
   - B000-PROC Section checks for valid record code and sequence, calculates stock value, prints the output record, and reads the next record. If the routine were larger and more complex, it could be divided into smaller Sections.
   - H000-HEAD performs the page headings.
   - T000-TOTAL prints final totals at the end of the run.

   The main logic section represents the overall program structure. Each subsidiary Section contains logical processing that is related only to its section of code. Thus, H000-HEAD is concerned only with the printing of headings, and T000-TOTAL is concerned only with the printing of final totals.

   Note that each Section is coded independently, and that the program executes a Section only by means of a PERFORM. Because on some compilers a Section executes through its EXIT statement and up to the next Section name, Sections should be coded clearly one after the other following the main logic.

3. *Working-Storage.* There is one level 01 group in Working-Storage for all arithmetic items:

   ```
   01  ARITHMETIC-FIELDS     COMP-3.
   ```

   All items within this group are given the COMP-3 attribute. This practice saves coding COMP-3 (or COMP) repetitively for each arithmetic item and ensures that similar fields are defined together.

4. *Condition Names.* There are two condition names used, one for the record code on the input record (CODE-IN), and the other in Working-Storage for the end-of-file condition.

PAGE OVERFLOW

Continuous printout paper forms usually have a perforation every 11 inches, allowing, at 6 lines per inch, up to 66 lines per page. Since the printer can print past this perforation, you code a program to count the lines printed and spaced, and when

```
00004              ENVIRONMENT DIVISION.
00005              CONFIGURATION SECTION.
00006              SPECIAL-NAMES.
00007                  C01 IS TOP-PAGE.
00008              INPUT-OUTPUT SECTION.
00009              FILE-CONTROL.
00010                  SELECT STOCK-FILE. ASSIGN TO SYS015-UR-25L1-S.
00011                  SELECT PRINT-FILE. ASSIGN TO SYS014-UR-1403-S.

00013              DATA DIVISION.
00014              FILE SECTION.
00015              FD  STOCK-FILE
00016                  LABEL RECORDS ARE OMITTED
00017                  DATA RECORD IS STOCK-RECORD.
00018              01  STOCK-RECORD.
00019                  03  CODE-IN          PIC XX.
00020                      88  VALID-STOCK-CODE         VALUE '12'.
00021                  03  FILLER           PIC XX.
00022                  03  STOCK-IN         PIC X(5).
00023                  03  QTY-IN           PIC S999.
00024                  03  UNCOST-IN        PIC S99V99.
00025                  03  DESCRIP-IN       PIC X(20).
00026                  03  FILLER           PIC X(44).

00028              FD  PRINT-FILE
00029                  LABEL RECORDS ARE OMITTED
00030                  DATA RECORD IS PRINT-RECORD.
00031              01  PRINT-RECORD    PIC X(133).

00033              WORKING-STORAGE SECTION.
00034              77  EOF-FLAG          PIC X(3)         VALUE ' '.
00035                  88  END-FILE                       VALUE 'END'.
00036              77  PREV-STOCK        PIC X(5)         VALUE LOW-VALUES.

00038              01  ARITHMETIC-FIELDS   COMP-3.
00039                  03  LINE-CTR       PIC S999        VALUE +003.
00040                      88  END-PAGE                    VALUE +15 THRU +99.
00041                  03  PAGE-CTR       PIC S999        VALUE +001.
00042                  03  STOCK-VALUE    PIC S9(5)V99    VALUE +0.
00043                  03  TOTAL-VALUE    PIC S9(7)V99    VALUE +0.

00045              01  HEADING-LINE.
00046                  03  FILLER         PIC X(15)   VALUE ' '.
00047                  03  FILLER         PIC X(10)   VALUE 'STOCK'.
00048                  03  FILLER         PIC X(24)   VALUE 'DESCRIPTION'.
00049                  03  FILLER         PIC X(23)   VALUE 'QTY      UNCOST'.
00050                  03  FILLER         PIC X(10)   VALUE 'VALUE'.
00051                  03  DATE-PR        PIC X(22)   VALUE ' '.
00052                  03  FILLER         PIC X(6)    VALUE 'PAGE'.
00053                  03  PAGE-PR        PIC ZZ9.

00055              01  DETAIL-LINE.
00056                  03  FILLER         PIC X(15)   VALUE ' '.
00057                  03  STOCK-PR       PIC X(5).
00058                  03  FILLER         PIC X(5)    VALUE ' '.
00059                  03  DESCRIP-PR     PIC X(24).
00060                  03  QTY-PR         PIC ZZ9-.
00061                  03  FILLER         PIC X(5)    VALUE ' '.
00062                  03  UNCOST-PR      PIC ZZ.99.
00063                  03  FILLER         PIC X(5)    VALUE ' '.
00064                  03  VALUE-PR       PIC ZZ,ZZZ.99CR.
00065                  03  ERR-MESS-PR    PIC X(54)   VALUE ' '.
```

FIGURE 6-1 Use of the PERFORM Statement.

118

```
00067          01   TOTAL-LINE.
00068               03   FILLER           PIC X(52)     VALUE ' '.
00069               03   FILLER           PIC X(14)     VALUE 'TOTAL VALUE ='.
00070               03   TOTAL-VALUE-PR   PIC ZZZZ,ZZZ.99CR.
00071               03   FILLER           PIC X         VALUE '*'.

00073          PROCEDURE DIVISION.
00074     ***  M A I N   L O G I C
00075          A000-MAIN-LOGIC SECTION.
00076               OPEN INPUT   STOCK-FILE, OUTPUT PRINT-FILE.
00077               PERFORM H000-HEAD.
00078               READ STOCK-FILE, AT END MOVE 'END' TO EOF-FLAG.
00079               PERFORM B000-PROC UNTIL END-FILE.
00080               PERFORM T000-TOTAL.
00081               CLOSE STOCK-FILE, PRINT-FILE.
00082               STOP RUN.
00083          A999-END. EXIT.

00085     ***  P R O C E S S I N G   R O U T I N E
00086          B000-PROC SECTION.
00087               IF END-PAGE PERFORM H000-HEAD.
00088               IF NOT VALID-STOCK-CODE
00089                   MOVE 'INVALID STOCK RECORD CODE' TO ERR-MESS-PR
00090               ELSE
00091                   IF STOCK-IN NOT > PREV-STOCK
00092                       MOVE 'EQUAL OR LOW SEQ' TO ERR-MESS-PR
00093                   ELSE
00094                       MOVE STOCK-IN TO PREV-STOCK
00095                       MOVE QTY-IN TO QTY-PR
00096                       MOVE UNCOST-IN TO UNCOST-PR
00097                       COMPUTE STOCK-VALUE = QTY-IN * UNCOST-IN
00098                       MOVE STOCK-VALUE TO VALUE-PR
00099                       ADD STOCK-VALUE TO TOTAL-VALUE.
00100               MOVE DESCRIP-IN TO DESCRIP-PR.
00101               MOVE STOCK-IN TO STOCK-PR.
00102               MOVE DETAIL-LINE TO PRINT-RECORD.
00103               WRITE PRINT-RECORD AFTER ADVANCING 1 LINES.
00104               ADD 1 TO LINE-CTR.
00105               MOVE SPACES TO DETAIL-LINE.
00106               READ STOCK-FILE, AT END MOVE 'END' TO EOF-FLAG.
00107          B999-RETURN. EXIT.

00109     ***  H E A D I N G   R O U T I N E
00110          H000-HEAD SECTION.
00111               MOVE PAGE-CTR TO PAGE-PR.
00112               MOVE HEADING-LINE TO PRINT-RECORD.
00113               WRITE PRINT-RECORD AFTER ADVANCING TOP-PAGE.
00114               MOVE 3 TO LINE-CTR.
00115               ADD 1 TO PAGE-CTR.
00116               MOVE SPACES TO PRINT-RECORD.
00117               WRITE PRINT-RECORD AFTER ADVANCING 1 LINES.
00118          H999-RETURN. EXIT.

00120     ***  T O T A L   P R O C E S S I N G
00121          T000-TOTAL SECTION.
00122               MOVE TOTAL-VALUE TO TOTAL-VALUE-PR.
00123               MOVE TOTAL-LINE TO PRINT-RECORD.
00124               WRITE PRINT-RECORD AFTER ADVANCING 2 LINES.
00125          T999-RETURN. EXIT.
```

FIGURE 6-1   (Cont.)

this count exceeds a predetermined number of lines, the program will skip to the top of the next page. The usual procedure is to print a heading with a page number and to reset the line counter.

In Figure 6-1, the first statement in B000-PROC Section checks the contents of LINE-CTR. If its contents exceeds 15, the program PERFORMs the heading routine (H000-HEAD). The statements that define the top of the page, skip to the top of the next page, and write the heading are as follows:

```
SPECIAL-NAMES.
    C01 IS TOP-PAGE.
    .
    .
WRITE PRINT-RECORD AFTER ADVANCING TOP-PAGE.
```

TOP-PAGE is defined in the Environment Division under a new paragraph, SPECIAL-NAMES, that contains the entry C01 (channel 1, or the top line of the forms). C01 is an IBM COBOL reserved word that differs by COBOL version. TOP-PAGE is any unique descriptive name.

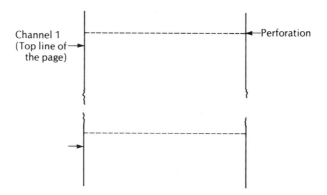

Note: Some COBOL compilers skip to a new page if the LINES option contains 0, as

```
      WRITE PRINT-RECORD AFTER 0 LINES.
OR    WRITE PRINT-RECORD POSITION 0.
```

END-OF-PAGE

COBOL provides an END-OF-PAGE option in the WRITE statement as follows:

```
WRITE PRINT-RECORD AFTER ADVANCING 2 LINES
    AT END-OF-PAGE PERFORM H000-HEADING.
```

This option directs the program to test for channel 12 at the bottom of a page, and to be effective requires a hole punched in channel 12 of a paper tape on the printer. Often, the tape is punched only for channel 1, and a test for channel 12 will not work. Consequently, most programmers simply count the lines spaced and check for a maximum count, as in Figure 6-1. Systems using SPOOLING or an off-line printer may not accept this option.

ADVANCED IF LOGIC

Earlier chapters covered relatively simple uses of IF logic that provide for many typical business programming situations. This section introduces other logic features: THEN, OTHERWISE, and NEXT SENTENCE clauses, arithmetic expressions, nested IFs, compound IFs, and implied subjects.

1. *THEN.* IBM 370 and CDC COBOL allow the use of the word THEN optionally in an IF statement:

    ```
    ANS COBOL:
        IF QUANTITY IS NOT = 0
            COMPUTE AVERAGE-COST = TOTAL-COST / QUANTITY.

    IBM 370 with optional THEN:
        IF QUANTITY IS NOT = 0 THEN
            COMPUTE AVERAGE-COST = TOTAL-COST / QUANTITY.
    ```

2. *OTHERWISE.* In any COBOL version the ELSE clause is optional. Some versions allow the reserved word OTHERWISE in its place.

3. *Arithmetic Expression.* An arithmetic expression can be used in an IF statement, as in the following:

    ```
    IF VALUE = FACTOR * .25 . . .
                Arithmetic expression
    ```

4. *NEXT SENTENCE.* The NEXT SENTENCE option causes the program to continue execution with the first statement following the period. The general format of the IF with its options is as follows:

    ```
    IF condition  {statement-1     }  {ELSE       }  {Statement-2
                  {NEXT SENTENCE   }  {OTHERWISE  }  {NEXT SENTENCE
    ```

    The following example tests the line counter to determine if the end of the page has (not) been reached by using the NEXT SENTENCE option. In this case, if the line counter is less than 55, the program bypasses the ELSE condition:

```
IF LINE-CTR < 55 NEXT SENTENCE
ELSE PERFORM H000-HEAD.
```

However, with a more sensible organization of the IF logic you can often avoid using the NEXT SENTENCE option:

```
IF LINE-CTR NOT < 55 PERFORM H000-HEAD.
```

The result of this last example is simple, clear code—always an objective in programming.

5. *Nested IF.* It is possible for the condition of one IF statement to be another IF statement. The ELSE clause is associated with the closest preceding IF that is not already paired with another IF. For example:

```
IF RECORD-CODE = '23'
    IF CUSTOMER-NO > PREV-CUSTOMER
        PERFORM C000-CALC-CUST
    ELSE
        PERFORM R000-ERROR-ROUTINE.
```

For clarity, the nested IF is indented, and its related ELSE is indented to appear directly under it. This particular example has an ELSE related to the second IF, but none is related to the first IF. The example also nests one IF statement inside another IF statement. If you want the ELSE to apply to the first IF instead of the second IF, you could use a NEXT SENTENCE clause with slightly different logical results:

```
IF RECORD-CODE = '23'
    IF CUSTOMER-NO > PREV-CUSTOMER
        PERFORM C000-CALC-CUST
    ELSE NEXT SENTENCE
ELSE
    PERFORM R000-ERROR-ROUTINE.
```

It is possible to continue nesting IF statements, although the logic may become incomprehensible, and because of indenting, the statements may run off the coding sheet. In such cases, the solution may be to divide the logic into smaller pieces, or to use one of the following features.

6. *Compound IF.* You can combine two or more simple conditions using the logical operators AND and OR, optionally combined with the logical operator NOT. In IF logic, AND implies that *both* conditions must be true, whereas OR implies that *either one* or *both* conditions must be true. This difference between AND and OR is an important distinction in programming logic.

The following two examples provide the same logic as the preceding nested IF statement, testing for valid record code and customer sequence:

Example 1. Use of AND:

```
IF RECORD-CODE = '23' AND CUSTOMER-NO > PREV-CUSTOMER
    PERFORM C000-CALC-CUST
ELSE
    PERFORM R000-ERROR-ROUTINE.
```

If the code is 23 and the customer number is higher than the previous number, then both conditions are true, and the program performs the calculation routine. Otherwise, there is an error condition.

Example 2. Use of OR:

```
IF RECORD-CODE NOT = '23' OR CUSTOMER-NO NOT > PREV-CUSTOMER
    PERFORM R000-ERROR-ROUTINE
ELSE
    PERFORM C000-CALC-CUST.
```

Example 2 uses OR to achieve the same effect as example 1 using AND, but note that example 2 recasts the IF conditions with NOT operators. There is a shift in the logical approach, with the two PERFORMs reversed. (Check the result if the PERFORMs were in the same sequence as in example 1.) NOT operators coupled with OR as in example 2 can cause problems in COBOL by generating unexpected illogical results, and experienced COBOL programmers have learned to avoid this combination.

7.   *Implied Subject.* Consider the following compound IF statement:

```
IF QTY-ON-HAND > 25 AND QTY-ON-HAND < RE-ORDER-POINT
    PERFORM G000-RE-ORDER-ROUTINE.
```

This statement has two conditional expressions, both with the same subject, QTY-ON-HAND. In such a case, you can *imply* the subject for the second condition, as follows:

```
IF QTY-ON-HAND > 25 AND < RE-ORDER-POINT
    PERFORM G000-RE-ORDER-ROUTINE.
```

The use of an *implied subject* does not affect efficiency of execution. The choice of its use is up to the programmer: Is the statement clearer to read? Sometimes the statement is clearer if the conditions are in parentheses (although not necessarily clearer in this case):

```
IF (QTY-ON-HAND > 25) AND (QTY-ON-HAND < RE-ORDER-POINT)
    PERFORM G000-RE-ORDER-ROUTINE.
```

8.   *Implied Operator.* You can also imply the operator (=, >, <) in a COBOL IF statement. Consider this example in which the subject is implied:

```
IF CUSTOMER-BALANCE > 100.00 AND > CREDIT-LIMIT
    PERFORM ...
```

Since the *greater than* (>) operator is the same for each condition, you can imply it also:

```
IF CUSTOMER-BALANCE > 100.00 AND CREDIT-LIMIT
   PERFORM ...
```

In a complex IF statement, implied subjects and operators may be confusing, and often the clearest approach is to spell out each condition entirely. Note: The sign (NEGATIVE, POSITIVE, or ZERO) condition and class (NUMERIC or ALPHABETIC) condition tests cannot have implied subjects or operators.

THE GO TO STATEMENT

In COBOL, the PERFORM statement causes program control to leave a routine and to enter another one. The normal return from the executed subroutine is to the statement immediately following the PERFORM. COBOL also provides a GO TO statement that enables the program to branch directly to any other part of the program with no automatic return. In general, there is seldom use for the GO TO statement, although in a program with complex logic, and with the limitations of the COBOL IF statement, a GO TO may be occasionally necessary.

Basically, the GO TO branches to a Paragraph name (Technically, GO TO can also branch to a Section name, although Sections should be reserved as complete subroutines that the program executes only through a PERFORM.) A GO TO may be unconditional or conditional. The general formats are:

```
unconditional:   GO TO paragraph-name.
conditional:     IF condition GO TO paragraph-name.
```

A simple example follows:

```
IF HOURS = ZERO GO TO C300-BYPASS.
DIVIDE HOURS INTO KMS GIVING RATE-OF-SPEED.
MOVE RATE-OF-SPEED TO SPEED-PR.
WRITE PRINT-RECORD...
C300-BYPASS.
   MOVE ...
```

The IF statement causes the program to GO TO C300-BYPASS if the divisor (HOURS) contains zero. In this case, C300-BYPASS is a Paragraph name. The GO TO statement branches to this address (to the statement immediately following), and the WRITE itself drops directly into the Paragraph name. The program could avoid the GO TO by use of an IF statement using NOT:

```
IF HOURS NOT = ZERO
   DIVIDE HOURS INTO KMS GIVING RATE-OF-SPEED
   MOVE RATE-OF-SPEED TO SPEED-PR
   WRITE PRINT-RECORD... .
MOVE ...
```

Another solution, less efficient, could use a PERFORM:

```
IF HOURS NOT = ZERO
   PERFORM D100-DIVIDE.
```

The subroutine D100-DIVIDE would be a Section containing the DIVIDE, MOVE, and WRITE statements.

NOTE: If you must use GO TO, for program clarity be sure that it branches *forward* in the program to a Paragraph name in the same Section, preferably the EXIT.

GO TO DEPENDING

You may find an occasional use for the GO TO DEPENDING statement. Its general format is as follows:

GO TO procedure-1, procedure-2, . . ., DEPENDING ON data-item.

As an example, assume that a wholesale supply company has three discount rates based on volume of customer sales. The rate codes are 1, 2, and 3 and are stored in a field named DISCO-CODE. The following routine using GO TO DEPENDING stores the correct discount rate depending on the code:

```
77   DISCO-CODE           PIC 9.
       .
       .
       .
     GO TO D100, D200, D300 DEPENDING ON DISCO-CODE.
     MOVE .00 TO DISCO-RATE.
     GO TO D500.
D100.
     MOVE .05 TO DISCO-RATE.
     GO TO D5CC.
D200.
     MOVE .03 TO DISCO-RATE.
     GO TO D500.
D300.
     MOVE .02 TO DISCO-RATE.
D500.
     COMPUTE DISCO-AMT ROUNDED = SALES-AMT * DISCO-RATE.
```

If the code contains 1, the program goes to the first address specified (D100), if 2, to the second address, and if 3, to the third address. If the code is none of these, the program continues to the statement that follows. Although most of the coding is clear, GO TO DEPENDING often involves a lot of GO TO statements. Therefore, make sure that the GO TO statements branch forward to addresses that are in the same Section of coding as the statements themselves.

DATE

Most reports are designed to accommodate one or two dates. The most common date is the *effective date* of a report, such as March 31, 19xx. Many transactions that occur prior to this date are not received and entered until after the date, and although a report is effective as of March 31, it may be run several days later. Because the program may be run on almost any day, the common procedure is to enter the date as a data record, often as a special date card preceding the input data. A special code in a preassigned column identifies the date card. Many installations use a standard date card format that all programs must read. The following example date card is identified by the character D in column one:

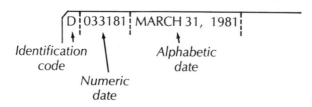

This example date card contains two dates: the alphabetic date is useful for a report heading, and the numeric date is useful to check the accuracy of the dates on input transaction records and in calculations, such as for delinquent payments, discounts, and interest. In the File Section, a program must define the date record, and in the Procedure Division it must test for the presence of the date record and process it.

Another useful date is the *run date*. It indicates when a report was actually run and is easily extracted from the main storage of many computer systems (the date may not be available on small systems). IBM 360/370 COBOL uses the reserved word CURRENT-DATE (so it need not be defined). The date record is coded as follows:

```
WORKING-STORAGE SECTION.
77   TO-DAY                 PIC X(8).

PROCEDURE DIVISION.
     MOVE CURRENT-DATE TO TO-DAY.
```

The computer system provides the current date in one of two formats (including two slashes) depending on the installation:

dd/mm/yy   mm/dd/yy

Other COBOL versions use the reserved word DATE with a format of yymmdd. Chapter 7 includes a program that reads and processes the date card.

ERROR PREVENTION

Advanced COBOL logic and organization involves the following error prevention points:

1.   Use condition names to make program logic clearer. A condition name should be meaningful and should be used for only one purpose.

2.   Use PERFORM statements that execute separate Sections to improve program clarity. Be sure that each Section has one clear entry point and exit and is clearly isolated from all other Sections.

3.   Employ the following IF logic rules:
- Avoid NOT in conjunction with OR.
- Avoid nesting IF statements to deep levels.
- Use parentheses to make the logic clearer.
- Avoid complex logical expressions, and if necessary recast them into separate statements.
- Provide data that tests every condition of program logic. This practice is the only way to ensure that what looks possible in theory will actually work.

4.   Watch for punctuation in an IF statement. The following code is supposed to test each condition separately:

```
IF CODE-IN NOT = '21'
    MOVE 'INVALID CODE' TO CODE-MESS-PR
IF ACCT-NO-IN < PREV-ACCT
    MOVE 'OUT OF SEQUENCE' TO SEQ-MESS-PR.
```

— Missing period

The first MOVE does not end with a period. As a result, the compiler mistakenly treats the second IF as nested within the first. The second IF executes only if CODE-IN is not equal to '21'.

PROBLEMS

6–1. What is the advantage of using condition names instead of explicitly coding literals?

6–2. An input record contains the current month in a field named MONTH-IN PIC XX. If the month is December (12), the program is to move "YEAR END" to HEADING. Code MONTH-IN, the condition name, and the IF logic.

6–3. What is the purpose of the PERFORM statement?

6–4. What normally terminates the following PERFORM statements?
(a) PERFORM paragraph-name.
(b) PERFORM paragraph-name-1 THRU paragraph-name-2.
(c) PERFORM section-name.
(d) PERFORM name 25 TIMES.
(e) PERFORM name UNTIL COUNT = TOTAL.

6–5. The following is a logic problem. If ACCUM is zero and TOTAL is negative, move N to PRINT-SIGNAL. If the sum of TOTAL and ACCUM is greater than zero, go to C25. If both TOTAL and ACCUM are greater than zero, move Y to PRINT-SIGNAL and go to C35. Code the logic using nested IF statements or compound IFs as required.

6–6. Revise a recent program, reorganizing it into PERFORM statements and Sections. Use condition names where appropriate.

CHAPTER 7

PROGRAMMING STRATEGY AND STYLE

OBJECTIVE: To examine programming style and techniques for more maintainable and efficient programs.

INTRODUCTION

In an installation, programs must be revised because of errors and because of changes in specifications. The original programmer and others spend much time rereading programs to make these changes. Installations have thrown out many sloppy programs because they were easier to rewrite than to correct. As a result, one objective of writing a program should be to ensure that it is maintainable.

Style and technique are important features of improving readability and maintainability. As programs become more complex, it is increasingly necessary to adopt recognizable conventions and to use the clearest, most readable programming style. There are generally accepted techniques that apply to all programming languages, and those that apply to a particular one. In this regard, this chapter covers the structured programming approach, program objectives, specific good COBOL practices, and programming efficiency.

STRUCTURED PROGRAMMING

"Structured programming" originated as a response to the need for readable programs. In established installations, some 60 to 80 percent of programming effort has been devoted to maintenance—correcting and revising existing programs. In many cases, programs were found to be incomprehensible, with peculiar names, little apparent organization, and GO TO statements branching from page to page. What was needed to remedy the situation was a more systematic approach to programming, and what materialized was 'structured programming.' The net effect reported by those who have adopted it has been a dramatic improvement in programming performance.

Structured programming involves an approach that results in well-organized and easily maintained code. This section covers the basic ideas of structured programming. Since there are a number of textbooks devoted exclusively to this topic, this one will not attempt to belabor the subject nor give it the pretence of scientific method.

Any reader who has understood the material to this point will have no trouble with the topic. The previous program examples are all structured in style: organized into logical modules, containing indented subsidiary statements, and lacking GO TO statements. A true structured program has the following features:

1.   *Three Basic Control Structures.* A structured program consists of three basic control structures that can perform any function:

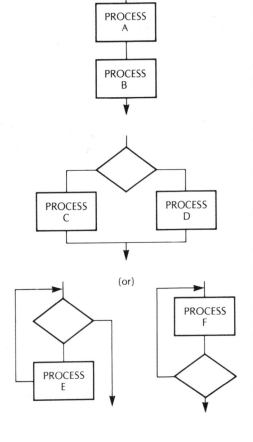

- *Simple Sequence.* One operation directly follows another, with no logic tests to change the sequence. A simple example is "Move data to the print area" followed by "Print a line."

- *Selection.* The program branches conditionally to one of two processes and returns. COBOL expresses this logic as

    IF . . . ELSE . . .

- *Repetition.* The program repeats an operation (or series of operations) a specified number of times. There are two variations on the test. COBOL expresses the logic as

    PERFORM . . . UNTIL . . .

2. *Elimination of GO TO Statements.* The GO TO (or unconditional branch operation) is said to be the greatest cause of adding to program complexity. COBOL has the powerful PERFORM statement to permit looping without the use of GO TOs, and to execute separate routines. It is therefore possible to eliminate jumping forward and backward between routines. Basically, the flow of logic should be *forward.* The mind can more easily follow code that moves forward in a linear fashion rather than code that jumps back and forth between pages.

3. *Organization into Logical Modules.* A program should have a section of main logic and various subsidiary sections of related logic. The routines are localized so that each routine performs only operations that are relevant to that routine. The main logic routine performs the subsidiary routines as required, and subsidiary routines can perform other subsidiary routines at a lower level. Each routine has one entry point (at the top) and one exit point (at the bottom). (There may be some exceptions for exits, especially on serious error conditions.) Each routine is restricted to 50–60 lines per printed page, and fewer lines on a visual display terminal.

4. *Indentation.* To clarify the program logic, statements that are subsidiary to others should be indented. The following are two examples of an IF statement, the first not indented, and the second indented:

```
IF STOCK-QTY < RE-ORDER-POINT            IF STOCK-QTY < RE-ORDER POINT
IF QTY-ON-ORDER = ZERO                        IF QTY-ON-ORDER = ZERO
MOVE 'RE-ORDER STOCK' TO MESS-PR.                MOVE 'RE-ORDER STOCK' TO MESS-PR.
```

The first example does not clearly indicate that the three statements are uniquely related, whereas in the second example, the relationship is made quite clear.

5. *Top-down Approach.* The small programs presented to this point have required little special organization, but large programs are complex and should be organized, coded, and tested in segments. The program is designed around a main logic routine with various subsidiary routines, which are at any low level:

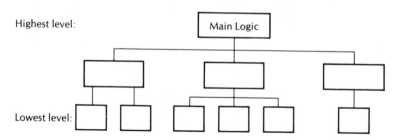

The main logic, the highest level, provides the skeleton of the program and should be coded and tested first. Even if there is little output, the test will help to validate the overall logic. As the routines of the next lower level are coded, they are attached to the main logic for testing. Since the main logic is known to work, any error is quickly located in its subsidiary routine. Routines of lower levels are coded and tested until in time there is a fully working program. An alternative method that was once commonly used is to code routines of the lowest level first and test them with "test drivers"—all with their own input/output logic. This method requires more coding and debugging because the additional input/output must also be debugged. Also, when all the routines that work alone are finally organized into one large program, it is likely to collapse.

Structured programming may require more initial coding effort, but users who have seriously adopted it claim that their programs are more readable, have fewer errors, and are easier to maintain. The net result is a shorter time period in which programs become operational. Fortunately, COBOL lends itself very well to the structured programming style.

PROGRAM CONTROL

The program in Chapter 6 used the structured programming technique to handle input logic by using an initial READ and a PERFORM of a Section that processed a record and then read the next record. The approach merits further explanation. Assume the following code, with no initial READ, but with the READ at the beginning of B000-PROC:

```
PERFORM B000-PROC UNTIL END-FILE.
        .
        .
        .
B000-PROC SECTION.
    READ STOCK-FILE,
        AT END MOVE 'END' TO END-FILE-FLAG.
        .
        .
        .
B999-RETURN. EXIT.
```

In this case, the program will read and process correctly until reaching the end-of-file in B000-PROC. At this point, however, it will move 'END' to END-FILE-FLAG and *continue processing* through to the EXIT. Because no new record is read, it reprocesses the last input record (that was already processed prior to reaching end-of-file and is still in the input area) before reaching the EXIT and returning to the main logic. A solution would be to change the AT END to include a GO TO:

```
READ STOCK-FILE,
    AT END MOVE 'END' TO END-FILE-FLAG,
    GO TO B999-RETURN.
```

Because this solution uses the much-maligned GO TO statement, a structured programming purist would adopt the approach taken in this text where the READ immediately precedes the EXIT.

PROGRAMMING OBJECTIVES

The objectives of a computer program are accuracy, efficiency, and maintainability.

Accuracy.   Obviously, a program should produce correct answers. This objective is first and foremost because a program that is inaccurate is useless. Unfortunately, the larger the program, the less certainty there is of its accuracy.

Efficiency.   Subject to the deadline allowed to get the program working accurately, a program should be efficient. A good programmer can code the problem using less storage and less execution time, even without spending much (if any) more coding time.

Maintainability.   A program must be revised constantly to meet new conditions and new technological releases. As a result, a program should be written with the knowledge that it will eventually have to be rewritten.

Many beginning programmers think that accuracy is the only objective in programming. Their attitude is, in effect, "the program works—what more do you want?" A more experienced programmer takes great pride in manipulating coding to produce the most efficient program imaginable, but at some cost in time and comprehensibility. The difference between these two and the professional programmer is the long-term outlook: the professional is concerned not only with accuracy and efficiency, but also with maintainability. The program must not only work well today, it must also be written to work well throughout its life.

Accuracy and efficiency result from a thorough working knowledge of the computer and its language, and from painstaking care in coding and testing. Maintainability results from a good approach and attitude to programming and may be accomplished by the following:

Clarity.   Use program comments wherever necessary to explain what a routine is supposed to accomplish, especially calculations and logic. Use meaningful, descriptive names for data areas. Adopt standards regarding the names of data areas, instructions, documentation, and programming style. Ensure that the coding matches the flow and logic in the flowchart. Keep in mind that the simple solution is always the best one.

Organization

A good program is well organized. Organize the coding into logical sections; keep related operations together. If possible, limit each Section to one page of computer listing (about 60 lines). What is best understood is what the eye can see all at once and held in the mind. Organize Sections into a logical sequence so that the commonly performed routines are first, and the seldom-performed routines are last. Avoid instructions that jump from one routine to another and back.

Coding Techniques

Whereas organization is concerned with the approach to programming, coding techniques involve the use of instructions. Every programming language has its peculiarities and its pitfalls of redundancy. The best program is always simple and clear and avoids using complicated, tricky routines to solve relatively simple problems. For example, a programmer could code an extremely sophisticated COBOL routine consisting of loops within loops to scan a table of data for some specified code; however, the programmer could accomplish the same results in one statement by using the COBOL PERFORM UNTIL statement.

Portability

It is often desirable to avoid becoming locked in to the computer of one particular manufacturer. Such a situation occurs when the programs in an installation are written in a language that is rarely used elsewhere. If the installation decides to switch to a different manufacturer, all the programs must be rewritten at considerable cost. Many installations have chosen a universal high-level language like COBOL because if they change manufacturer, they only need make minor programming changes.

Flexibility and Expandability

Programs should be written with the knowledge that program requirements will change in the future. For example, file sizes grow and price levels increase. Defined field lengths should provide for future larger values. Main storage is cheaper than programming time (up to a point), and defining a few extra bytes for larger field lengths is low-cost insurance against program revisions.

COBOL PROGRAMMING PRACTICES

Because of debugging and revising, programmers spend more time reading a program than writing a program. As a result, there is a need for readability—simple code, meaningful names, elimination of redundant words and statements, and clear, straightforward flow of logic. Programmers were once proud of tricky, technical code; today they are more likely to exhibit their programs as examples of clear and elegant style.

Identification Division

PROGRAM-ID.   A program should be named according to installation standards, and if there are no standards, the name should at least be descriptive. Since many programs can access one data file, program names can be ambiguous. To prevent this many installations use *project codes*. Thus, an "Order Entry" project is numbered 240, and programs within this project are numbered 240001, 240002, etc. Programs within an inventory project numbered 425 are also numbered serially, as 425001, 425002, etc. Programs are therefore easily identified and filed according to project code.

AUTHOR.   This entry is useful to identify and locate the original programmer in case of revisions or inquiries.

REMARKS.   This paragraph should clearly and simply explain the purpose of the program. Several paragraphs may be necessary for large programs.

Data Division

Spacing.   Insert blank lines between Divisions, Sections, and Paragraphs, and anywhere else to break up the cluttered appearance of a program.

Alignment.   Align level numbers (01, 05, etc.), PICTURE, and VALUE clauses consistently.

Indentation.   Indent subfields (03, 05, etc.) consistently and increment level numbers according to installation standards.

Literals.   Use named constants in Working-Storage rather than literals. The name of a constant can better indicate its purpose. Also, if its value must be changed, you need to change only the constant in Working-Storage, and not every use of the literal in the program. In the following, the first statement uses a numeric literal, whereas the second statement references a named constant defined in Working-Storage:

```
COMPUTE CHARGE ROUNDED = AMOUNT * 0.03245.
COMPUTE CHARGE ROUNDED = AMOUNT * ADJUSTMENT-FACTOR.
```

Data Names.   Avoid meaningless names like A, B, and X, or even AMOUNT-1 and SWITCH. There is a trade-off between meaningful names (often long) and a natural reluctance to repeatedly spell out long names. It is advisable to use clear abbreviations in order to reduce verbiage and spelling errors. Thus, the name PREVIOUS-CUSTOMER-NUMBER is still clear when coded as PREV-CUST-NO. But be careful of ambiguities: TEMP could mean temporary or temperature, and INV could mean inventory or invoice. Adopt COBOL abbreviations and delete redundant words. Consider two examples that define the same field, TOTAL-SALES:

```
77   TOTAL-SALES PICTURE IS S99999V99 USAGE IS COMPUTATIONAL-3
                                       VALUE IS ZERO.
77   TOTAL-SALES PIC S9(5)V99 COMP-3 VALUE ZERO.
```

To a nonprogrammer, neither statement makes much sense, despite COBOL's claim of readability. To a programmer, the second statement is just as clear as the first (perhaps clearer because of the lack of redundant information).

Condition Names.   Here are some useful guidelines regarding condition names:

* Use condition names only where necessary.
* Define them with meaningful names.
* Assign meaningful values such as END or YES, rather than 0 or 1.
* Use each condition name for one purpose only.

Procedure Division

Organization.   Code only one statement per line, and avoid continuing literals onto a second line. Organize program logic into various routines, such as

* Initialization
* Main Processing
* Termination

Code routines as Sections or Paragraphs that are executed by PERFORM statements. Each Section should have one entry point (the first statement) and one exit point through the last statement (with a possible exception of exiting on a disastrous error). Each Section should consist of logic related only to that routine, and should be limited to about 50–60 lines.

Comments.   Use well-organized coding that is clear and self-documenting to minimize the need for elaborate comments. Any comment should add to the clarity of a program. The beginning of each Section should contain a comment that explains the purpose of the routine and any unusual logic or computation.

Section and Paragraph Names.   Code Section and Paragraph names (Procedure names) in ascending sequence to reduce the chances of coding duplicate names. A descriptive suffix helps to clarify the purpose of a routine. A name stands out more clearly if coded on its own separate line. The following is one suggested method used in this text:

```
H000-PAGE-HEADING SECTION.
        •
        •
        •
H999-RETURN. EXIT.
```

Section names in the Procedure Division are in ascending sequence, with a descriptive suffix (PAGE-HEADING).

Paragraph names in the Section use the same first letter (H) and are in ascending order.

Each Paragraph name within H000 contains a sequentially higher number, perhaps incremented by 100, as H100, H200. The last Paragraph containing EXIT is numbered 999 to indicate the highest and last statement in the Section.

Punctuation.   Because of the similarity of commas and semicolons to periods, some authorities advise against their use (although this text uses commas extensively). In the following, the programmer coded a comma that was keyed as a period. The effect is that the WRITE statement will always execute whether LINE-COUNT is high or not high:

```
IF LINE-COUNT > END-PAGE
   MOVE ZERO TO LINE-COUNT.⟋ Keyed as period in error
WRITE PRINT-RECORD FROM HEADING-LINE.
```

MULTIPLY.   The MULTIPLY statement with no GIVING option is unclear by its nature. Consider:

```
MULTIPLY HOURS BY RATE.
```

Although the reader expects the program to store the product in HOURS, instead it is in RATE. The use of GIVING or COMPUTE designates the receiving field more clearly:

```
MULTIPLY HOURS BY RATE GIVING WAGE.
(OR) COMPUTE WAGE = HOURS * RATE.
```

ALTER.   Many installations have a rule against using the ALTER statement. When revising an old program, you may encounter an ALTER. The program will have a GO TO attached to a Paragraph name:

```
D200-GO.
   GO TO F000-CALC.
D299-GONE.
```

Elsewhere the program can ALTER the GO TO at D200-GO so that the program will GO TO a different address on execution:

```
ALTER D200-GO TO PROCEED TO G300-ERROR.
```

After reaching D200-GO, the program will GO TO G300-ERROR instead of F000-CALC. But unfortunately, the reader cannot easily see that the GO TO statement is a "switch" that can change its address, nor is it readily apparent what the address(es) is. If possible, eliminate the ALTER and devise a more comprehensible method. Often, a condition name or a PERFORM will produce clearer code in such cases.

GO TO. Minimize the use of GO TO and GO TO DEPENDING ON. The intelligent use of PERFORM statements and nested IF logic can substitute for GO TO in most cases. In this way, you can design programs that progress forward in a linear sequence and are simple to understand. If used, a GO TO should go down a Section, not back up. The following statement uses an unnecessary GO TO:

```
IF LINE-CTR < 55 GO TO C200-NEXT
ELSE PERFORM H000-PAGE-HEADING.
C200-NEXT.
```

A minor rearrangement of this logic can avoid the GO TO and the Paragraph name:

```
IF LINE-CTR > 54 PERFORM H000-PAGE-HEADING.
```

There is an advantage in disposing of Paragraph names: it is not always apparent if there are PERFORMs or GO TOs referencing them. Occasionally, eliminating a GO TO is not so simple and may require more time and ingenuity than many programmers are prepared to devote.

IF Logic. There are many ways to keep IF logic clear and simple:

- Indent subsidiary statements and nested IFs to make the hierarchy clear.
- Minimize the use of compound IFs.
- Keep ELSE statements reasonably close to their related IF statements.
- Avoid deep nesting of IFs.
- Avoid the use of NOT with OR.
- Watch out for logical impossibilities, especially with AND:

```
IF AMOUNT > 25.00 AND < ZERO ...    (never true)
```

or logical redundancies, especially with OR:

```
IF COUNT = 0 OR COUNT NOT = 0 ...   (always true)
```

In a large program, the reader must plow through hundreds or thousands of words. In the statement

```
IF AMOUNT IS NOT GREATER THAN ZERO ...
```

the words IS and THAN are redundant; most compilers permit the operator $>$ in place of GREATER. The following is shorter and just as clear:

```
IF AMOUNT NOT > ZERO ...
```

The following is dreadful code, the kind that you might find buried in some installation and written by a beginner:

```
    IF CUSTOMER-BALANCE IS GREATER THAN CREDIT-LIMIT GO TO
        ALICE. GO TO BOB.
CAROL. MOVE 'PLEASE PAY ACCOUNT' TO MESSAGE-AREA. GO TO
        Z-OUT.                                                  Ugly,
BOB. IF CUSTOMER-BALANCE IS GREATER THAN 250.00 GO TO CAROL.    nasty
        GO TO Z-OUT.                                            code
ALICE. IF DATE-PAID IS EQUAL TO THIS-MONTH GO TO Z-OUT ELSE
        GO TO BOB.
Z-OUT. ...
```

It requires considerable concentration to determine just what this routine is trying to accomplish. You can easily recast the logic, disposing of all seven GO TOs and all four Paragraph names:

```
IF CUSTOMER-BALANCE > CREDIT-LIMIT AND > 250.00        Neat,
    IF DATE-PAID NOT = THIS-MONTH                      elegant
        MOVE 'PLEASE PAY ACCOUNT' TO MESSAGE-AREA.     code
```

Sometimes a solution to difficult programming logic requires certain ingenuity. Assume that a customer record contains aged balances owing: current due, 31–60 days, 61–90 days, and over 90 days due. Any payment that the customer makes applies to the oldest amount—first to over 90, then to 61–90, then to 31–60, then to current due. For example, a customer's balance is:

current	31–60	61–90	over 90 days
$200	$125	$75	$105

A payment of $250 erases the over 90 days ($105), then the 61–90 balance ($75), and finally part of the 31–60 ($70). The account is now:

current	31–60	61–90	over 90 days
$200	$55	$0	$0

A quick but uninspired programming solution could be as shown in Figure 7-1.

```
        SUBTRACT AMOUNT FROM OVER90-DUE.
        IF OVER90-DUE IS NOT NEGATIVE GO TO P900-RETURN.
        MOVE OVER90-DUE TO AMOUNT.
        MOVE ZEROS TO OVER90-DUE.
        ADD AMOUNT TO OVER60-DUE.
        IF OVER60-DUE IS NOT NEGATIVE GO TO P900-RETURN.
        MOVE OVER60-DUE TO AMOUNT.
        MOVE ZEROS TO OVER60-DUE.
        ADD AMOUNT TO OVER30-DUE.
        IF OVER30-DUE IS NOT NEGATIVE GO TO P900-RETURN.
        MOVE OVER30-DUE TO AMOUNT.
        MOVE ZEROS TO OVER30-DUE.
        ADD AMOUNT TO CURR-DUE.
P900-RETURN.  ...
```

FIGURE 7-1   Paying Aged Balances—Unstructured Code.

The routine contains some redundant code: the statements that MOVE to AMOUNT and ADD AMOUNT can be combined. Also, nested IF statements can be used to eliminate the three GO TO statements, as shown in Figure 7-2.

```
        SUBTRACT AMOUNT FROM OVER90-DUE.
        IF OVER90-DUE IS NEGATIVE
            ADD OVER90-DUE TO OVER60-DUE
          MOVE ZEROS TO OVER90-DUE
          IF OVER60-DUE IS NEGATIVE
              ADD OVER60-DUE TO OVER30-DUE
            MOVE ZEROS TO OVER60-DUE
            IF OVER30-DUE IS NEGATIVE
                ADD OVER30-DUE TO CURR-DUE
              MOVE ZEROS TO OVER30-DUE.
```

FIGURE 7-2   Paying Aged Balances—Structured Code.

The revised solution is consistent and certainly clearer than the previous one. (A possibility, however, is that the nested IFs could reach past the right margin of the coding sheet or display screen, or the logic could run on past a page or two.) Note in this case the difference between nested IFs and IF . . . ELSE . . . . The use of ELSE in this example would produce an incorrect result, as shown in Figure 7-3. ELSE clauses would make the program logic bypass required steps. For example, a payment makes over 90 negative. The program adds the negative balance to 61–90 and clears over 90 to zero. But instead of checking 61–90 for negative, the program bypasses the rest of the routine.

```
SUBTRACT AMOUNT FROM OVER90-DUE.
IF OVER90-DUE IS NEGATIVE
    ADD OVER90-DUE TO OVER60-DUE
    MOVE ZEROS TO OVER90-DUE
ELSE
    IF OVER60-DUE IS NEGATIVE
        •
        •
        •
```

FIGURE 7-3   Paying Aged Balances—Incorrect Use of ELSE.

PROGRAM EFFICIENCY

Today, the major concern of most computer installations is *user* efficiency rather than computer efficiency. Because programming costs are increasing and computer costs are declining, the former has become the largest share of the installation budget. It is justifiable, therefore, to place an emphasis on programmer efficiency. However, if two programmers were each to write a program to solve the same problem, one program could be very efficient in its use of storage and execution time, whereas the other could be extravagant in space and execution time. If both programs require the same time to code and are equally clear and maintainable, then why not maintain the practices that produced the efficient program? Only the manufacturer gains from inefficient coding because eventually the installation will require a faster, larger CPU, resulting in higher rental costs.

Some practices that generate efficient code include the following:

- *Initialization.* Initialize PICTURE values with blanks or zeros rather than MOVE such values at the start of the Procedure Division.
- *Field Length.* Define as the same length fields that are to be moved or compared one to the other.
- *Arithmetic Fields.* Arithmetic PICTURE fields should contain an S sign. For the 360/370, arithmetic fields should be defined as an odd number of digits.* All fields being added or compared should have an equal number of decimal places and the same format (such as COMP or COMP-3 depending on the computer and the field's use). Working-Storage fields should be defined as COMP or COMP-3. Use COMPUTE instead of ADD, SUBTRACT, MULTIPLY, or DIVIDE.

*The IBM 360/370 stores arithmetic fields in packed format, two digits per byte, plus a half-byte for the sign. The following depicts 2-, 3-, and 4-byte fields respectively containing 3, 5, and 7 digits (this is the format for decimal (COMP-3) arithmetic, not binary):

| 12 | 3+ | | |

| 12 | 34 | 5+ | |

| 12 | 34 | 56 | 7+ |

Minimize the use of ON SIZE ERROR, which generates a lot of machine code. For DIVIDE, ON SIZE checks only for a zero divisor, a test that the program can perform better. When possible, use MULTIPLY rather than DIVIDE; instead of dividing a value by 2, multiply by its reciprocal, .5. Use ROUNDED and REMAINDER only where necessary.

Match literals to fields according to sign, length, and decimal position:

```
77   COUNTER       PIC S99V9 COMP-3 VALUE +00.0.
     .
     .
     .
ADD +01.0 TO COUNTER.
```

In an arithmetic expression, perform division last if possible. For example, in an expression such as

$$10 * (3 / 6)$$

the divide executes first. It generates a temporary work field of PIC S9 format (on some compilers) that is too small for the actual quotient 0.5. The stored quotient is zero, and the product becomes $10 \times 0 = 0$. The expression would execute correctly as

$$(10 * 3) / 6.$$

- *Nonarithmetic Fields.* Nonarithmetic fields should be defined or allowed to default to DISPLAY, and defined as PICTURE X.
- *Input/Output.* Use READ and WRITE for all input/output, and ACCEPT and DISPLAY only if necessary (such as for terminal I/O processing).
- *Comparison.* Compare fields of the same data format: numeric to numeric and alphanumeric to alphanumeric.

Become familiar with the computer's Assembler (low-level) language to gain an insight into the machine's operation, storage handling of data, and generated machine code.

PROGRAM EXAMPLE

The program example in Figure 7-4 illustrates a fully structured program, including the use of a date card. Up to now, programs have processed only one type of input record. Figure 7-4 provides for an additional record type, a date card. The File Section in this example defines the date card as DATE-RECORD and indicates and defines two record formats in the FD statement:

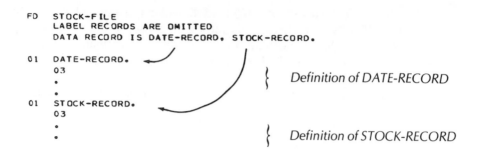

```
FD   STOCK-FILE
     LABEL RECORDS ARE OMITTED
     DATA RECORD IS DATE-RECORD, STOCK-RECORD.

01   DATE-RECORD.
     03
      .
      .
01   STOCK-RECORD.
     03
      .
      .
```

{ Definition of DATE-RECORD

{ Definition of STOCK-RECORD

```
00001              IDENTIFICATION DIVISION.
00002              PROGRAM-ID. CHAPT07.
00003           *          STRUCTURED PROGRAM USING A DATE CARD.

00005              ENVIRONMENT DIVISION.
00006              CONFIGURATION SECTION.
00007              SPECIAL-NAMES.
00008                  C01 IS TOP-PAGE.
00009              INPUT-OUTPUT SECTION.
00010              FILE-CONTROL.
00011                  SELECT INPUT-FILE, ASSIGN TO SYS015-UR-2501-S.
00012                  SELECT PRINT-FILE, ASSIGN TO SYS014-UR-1403-S.

00014              DATA DIVISION.
00015              FILE SECTION.
00016              FD   INPUT-FILE
00017                  LABEL RECORDS ARE OMITTED
00018                  DATA RECORD IS DATE-RECORD, STOCK-RECORD.

00020              01   DATE-RECORD.
00021                  03  DATE-CODE-IN     PIC XX.
00022                      88 VALID-DATE-CODE           VALUE 'DR'.
00023                  03  NUMERIC-DATE-IN.
00024                      05  MONTH-IN     PIC XX.
00025                      05  DAY-IN       PIC XX.
00026                      05  YEAR-IN      PIC XX.
00027                  03  ALPHA-DATE-IN    PIC X(18).
00028                  03  FILLER           PIC X(54).

00030              01   STOCK-RECORD.
00031                  03  CODE-IN          PIC XX.
00032                  03  FILLER           PIC XX.
00033                  03  STOCK-IN         PIC X(5).
00034                  03  QTY-IN           PIC S999.
00035                  03  UNCOST-IN        PIC S99V99.
00036                  03  DESCRIP-IN       PIC X(20).
00037                  03  FILLER           PIC X(44).

00039              FD   PRINT-FILE
00040                  LABEL RECORDS ARE OMITTED
00041                  DATA RECORD IS PRINT-RECORD.
00042              01   PRINT-RECORD         PIC X(133).
```

FIGURE 7-4   Structured Program with Date Card.

```
00044              WORKING-STORAGE SECTION.
00045              77  EOF-FLAG           PIC X(3)          VALUE ' '.
00046                  88  NOT-END-FILE                     VALUE ' '.
00047                  88  END-FILE                         VALUE 'END'.
00048              77  PREV-STOCK         PIC X(5)          VALUE LOW-VALUES.

00050              01  ARITHMETIC-FIELDS  COMP-3.
00051                  03  LINE-CTR       PIC S999          VALUE +3.
00052                      88  END-PAGE                     VALUE +15 THRU +99.
00053                  03  PAGE-CTR       PIC S999          VALUE +1.
00054                  03  SPACE-CTL      PIC S9            VALUE +2.
00055                  03  STOCK-VALUE    PIC S9(5)V99      VALUE +0.
00056                  03  TOTAL-VALUE    PIC S9(7)V99      VALUE +0.


00058              01  HEADING-LINE.
00059                  03  FILLER         PIC X(15)    VALUE ' '.
00060                  03  FILLER         PIC X(10)    VALUE 'STOCK'.
00061                  03  FILLER         PIC X(24)    VALUE 'DESCRIPTION'.
00062                  03  FILLER         PIC X(23)    VALUE 'QTY      UNCOST'.
00063                  03  FILLER         PIC X(10)    VALUE 'VALUE'.
00064                  03  DATE-PR        PIC X(22)    VALUE ' '.
00065                  03  FILLER         PIC X(6)     VALUE 'PAGE'.
00066                  03  PAGE-PR        PIC ZZ9.

00068              01  DETAIL-LINE.
00069                  03  FILLER         PIC X(15)    VALUE ' '.
00070                  03  STOCK-PR       PIC X(5).
00071                  03  FILLER         PIC X(5)     VALUE ' '.
00072                  03  DESCRIP-PR     PIC X(24).
00073                  03  QTY-PR         PIC ZZ9-.
00074                  03  FILLER         PIC X(5)     VALUE ' '.
00075                  03  UNCOST-PR      PIC ZZ.99.
00076                  03  FILLER         PIC X(5)     VALUE ' '.
00077                  03  VALUE-PR       PIC ZZ,ZZZ.99CR.
00078                  03  ERR-MESS-PR    PIC X(54)    VALUE ' '.

00080              01  TOTAL-LINE.
00081                  03  FILLER         PIC X(52)    VALUE ' '.
00082                  03  FILLER         PIC X(14)    VALUE 'TOTAL VALUE ='.
00083                  03  TOTAL-VALUE-PR PIC ZZZZ,ZZZ.99CR.
00084                  03  FILLER         PIC X        VALUE '*'.

00086              PROCEDURE DIVISION.
00087              ***  M A I N   L O G I C
00088              A000-MAIN-LOGIC SECTION.
00089                  OPEN INPUT INPUT-FILE, OUTPUT PRINT-FILE.
00090                  READ INPUT-FILE, AT END MOVE 'END' TO EOF-FLAG.
00091                  IF NOT-END-FILE PERFORM D000-DATE.
00092                  PERFORM H000-HEAD.
00093                  PERFORM B000-PROC UNTIL END-FILE.
00094                  PERFORM T000-TOTAL.
00095                  CLOSE INPUT-FILE, PRINT-FILE.
00096                  STOP RUN.
00097              A999-END. EXIT.
```

FIGURE 7-4   (Cont.)

```
00099              ***  P R O C E S S I N G   R O U T I N E
00100              B000-PROC SECTION.
00101                  IF END-PAGE PERFORM H000-HEAD.
00102                  IF STOCK-IN NOT > PREV-STOCK
00103                      MOVE 'EQUAL OR LOW SEQUENCE' TO ERR-MESS-PR
00104                  ELSE
00105                      MOVE STOCK-IN TO PREV-STOCK
00106                      MOVE QTY-IN TO QTY-PR
00107                      MOVE UNCOST-IN TO UNCOST-PR
00108                      COMPUTE STOCK-VALUE = QTY-IN * UNCOST-IN
00109                      MOVE STOCK-VALUE TO VALUE-PR
00110                      ADD STOCK-VALUE TO TOTAL-VALUE.
00111                  MOVE DESCRIP-IN TO DESCRIP-PR.
00112                  MOVE STOCK-IN TO STOCK-PR.
00113                  MOVE DETAIL-LINE TO PRINT-RECORD.
00114                  WRITE PRINT-RECORD AFTER ADVANCING SPACE-CTL LINES.
00115                  MOVE SPACES TO DETAIL-LINE.
00116                  ADD 1 TO LINE-CTR.
00117                  MOVE 1 TO SPACE-CTL.
00118                  READ INPUT-FILE, AT END MOVE 'END' TO EOF-FLAG.
00119              B999-RETURN. EXIT.

00121              ***  D A T E   C A R D   P R O C E S S I N G
00122              D000-DATE SECTION.
00123                  IF VALID-DATE-CODE
00124                      MOVE ALPHA-DATE-IN TO DATE-PR
00125                  ELSE MOVE ALL '*' TO DATE-PR.
00126                  READ INPUT-FILE, AT END MOVE 'END' TO EOF-FLAG.
00127              D999-RETURN. EXIT.

00129              ***  H E A D I N G   R O U T I N E
00130              H000-HEAD SECTION.
00131                  MOVE PAGE-CTR TO PAGE-PR.
00132                  MOVE HEADING-LINE TO PRINT-RECORD.
00133                  WRITE PRINT-RECORD AFTER ADVANCING TOP-PAGE.
00134                  MOVE 3 TO LINE-CTR.
00135                  ADD 1 TO PAGE-CTR.
00136                  MOVE 2 TO SPACE-CTL.
00137              H999-RETURN. EXIT.

00139              ***  T O T A L   P R O C E S S I N G
00140              T000-TOTAL SECTION.
00141                  MOVE TOTAL-VALUE TO TOTAL-VALUE-PR.
00142                  MOVE TOTAL-LINE TO PRINT-RECORD.
00143                  WRITE PRINT-RECORD AFTER ADVANCING 2 LINES.
00144              T999-RETURN. EXIT.
```

FIGURE 7-4   (Cont.)

Although two records are defined, there is actually only one input area because there is only one input file. DATE-RECORD and STOCK-RECORD define the same input area in two different ways. The program reads a record into the single input area and then checks the code to determine the type of record. The code for each type should be in the same position in each record (in the figure, positions 1 and 2). (Later chapters show how to define and process more than one input file in a program.)

```
Printed Report:


STOCK      DESCRIPTION     QTY     UNCOST        VALUE      JUNE 30, 1983  PAGE 1

00230      RIVETTERS         1       1.00          1.00
00236      ASSEMBLERS       15        .35          5.25
00245      RE-INFORCERS    100      15.25      1,525.00
00277      CO-ORDINATORS   525       3.75      1,968.75
00416      COMBINERS       256       2.77        709.12
00524      BINARIES          9      25.33        227.97
00584      BAILING UNITS    36       3.68        132.48
00845      CONTROLLERS     362        .35        126.70
01238      LIFTERS         632       5.22      3,299.04
01326      COMPILERS       947      82.61     78,231.67
01397      RESISTORS         2      25.25         50.50
02164      ACCESSORS       25-      10.52        263.00CR




STOCK      DESCRIPTION     QTY     UNCOST        VALUE      JUNE 30, 1983  PAGE 2

00957      MAXIMIZERS                                     EQUAL OR LOW SEQUENCE
02247      OPTIMIZERS      633        .75        474.75

                          TOTAL VALUE =     86,489.23  *
```

FIGURE 7-4   (Cont.)

The addition of another record type adds slightly to main logic complexity, as the example program indicates. A new subroutine, D000-DATE, tests for the date card and if valid, stores the date and reads another input record.

Another new feature is the use of a variable to control line spacing, called SPACE-CTL in Working-Storage. Note that B000-CALC now contains the statement

```
WRITE PRINT-RECORD AFTER ADVANCING SPACE-CTL LINES.
```

Because SPACE-CTL can contain any numeric value 0 through 9, the WRITE works for any normal spacing requirement. To cause the program to double-space on the first line following a heading, the program initializes SPACE-CTL with 2 in Working-Storage and H000-HEAD. In B000-PROC, after printing a line, the program stores 1 in SPACE-CTL to force detail lines to single-space.

PROBLEMS

7-1. What are the features of a structured program?

7-2. What are the objectives of a computer program?

7–3. What practices can make programs more easily maintained? Explain.

7–4. What are the advantages of organizing a program into a main logic section with separate routines?

7–5. Why does current thinking consider the use of GO TO statements undesirable?

7–6. Revise your most recent program to provide for reading and processing a date card.

7–7. Code the following program that calculates annual depreciation on company assets. Records are in sequence of Asset number.

COL.

1–2	Record code (84)
6–9	Asset number
10–29	Description
30–31	Year purchased
32–33	Life expectancy in years
34–39	Original cost (no cents)
40–45	Salvage value (no cents)
46–80	Unused

There is only one record per asset number. Each record requires calculation of a depreciation rate. Show all details on the print line, including description and calculated rate.

The company uses the "sum of years' digits" depreciation method. Assume that an asset purchased in 1984 for $1,000 has a life expectancy of five years and an estimated salvage value at the end of five years of $200. The calculation of depreciation for each year based on $800 ($1,000 − 200) is:

YEAR		ANNUAL RATE	DEPRECIATION	
1984	1	5/15	$266.67	(5/15 × $800)
1985	2	4/15	213.33	
1986	3	3/15	160.00	
1987	4	2/15	106.67	
1988	5	1/15	53.33	
Totals		15/15	$800.00	

The sum of digits formula, where n = life expectancy, is

$$\frac{n(n+1)}{2} = \frac{5(5+1)}{2} = \frac{30}{2} = 15$$

The formula for the depreciation rate is

$$r = \frac{\text{number of remaining years}}{\text{sum of digits of life in years}}$$

In the example, if the current year is 1986, there are three years remaining. Current year's depreciation is

$$\frac{3}{15} \times \$800 = \$160.00$$

For each asset, calculate depreciation only for the current year. Provide test data with various years of purchase, life expectancy, original cost, and salvage value. For assets that are already fully depreciated (for example, purchased 12 years ago with a life expectancy of ten years), calculate zero depreciation. At end-of-file, print total depreciation for all records. You will need a date card as the first record to provide the current year.

CHAPTER 8

REPORT DESIGN

OBJECTIVE: To study the design of computer program reports.

INTRODUCTION

A computer program consists of three basic stages: input, processing, and output. The output stage, the subject of this chapter, may vary considerably by program because programs can display information on a display screen, print information on paper, or store information on disk.

COMPUTER PRINTOUTS

The most common computer output is the *printed report,* which is a permanent hard copy that can be read and filed. Some reports are intended to remain within a company's computer department, such as the output of a program that validates new input records by checking for invalid data. Some reports are produced for various departments within a company, such as a current listing of customer balances owed. And some reports are produced to be sent outside a company, such as invoices to customers and payments to suppliers.

The paper used to print a computer report is called *continuous forms* and consists of pages of paper that are connected together and separated by perforations. It is supplied in single part, or multipart with carbons, and is usually 11 inches long by 14 or 15 inches wide. The left and right margins of the paper contain holes that align in the printer device. The forms may be preprinted for special reports, such as invoices, but many reports, such as customer listings and company general ledgers, do not require a preprinted form and are printed on plain forms that are either blank or horizontally striped. Plain continuous forms are called *stock tab* (for stock tabulating forms) and *continuous printout,* or *C.P.O.* When using plain forms, a program must print headings and any descriptive information necessary to make the report readable.

Printer characteristics vary considerably, with typical speeds of 600, 1000, or 2000 lines per minute. The number of positions that may be printed on a line also varies, for example, 120, 132, or 144 positions. Printable characters include digits 0–9, letters A–Z, and special characters such as $, +, %, and *. Most printers print an entire line at once by using a chain, drum, or bar. Vertical spacing is generally six or eight lines per inch.

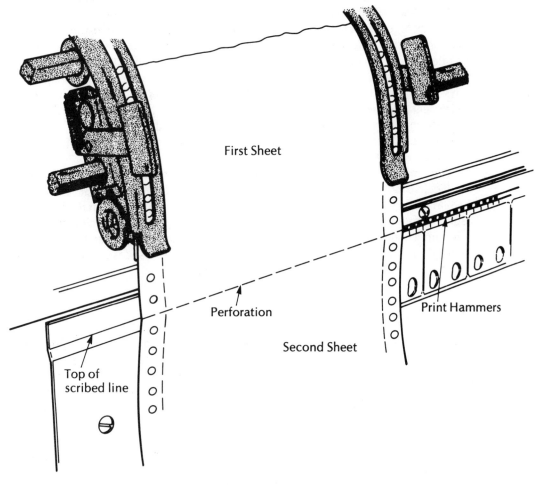

FIGURE 8-1   Printer Forms.

PRINCIPLES OF GOOD REPORT DESIGN

One of the arts of successful programming that merits considerable effort is report design, and special forms are available to help design these reports. If a report is to be used only within a data processing department, then an analyst designs a simple report to suit the computer operators and control personnel. At the other extreme, a program may require a skillfully prepared preprinted form, designed by a forms specialist (such design is outside the scope of this text, which is concerned with the common computer report prepared for the various departments throughout the company).

Often, the recipient of a report may lay out the initial design. A programmer-analyst will then determine if the necessary data are available in the computer system and design the final report layout to suit the user; but the recipient does not always have the technical expertise to realize that some of the analyst's stipulations may be quite unnecessary. As an example, assume that a computer system stores the current date internally in this format: yy/mm/dd. An analyst then compels the user of a report to accept the output with the date in the same format: yy/mm/dd. Although the analyst may claim that "this is the way the computer does it," such a rigid format requirement is quite unnecessary, and it is easy to program a computer to arrange the date into any reasonable format that the user desires. Also, if necessary, the program can easily translate a numeric month into alphabetic to clarify which field is the month and which is the day.

The importance of good report design cannot be underestimated. The report is the *objective* of the computer system, and it is generally designed *first,* before the program coding is even attempted. The following are useful practices that will help to ensure a final report layout that is clear, concise, and logical. Within an installation, all reports should adhere to certain standards, especially regarding the layout of headings and control totals. Ideally, one person should be responsible for approving all layouts. The next sections discuss various standards.

Headings

Headings should contain only essential information and should suppress redundant information. For example, if a report is to remain within a company, then it should not contain the company name—presumably the employees know the name of their employer!

Ideally, a heading should contain two dates: the *effective date* of the report, such as March 31, 19xx, and which includes all data up to that time; and the *run date,* such as April 7, 19xx, which is the day on which the report happens to be run. Because it takes extra time to accumulate a month's data, the run date will ordinarily be a few days after the effective date. A program may obtain these dates from a date card. Some computers maintain today's date in the Supervisor area, and any program can access it.

All pages should be numbered to ensure that they stay in sequence because after the pages are printed they are usually separated (burst) and filed. Also, some installations print the program number in the heading for identification. The headings should be aligned carefully with the detail information. Some analysts center headings above each detail field, whereas other analysts arrange headings to left-adjust over alphabetic detail and right-adjust over numeric detail.

Detail Lines

Many reports require information from every record to be printed, in effect, detail information. Because many printers can print 120 positions equally as fast as 60 positions, each report line should contain as much useful information as possible without jamming or cluttering the line. For each line, descriptive information (such as account number and name) should be on the left, and amount fields should be on the right.

Ensure that amount fields provide for the largest possible value that could occur. Also, because most amount fields are subject to correcting and reversing entries, they may be either positive or negative; therefore, the fields should allow for editing with the CR (credit) or − (minus) symbol on the right. Other common editing includes suppression of leftmost zeros (replacement with blanks) and insertion of commas and decimal points. For example, 1234567 may print as 12,345.67 and 0000125 as 1.25. The dollar sign is limited to specialized purposes such as printing customer invoices and checks. Many analysts consider it redundant to list dollar signs vertically down every line of a report.

Totals

Reports should usually display totals for every dollar amount field. In Figure 8-2, the total of VALUE is important; a total of UNIT COST would be meaningless, but a total of QTY could be used for control purposes. A program may print a total of the number of records in a file, which is a useful figure if records become lost.

```
                STOCK STATUS AS AT APRIL 30, 19XX        PAGE    1

       STOCK#   DESCRIPTION         QTY   UNIT COST($) VALUE($)

         128    TAPE 8-TRACK        127        5.32      675.64
         132    TAPE - CASSETTE      26        4.20      109.20
         168    RECORDS             103        3.91      402.73
         253    STEREO RECEIVERS      5      253.25    1,266.25

                TOTAL VALUE                            2,453.82
```

FIGURE 8-2   Report Featuring Total Value.

Note in Figure 8-2 that alphabetic fields like DESCRIPTION align on the left side of the description column (left-adjust):

RECORDS
STEREO RECEIVERS
Left-adjusted ↑

Arithmetic fields, however, align on the right (right-adjust) and align detail and totals according to the decimal point:

402.73
1,266.25
↑ *Right-adjusted*

Arithmetic fields should allow for the largest possible amount that could occur, and totals should generally be longer than detail fields.

DESIGN FEATURES

Total Levels

The report in Figure 8-2 provides only a total of VALUE at the end of the run. Many reports, however, require totals at points throughout a run; the following terms apply to such *control breaks:*

LEVEL	TERM	COMMON INDICATION
1. (lowest)	Minor total	*
2.	Intermediate total	**
3. (highest)	Major total	***

The asterisks, if used, print to the right of a total and indicate the total level. Some reports place asterisks beside each total on a line, but other reports place asterisks only beside the rightmost total (the choice is dependent on space and preference). A final total line is in a sense a control break, but it need not be indicated by asterisks because it is obviously a final total.

If there are only two total levels, they are called *minor* and *major*. There is no common term for any additional level, although such terms as intermediate-1 and intermediate-2 are acceptable.

The report in Figure 8-3 lists sales for the current month, and the following totals are required.

1.   Total sales by each salesman (minor)

2.   Total sales by all salesmen in a district (major)

3.   Final total sales at the end of the run

The input for this program, whether cards, tape, or disk, will have the sales districts in ascending sequence, and the salesmen in sequence within districts. The output is a *multiple control break,* which is discussed in Chapter 10.

```
          SALES ANALYSIS FOR THE MONTH ENDED AUGUST 31, 19XX    PAGE   1

DISTRICT SALESMAN                ITEM    QTY       PRICE      VALUE($)

   01     023    ANDERSON        418      27        1.25        33.75
   01     023    ANDERSON        653      19       20.50       389.50
   01     023    ANDERSON        684     116        9.95      1,154.20
                                                              1,577.45 *

   01     226    BERNSTEIN       127      86        5.50       473.00
   01     226    BERNSTEIN       418     130        1.25       162.50
                                                               635.50 *

          TOTAL DISTRICT 01                                  2,212.95 **

   02     002    SAUNDERS        418     152        1.25       190.00
   02     002    SAUNDERS        653      46       20.50       943.00
                                                              1,133.00 *

   02     034    BAKER           127     163        5.50       896.50
   02     034    BAKER           418      40        1.25        50.00
   02     034    BAKER           684      83        9.95       825.85
                                                              1,772.35 *

          TOTAL DISTRICT 02                                  2,905.35 **

          *** FINAL TOTAL ***                                5,118.30
```

FIGURE 8-3   Control Totals.

The report in Figure 8-3 shows salesmen 023 and 226 in district 01, and salesmen 002 and 034 in district 02. Note that the detail lines (each sale) are single-spaced and, for purposes of clarity, the totals are double-spaced.

If there is sufficient room on a line, you can offset the totals in a separate column as in Figure 8-4. In this case, the asterisk denoting total salesman is not necessary.

```
DISTRICT SALESMAN          ITEM    QTY       PRICE      VALUE($)  TOTAL($)

   01     023    ANDERSON   418      27        1.25        33.75
   01     023    ANDERSON   653      19       20.50       389.50
   01     023    ANDERSON   684     116        9.95      1,154.20  1,577.45
```

FIGURE 8-4   Offset Totals.

Group Indication

Some analysts prefer to design a report with *group indication,* which indicates the district, salesman number, and salesman name only on the first line of a group of items. The program prints the group indication only on the first line of the group and on the first line of each following page.

DISTRICT	SALESMAN		ITEM	QTY	PRICE	VALUE($)
01	023	ANDERSON	418	27	1.25	33.75
			653	19	20.50	389.50
			684	116	9.95	1,154.20
						1,577.45 *
	226	BERNSTEIN	127	86	5.50	473.00
			418	130	1.25	162.50
				ETC...		

FIGURE 8-5   Group Indication.

Group or Summary Printing

The preceding reports were detailed listings with control totals. Some users require only the control totals, not the detail information; these reports are called *group,* or *summary printing* as shown in Figure 8-6. Note the change in the use of the asterisks. The salesman's level does not require an asterisk because it is now, in effect, a detail line.

DISTRICT	SALESMAN		TOTAL SALES
01	023	ANDERSON	1,577.45
	226	BERNSTEIN	635.50
	TOTAL DISTRICT 01		2,212.95 *
02	002	SAUNDERS	1,133.00
	034	BAKER	1,772.35
	TOTAL DISTRICT 02		2,905.35 *
	FINAL TOTAL		5,118.30 **

FIGURE 8-6   Group Printing.

Staggered Totals

If the total fields are considerably larger than the detail fields, it may not be possible to fit all the totals on one line so that they align properly with the detail fields. Therefore, you can stagger the totals on two lines so that they are aligned as shown in Figure 8-7.

```
STOCK  NO.    DESCRIPTION        OLD  VALUE   RECEIPTS      ISSUES   NEW  VALUE

   XXXXX       X--------X         2,650.20      523.20      60.35    3,113.05
                                      •            •           •         •
                                      •            •           •         •
              ***  TOTALS  ***    1,206,351.80           151,571.93
                                          151,918.28          1,206,698.15  *
```

FIGURE 8-7   Staggered Totals.

List-Ups

Some reports are simple listings that are hundreds of pages long. In many cases, it is quite possible for these reports to provide the same information in a fewer number of pages. Consider the listing of customer payments in Figure 8-8.

```
              CUST  NO.    DOCUMENT      AMOUNT($)

                 16322      64635        520.00
                 16326      64620        100.00
                 16345      64600         55.00      ETC...
```

FIGURE 8-8   Listing of Payments.

This report uses only about 30 print positions out of 120 or more positions on the printer form. With a little programming effort, it is often possible to print three or four payments on one line:

```
CUST  NO.   DOCUM'T  AMT($)    CUST  NO.   DOCUM'T  AMT($)    CUST  NO.   DOCUM'T  AMT($)

  16322      64635   520.00      16326      64620   100.00      16345      64600    55.00
```

Such a report is often called *three-up* (or four-up, as the case may be). Data processing installations often fail to take advantage of such cost-saving techniques—the saving?—less computer time spent in printing, less paper used, and less filing space.

District Reports

The sales analysis report in Figure 8-3 showed totals by salesman within district. Sometimes a company needs to issue each district a copy of only its own (district) sales figures. The report in Figure 8-3, as designed, would not enable a company to issue separate district reports. A simple solution is to skip to a new page after printing a district total, and to print a new heading for each district on each page. Final totals may be printed at the end on a separate page. Also, the district number should be printed *in the heading,* rather than repetitively down the page. This practice, shown in Figure 8-9, makes the report less cluttered with repetitious information, and allows space for additional information.

```
DISTRICT 01   SALES ANALYSIS FOR THE MONTH ENDED AUGUST 31, 19XX    PAGE   1

        SALESMAN                 ITEM    QTY        PRICE         VALUE($)

        023     ANDERSON          418     27         1.25          33.75
                                  653     19        20.50         389.50
                                   •       •           •             •
                                   •       •           •             •
                                                                  ETC...
```

FIGURE 8-9   District Report.

File Update Reports

A general rule governing the updating of a master file with transactions is to *never print a detailed report during an initial file update.* The reasons for this rule are as follows:

1. There is a possibility that the initial update run will have an error and will have to be rerun.
2. A detailed listing processes slowly because the program prints every input record.
3. There may be a lot of expense in wasted paper, especially if the report is run on costly preprinted multipart forms.

When an updated file has proved to be valid, *then* a detail report should be run. Consider an inventory master file that is to be updated with the current month's stock receipts and issues, as shown in Figure 8-10:

```
              INVENTORY BALANCE AS AT AUGUST 31, 19XX            PAGE  XX

   STOCK#   DESCRIPTION        OLD VALUE   RECEIPTS    ISSUES  NEW VALUE

   01249   TELEVISION          5,260.15   1,127.13    516.18   5,871.10
   01425   RECORD PLAYERS        127.40       0.00     15.00     112.40
   01563   STEREO AMPLIFIERS       0.00     516.15    516.15       0.00
   02314   RECEIVERS             964.25     275.00    524.60     714.65

           *** TOTALS ***      6,351.80   1,918.28  1,571.93   6,698.15 *
```

FIGURE 8-10   File Updating Report.

In the example, the old balance is on the left, the transactions are in the middle, and the new updated balance is on the right, so that the report reads logically as follows:

OLD BALANCE + RECEIPTS − ISSUES = NEW BALANCE

PRINTER LAYOUT

Figure 8-11 illustrates a printer layout for the preceding district/salesman report. (This example is quite simple—most business reports are more complex.) The following approach is recommended for designing printer layouts.

- Design the printer layout prior to flowcharting and coding, using a standard layout form.
- Enter each descriptive heading and field exactly as they appear on the layout form. It is often necessary to make several attempts at a design before reaching one that is satisfactory, so the early designs may be rough.
- Center the report on the page, and evenly arrange the fields. If the report is to be bound on the left, information printed on the extreme left may be concealed.
- Space each line on the report layout exactly as the program is to space the lines.
- Show everything that the program will print, including complete error messages, if any.
- Show minus signs or CRs to indicate a possible negative value (remember, there are often reversing and correcting entries).

Some users file their reports in 8½ by 11 inch binders. Consequently, it is often desirable to design a report so that it can be cut to the 8½-inch width. Photoreduction is another possible consideration that can facilitate filing and binding.

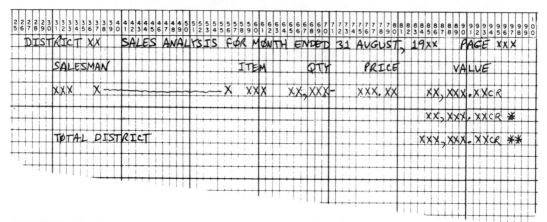

FIGURE 8-11   Printer Layout.

CONTROL REGISTER

Most installations maintain a control register for entering control totals. Consider the control register in Figure 8-12.

CONTROL REGISTER—CUSTOMER ACCOUNTS						
					Branch 10	
Date	Old Balance		Sales		Payments	
Mo Day	$ Amount	# Recs	$ Amount	# Recs	$ Amount	# Recs
03/14	6,200.–	7	625.–	4	500.–	4
03/15	6,325.–	7	675.–	5	1,000.–	6
03/16	6,000.–	7				

FIGURE 8-12   Control Register.

On 03/15, when the sales of $675 and payments of $1,000 are applied to the old balance, the new balance becomes $6,000. You enter this figure in the old balance for 03/16. On 03/16, assume that there are four sales for $1,400 and five payments for $1,050; you enter these figures in the control register prior to the update:

03/16	6,000.–	7	1,400.–	4	1,050.–	5
03/17	6,350.–					

The file update program should produce a new balance of $6,350 for Branch 10. A listing for Branch 10 in Figure 8-13 shows the program output (cents are deleted for clarity).

```
                          ACCOUNTS RECEIVABLE              MARCH 17,  19XX

     BRANCH ACCOUNT       OLD BAL.      SALES     PAY'TS    NEW BAL.

        10      200           500          0          0         500
                202         1,000         50        250         800
                203           500          0        100         400
                205         1,000        200          0       1,200
                210         1,000        600        200       1,400
                212         1,500          0        400       1,100
                213          500          550        100         950

     TOTAL AMOUNT          6,000 *      1,400 *    1,050 *    6,350 *

     TOTAL RECORDS             7            4          5           7
```

FIGURE 8-13   Control Totals.

A control clerk should check all totals with the control register and they should all agree. If the new balance is incorrect, it is easy to determine the cause—either the old balance, sales, or payments.

SUMMARY

This chapter has only shown the most common reports that a business programmer is likely to encounter, including the basic principles that apply to most financial statements. There are many other more complicated business problems that a programmer will encounter.

Remember that a report is all that a user sees, and that the user will judge the data processing department from the report. Despite expensive hardware and high-priced technical experts, poorly designed reports can only create a bad impression.

PROBLEMS

8–1. What are the two dates that many programs require on a report? how do they differ? and what is their origin?

8–2. What is a detail line?

8–3. How are alphabetic and numeric fields usually aligned?

8–4. What is a multiple control break?

8–5. What is group indication?

8–6. What is the solution to too many crowded, overlapping totals on one line?

8–7. What is an efficient way to print information that requires 20 or 30 print positions for each output record?

8–8. Comment on the practice of printing a detailed listing during a file update run.

CHAPTER 9

CONTROL BREAK LOGIC—I

OBJECTIVE: To present the input logic for sequence checking and simple control breaks.

INTRODUCTION

There are a number of standard activities with which business programs are concerned. These include the following:

- *Data Validation:* Preediting new data to ensure its reasonableness and accuracy.
- *Sorting:* Resequencing records in a file into some required order.
- *File Maintenance:* Correcting data on a file.
- *File Updating:* Applying various transactions to update a file.
- *Information Reporting:* Producing reports using data files to provide current information to management.

This chapter is mostly concerned with information reporting, although the logical approach as presented applies to all business programming activities. To produce a report, a file must be in some predetermined sequence, and a program must be coded to process the file accordingly. The program should check the file sequence in order to terminate a run before it produces pages of "garbage." Each record in a file contains one or more control fields that the program checks to determine what action to take. This chapter is concerned with the strategy of testing those control fields and determining the necessary action.

SEQUENCE CHECKING

In a typical file processing program, the basic decision around which the program logic pivots is the sequence check. Because most files contain records stored in ascending sequence by a control word (customer number, inventory number), an input record control word is higher than, equal to, or lower than the control word of the previously processed record. Therefore, the sequence test is a major determinant in the direction of program logic. As a general rule in data processing, every program that processes a file sequentially will also test that file's sequence. For a file in ascending sequence, two special conditions may exist:

1. *Record control number is unique.* In an inventory master file, no two stock numbers may be the same. As shown in Figure 9-1A, each succeeding record that the program reads must be high—an equal number indicates a duplicate record, and a low number indicates an out of sequence record.
2. *Record control number is not unique.* In this case, there may be more than one record for each control word, such as stock issue and receipt transactions for the same stock item. As shown in Figure 9-1B, a succeeding record may be validly high or equal, but a low record is still an error.

When embarking upon a new programming problem, concern your initial strategy with the sequence of the input file(s). You can then design the associated flowchart logic around this fundamental test. In all the examples in this and the next chapter, the sequence check is the central instruction.

FILE PROCESSING AND CONTROL BREAKS

A *file* or *data set* is a group of related records stored on punched cards, tape, or disk. There are two main types of files in batch processing: the *master file* contains semipermanent records for each customer, inventory item, employee, etc.; the *transaction file* contains temporary current records used to update the master file at regular intervals.

A program can read a single file on one input device, two merged files on one input device, or two or more files on two or more input devices. The programming to handle these situations should be systematic and consistent. The next sections give the flowcharting techniques appropriate to each type of problem. By recognizing the nature of a problem, you can approach the solution with a sound strategy and develop accurate, efficient, and more easily maintained programs.

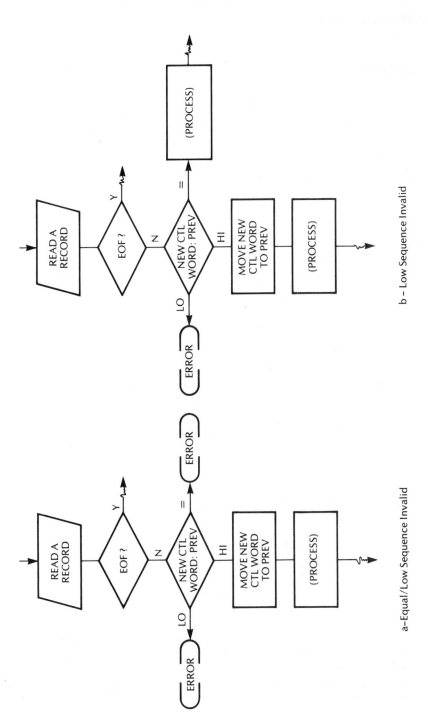

a—Equal/Low Sequence Invalid

b – Low Sequence Invalid

FIGURE 9-1   Sequence Checking.

Single Control Break

A *control break* occurs when a program encounters a high sequence on a control word and prints (or writes on an output device) totals to that point. For example, assume that there are any number of payments per customer for a file of customer payment transactions. A program requires the total amount paid by each customer. The basic program logic checks the customer sequence for each input record by comparing a new customer number to a previously read (and stored) customer number:

SEQUENCE CHECK NEW CUSTOMER NO. : PREVIOUS CUSTOMER	ACTION
Equal	Add payment to customer total.
High	Control break—print total payments for previous customer.
Low	Error—customer out of sequence.

In the flowchart in Figure 9-2, note the following. For each newly read customer number that is equal to the one previously read, the program adds a payment to the customer's total. On a high sequence there is a control break; the program must print the total payments for the *previously stored* customer. It then adds those total payments to a final total and clears to zero the customer payment total. You should now avoid two common programming errors: First, it is necessary now to initialize the sequence check for the next input record; you must store the new customer number in a field designated as "previous" customer number. Second, the record that caused the control break is still in the input area and has not yet been processed. The program must now execute the instructions that process a new customer (add the payment to the customer total):

```
READ CUSTOMER-FILE, AT END ...
IF CUST-IN > PREV-CUST PERFORM 0000-HIGH.
IF CUST-IN < PREV-CUST
    MOVE 'OUT OF SEQUENCE' TO ERR-MESS-PR
ELSE ADD PAYMENT-IN TO CUST-TOTAL.
```

The flowchart is incomplete for two reasons: First, the first input record will cause a *false control break.* Assuming that the "previous" customer is initialized to LOW-VALUES, the first record will always be higher than the "previous" customer, and the program will break control and print zero totals for the first "stored" customer. Second, the end-of-file condition is not complete. On end-of-file, if you simply print final totals, you will fail to print the stored totals for the last customer. Both first record and end-of-file conditions are the cause of many programming errors and require special treatment.

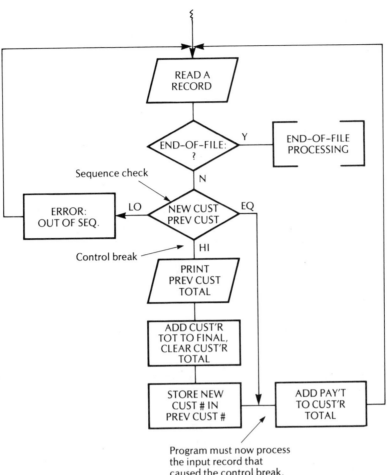

FIGURE 9-2   Simple Control Break (incomplete).

First Record Condition.   On a sequence check, the first input record will cause a false control break. The following are two ways to avert this situation:

1.   If the "previous" control word is initialized with LOW-VALUES, you can test its contents on a high control break and bypass printing the total level:

```
        IF  CUST-IN  >  PREV-CUST  PERFORM  C000-HIGH-CUST.
              .
              .
              .
        C000-HIGH-CUST SECTION.
            IF  PREV-CUST = LOW-VALUES GO TO C999-RETURN.
              .
              .
        C999-RETURN.  EXIT.
```

2.   If the main logic initialization has a READ operation, you can avoid use of LOW-VALUES entirely by storing the new input control word in the "previous" control word:

```
OPEN INPUT CUSTOMER-FILE ...
READ CUSTOMER-FILE, AT END ...
MOVE CUST-IN TO PREV-CUST.
PERFORM ... UNTIL END-FILE.
CLOSE CUSTOMER-FILE ...
STOP RUN.
```

With the new customer number assigned to PREV-CUST, the first sequence test will always generate an equal condition. Thus, there is no false control break and no need to test for one on a high condition. Also, since the initialization statement stores CUST-IN in PREV-CUST, there is no need to use LOW-VALUES for this purpose.

The program examples in this chapter use both approaches to handling the first record and its possible false control break.

End-of-file Condition.   Although a program has processed all input records when the end-of-file occurs, it does not mean that the program has completed all processing to that point—the program has not yet printed the stored total for the last customer in the file. It may help to think of the end-of-file condition as a special control break requiring the printing of all stored totals to that point.

You can approach end-of-file processing in several ways. The simplest solution prints the last stored customer total and then prints the final total. This solution may be adequate if there is little processing on the control break, but programs often have many instructions involved in the printing of totals. Recoding these instructions means additional coding time, more debugging, and larger program size.

A better approach to handling end-of-file totals is to use the routine that printed customer totals. Therefore, the flowchart logic directs the end-of-file condition to the control break routine, and the flowchart would appear as in Figure 9-3. If this logic were incorporated into the previous flowchart in Figure 9-2, there would be a complication. After printing the last customer total, the program would return to process the "input record" that presumably caused the control break. The program would then read another input record—but there is no valid record. This attempt to read a nonexistent record would be a disaster, especially on a system that uses job control records between jobs. The solution to this is to organize the program into a main logic routine and various related subroutines. The printing of customer totals would then be one of the subroutines that the program performs on both a high control break and an end-of-file.

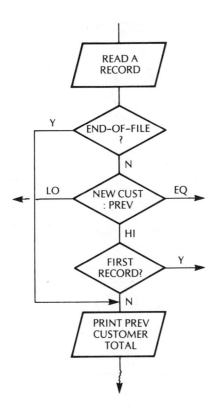

FIGURE 9-3   End-of-file Processing.

PROGRAM EXAMPLE

Figure 9-4 shows the flowchart for a program example that handles the control break on customer number. In this and all following program examples, the flowchart depicts the general logic and does not indicate every operation that the program executes, such as clearing the print line and adding to the line count (simple operations that almost every program performs). Many of the instructions, although important to the program's execution, are logically unimportant. Many experienced programmers (if they draw a flowchart at all) only design the basic logical pattern, from which they code the detailed instructions.

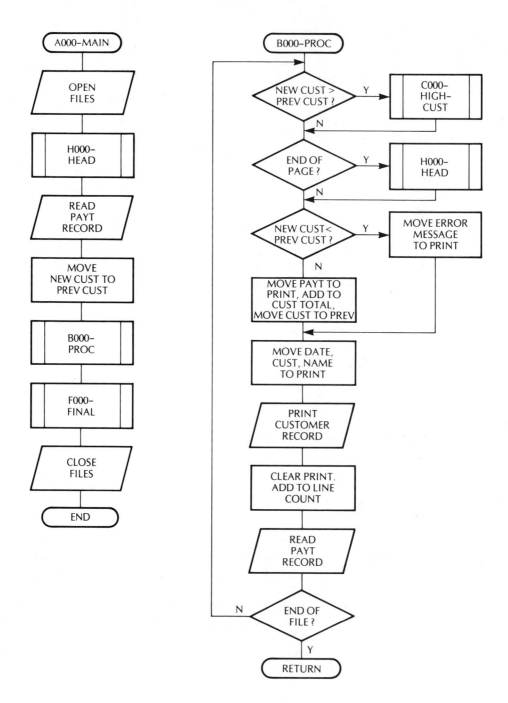

FIGURE 9-4   Flowchart for Simple Control Break.

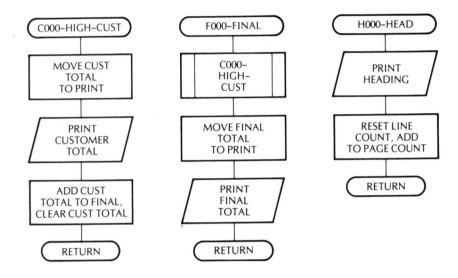

FIGURE 9-4   (Cont.)

Figure 9-5 shows the program listing for the flowchart in Figure 9-4. In A000-MAIN, after the initial READ, there is a MOVE statement that stores CUST-IN in PREV-CUST. As a result, on the first sequence check in B000-PROC-CUST, the first record tests as equal. There is no false control break and no need to provide a special test for first record.

The test for low sequence, B000-PROC-CUST, would normally cause the program to terminate on an error, a common practice as explained in the next section. The error termination routine would print an error message, run out the rest of the input file if necessary, close the files, and stop the run. In these examples, however, the programs print the error message and continue processing. The reason for continuing is that during program testing you can fully test a program each run if it does not cancel. Following the program listing is a printout of the input data and the printed output from the program's execution.

ERROR TESTING

Although the only error test that Figure 9-5 makes is for low sequence, a common test is for valid record code. It is a good programming practice to check these items soon after reading a record, and before doing any significant processing of the record. In a production environment, when a serious error occurs (especially out-of-sequence) the practice is to cancel the job. Such a procedure is easy to code:

```
IF NOT VALID-CODE PERFORM R100-CODE-ERROR.
IF CUST-IN < PREV-CUST PERFORM R200-SEC-ERROR.
```

```
00001              IDENTIFICATION DIVISION.
00002              PROGRAM-ID. CHAPT9A.
00003              REMARKS.  ONE-LEVEL CONTROL BREAK ON CUSTOMER NUMBER.

00005              ENVIRONMENT DIVISION.
00006              CONFIGURATION SECTION.
00007              SPECIAL-NAMES.
00008                  C01 IS TOP-PAGE.
00009              INPUT-OUTPUT SECTION.
00010              FILE-CONTROL.
00011                  SELECT  PAYT-FILE, ASSIGN TO SYS015-UR-2501-S.
00012                  SELECT PRINT-FILE, ASSIGN TO SYS014-UR-1403-S.

00014              DATA DIVISION.
00015              FILE SECTION.
00016          FD  PAYT-FILE
00017              LABEL RECORDS ARE OMITTED
00018              DATA RECORD IS  PAYT-RECORD.
00019          01  PAYT-RECORD.
00020              03  FILLER          PIC X(5).
00021              03  CUST-IN         PIC X(5).
00022              03  NAME-IN         PIC X(20).
00023              03  PAYT-IN         PIC S9(4)V99.
00024              03  DATE-IN         PIC 9(6).
00025              03  FILLER          PIC X(38).

00027          FD  PRINT-FILE
00028              LABEL RECORDS ARE OMITTED
00029              DATA RECORD IS PRINT-RECORD.
00030          01  PRINT-RECORD        PIC X(133).

00032              WORKING-STORAGE SECTION.
00033          01  ALPHANUMERIC-ITEMS  DISPLAY.
00034              03  EOF-FLAG        PIC X(3)          VALUE ' '.
00035                  88  END-FILE                      VALUE 'END'.
00036              03  PREV-CUST       PIC X(5)     VALUE LOW-VALUES.

00038          01  ARITHMETIC-ITEMS    COMP-3.
00039              03  CUST-TOTAL      PIC S9(5)V99     VALUE +0.
00040              03  FINAL-TOTAL     PIC S9(7)V99     VALUE +0.
00041              03  LINE-COUNT      PIC S999         VALUE +0.
00042                  88  END-PAGE                     VALUE +25 THRU +999.
00043              03  PAGE-COUNT      PIC S999         VALUE +1.
00044              03  SPACE-CTL       PIC S9           VALUE +2.

00046          01  HEADING-LINE.
00047              03  FILLER          PIC X(20)         VALUE ' '.
00048              03  FILLER          PIC X(07)         VALUE 'CUSTR'.
00049              03  FILLER          PIC X(23)         VALUE 'NAME'.
00050              03  FILLER          PIC X(13)         VALUE 'PAYMENT'.
00051              03  FILLER          PIC X(14)         VALUE 'DATE      PAGE'.
00052              03  PAGE-HD-PR      PIC ZZ9.

00054          01  CUST-PAYT-LINE.
00055              03  FILLER          PIC X(20)         VALUE ' '.
00056              03  CUST-PR         PIC X(7).
00057              03  NAME-PR         PIC X(21).
00058              03  PAYT-PR         PIC ZZ,ZZ9.99CR.
00059              03  FILLER          PIC X(2)          VALUE ' '.
00060              03  DATE-PR         PIC 99B99B99.
00061              03  ERR-MESS-PR     PIC X(20)         VALUE ' '.

00063          01  TOTAL-PAYT-LINE.
00064              03  FILLER          PIC X(46)         VALUE ' '.
00065              03  CUST-TOT-PR     PIC ZZZZ,ZZ9.99CR.
00066              03  ASTERISK-PR     PIC X(2)          VALUE '*'.
```

FIGURE 9-5   Simple Control Break.

```
00068          PROCEDURE DIVISION.
00069     ***  M A I N   L O G I C
00070          A000-MAIN SECTION.
00071              OPEN INPUT PAYT-FILE, OUTPUT PRINT-FILE.
00072              PERFORM H000-HEAD.
00073              READ PAYT-FILE, AT END MOVE 'END' TO EOF-FLAG.
00074              MOVE CUST-IN TO PREV-CUST.
00075              PERFORM B000-PROC-CUST UNTIL END-FILE.
00076              PERFORM F000-FINAL.
00077              CLOSE PAYT-FILE, PRINT-FILE.
00078              STOP RUN.
00079          A199-END. EXIT.

00082     ***  C U S T O M E R   P R O C E S S I N G
00083          B000-PROC-CUST SECTION.
00084              IF CUST-IN > PREV-CUST PERFORM C000-HIGH-CUST.
00085              IF END-PAGE PERFORM H000-HEAD.
00086              IF CUST-IN < PREV-CUST
00087                  MOVE 'OUT OF SEQUENCE' TO ERR-MESS-PR
00088              ELSE
00089                  MOVE PAYT-IN TO PAYT-PR
00090                  ADD  PAYT-IN TO CUST-TOTAL
00091                  MOVE CUST-IN TO PREV-CUST.
00092              MOVE DATE-IN TO DATE-PR.
00093              MOVE CUST-IN TO CUST-PR.
00094              MOVE NAME-IN TO NAME-PR.
00095              WRITE PRINT-RECORD FROM CUST-PAYT-LINE AFTER ADVANCING
00096                  SPACE-CTL LINES.
00097              MOVE SPACES TO CUST-PAYT-LINE.
00098              ADD SPACE-CTL TO LINE-COUNT.
00099              MOVE 1 TO SPACE-CTL.
00100              READ PAYT-FILE, AT END MOVE 'END' TO EOF-FLAG.
00101          B999-RETURN. EXIT.

00103     ***  C U S T O M E R   T O T A L S
00104          C000-HIGH-CUST SECTION.
00105              MOVE CUST-TOTAL TO CUST-TOT-PR.
00106              MOVE TOTAL-PAYT-LINE TO PRINT-RECORD.
00107              WRITE PRINT-RECORD AFTER ADVANCING 1 LINES.
00108              ADD CUST-TOTAL TO FINAL-TOTAL.
00109              MOVE ZEROS TO CUST-TOTAL.
00110              ADD 2 TO LINE-COUNT.
00111              MOVE 2 TO SPACE-CTL.
00112          C999-RETURN. EXIT.

00114     ***  F I N A L   T O T A L S
00115          F000-FINAL SECTION.
00116              PERFORM C000-HIGH-CUST.
00117              MOVE FINAL-TOTAL TO CUST-TOT-PR.
00118              MOVE '**' TO ASTERISK-PR.
00119              WRITE PRINT-RECORD FROM TOTAL-PAYT-LINE
00120                  AFTER ADVANCING 2 LINES.
00121          F999-RETURN. EXIT.

00123     ***  P A G E   H E A D I N G
00124          H000-HEAD SECTION.
00125              MOVE PAGE-COUNT TO PAGE-HD-PR.
00126              WRITE PRINT-RECORD FROM HEADING-LINE
00127                  AFTER ADVANCING TOP-PAGE.
00128              MOVE 3 TO LINE-COUNT.
00129              MOVE 2 TO SPACE-CTL.
00130              ADD 1 TO PAGE-COUNT.
00131          H999-RETURN. EXIT.
```

FIGURE 9-5   (Cont.)

Input Data:

```
        Cust.                      Payment Date
        00123 ADAM  SMITH          010000 051280
        00123 ADAM  SMITH          001235 051480
        00245 JP  ANDERSON         002500 050980
        00245 JP  ANDERSON         010000 051980
        00245 JP  ANDERSON         002500 052280
        01530 N  DENNIS            000500 042980
        02233 AB  ROBINSON         035000 060380
        02233 AB  ROBINSON         250000 072680
        02575 FD  MONROE           025000 062280
        02575 FD  MONROE           003525 061580
        02575 FD  MONROE           010000 051480
```

Printed Report:

```
    CUSTR   NAME                   PAYMENT      DATE      PAGE      1

    00123   ADAM  SMITH            100.00      05 12 80
    00123   ADAM  SMITH             12.35      05 14 80
                                   112.35   *

    00245   JP  ANDERSON            25.00      05 09 80
    00245   JP  ANDERSON           100.00      05 19 80
    00245   JP  ANDERSON            25.00CR    05 22 80
                                   100.00   *

    01530   N  DENNIS                5.00      04 29 80
                                     5.00   *

    02233   AB  ROBINSON           350.00      06 03 80
    02233   AB  ROBINSON         2,500.00      07 26 80
                                 2,850.00   *

    02575   FD  MONROE            250.00       06 22 80




    CUSTR   NAME                   PAYMENT      DATE      PAGE      2

    02575   FD  MONROE             35.25       06 15 80
    02575   FD  MONROE            100.00       05 14 80
                                  385.25    *

                                3,452.60    **
```

FIGURE 9-5   (Cont.)

Both subroutines could print an error message and cancel the run (CLOSE files, STOP RUN). Punched-card input, however, should be run out before the CLOSE, as follows:

```
R10C-CODE-ERROR SECTION.
    MOVE 'INVALID RECORC CODE' TC ERR-MESS-PR.
    WRITE PRINT-LINE.
    PERFORM S00U-RUN-OUT UNTIL ENC-FILE.
    CLOSE PAYT-FILE, PRINT-FILE.
    STOP RUN.
R199-END. EXIT.

S00G-RUN-OUT SECTION.
    READ PAYT-FILE
        AT END MOVE 'END' TO ENC-FILE-FLAG.
S999-RETURN. EXIT.
```

If the program is to continue processing rather than cancel, the structured programming may require some ingenuity to avoid GO TOs. On invalid code and low sequence, you may want to insert an error message in the print area and bypass both adding the payment to the customer total and storing the new customer number in "previous" customer. The following is one of many possible solutions. The error message field, ERR-MESS-PR, now contains condition names; after testing, if the field is blank, it is a VALID-RECORD; but if it contains an error message, it is an INVALID-RECORD.

```
01   CUST-PAYT-LINE.
     ...
     03  ERR-MESS-PR       PIC X(20)     VALUE ' '.
         88  VALID-RECORD                VALUE ' '.
         88  INVALID-RECORD              VALUE 'INVALID RECORD CODE'
                                               'OUT OF SEQUENCE'.
C000-PROC SECTION.
    IF END-PAGE PERFORM H000-HEAD.
    IF NOT VALID-CODE
        MOVE 'INVALID RECORD CODE' TO ERR-MESS-PR
    ELSE
    IF CUST-IN < PREV-CUST
        MOVE 'OUT OF SEQUENCE' TO ERR-MESS-PR.
    IF VALID-RECORD AND BRANCH-IN > PREV-BRANCH
        PERFORM C000-HIGH.
    IF VALID-RECORD
        MOVE PAYT-IN TO PAYT-PR
        ADD  PAYT-IN TO CUST-TOTAL
        MOVE CUST-IN TO PREV-CUST.
```

TOTALS ONLY

The program in Figure 9-5 illustrated a detail listing in which every input record was printed. It is often necessary to print only the total lines. Therefore, rather than print each detail line, the program should accumulate the customer payments and print only total payments:

```
CUST#   NAME                PAYMENTS

00245   JP ANDERSON          100.00
00312   JL BROWN             647.50
01422   RL CARTER          3,145.25
01530   N  DENNIS              5.00    ETC...
```

To accomplish this, the program in Figure 9-5 requires a number of minor changes. You should eliminate the definition of the detail customer payment line (CUST-PAYT-LINE) and alter the total line (TOTAL-PAYT-LINE) to include customer number and name. A field is required to save the customer name (PREV-NAME) for printing on a control break. You can no longer move NAME-IN directly into NAME-PR because on a control break NAME-IN contains the name of the following customer, not the name that is to print. Also, eliminate printing a detail line for each payment in B000-PROC. Other minor adjustments include deleting the asterisk on total customer payments (it is now the lowest level) and modifying SPACE-CTL. Figure 9-6 lists the revised program.

The next chapter continues with input logic by introducing the two-level and three-level control break. It also clarifies the placement of the page overflow test in a complex program and covers more programming strategy.

```
00001           IDENTIFICATION DIVISION.
00002           PROGRAM-ID. CHAPT9B.
00003           REMARKS. ONE-LEVEL CONTROL BREAK, TOTALS BY CUSTOMER ONLY.

00005           ENVIRONMENT DIVISION.
00006           CONFIGURATION SECTION.
00007           SPECIAL-NAMES.
00008               C01 IS TOP-PAGE.
00009           INPUT-OUTPUT SECTION.
00010           FILE-CONTROL.
00011               SELECT  PAYT-FILE, ASSIGN TO SYS015-UR-2501-S.
00012               SELECT PRINT-FILE, ASSIGN TO SYS014-UR-1403-S.

00014           DATA DIVISION.
00015           FILE SECTION.
00016           FD   PAYT-FILE
00017               LABEL RECORDS ARE OMITTED
00018               DATA RECORD IS  PAYT-RECORD.
00019           01   PAYT-RECORD.
00020               03   FILLER         PIC X(5).
00021               03   CUST-IN        PIC X(5).
00022               03   NAME-IN        PIC X(20).
00023               03   PAYT-IN        PIC S9(4)V99.
00024               03   DATE-IN        PIC 9(6).
00025               03   FILLER         PIC X(38).
```

FIGURE 9-6   Printing of Totals Only.

```
00027          FD  PRINT-FILE
00028              LABEL RECORDS ARE OMITTED
00029              DATA RECORD IS PRINT-RECORD.
00030          01  PRINT-RECORD          PIC X(133).


00032          WORKING-STORAGE SECTION.
00033          01  ALPHANUMERIC-FIELDS DISPLAY.
00034              03   EOF-FLAG          PIC X(3)       VALUE ' '.
00035                   88   END-FILE                    VALUE 'END'.
00036              03   PREV-CUST         PIC X(5)       VALUE LOW-VALUES.
00037              03   PREV-NAME         PIC X(20)      VALUE ' '.


00039          01  ARITHMETIC-FIELDS    COMP-3.
00040              03   CUST-TOTAL       PIC S9(5)V99   VALUE +0.
00041              03   FINAL-TOTAL      PIC S9(7)V99   VALUE +0.
00042              03   LINE-COUNT       PIC S999       VALUE +0.
00043                   88   END-PAGE                   VALUE +25 THRU +999.
00044              03   PAGE-COUNT       PIC S999       VALUE +1.
00045              03   SPACE-CTL        PIC S9         VALUE +2.
00046
00047          01  HEADING-LINE.
00048              03   FILLER           PIC X(20)      VALUE ' '.
00049              03   FILLER           PIC X(07)      VALUE 'CUSTR'.
00050              03   FILLER           PIC X(24)      VALUE 'NAME'.
00051              03   FILLER           PIC X(21)      VALUE 'PAYMENT'.
00052              03   FILLER           PIC X(06)      VALUE 'PAGE'.
00053              03   PAGE-HD-PR       PIC ZZ9.


00055          01  TOTAL-PAYT-LINE.
00056              03   FILLER           PIC X(20)      VALUE ' '.
00057              03   CUST-PR          PIC X(7).
00058              03   NAME-PR          PIC X(20).
00059              03   CUST-TOT-PR      PIC ZZZZ,ZZ9.99CR.
00060              03   ASTERISK-PR      PIC X          VALUE ' '.
00061              03   FILLER           PIC X(2)       VALUE ' '.
00062              03   ERR-MESS-PR      PIC X(20)      VALUE ' '.


00064          PROCEDURE DIVISION.
00065          *** M A I N   L O G I C
00066          A000-MAIN SECTION.
00067              OPEN INPUT PAYT-FILE, OUTPUT PRINT-FILE.
00068              PERFORM H000-HEAD.
00069              READ PAYT-FILE, AT END MOVE 'END' TO EOF-FLAG.
00070              MOVE CUST-IN TO PREV-CUST.
00071              PERFORM B000-PROC-CUST UNTIL END-FILE.
00072              PERFORM F000-FINAL.
00073              CLOSE PAYT-FILE, PRINT-FILE.
00074              STOP RUN.
00075          A199-END. EXIT.
```

FIGURE 9-6   (Cont.)

```
00077            ***  C U S T O M E R   P R O C E S S I N G
00078            B000-PROC-CUST SECTION.
00079                IF CUST-IN > PREV-CUST
00080                    PERFORM C000-HIGH-CUST.
00081                IF END-PAGE PERFORM H000-HEAD.
00082                IF CUST-IN < PREV-CUST
00083                    MOVE 'OUT OF SEQUENCE' TO ERR-MESS-PR
00084                    MOVE CUST-IN TO CUST-PR
00085                    WRITE PRINT-RECORD FROM TOTAL-PAYT-LINE
00086                        AFTER ADVANCING SPACE-CTL LINES
00087                    MOVE SPACES TO TOTAL-PAYT-LINE
00088                ELSE
00089                    ADD  PAYT-IN TO CUST-TOTAL
00090                    MOVE NAME-IN TO PREV-NAME
00091                MOVE CUST-IN TO PREV-CUST.
00092                READ PAYT-FILE, AT END MOVE 'END' TO EOF-FLAG.
00093            B999-RETURN. EXIT.

00095            ***  C U S T O M E R   T O T A L S
00096            C000-HIGH-CUST SECTION.
00097                MOVE PREV-NAME TO NAME-PR.
00098                MOVE PREV-CUST TO CUST-PR.
00099                MOVE CUST-TOTAL TO CUST-TOT-PR.
00100                MOVE TOTAL-PAYT-LINE TO PRINT-RECORD.
00101                WRITE PRINT-RECORD AFTER ADVANCING SPACE-CTL LINES.
00102                MOVE SPACES TO TOTAL-PAYT-LINE.
00103                ADD CUST-TOTAL TO FINAL-TOTAL.
00104                MOVE ZEROS TO CUST-TOTAL.
00105                ADD SPACE-CTL TO LINE-COUNT.
00106                MOVE 1 TO SPACE-CTL.
00107            C999-RETURN. EXIT.

00109            ***  F I N A L   T O T A L S
00110            F000-FINAL SECTION.
00111                PERFORM C000-HIGH-CUST.
00112                MOVE 'FINAL TOTAL =' TO NAME-PR.
00113                MOVE FINAL-TOTAL TO CUST-TOT-PR.
00114                MOVE '*' TO ASTERISK-PR.
00115                WRITE PRINT-RECORD FROM TOTAL-PAYT-LINE
00116                        AFTER ADVANCING 2 LINES.
00117            F999-RETURN. EXIT.

00119            ***  P A G E   H E A D I N G
00120            H000-HEAD SECTION.
00121                MOVE PAGE-COUNT TO PAGE-HD-PR.
00122                WRITE PRINT-RECORD FROM HEADING-LINE
00123                    AFTER ADVANCING TOP-PAGE.
00124                MOVE 3 TO LINE-COUNT.
00125                MOVE 2 TO SPACE-CTL.
00126                ADD 1 TO PAGE-COUNT.
00127            H999-RETURN. EXIT.
```

Printed Report:

```
    CUSTR  NAME                    PAYMENT              PAGE    1

    00123  ADAM SMITH              112.35
    00245  JP ANDERSON             100.00
    01530  N DENNIS                  5.00
    02233  AB ROBINSON           2,850.00
    02575  FD MONROE               385.25

           FINAL TOTAL =         3,452.60   *
```

FIGURE 9-6   (Cont.)

176

ERROR PREVENTION

The following are error prevention points pertaining to sequence checking and control breaks.

1. Ensure that the first input record does not cause a false control break.
2. Ensure that the end-of-file properly handles the last stored data.
3. After a control break, ensure that the program returns to process the input record that caused the control break.
4. On a control break, the program usually adds the accumulated totals to the next higher level, such as final total. Be sure to clear the lower level accumulated totals to zero.

PROBLEMS

9-1. Describe two ways to avoid a false control break on the first input record.

9-2. Draw the flowchart logic for the following: The input record contains supplier number, supplier name, and amount payable. The program prints each record with totals for each supplier, and at the end of the run, a total amount payable for all suppliers. Provide for page overflow.

9-3. Code and test the program in Problem 9-2 using full structured programming conventions and supply enough data to force page overflow.

9-4. Revise the program in Problem 9-3 so that it omits the printing of each supplier record.

CHAPTER 10

CONTROL BREAK LOGIC—II

OBJECTIVE: To continue the logic for two- and three-level control breaks, and to emphasize sound programming strategy.

INTRODUCTION

The previous chapter covered the essentials of sequence checking and simple control breaks using one control field. But many records contain more than one control field, and a control break may be required for each field. Thus, a file could consist of records with customer numbers within store, or employees within department. This chapter deals with control words of more than one field, and control breaks of more than one level. It also presents a sound logical strategy to handle input records.

TWO-LEVEL CONTROL BREAKS

The program example in Chapter 9 used only customer number for the control word. A control word, however, may consist of more than one field. Consider a sales file containing records in sequence by department number (major) and product number (minor). The input record is as follows:

| DEPT | PROD | DESCRIPTION | QTY | $SALES |

Control fields

There may be any number of sales for a product within a department. Since product numbers are in ascending sequence within department, the first product number of a department may be lower than the last product number of the preceding department. A program to produce a report listing each sale for a product and control totals of sales by product and department is shown in Figure 10-1.

```
                      SALES REPORT

  DEPT    PROD    DESCRIPTION      QTY     SALES($)

  025     2430    TURNTABLES        1        243.00
          2430    TURNTABLES        3        645.25
          2430    TURNTABLES        1        119.00
                                           1,007.25 *  ◄
                                                            totals by
          2628    RECEIVERS         1        226.00          Product
          2628    RECEIVERS         2        314.00
          2628    RECEIVERS         1        140.50
                                             680.50 *
                                           1,687.75 **  ◄
                                                            total by
  040     0320    PROCESSORS        1      2,164.00          Department
                                                  ETC...
```

FIGURE 10-1   Report with Two-level Totals.

Because a file may contain any number of sales for a product in a department, there is little advantage in comparing a new record to a previous record by product number only:

NEW PROD	ACTION
High	Print the previous product total.
Equal	Add to product total (but is this the same department?).
Low	Out of sequence? or valid product for the next department?

A more logical approach is to compare department numbers first:

NEW DEPT	ACTION
High	Print product totals, then department totals.
Equal	Same department, but could be a new product.
Low	Department is out of sequence.

On a high department sequence, the program prints the total for the last stored product and then the total for the stored department, and then continues with normal processing of the input record. But if the comparison of department is equal, the program should check for a change of product. If high, product totals would be printed, and the program would continue with processing the input record.

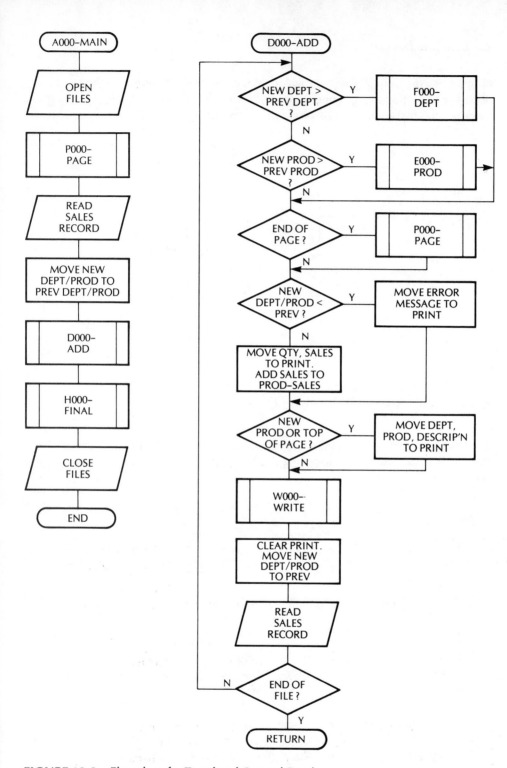

FIGURE 10-2 Flowchart for Two-level Control Break.

PROGRAM EXAMPLE

Figure 10-2 provides the new flowchart, which is similar in approach to the single control break in Chapter 9. Figure 10-3 is the program listing. Note how Section D000-ADD tests the department/product field for low sequence:

```
FILE SECTION.
    •
    •
 03   DEPT-PROD-IN.
      05   DEPT-IN       PIC X(3).
      05   PROD-IN       PIC X(4).
    •
    •
WORKING-STORAGE SECTION.
    •
    •
 03   PREV-DEPT-PROD.
      05   PREV-DEPT     PIC X(3).
      05   PREV-PROD     PIC X(4).
    •
    •
PROCEDURE DIVISION.
    •
    •
 IF DEPT-PROD-IN < PREV-DEPT-PROD
      MOVE 'OUT OF SEQUENCE' TO ERR-MESS-PR.
```

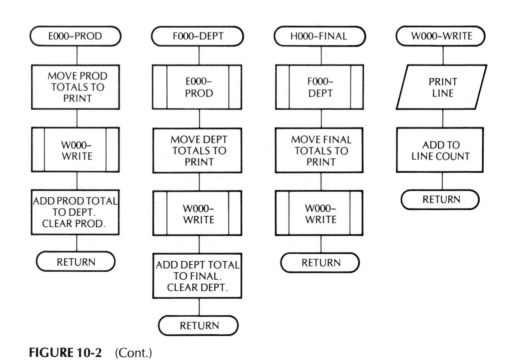

FIGURE 10-2   (Cont.)

```
00001              IDENTIFICATION DIVISION.
00002              PROGRAM-ID. CHAP10A.
00003              REMARKS.  TWO-LEVEL CONTROL BREAK BY DEPARTMENT/PRODUCT.

00005              ENVIRONMENT DIVISION.
00006              CONFIGURATION SECTION.
00007              SPECIAL-NAMES.
00008                  C01 IS TOP-PAGE.
00009              INPUT-OUTPUT SECTION.
00010              FILE-CONTROL.
00011                  SELECT SALES-FILE, ASSIGN TO SYS015-UR-2501-S.
00012                  SELECT PRINT-FILE, ASSIGN TO SYS014-UR-1403-S.

00014              DATA DIVISION.
00015              FILE SECTION.
00016          FD  SALES-FILE
00017              LABEL RECORDS ARE OMITTED
00018              DATA RECORD IS SALES-RECORD.
00019          01  SALES-RECORD.
00020              03  CODE-IN           PIC X(2).
00021              03  FILLER            PIC X(2).
00022              03  DEPT-PROD-IN.
00023                  05 DEPT-IN        PIC X(3).
00024                  05 PROD-IN        PIC X(4).
00025              03  DESCRIP-IN        PIC X(20).
00026              03  QTY-IN            PIC S999.
00027              03  SALES-IN          PIC S9(5)V99.
00028              03  FILLER            PIC X(39).

00030          FD  PRINT-FILE
00031              LABEL RECORDS ARE OMITTED
00032              DATA RECORD IS PRINT-LINE.
00033          01  PRINT-LINE            PIC X(133).

00035              WORKING-STORAGE SECTION.
00036          01  ALPHANUMERIC-ITEMS   DISPLAY.
00037              03  PREV-DEPT-PROD.
00038                  05  PREV-DEPT     PIC X(3).
00039                  05  PREV-PROD     PIC X(4).
00040              03  EOF-FLAG          PIC X(3)      VALUE ' '.
00041                  88  END-FILE                    VALUE 'END'.

00043          01  ARITHMETIC-ITEMS     COMP-3.
00044              03  DEPT-SALES        PIC S9(7)V99 VALUE +0.
00045              03  FINAL-SALES       PIC S9(7)V99 VALUE +0.
00046              03  LINE-CTR          PIC S999     VALUE +0.
00047                  88 END-PAGE                     VALUE +55 THRU +999.
00048              03  PROD-SALES        PIC S9(7)V99 VALUE +0.
00049              03  SPACE-CTL         PIC S9       VALUE +0.

00051          01  HEADING-LINE.
00052              03  FILLER            PIC X(25)    VALUE ' '.
00053              03  FILLER            PIC X(13)    VALUE 'DPT    PROD'.
00054              03  FILLER            PIC X(23)    VALUE 'DESCRIPTION'.
00055              03  FILLER            PIC X(16)    VALUE 'QTY     SALES($)'.
```

FIGURE 10-3   Two-level Control Break.

```
00057          01   SALES-LINE.
00058               03   FILLER          PIC X(25)     VALUE ' '.
00059               03   DEPT-PR         PIC X(06).
00060               03   PROD-PR         PIC X(07).
00061               03   DESCRIP-PR      PIC X(23).
00062               03   QTY-PR          PIC ZZ9-.
00063               03   FILLER          PIC X(3)      VALUE ' '.
00064               03   SALES-PR        PIC ZZ,ZZ9.99CR.
00065               03   ERR-MESS-PR     PIC X(20)     VALUE ' '.

00067          01   TOTAL-LINE.
00068               03   FILLER          PIC X(66)     VALUE ' '.
00069               03   TOTAL-SALES-PR  PIC ZZZZ,ZZ9.99CR.
00070               03   ASTERISK-PR     PIC X(3)      VALUE '*'.

00072          PROCEDURE DIVISION.
00073          *** M A I N   L O G I C
00074          A000-MAIN SECTION.
00075              OPEN INPUT SALES-FILE, OUTPUT PRINT-FILE.
00076              PERFORM P000-PAGE.
00077              READ SALES-FILE, AT END MOVE 'END' TO EOF-FLAG.
00078              MOVE DEPT-PROD-IN TO PREV-DEPT-PROD.
00079              PERFORM D000-ADD UNTIL END-FILE.
00080              PERFORM H000-FINAL.
00081              CLOSE SALES-FILE, PRINT-FILE.
00082              STOP RUN.
00083          A199-END. EXIT.



00085          *** P R O C E S S   P R O D U C T
00086          D000-ADD SECTION.
00087              IF DEPT-IN > PREV-DEPT PERFORM F000-DEPT
00088              ELSE
00089                  IF PROD-IN > PREV-PROD PERFORM E000-PROD.
00090              IF END-PAGE PERFORM P000-PAGE.
00091              IF DEPT-PROD-IN < PREV-DEPT-PROD
00092                  MOVE 'OUT OF SEQUENCE' TO ERR-MESS-PR
00093              ELSE
00094                  MOVE QTY-IN TO QTY-PR
00095                  MOVE SALES-IN TO SALES-PR
00096                  ADD SALES-IN TO PROD-SALES.
00097              IF DEPT-PROD-IN NOT = PREV-DEPT-PROD OR LINE-CTR = 3
00098                  MOVE DESCRIP-IN TO DESCRIP-PR
00099                  MOVE PROD-IN TO PROD-PR
00100                  MOVE DEPT-IN TO DEPT-PR.
00101              MOVE SALES-LINE TO PRINT-LINE.
00102              PERFORM W000-WRITE.
00103              MOVE 1 TO SPACE-CTL.
00104              MOVE SPACES TO SALES-LINE.
00105              MOVE DEPT-PROD-IN TO PREV-DEPT-PROD.
00106              READ SALES-FILE, AT END MOVE 'END' TO EOF-FLAG.
00107          D999-RETURN. EXIT.
```

FIGURE 10-3 (Cont.)

183

```
00109          ***  P R O D U C T   T O T A L
00110          E000-PROD SECTION.
00111              MOVE PROD-SALES TO TOTAL-SALES-PR.
00112              MOVE '*' TO ASTERISK-PR.
00113              MOVE TOTAL-LINE TO PRINT-LINE.
00114              PERFORM W000-WRITE.
00115              MOVE SPACES TO TOTAL-LINE.
00116              MOVE 2 TO SPACE-CTL.
00117              ADD PROD-SALES TO DEPT-SALES.
00118              MOVE ZEROS TO PROD-SALES.
00119          E999-RETURN. EXIT.


00121          ***  D E P A R T M E N T   T O T A L
00122          F000-DEPT SECTION.
00123              PERFORM E000-PROD.
00124              MOVE DEPT-SALES TO TOTAL-SALES-PR.
00125              MOVE '**' TO ASTERISK-PR.
00126              MOVE TOTAL-LINE TO PRINT-LINE.
00127              PERFORM W000-WRITE.
00128              MOVE SPACES TO TOTAL-LINE.
00129              ADD DEPT-SALES TO FINAL-SALES.
00130              MOVE ZEROS TO DEPT-SALES.
00131          F999-RETURN. EXIT.


00133          ***  F I N A L   T O T A L
00134          H000-FINAL SECTION.
00135              PERFORM F000-DEPT.
00136              MOVE FINAL-SALES TO TOTAL-SALES-PR.
00137              MOVE TOTAL-LINE TO PRINT-LINE.
00138              PERFORM W000-WRITE.
00139          H999-RETURN. EXIT.


00141          ***  P A G E   H E A D I N G
00142          P000-PAGE SECTION.
00143              MOVE HEADING-LINE TO PRINT-LINE.
00144              WRITE PRINT-LINE AFTER ADVANCING TOP-PAGE.
00145              MOVE 3 TO LINE-CTR.
00146              MOVE 2 TO SPACE-CTL.
00147          P999-RETURN. EXIT.


00149          ***  C O M M O N   P R I N T
00150          W000-WRITE SECTION.
00151              WRITE PRINT-LINE AFTER ADVANCING SPACE-CTL LINES.
00152              ADD SPACE-CTL TO LINE-CTR.
00153          W999-RETURN. EXIT.
```

FIGURE 10-3   (Cont.)

Input Data:

```
       Code  Dpt Prod                        Qty Amount
       0501 025 2430 TURNTABLES              0010 0024300
       0501 025 2430 TURNTABLES              0030 0064535
       0501 025 2430 TURNTABLES              0010 0011900
       0501 025 2628 RECEIVERS               0010 0022600
       0501 025 2628 RECEIVERS               0020 0014050
       0501 025 2628 RECEIVERS               0010 0068050
       0504 030 0320 PROCESSORS              0010 0216400
       0504 040 0440 DISK STORAGE            0040 0184750
       0504 040 0440 DISK STORAGE            0060 0324290
       0504 040 1623 TERMINALS               0150 0662735
       0504 040 1623 TERMINALS               0030 0122530
       0501 125 0347 RECORDS                 0200 0008560
       0501 125 0392 CASSETTE TAPE           0120 0004912
       0501 125 0395 8-TRACK TAPE            0070 0002520
```

Printed Report:

```
    DPT    PROD    DESCRIPTION          QTY      SALES($)

    025    2430    TURNTABLES            1         243.00
                                         3         645.35
                                         1         119.00
                                                 1,007.35   *

    025    2628    RECEIVERS             1         226.00
                                         2         140.50
                                         1         680.50
                                                 1,047.00   *

                                                 2,054.35   **

    030    0320    PROCESSORS            1       2,164.00
                                                 2,164.00   *

                                                 2,164.00   **

    040    0440    DISK STORAGE          4       1,847.50
                                         6       3,242.90
                                                 5,090.40   *

    040    1623    TERMINALS            15       6,627.35
                                         3       1,225.30
                                                 7,852.65   *

                                                12,943.05   **

    125    0347    RECORDS              20          85.60
                                                    85.60   *

    125    0392    CASSETTE TAPE        12          49.12
                                                    49.12   *

    125    0395    8-TRACK TAPE          7          25.20
                                                    25.20   *

                                                   159.92   **

                                                17,321.32
```

FIGURE 10-3 (Cont.)

185

On a change of department, there is always automatically a change of product. When the program detects a high department, it performs the department total routine, F000-DEPT. But product total must print before department total; therefore, the first statement within F000-DEPT PERFORMs product total, E000-PROD. After printing the product total, the program *unwinds* and returns to print the department total. On end-of-file, the program PERFORMs H000-FINAL, which PERFORMs F000-DEPT, which in turn PERFORMs E000-PROD. Thus, the program prints the last product total, unwinds for the last department total, and then unwinds for the final total. Keep this logic clearly in mind because the next program example takes control breaks one step further to three levels.

Group Indication

A simple program can print department numbers repetitively down a page, as shown below on the left. A more elegant approach prints a department number only for the first product of each set, as shown on the right:

DEPT	PROD		DEPT	PROD
001	2430		001	2430
001	2430			2430
001	2430			2430

A program may handle the suppression of control words by printing them only at the top of a page and for the first product of a department:

```
IF DEPT-PROD-IN NOT = PREV-DEPT-PROD      (If new department/product)
    OR LINE-CTR = 3                        (If top of page)
        MOVE DEPT-IN TO DEPT-PR.
```

THREE-LEVEL CONTROL BREAKS

Extending program logic to handle three or more control fields is relatively simple, if you adhere to a sound, consistent strategy. Test the control fields jointly to determine the high/low/equal condition: If high, there is a control break at least of the lowest level; if equal, you process the record (add or print, as required); and if low, the record is out of sequence. There is little difficulty if a program is organized to handle the control levels properly, such as a major total always forcing a minor total level first.

Figure 10-4 depicts a sales report with three total levels: branch (major), department (intermediate), and product (minor). Sales are accumulated (not listed) to show total sales by product, then by department, then by branch, with a final total at the end of the run. The program to handle this problem is in Figure 10-5. It tests for control breaks as follows:

A CHANGE OF	CAUSES THE PROGRAM TO PRODUCE
Branch	Product, then department, then branch totals.
Department	Product, then department totals.
Product	Product totals only.

Thus, a control break at any level (including end-of-file) automatically triggers control breaks at all lower levels. To reduce space and to simplify, a number of features have been deleted. A normal program would include, for example, a page overflow test and a check for valid record code.

```
        BRANCH   DEPT    PROD    DESCRIPTION           SALES($)

          01      001     2430    TURNTABLES           1,500.00
                          2628    RECEIVERS              125.00
                          2635    SPEAKERS               205.00
                                                       1,830.00 *

          01      004     2365    RECORDS                750.00
                          2386    8-TRACK TAPE           550.00
                                                       1,300.00 *

                                                       3,130.00 **

          02      001     2430    TURNTABLES             860.00
                          2628    RECEIVERS            1,000.00
                          2635    SPEAKERS               500.00
                                                       2,360.00 *   ETC...
```

FIGURE 10-4   Report with Three-level Totals.

The input logic has become more complicated, and a separate logic routine could be justified. In Figure 10-5 the Section in the Procedure Division called A200-SEQ handles the sequence-checking logic and the READ. In effect, program execution pivots around this routine, which selects the Section to be processed— product, department, or branch. Such a separate routine can make a program clearer, particularly when input logic is complex.

```
00001              IDENTIFICATION DIVISION.
00002              PROGRAM-ID. CHAP10B.
00003              REMARKS.  THREE-LEVEL CONTROL BREAK BY BRANCH/DEPT/PRODUCT.

00005              ENVIRONMENT DIVISION.
00006              CONFIGURATION SECTION.
00007              SPECIAL-NAMES.
00008                  C01 IS TOP-PAGE.
00009              INPUT-OUTPUT SECTION.
00010              FILE-CONTROL.
00011                  SELECT SALES-FILE. ASSIGN TO SYS015-UR-2501-S.
00012                  SELECT PRINT-FILE. ASSIGN TO SYS014-UR-1403-S.

00014              DATA DIVISION.
00015              FILE SECTION.
00016              FD  SALES-FILE
00017                  LABEL RECORDS ARE OMITTED
00018                  DATA RECORD IS SALES-RECORD.
00019              01  SALES-REC.
00020                  03  CODE-IN        PIC X(2).
00021                  03  BRAN-DEPT-PROD-IN.
00022                      05  BRAN-IN    PIC X(2).
00023                      05  DEPT-IN    PIC X(3).
00024                      05  PROD-IN    PIC X(4).
00025                  03  DESCRIP-IN     PIC X(20).
00026                  03  QTY-IN         PIC S999.
00027                  03  SALES-IN       PIC S9(5)V99.
00028                  03  FILLER         PIC X(39).

00030              FD  PRINT-FILE
00031                  LABEL RECORDS ARE OMITTED
00032                  DATA RECORD IS PRINT-LINE.
00033              01  PRINT-LINE         PIC X(133).

00035              WORKING-STORAGE SECTION.
00036              01  ALPHANUMERIC-ITEMS  DISPLAY.
00037                  03  PREV-BRAN-DEPT-PROD.
00038                      05  PREV-BRAN  PIC X(2).
00039                      05  PREV-DEPT  PIC X(3).
00040                      05  PREV-PROD  PIC X(4).
00041                  03  EOF-FLAG       PIC X(3)      VALUE ' '.
00042                      88  END-FILE                 VALUE 'END'.

00044              01  ARITHMETIC-ITEMS    COMP-3.
00045                  03  LINE-CTR       PIC S999      VALUE +0.
00046                      88 END-PAGE                  VALUE +25 THRU +999.
00047                  03  SPACE-CTL      PIC S9        VALUE +0.
00048                  03  PROD-SALES     PIC S9(7)V99 VALUE +0.
00049                  03  DEPT-SALES     PIC S9(7)V99 VALUE +0.
00050                  03  BRAN-SALES     PIC S9(7)V99 VALUE +0.
00051                  03  FINAL-SALES    PIC S9(7)V99 VALUE +0.
```

FIGURE 10-5   Three-level Control Break.

```cobol
00053              01   SALES-LINE.
00054                   03   FILLER          PIC X(20)    VALUE ' '.
00055                   03   BRAN-PR         PIC X(05).
00056                   03   DEPT-PR         PIC X(06).
00057                   03   PROD-PR         PIC X(07).
00058                   03   DESCRIP-PR      PIC X(23).
00059                   03   QTY-PR          PIC ZZ9-.
00060                   03   FILLER          PIC X(3)     VALUE ' '.
00061                   03   SALES-PR        PIC ZZ,ZZ9.99CR.
00062                   03   ERR-MESS-PR     PIC X(20)    VALUE ' '.

00064              01   TOTAL-LINE.
00065                   03   FILLER          PIC X(66)    VALUE ' '.
00066                   03   TOTAL-SALES-PR  PIC ZZZZ,ZZ9.99CR.
00067                   03   ASTERISK-PR     PIC X(3)     VALUE '*'.

00069              PROCEDURE DIVISION.
00070         ***   M A I N   L O G I C
00071         A000-MAIN SECTION.
00072              OPEN INPUT SALES-FILE, OUTPUT PRINT-FILE.
00073              READ SALES-FILE, AT END MOVE 'END' TO EOF-FLAG.
00074              MOVE BRAN-DEPT-PROD-IN TO PREV-BRAN-DEPT-PROD.
00075              PERFORM A200-SEQ UNTIL END-FILE.
00076              PERFORM H000-FINAL.
00077              CLOSE SALES-FILE, PRINT-FILE.
00078              STOP RUN.
00079         A199-END. EXIT.

00081         ***   S E Q U E N C E   L O G I C
00082         A200-SEQ SECTION.
00083              IF BRAN-IN > PREV-BRAN PERFORM G000-BRAN
00084              ELSE
00085                  IF DEPT-IN > PREV-DEPT PERFORM F000-DEPT
00086                  ELSE
00087                      IF PROD-IN > PREV-PROD PERFORM E000-PROD.
00088              PERFORM D000-ADD.
00089              READ SALES-FILE, AT END MOVE 'END' TO EOF-FLAG.
00090         A299-RETURN. EXIT.

00092         ***   P R O C E S S   P R O D U C T
00093         D000-ADD SECTION.
00094              IF BRAN-DEPT-PROD-IN < PREV-BRAN-DEPT-PROD
00095                  MOVE 'OUT OF SEQUENCE' TO ERR-MESS-PR
00096              ELSE
00097                  MOVE QTY-IN TO QTY-PR
00098                  MOVE SALES-IN TO SALES-PR
00099                  ADD SALES-IN TO PROD-SALES.
00100              MOVE DESCRIP-IN TO DESCRIP-PR.
00101              MOVE PROD-IN TO PROD-PR.
00102              MOVE DEPT-IN TO DEPT-PR.
00103              MOVE BRAN-IN TO BRAN-PR.
00104              MOVE SALES-LINE TO PRINT-LINE.
00105              PERFORM W000-WRITE.
00106              MOVE 1 TO SPACE-CTL.
00107              MOVE SPACES TO SALES-LINE.
00108              MOVE BRAN-DEPT-PROD-IN TO PREV-BRAN-DEPT-PROD.
00109         D999-RETURN. EXIT.
```

FIGURE 10-5 (Cont.)

189

```
00111.        ***  P R O D U C T  T O T A L
00112            E000-PROD SECTION.
00113                MOVE PROD-SALES TO TOTAL-SALES-PR.
00114                MOVE '*' TO ASTERISK-PR.
00115                MOVE TOTAL-LINE TO PRINT-LINE.
00116                PERFORM W000-WRITE.
00117                MOVE SPACES TO TOTAL-LINE.
00118                MOVE 2 TO SPACE-CTL.
00119                ADD PROD-SALES TO DEPT-SALES.
00120                MOVE ZEROS TO PROD-SALES.
00121            E999-RETURN. EXIT.

00123        ***  D E P A R T M E N T  T O T A L
00124            F000-DEPT SECTION.
00125                PERFORM E000-PROD.
00126                MOVE DEPT-SALES TO TOTAL-SALES-PR.
00127                MOVE '**' TO ASTERISK-PR.
00128                MOVE TOTAL-LINE TO PRINT-LINE.
00129                PERFORM W000-WRITE.
00130                MOVE SPACES TO TOTAL-LINE.
00131                ADD DEPT-SALES TO BRAN-SALES.
00132                MOVE ZEROS TO DEPT-SALES.
00133            F999-RETURN. EXIT.

00135        ***  B R A N C H  T O T A L
00136            G000-BRAN SECTION.
00137                PERFORM F000-DEPT.
00138                MOVE BRAN-SALES TO TOTAL-SALES-PR.
00139                MOVE '***' TO ASTERISK-PR.
00140                MOVE TOTAL-LINE TO PRINT-LINE.
00141                PERFORM W000-WRITE.
00142                MOVE SPACES TO TOTAL-LINE.
00143                ADD BRAN-SALES TO FINAL-SALES.
00144                MOVE ZEROS TO BRAN-SALES.
00145            G999-RETURN. EXIT.

00147        ***  F I N A L  T O T A L
00148            H000-FINAL SECTION.
00149                PERFORM G000-BRAN.
00150                MOVE FINAL-SALES TO TOTAL-SALES-PR.
00151                MOVE TOTAL-LINE TO PRINT-LINE.
00152                PERFORM W000-WRITE.
00153            H999-RETURN. EXIT.

00155        ***  C O M M O N  P R I N T
00156            W000-WRITE SECTION.
00157                WRITE PRINT-LINE AFTER ADVANCING SPACE-CTL LINES.
00158            W999-RETURN. EXIT.
```

FIGURE 10-5 (Cont.)

190

Printed Report:

```
01   025   2430   TURNTABLES           1        243.00
01   025   2430   TURNTABLES           3        645.35
01   025   2430   TURNTABLES           1        119.00
                                              1,007.35   *

01   025   2628   RECEIVERS            1        226.00
01   025   2628   RECEIVERS            2        140.50
01   025   2628   RECEIVERS            1        680.50
                                              1,047.00   *

                                              2,054.35   **

01   125   0347   RECORDS             20         85.60
                                                 85.60   *

01   125   0392   CASSETTE TAPE       12         49.12
                                                 49.12   *

01   125   0395   8-TRACK TAPE         7         25.20
                                                 25.20   *

                                                159.92   **

                                              2,214.27   ***

04   030   0320   PROCESSORS           1      2,164.00
                                              2,164.00   *

                                              2,164.00   **

04   040   0440   DISK STORAGE         4      1,847.50
04   040   0440   DISK STORAGE         6      3,242.90
                                              5,090.40   *

04   040   1623   TERMINALS           15      6,627.35
04   040   1623   TERMINALS            3      1,225.30
                                              7,852.65   *

                                             12,943.05   **

                                             15,107.05   ***

                                             17,321.32
```

FIGURE 10-5 (Cont.)

191

PAGE OVERFLOW

Chapter 6 covered page overflow for a simple program with no control breaks. In a complex program, placement of the page overflow test is critical. Many installations prefer to avoid printing total lines immediately at the top of a page. In the following example, the page begins with two total lines for plant and department, but the totals do not clearly indicate the set of data to which they belong:

```
PLANT    DEPARTMENT    NAME        HOURS    RATE        WAGE

                                               52,325.38 *
                                              265,547.97 **
```

Many programmers feel that such totals should be printed at the bottom of the previous page, or with at least one detail line (in this case employee) at the top of the page. On most reports, the strategy for handling page overflows, regardless of the number of control break levels, is relatively simple:

1. Set the line count maximum to several lines fewer than a page can accommodate (usually about 55). This practice allows for space at the bottom of a page for totals.
2. Count every line printed and spaced.
3. Insert the test for page overflow in one place only—before printing a detail line (a *detail line* is the lowest level of printing in the program). Although there may be two or three control break levels, it is not necessary to test for page overflow everywhere a program prints totals.
4. Do not test if the line count *equals* a maximum value. If a program increments the line count by one, two, or three depending on spacing, it is possible to bypass the maximum value and to continue through the perforation without ejecting to a new page. Instead, test if the line count *exceeds* a maximum value.

Most programs should require only two PERFORMs of the page heading routine: one at the time of initialization and another prior to printing a detail line. This procedure will ensure that a program will never print totals on the first line of a page—at least one detail line will always immediately precede a total line.

In the first program example in this chapter with the two-level control break, the page overflow test should be in D000-ADD Section prior to moving the detail line to PRINT-RECORD. For the second program example with the three-level control break, since no detail sales record is printed (total product sales is the lowest level), the test should be at the start of E000-PROD, the lowest level of printing.

PROGRAMMING STRATEGY

When attempting to organize and write a program, you may find it difficult to know where to begin. Usually there are many special conditions and exceptions that complicate a solution and confuse the relatively simple strategy in approaching the problem. It is important to define the essential problem that is to be solved. You do this by ignoring all exceptions, error conditions, and complex calculations. *Isolate the main logic first and build the program around this skeleton.* The main logic is the main loop of a program, which almost always centers upon the input logic. Once you have determined the input logic, you may realize that the program is a typical multiple control break or a file update problem with a standard solution.

You will find that the remainder of the program arranges itself into logical sections. These sections should be coded so that they are approximately in the sequence in which the program will execute them. The exceptions to this sequence are the page heading routine (generally similar from program to program) and error routines (which occur infrequently). These less important routines should be separated toward the end where they do not clutter the main logic of a program. As an example, consider the preceding program with the three-level control break. The program accumulates sales by product, department, and branch and is simpler than the typical business problem. It has a number of subroutines, all subsidiary to the main logic. Although there are many ways to organize a program, especially the main processing routines, the program begins with main logic that can be applied to most programs:

- OPEN files.
- READ the first record.
- PERFORM sequencing and reading until end-of-file.
- PERFORM final processing.
- CLOSE files.
- STOP run.

Since this program has some complex input logic, the sequencing Section handles the decision making and is in a sense part of the Main Logic:

```
IF high Branch, PERFORM Branch-Totals,
ELSE
   IF high Department, PERFORM Department-totals,
   ELSE
      IF high Product, PERFORM Product-totals.
PERFORM Product-Processing.
READ next record.
```

This strategy can be applied to many business programs. Although there are other approaches, the best approach is to organize a program into logical sections.

A program should consist of a main logic routine and any number of subroutines. A subroutine may execute from more than one point, or from only one point. It is also possible for one subroutine to link to another subroutine and to return (a practice to be used with great care).

Ideally, you should organize a program—main logic and subroutines—according to some logical, consistent strategy. For example, assume a program that performs calculations and prints totals by minor and major level. You should code the program in independent sections, with the most important and most commonly used routines first:

Program
Organization:

| Initialization |

Initialization must be done first. (It could also be combined with the main logic routine.)

| Main Logic |

The program "rotates" on this routine, which consists of tests to determine which subroutine to invoke.

| Calculation |

These subroutines are organized in order of importance, from the most commonly executed to the least commonly executed. They are basically in the sequence in which the program executes them.

| Minor Totals |

An advantage of this sequence—detail calculations, minor total, major total, and final total—is that any subroutine can be easily located.

| Major Totals |

Subroutines are usually restricted in size to a maximum of one page of computer printout so that no one subroutine is too complicated. There is usually only one entry point and one exit point.

| Final Totals |

| Page Heading |

Page overflow occurs only periodically.

| Error Routines |

Errors and other miscellaneous routines rarely occur. They are least important in terms of execution and should be coded at the end of the program.

SUMMARY

This chapter extends the material that the previous chapter introduced. The new concept introduced is the technique of breaking control on two or more levels; a high control break automatically triggers breaks on lower levels.

The handling of page overflow takes some care, especially to ensure that the program does not print a total at the top of a page.

This chapter concludes the basic material on logic and control breaks. The next part introduces many advanced programming techniques. The only other material on input logic is in Chapter 15, which covers the logic for handling more than one input file.

PROBLEMS

10-1. Draw a flowchart for the following: Input records contain department, employee number, employee name, and monthly earnings. Each employee has only one record. Total earnings are required for department and end-of-file. Provide for page overflow with no totals at the top of a page.

10-2. Revise Problem 10-1 for one more control level. As well as department and employee, provide for plant totals as employee, department, plant, and end-of-file.

10-3. Code and test the program in Problem 10-2 using full structured programming conventions and supply enough data to force page overflows.

PART IV
ADVANCED TOPICS

PART IV

ADVANCED TOPICS

CHAPTER 11

TABLE PROCESSING—I

OBJECTIVE: To introduce the concept of tables, their definition, and the techniques involved in processing data in tables.

INTRODUCTION

Many business programs require the use of a *table* (also known as an *array*). A table is a set of related data of relatively permanent nature, although a table may consist of a series of adjacent blank or zero fields defined to hold related data. An income tax table is an obvious example, but there are many others as this chapter and the next illustrate. The content of a table may be numeric (as is an income tax table) or descriptive (as are the names of departments in a company). This chapter introduces some new COBOL statements and a number of important programming concepts and techniques.

DEFINING TABLES

Consider a table of the twelve months:

```
' JANUARY  '
'FEBRUARY  '
'MARCH     '
     •
     •
     •
'DECEMBER  '
```

A program is required to print the descriptive names of each month. It is a simple matter in COBOL to define such a table of months and to code the instruction(s) to access the name from the table. In COBOL, two special clauses are used to define a table: REDEFINES and OCCURS. Figure 11-1 defines a table containing the names of the twelve months, coded to permit the use of *direct table addressing*.

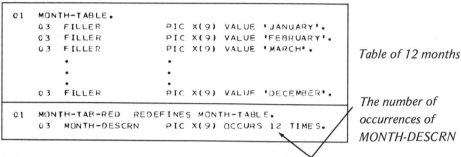

```
01    MONTH-TABLE.
      03   FILLER            PIC X(9)  VALUE 'JANUARY'.
      03   FILLER            PIC X(9)  VALUE 'FEBRUARY'.
      03   FILLER            PIC X(9)  VALUE 'MARCH'.
               •                   •
               •                   •
               •                   •
      03   FILLER            PIC X(9)  VALUE 'DECEMBER'.
01    MONTH-TAB-RED   REDEFINES MONTH-TABLE.
      03   MONTH-DESCRN      PIC X(9)  OCCURS 12 TIMES.
```

Table of 12 months

The number of occurrences of MONTH-DESCRN

FIGURE 11-1   Table Definition.

MONTH-TABLE is a conventional definition of the twelve months. Each entry is defined as FILLER rather than with a unique name, and of the same length. As MONTH-TABLE stands, you cannot use it as a table. But by using the REDEFINES clause, it is possible to *redefine* MONTH-TABLE so that you can reference any of the twelve entries through use of a *subscript*. MONTH-TAB-RED redefines MONTH-TABLE, using the OCCURS clause; thus, MONTH-TAB-RED indicates that there are twelve similarly declared entries in MONTH-TABLE (PIC X(9)), and that you may reference any entry using the name MONTH-DESCRN coupled with an appropriate subscript (n). Thus, MONTH-DESCRN (1) references the first entry (January), and MONTH-DESCRN (10) references the tenth entry (October). The valid subscript values in this case are 01 through 12. You can extract the alphabetic month with a simple MOVE statement. Assume that MONTH-PR is defined in the heading area, and you want to move the fifth month description (May) to MONTH-PR:

```
MOVE MONTH-DESCRN (5) TO MONTH-PR.
```
                                        subscript

This coding does not accomplish much because if you already know the month, you can simply move the literal 'MAY' to MONTH-PR. But if an input record contains a numeric month, you can use this numeric value to locate and extract the description:

```
03   MONTH-IN          PIC 99.

MOVE MONTH-DESCRN (MONTH-IN) TO MONTH-PR.
```

                        subscript variable, containing value 1–12

This coding works, but the program would be more efficient if the subscript had the attributes COMPUTATIONAL (COMP, not COMP-3) and SYNC to provide correct boundary alignment of the subscript on the 360/370 and some other computers. Defining COMP generates an arithmetic value in binary format, which, for subscripts, is more efficient than other formats. SYNC, or SYNCHRONIZED, causes the compiler to align a defined binary field so that it begins on a particular storage address, such as an even numbered location on IBM 360/370. This feature results in more efficient execution of machine language. You do not normally apply these attributes to an input field, but you can move an input field to another field that is defined with COMP and SYNC, which is named SUBSCR in the following:

```
77   SUBSCR              PIC S99 COMP SYNC.

MOVE MONTH-IN TO SUBSCR.
MOVE MONTH-DESCRN (SUBSCR) TO MONTH-PR.
```

OCCURS Clause

OCCURS designates the number of repetitions of a table entry and must specify a positive integer value, such as 12 or 100. All table entries must have similar definitions, the same format (alphanumeric or numeric), and the same length. OCCURS cannot contain a VALUE clause and can be only levels 02 through 49 (not 01, 66, 77, or 88).

The preceding example involves direct table addressing, a relatively simple feature in COBOL. The only danger in this is that MONTH-IN could contain a value other than 01 through 12, causing a serious execution error (a subscript value outside the range of the table). Before using a subscript, check that it is valid, as in the following:

```
MOVE MONTH-IN TO SUBSCR.
IF SUBSCR < 01 OR > 12 PERFORM Z200-MONTH-ERROR
ELSE MOVE MONTH-DESCRN (SUBSCR) TO MONTH-PR.
```

Most tables do not have such a neat one-for-one relationship with the subscript and require a methodical table lookup.

SEQUENTIAL TABLES

Consider the following situation. A firm has five inventory stock items for sale with the following prices:

STOCK ITEM	SELLING PRICE
203	$ 2.25
206	5.27
240	0.25
244	10.37
265	3.25

The company sells various quantities of each item and uses the sales as source documents to key-enter the stock number and the quantity sold. Rather than key in selling price and value, a computer program is to check the stock number, determine its selling price, and calculate value sold. Figure 11-2 illustrates the program logic.

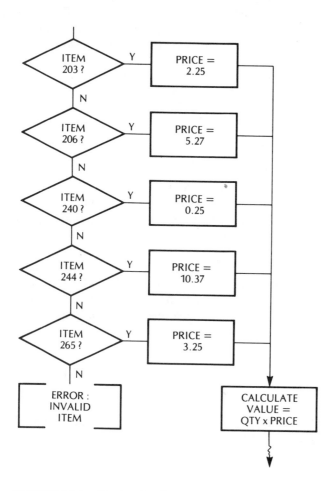

FIGURE 11-2   Testing Stock Item Numbers.

The programming is straightforward. However, what if the company sold 200 items or more? Coding a program to test for 200 items separately is grossly inefficient. The ideal solution uses only one compare, repetitive processing, and the stored program's ability to "modify" its own instructions. Therefore, it is necessary to define the stock items and selling prices into an orderly arrangement in a table. The table consists of two parts: the list of stock items, called the *table argument,* and the list of prices, called the *function*. The program reads input records containing stock number and quantity sold and uses the input stock item number, called the *search argument*, to locate an item in the table of arguments and the appropriate price in the table of functions. The program then calculates the value sold by multiplying quantity sold from the input record by the located price in the table.

All search arguments and table arguments must be defined identically with the same length and data type (arithmetic or character). The functions may have any suitable definition, but must be defined identically, and there must be one function for each table argument. Within a table, the arguments are arranged in one of two ways, as *unique entries* or as *steps*.

Tables with Unique Entries

A table with unique entries includes such arguments as stock numbers, employee numbers, and electric rate codes. The table arguments need not be consecutive (one argument immediately following another, as 7, 8, 9) or sequential (each argument higher than the preceding one), although a sequential arrangement is more common. Each argument value, however, should occur only once in the table.

Assume a stock table as before, with the stock items as the arguments in ascending sequence. A program reads an input record and successively compares its stock number against each stock item table argument. This procedure is called a *table lookup* or *table search*. Figure 11-3 shows the programming logic. In the flowchart, the key instruction in the loop is the compare operation. The result of comparing a search argument against a table argument is as follows:

- Equal   Argument is found, extract the function.
- High   Argument may be a higher entry in the table—increment for the next entry.
- Low   Because the arguments are in ascending sequence, the argument is not in the table.

The last result, low, requires further examination. Consider the table argument entries 203, 206, 240, 244, and 265. If the search argument is 165, then the result of the first compare is low, and by definition the argument is not in the table because all arguments are higher. If the search argument is 204, then the first compare is high, but the second compare is low. However, a problem occurs when a search argument is higher than any entry in the table—the program will continue comparing past the end of the table. To prevent this, it must have a *stopper*. One simple way to provide a stopper is to insert a "high" value as the last table argument—9s for arithmetic arguments and HIGH-VALUES for alphanumeric arguments. No search argument can exceed this value, and in most cases can never equal it. A comparison to the "high" argument will therefore deliver a low, error condition. A second method to

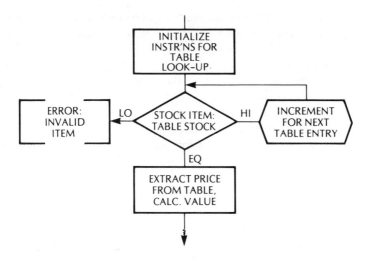

FIGURE 11-3   Table Lookup on Stock Number.

force termination of a search is to count the number of times the loop is executed. If the count exceeds the number of entries in the table, then the program concludes that the argument is not in the table. In a third method of forcing termination, a program inserts the search argument into the last entry in the table, a position reserved for this purpose. Consequently, the loop will always find an equal and must check if the compare is at the last entry position. The advantage of the second and third methods is that the table need not be in ascending sequence.

Note: Often in business applications, 20 percent of the table items involves 80 percent of the activity. Therefore, it may be more efficient to insert the most commonly used items at the start of a table. The table will no longer be in ascending sequence, and the compare will test only for equal or unequal. Determining if an item is not in the table will involve a search against all arguments through to the end.

Tables with Steps

In a table with arguments arranged in steps, the arguments represent a range of values. Consider the following income tax table:

ANNUAL TAXABLE INCOME	TAX FORMULA
up to $ 2,500	10% of Taxable Income
2,501 to 5,000	12% of Taxable Income less $ 50
5,001 to 8,000	15% of Taxable Income less 200
8,001 to 12,000	19% of Taxable Income less 520
12,001 to 20,000	24% of Taxable Income less 1,120
20,001 and over	30% of Taxable Income less 2,320

The taxable income is the argument, and the tax formula, consisting of two parts, is the function. The function may have to be defined in two parts, one for the rate and one for a *correction factor*. The simplest way to arrange the arguments is with the high values of each step as follows:

$$2,500$$
$$5,000$$
$$8,000$$
$$12,000$$
$$20,000$$
$$99,999$$

Accordingly, you write a routine to successively compare an employee's annual taxable income against each table argument. If an employee's income is $2,500 or less, then the tax is 10% of income; for an income of $3,000, for example, the table search stops on the second step where $3,000 is lower than $5,000. The calculation, therefore, is as follows:

$$\text{Tax} = \$3,000 \times 12\% - \$\ 50$$
$$= \quad \$360 \quad - \$\ 50 = \$310$$

In the table, as shown in Figure 11-4 and the calculation, either an equal or a low condition means that the argument is found. And as long as the highest possible value (in this case arithmetic 9s) is the last entry and arguments are in ascending sequence, any possible taxable income by definition is always equal to, or lower than, at least one of the table arguments.

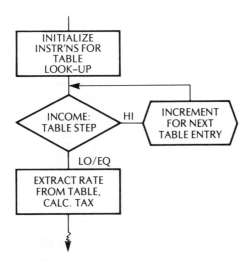

FIGURE 11-4   Table Lookup on Tax Steps.

TABLE SEARCHING

A table search involves table arguments and functions. Again, consider a table of stock item numbers (the table argument) and associated prices (the function). In Figure 11-5 STOCK-TAB-VALUES defines each stock item and its price in the same VALUE clause. The last entry contains a value of 9s as a table search stopper for arithmetic arguments. The REDEFINES clause, however, has separate entries for item and price, so that you may reference each field separately. It is now possible to search the table by initializing a subscript and looping until the required item is found. The figure assumes that table items are in ascending sequence and that STOCK-IN contains a stock number from an input record.

```
01    STOCK-TAB-VALUES.                          ITEM PRICE
      03  FILLER      PIC X(7) VALUE '2030225'.   203  2.25
      03  FILLER      PIC X(7) VALUE '2060527'.   206  5.27
      03  FILLER      PIC X(7) VALUE '2400025'.   240  0.25
      03  FILLER      PIC X(7) VALUE '2441037'.   244 10.37
      03  FILLER      PIC X(7) VALUE '2650325'.   265  3.25
      03  FILLER      PIC X(7) VALUE '9990000'.   END OF TABLE

01    STOCK-TAB-RED REDEFINES STOCK-TAB-VALUES.
      03  STOCK-TAB-OCCUR OCCURS 6 TIMES.
          05   STOCK-ITEM-TAB  PIC X(3).
          05   STOCK-PRICE-TAB PIC S99V99.

77   END-SEARCH-SIGNAL    PIC X(3)    VALUE SPACES.
     88  END-SEARCH                   VALUE 'END'.
77   SUB           PIC S9(4) COMP SYNC.

     MOVE SPACES TO END-SEARCH-SIGNAL.
     MOVE 0 TO SUB.
     PERFORM T100-SEARCH UNTIL END-SEARCH.
          •
          •
          •
T100-SEARCH SECTION.
     ADD 1 TO SUB.
     IF STOCK-IN = STOCK-ITEM-TAB (SUB)
         MOVE STOCK-PRICE-TAB (SUB) TO STOCK-PRICE
         MOVE 'END' TO END-SEARCH-SIGNAL
     ELSE
     IF STOCK-IN < STOCK-ITEM-TAB (SUB)
         DISPLAY 'ITEM NOT IN TABLE'
         MOVE 'END' TO END-SEARCH-SIGNAL.
T999-RETURN. EXIT.
```

FIGURE 11-5   Table of Stock Items and Prices.

There are various ways to terminate the table lookup in Figure 11-5, but this example sets and tests a condition name, END-SEARCH. The search assumes that stock items are in ascending sequence in the table. The program sets END-SEARCH to 'END' on locating the table stock item, and therefore, prior to reusing the PERFORM, must initialize END-SEARCH to blank. Failure to initialize will cause PERFORM to recognize an 'END' condition, and T000-SEARCH will not execute.

Another variation on table lookup tests if the end of the table has been reached:

IF STOCK-ITEM-TAB (SUB) = '999' MOVE "END" TO SEARCH-FLAG. . .

You may also define a table without a stopper of 9s and test if the subscript value exceeds the table limit. The disadvantage of this method is that if you have to insert new stock items in the table, you must remember to change the IF statement:

IF SUB > 5 MOVE 'END' TO SEARCH-FLAG. . .

Subsequent examples use PERFORM with the VARYING option to initialize and increment a subscript.

INDEXES

The OCCURS clause provides for an INDEXED BY feature that automatically generates a subscript, called an *index,* so that the subscript is not defined:

```
01   STOCK-TAB-RED REDEFINES STOCK-TAB-VALUES.
     03   STOCK-TAB-OCCUR OCCURS 6 TIMES INDEXED BY ITEM-NDX.
```

In this case, the index is named ITEM-NDX (any unique name is valid) and is used as a subscript, but with one exception: the SET verb initializes and increments the index instead of MOVE and ADD:

```
SET ITEM-NDX TO 1.           Initialize index
SET ITEM-NDX UP BY 1.        Increment index
SET ITEM-NDX DOWN BY 1.      Decrement index
```

An index must contain a value only within the bounds of a table. For example, if the OCCURS clause specifies 6 TIMES, then an attempt to SET the index to zero or to increment the index to 7 causes an execution error.

The following differences between subscripts and indexes pertain to compiler and program execution:

1. *Subscript.* When a program adds to a subscript, there is a simple increment of the value (such as 6 + 1 = 7). When a subscript references a table location such as STOCK-ITEM-TAB (SUB), the storage address is then calculated. (The calculation is based on the starting address of the table plus the subscript value times the length of each entry.)

2.   *Index.* When a program adds to an index, it calculates the actual storage address. When an index references a table location, the storage address is already calculated.

Indexes have some restrictions. SET, SEARCH, and PERFORM can process an indexed item and change the index value. COBOL does not permit ADD to increment an index, and MOVE can only move the contents of one index to another index. DISPLAY and EXHIBIT can specify a subscript, but not an index. Consequently, a program using subscripts is often easier to debug than a program using indexes.

Constant recalculations of table addresses can be time consuming. A subscript is more efficient when incrementing the subscript value. An index is more efficient when it is used for addressing table items. However, since most table searches increment the subscript/index and use it to check the table entry, either method can be used. But if there are many table functions to be addressed, the use of indexes is usually more efficient.

It is also possible (but unnecessary) to define an index explicitly using the USAGE IS INDEX clause, but with no PICTURE:

```
        77  ITEM-NDX     USAGE IS INDEX.
```

The PERFORM VARYING and SEARCH examples next illustrate use of the index feature.

PERFORM VARYING STATEMENT

The PERFORM VARYING statement is particularly useful for COBOL table searches. Figure 11-6 uses the same table definition and index as before. The only new feature is the VARYING clause that

1.   Initializes the index (as was defined in the OCCURS) at the start of the search.
2.   Increments the index automatically for each step through the table.
The program in Figure 11-6 could also use a subscript instead of an index.

The general format for the PERFORM VARYING statement is as follows:

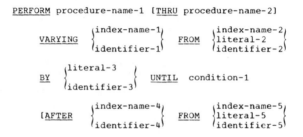

$$\text{BY} \begin{Bmatrix} \text{literal-6} \\ \text{identifier-6} \end{Bmatrix} \underline{\text{UNTIL}} \text{ condition-2}$$

$$[\underline{\text{AFTER}} \begin{Bmatrix} \text{index-name-7} \\ \text{identifier-7} \end{Bmatrix} \underline{\text{FROM}} \begin{Bmatrix} \text{index-name-8} \\ \text{literal-8} \\ \text{identifier-8} \end{Bmatrix}$$

$$\text{BY} \begin{Bmatrix} \text{literal-9} \\ \text{identifier-9} \end{Bmatrix} \underline{\text{UNTIL}} \text{ condition-3]]}$$

SEARCH STATEMENT

SEARCH provides a powerful table lookup facility using indexes and two new clauses: AT END and WHEN. Therefore, the table lookup in Figure 11-6 could be coded with SEARCH as follows:

```
1.  SET ITEM-NDX TO 1.                              Initialize index
2.  SEARCH STOCK-TAB-OCCUR                           Start search
3.     AT END PERFORM R000-NOT-IN-TABLE             Not in table
4.     WHEN STOCK-IN = STOCK-ITEM-TAB (ITEM-NDX)    Action if item
           MOVE STOCK-PRICE-TAB (ITEM-NDX) TO STOCK-PRICE.     found
```

1. SET must be coded first to initialize the index value.
2. SEARCH automatically steps through the table, one entry (or pair of entries) at a time.

```
77  END-SEARCH-SIGNAL    PIC X(3)    VALUE SPACES.
    88  END-SEARCH                    VALUE 'END'.

    MOVE SPACES TO END-SEARCH-SIGNAL.
    PERFORM T100-SEARCH VARYING ITEM-NDX FROM 1 BY 1
            UNTIL END-SEARCH.

T100-SEARCH SECTION.
    IF STOCK-IN = STOCK-ITEM-TAB (ITEM-NDX)
        MOVE STOCK-PRICE-TAB (ITEM-NDX) TO STOCK-PRICE
        MOVE 'END' TO END-SEARCH-SIGNAL
    ELSE
    IF STOCK-IN < STOCK-ITEM-TAB (ITEM-NDX)
        DISPLAY 'ITEM NOT IN TABLE'
        MOVE 'END' TO END-SEARCH-SIGNAL.
T999-RETURN. EXIT.
```

FIGURE 11-6 Use of Perform Varying.

3. If SEARCH has compared every item in the table without finding the required stock item, the program executes the AT END statement(s) and terminates the search. Consequently, the index will have no predictable value.

4. If the stock item is found, the WHEN condition is satisfied; the program executes the WHEN statement(s) (in this case the MOVE) and terminates the search. A SEARCH may contain more than one WHEN clause.

The table arguments (stock items) need not be in ascending sequence. Indeed, because often a few table entries have most of the activity, it may be more efficient to code the active items first in the table. There are, of course, many other variations on table search and search termination, but some installations adopt a table search standard; programs within the installation become easy to debug and maintain.

Formats for OCCURS and SEARCH

The OCCURS clause provides for entries in either ascending or descending sequence, as indicated in its general format:

```
OCCURS integer-2 TIMES

     ┌ASCENDING ┐
   [ │          │  KEY IS data-name-2 [data-name-3] ... ] ...
     └DESCENDING┘

     [INDEXED BY index-name-1[index-name-2] ... ]
```

The SEARCH statement allows more than one WHEN condition. Its general format is as follows:

```
SEARCH identifier-1 [VARYING  ┌index-name-1┐  ]
                              │            │
                              └identifier-2┘

   [AT END imperative-statement-1]

   WHEN condition-1    ┌imperative-statement-2┐
                       │                      │
                       └NEXT SENTENCE         ┘

   [WHEN condition-2   ┌imperative-statement-3┐  ]...
                       │                      │
                       └NEXT SENTENCE         ┘
```

PROGRAM EXAMPLE

Figure 11-7 is a structured COBOL program that performs a table search. The input employee time record contains record code (04), employee number, employee name, job number, and hours worked. The sequence is by employee number, with any number of records per employee. For each record, the program uses the job number to search a table of job numbers (argument) and rates-of-pay (function). The hours field (from the input record) is multiplied by rate (from the table) to calculate

```
00001              IDENTIFICATION DIVISION.
00002              PROGRAM-ID. CHAP11A.
00003              REMARKS. PROGRAM PERFORMS TABLE LOOKUP ON JOB NUMBER,
00004                       & CALCULATES WAGE = HOURS X RATE.

00006              ENVIRONMENT DIVISION.
00007              CONFIGURATION SECTION.
00008              SPECIAL-NAMES.
00009                  C01 IS TOP-PAGE.
00010              INPUT-OUTPUT SECTION.
00011              FILE-CONTROL.
00012                  SELECT TIME-FILE.   ASSIGN TO SYS015-UR-2501-S.
00013                  SELECT REPORT-FILE. ASSIGN TO SYS014-UR-1403-S.

00015              DATA DIVISION.
00016              FILE SECTION.
00017              FD  TIME-FILE
00018                  LABEL RECORDS ARE OMITTED
00019                  DATA RECORD IS TIME-RECORD.
00020              01  TIME-RECORD.
00021                  05  CODE-IN          PIC XX.
00022                  05  EMPNO-IN         PIC X(5).
00023                  05  NAME-IN          PIC X(15).
00024                  05  JOB-IN           PIC 99.
00025                  05  HOURS-IN         PIC S99V9.
00026                  05  FILLER           PIC X(53).

00028              FD  REPORT-FILE
00029                  LABEL RECORDS ARE OMITTED
00030                  DATA RECORD IS PRINT-RECORD.
00031              01  PRINT-RECORD         PIC X(133).

00033              WORKING-STORAGE SECTION.
00034              77  PREV-EMP             PIC X(5)      VALUE LOW-VALUES.
00035              77  EOF-FLAG             PIC X(3)      VALUE ' '.
00036                  88  END-FILE                       VALUE 'EOF'.
00037              77  SEARCH-FLAG          PIC X(3)      VALUE ' '.
00038                  88  END-SEARCH                     VALUE 'END'.

00040              01  ARITHMETIC-VALUES    COMP-3.
00041                  03  HOURS            PIC S99V9.
00042                  03  RATE             PIC S999V99.
00043                  03  WAGE             PIC S9(5)V99.
00044                  03  EMPLOYEE-HOURS   PIC S9(4)V9    VALUE +0.
00045                  03  EMPLOYEE-WAGE    PIC S9(5)V99   VALUE +0.
00046                  03  TOTAL-HOURS      PIC S9(4)V9    VALUE +0.
00047                  03  TOTAL-WAGE       PIC S9(5)V99   VALUE +0.
00048                  03  LINE-CTR         PIC S999       VALUE +0.
00049                  03  PAGE-CTR         PIC S999       VALUE +1.
00050                  03  PRINT-CTL        PIC S9         VALUE +1.

00052              01  JOB-TABLE.
00053                  05  FILLER           PIC X(6)      VALUE '010725'.
00054                  05  FILLER           PIC X(6)      VALUE '020615'.
00055                  05  FILLER           PIC X(6)      VALUE '040745'.
00056                  05  FILLER           PIC X(6)      VALUE '050855'.
00057                  05  FILLER           PIC X(6)      VALUE '060750'.
00058                  05  FILLER           PIC X(6)      VALUE '080925'.
00059                  05  FILLER           PIC X(6)      VALUE '100895'.
00060                  05  FILLER           PIC X(6)      VALUE '990000'.
```

FIGURE 11-7 Table Search Program.

211

```
00062        01   JOB-TABLE-DEF            REDEFINES JOB-TABLE.
00063             03   TABLE-ENTRIES       OCCURS 8 TIMES INDEXED BY NDX.
00064                  05   JOBNO-TAB       PIC 99.
00065                  05   RATE-TAB        PIC 99V99.

00067        01   HEADING-1.
00068             05   FILLER              PIC X(22)    VALUE ' '.
00069             05   FILLER              PIC X(22)    VALUE 'W E E K L Y   W A G E'
00070             05   FILLER              PIC X(13)    VALUE 'R E P O R T'.
00071             05   FILLER              PIC X(15)    VALUE ' '.
00072             05   FILLER              PIC X(06)    VALUE 'PAGE'.
00073             05   PAGE-PR             PIC ZZZ.

00075        01   HEADING-2.
00076             05   FILLER              PIC X(12)    VALUE ' '.
00077             05   FILLER              PIC X(26)    VALUE 'EMPLOYEE   NAME'.
00078             05   FILLER              PIC X(27)    VALUE 'JOB     RATE    HOURS'.
00079             05   FILLER              PIC X(04)    VALUE 'WAGE'.

00081        01   DETAIL-LINE.
00082             05   FILLER              PIC X(14)    VALUE ' '.
00083             05   EMPNO-PR            PIC X(08).
00084             05   NAME-PR             PIC X(17).
00085             05   JOB-PR              PIC X(02).
00086             05   RATE-PR             PIC ZZZ9.99.
00087             05   FILLER              PIC X(03)    VALUE ' '.
00088             05   HOURS-PR            PIC Z9.9-.
00089             05   FILLER              PIC X(04)    VALUE ' '.
00090             05   WAGE-PR             PIC ZZ,ZZ9.99CR.
00091             05   ERR-MESS-PR         PIC X(20)    VALUE ' '.

00093        01   TOTAL-LINE.
00094             05   FILLER              PIC X(48)    VALUE ' '.
00095             05   TOTAL-HOURS-PR      PIC Z,ZZ9.9-.
00096             05   ASTER1-PR           PIC X(02)    VALUE '*'.
00097             05   TOTAL-WAGE-PR       PIC ZZZZ,ZZ9.99CR.
00098             05   ASTER2-PR           PIC X(02)    VALUE '*'.

00100        PROCEDURE DIVISION.
00101        ***  M A I N   L O G I C
00102        A000-MAIN-LOGIC SECTION.
00103            OPEN INPUT TIME-FILE.
00104                 OUTPUT REPORT-FILE.
00105            PERFORM H000-HEAD.
00106            READ TIME-FILE, AT END MOVE 'EOF' TO EOF-FLAG.
00107            MOVE EMPNO-IN TO PREV-EMP.
00108            PERFORM B000-PROC UNTIL END-FILE.
00109            PERFORM E000-FINAL.
00110            CLOSE TIME-FILE, REPORT-FILE.
00111            STOP RUN.
00112        A199-END. EXIT.
```

FIGURE 11-7   (Cont.)

```
00114          *** E M P L O Y E E   P R O C E S S I N G
00115       B000-PROC SECTION.
00116          IF EMPNO-IN > PREV-EMP PERFORM D000-HIGH-EMP.
00117          IF LINE-CTR > 25 PERFORM H000-HEAD.
00118          IF EMPNO-IN < PREV-EMP
00119             MOVE 'OUT OF SEQUENCE' TO ERR-MESS-PR
00120          ELSE
00121             MOVE HOURS-IN TO HOURS
00122             MOVE ' ' TO SEARCH-FLAG
00123             PERFORM C000-SEARCH VARYING NDX FROM 1 BY 1
00124                UNTIL END-SEARCH
00125             MOVE WAGE TO WAGE-PR
00126             MOVE HOURS TO HOURS-PR
00127             MOVE RATE TO RATE-PR.
00128          MOVE JOB-IN   TO JOB-PR.
00129          IF EMPNO-IN NOT = PREV-EMP OR LINE-CTR = 5
00130             MOVE NAME-IN TO NAME-PR
00131             MOVE EMPNO-IN TO EMPNO-PR.
00132          MOVE DETAIL-LINE TO PRINT-RECORD.
00133          PERFORM  P000-PRINT.
00134          MOVE SPACES TO DETAIL-LINE.
00135          MOVE 1 TO PRINT-CTL.
00136          ADD HOURS TO EMPLOYEE-HOURS.
00137          ADD WAGE  TO EMPLOYEE-WAGE.
00138          MOVE EMPNO-IN TO PREV-EMP.
00139          READ TIME-FILE, AT END MOVE 'EOF' TO EOF-FLAG.
00140       B999-RETURN. EXIT.

00142          *** T A B L E   S E A R C H   &   C A L C   W A G E
00143       C000-SEARCH SECTION.
00144          IF JOB-IN = JOBNO-TAB (NDX)
00145             MOVE 'END' TO SEARCH-FLAG
00146             MOVE RATE-TAB (NDX) TO RATE
00147             COMPUTE WAGE ROUNDED = HOURS * RATE
00148          ELSE IF JOB-IN < JOBNO-TAB (NDX)
00149             MOVE 'END' TO SEARCH-FLAG
00150             MOVE 'JOB NO. NOT IN TABLE' TO ERR-MESS-PR
00151             MOVE ZEROS TO HOURS, RATE, WAGE.
00152       C999-RETURN. EXIT.

00154          *** E M P L O Y E E   T O T A L S
00155       D000-HIGH-EMP SECTION.
00156          MOVE EMPLOYEE-HOURS TO TOTAL-HOURS-PR.
00157          MOVE EMPLOYEE-WAGE  TO TOTAL-WAGE-PR.
00158          MOVE TOTAL-LINE TO PRINT-RECORD.
00159          PERFORM P000-PRINT.
00160          MOVE 2 TO PRINT-CTL.
00161          ADD EMPLOYEE-HOURS TO TOTAL-HOURS.
00162          ADD EMPLOYEE-WAGE  TO TOTAL-WAGE.
00163          MOVE 0 TO EMPLOYEE-HOURS, EMPLOYEE-WAGE.
00164       D999-RETURN. EXIT.

00166          *** F I N A L   T O T A L S
00167       E000-FINAL SECTION.
00168          PERFORM D000-HIGH-EMP.
00169          MOVE TOTAL-WAGE  TO TOTAL-WAGE-PR.
00170          MOVE TOTAL-HOURS TO TOTAL-HOURS-PR.
00171          MOVE '**' TO ASTER1-PR, ASTER2-PR.
00172          MOVE TOTAL-LINE TO PRINT-RECORD.
00173          MOVE 2 TO PRINT-CTL.
00174          PERFORM P000-PRINT.
00175       E999-RETURN. EXIT.
```

FIGURE 11-7   (Cont.)

213

```
00177            *** P A G E   H E A D I N G
00178            H000-HEAD SECTION.
00179                MOVE PAGE-CTR TO PAGE-PR.
00180                MOVE HEADING-1 TO PRINT-RECORD.
00181                WRITE PRINT-RECORD AFTER ADVANCING TOP-PAGE.
00182                MOVE HEADING-2 TO PRINT-RECORD.
00183                MOVE 2 TO PRINT-CTL.
00184                PERFORM P000-PRINT.
00185                MOVE 5 TO LINE-CTR.
00186                ADD 1 TO PAGE-CTR.
00187            H999-RETURN. EXIT.

00189            *** C O M M O N   P R I N T
00190            P000-PRINT SECTION.
00191                WRITE PRINT-RECORD AFTER ADVANCING PRINT-CTL LINES.
00192                ADD PRINT-CTL TO LINE-CTR.
00193            P999-RETURN. EXIT.
```

Printed report:

W E E K L Y   W A G E   R E P O R T   PAGE   1

EMPLOYEE	NAME	JOB	RATE	HOURS	WAGE	
11111	ANDERSON	04	7.45	10.5	78.23	
		01	7.25	21.5	155.88	
		01	7.25	31.5	228.39	
		01	7.25	10.5	76.13	
		04	7.45	10.5	78.23	
				84.5 *	616.85	*
22222	BROWN	02	6.15	40.0	246.00	
		02	6.15	50.0	307.50	
				90.0 *	553.50	*
22233	CARPENTER	01	7.25	99.9	724.28	
		04	7.45	1.0-	7.45CR	
		02	6.15	25.0	153.75	
				123.9 *	870.58	*
22235	DIXON	02	6.15	40.0	246.00	
				40.0 *	246.00	*
22240	EMMETT	01	7.25	15.0	108.75	
		01	7.25	15.0	108.75	
		04	7.45	5.0	37.25	
				35.0 *	254.75	*
22301	FLANDERS	01	7.25	25.5	184.88	
		01	7.25	25.5	184.88	
		03	0.00	0.0	0.00	JOB NO. NOT IN TABLE
		01	7.25	5.0	36.25	
				56.0 *	406.01	*
22355	GAROWSKI	04	7.45	1.5	11.18	
		04	7.45	1.5	11.18	
		04	7.45	1.5	11.18	
				4.5 *	33.54	*
22360	HENDERSON	02	6.15	8.0	49.20	
		02	6.15	8.0	49.20	
		02	6.15	8.0	49.20	
		02	6.15	8.0	49.20	
		02	6.15	8.0	49.20	
				40.0 *	246.00	*
				473.9 **	3,227.23	**

FIGURE 11-7 (Cont.)

wage. The program prints each input record, employee hours and wage totals, and final totals. For records that contain an error (invalid record code, invalid sequence, or invalid job number), the program prints an error message, omits calculation of wage, and continues processing with the next input record.

RELATED TABLES

Related arguments and functions may be defined in separate tables. In Figure 11-8, there are tables for both job number and rate-of-pay, each with its own unique index. (If the table lookup used a subscript, it could reference both tables.) For brevity, the table VALUE entries and their usual REDEFINES clauses are not coded.

```
01   JOB-TABLE.
     03   JOB-ENTRY            OCCURS 8 TIMES
                               INDEXED BY JOB-NDX
                               PIC 99.
01   RATE-TABLE.
     03   RATE-ENTRY           OCCURS 8 TIMES
                               INDEXED BY RATE-NDX
                               PIC 99V99.
            .
            .
            .
     SET JOB-NDX, RATE-NDX TO 1.
     SEARCH JOB-ENTRY VARYING RATE-NDX
          AT END PERFORM R000-ERROR
          WHEN JOB-IN = JOB-ENTRY (JOB-NDX)
               MOVE RATE-ENTRY (RATE-NDX) TO RATE.
```

FIGURE 11-8   Separately Defined Tables.

In Figure 11-8, the SEARCH routine automatically calculates the index JOB-NDX for the specified job table. In the SEARCH statement, the VARYING RATE-NDX also calculates the rate table index.

TWO- AND THREE-DIMENSIONAL TABLES

Tables up to now have been one dimensional—a single subscript or index references an entry. COBOL provides for tables of two and three dimensions. Consider an example of a two-dimensional table based on job numbers and rates-of-pay. This time there are three pay categories: day shift, night shift, and weekends. The pay rate varies not only by job number but also by category *within* job number:

JOB NO.	DAY RATE	NIGHT RATE	WEEKEND RATE
01	7.25	8.30	8.15
02	6.15	7.05	6.95
04	7.45	8.50	8.25
05	8.55	9.75	9.50
06	7.50	8.65	8.45
08	9.25	10.50	10.25
10	8.95	10.00	9.75

The table consists of seven jobs and three rates per job, or 21 entries. A reference to job 01, day shift is (1,1); to job 01, weekend is (1,3); to job 06, night shift is (5,2). Thus, the subscript/index consists of two parts: the first value indicates the *row* (in this case, job number), and the second value indicates the *column* (category).

Figure 11-9 illustrates the job table with the values for each rate category immediately following its related job number. In this example, two indexes are defined in the REDEFINES statement: JOB-NDX to reference the row (the job number), and RATE-NDX to reference the column (the job rate). These rates also require their own OCCURS clause. This table lookup example could also be coded using the PERFORM VARYING statement.

```
01   JOB-TABLE.
     05   FILLER           PIC X(14)    VALUE '010725083C0815'.
     05   FILLER           PIC X(14)    VALUE '0206150705C695'.
     05   FILLER           PIC X(14)    VALUE 'C4C745085CC825'.
     05   FILLER           PIC X(14)    VALUE '050855C975C950'.
     05   FILLER           PIC X(14)    VALUE 'C6C75CC865C845'.
     05   FILLER           PIC X(14)    VALUE '08C925105C1C25'.
     05   FILLER           PIC X(14)    VALUE '1CC89510CC0975'.
     05   FILLER           PIC X(14)    VALUE '99CCCCCCCCCCCC'.

01   JOB-TABLE-DEF         REDEFINES JCB-TABLE.
     03   TABLE-ENTRIES    CCCURS 8 TIMES INDEXED BY JOB-NDX.
          05   JOBNO-TAB   PIC 99.
          05   RATE-TAB    OCCURS 3 TIMES INDEXED BY RATE-NDX.
               1C   PAY-RATES PIC 99V99.
                         .
                         .
                         .
     IF CATEGORY-IN = 2 OR 3
          SET RATE-NDX TO CATEGORY-IN
     ELSE
          SET RATE-NDX TO 1.
     MOVE HOURS-IN TO HOURS.
     SET JOB-NDX TO 1.
     SEARCH TABLE-ENTRIES
          AT END
               MOVE 'JOB NO. NOT IN TABLE' TO ERR-MESS-PR
               MOVE ZEROS TO HOURS, RATE, WAGE
          WHEN JOB-IN = JOBNC-TAB (JOB-NDX)
               MOVE PAY-RATES (JOB-NDX, RATE-NDX) TO RATE
               COMPUTE WAGE ROUNDED = HOURS * RATE
               MOVE WAGE    TO WAGE-PR
               MOVE HOURS   TO HOURS-PR
               MOVE RATE    TC RATE-PR.
```

FIGURE 11-9   Searching a Two-dimensional Table.

To clear a two-dimensional table, assume a simple two-dimensional table defined for districts (rows 1–10) and months (columns 1–12):

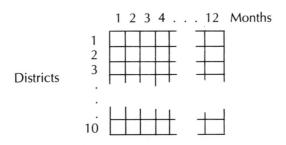

Assume also that the table, named SALES-TABLE, is intended to accumulate sales by district for 12 months. As defined in Figure 11-10, SALES-TABLE contains undefined data (uninitialized). In order to add sales amounts to the table, the entries must first be cleared. This program has one new feature: the AFTER clause. VARYING provides for the row subscript (SUB-DIS), and AFTER provides for the column subscript (SUB-MON). PERFORM processes the AFTER clause first and initializes both subscripts to 1. Then, the AFTER clause is processed 12 times, clearing all 12 month entries for district 1; SUB-DIS is incremented to 2, SUB-MON is reset to 1, and AFTER is processed 12 times for district 2. The PERFORM continues until all 12 months for each district are cleared successively. The PERFORM terminates when SUB-DIS exceeds 10.

Assume an input record with fields district (DISTR-IN), month (MONTH-IN), and amount sold (SALES-AMT). The instructions to add the amount sold in the previously defined table in Figure 11-10 are as follows:

```
MOVE DISTR-IN TO SUB-DIS.
MOVE MONTH-IN TO SUB-MON.
ADD SALES-AMT TO SALES-MONTH (SUB-DIS, SUB-MON).
```

The program should also ensure that both district and month contain valid values.

RULES FOR SUBSCRIPTING AND INDEXING

1. A table may contain one, two, or three dimensions.

2. Any reference to a table must specify one subscript or one index for each dimension.

3. On some compilers, subscripts and indexes may not be used in the same reference, as in TABLE (SUBSCR, INDX-1).

4. Commas are required between subscripts or indexes, as in (SUB-1, SUB-2) or (INDEX-1, INDEX-2, INDEX-3).

```
DATA DIVISION.
WORKING-STORAGE SECTION.
01  SUBSCRIPTS              COMP SYNC.
       05  SUB-DIS          PIC S9(4).
       05  SUB-MON          PIC S9(4).
01  SALES-TABLE.
       05  DIST-TAB         OCCURS 10 TIMES.
          10  MON-SALES-TAB OCCURS 12 TIMES
                            PIC S9(7)V99 COMP-3.
PROCEDURE DIVISION.
    PERFORM M100-CLEAR
         VARYING SUB-DIS FROM 1 BY 1 UNTIL SUB-DIS > 10
         AFTER   SUB-MON FROM 1 BY 1 UNTIL SUB-MON > 12.
    STOP RUN.

M100-CLEAR SECTION.
    MOVE ZEROS TO MON-SALES-TAB (SUB-DIS, SUB-MON).
M199-RETURN. EXIT.
```

FIGURE 11-10   Clearing a Two-dimensional Table.

5. Some compilers require precise coding of the subscript/index with no blank after the left parenthesis, a blank after the comma, and no blank before the right parenthesis.

DEBUGGING TIPS

1. *Table Definition.* Code the VALUE clauses and OCCURS clauses very carefully. If a program uses table entries as accumulators, be sure to initialize the entries to zeros. End a table with 9s or HIGH-VALUES to terminate a search.

2. *Subscripts.* Use subscripts rather than indexes because although you must define subscripts, they have fewer restrictions than indexes, and in the long run subscripts may cause less trouble. For efficiency, define subscripts as PIC 9(4), or on IBM as PIC S9(4), along with the COMP and SYNC attributes. Be sure to give subscripts descriptive names and to use them only for specific purposes. A subscript reference outside the table bounds causes an unpredictable error.

3. *Indexes.* Initialize or increment an index only with SET or PERFORM. Normally, use SET to initialize the index with the value 1. When you assign an index to a table, use it for that table only. An index reference outside the table bounds causes an execution error.

4. If PERFORM executes UNTIL some condition name is fulfilled, be sure to clear the condition name immediately before the PERFORM.

5. *Efficiency.* Subscripting and indexing generate a large amount of machine code. Therefore, if a table function is to be referenced more than once, it is more efficient to move the function from the table into an unsubscripted work

field for further processing. This practice is especially useful for two- or three-dimensional tables.

PROBLEMS

11–1. Define a sales table for twelve months. Each month's sales can total up to $150,000.00. Initialize the entries to zero.

11–2. Under what circumstance would arguments in a table not be in ascending sequence for a table lookup?

11–3. For table searches, there are two basic types of tables. What are these types and how do they differ?

11–4. What are three ways to ensure that a table lookup will terminate?

11–5. What is a subscript? How is it defined?

11–6. What is an index? How is it defined?

11–7. Distinguish between the role of a subscript and the role of an index.

11–8. For the following PERFORM statements, determine the number of iterations and the final value of SAM:

(a) PERFORM P250 VARYING SAM FROM 1 BY 1 UNTIL SAM > 25.

(b) PERFORM P350 VARYING SAM FROM −5 BY 2 UNTIL SAM > 5.

(c) PERFORM P450 VARYING SAM FROM 8 BY −2 UNTIL SAM < −10.

11–9. Define the following table for quantities sold and discount rates. A quantity up to 10 has no discount, from 11 to 25, a discount of 2% (.02), and so on.

QUANTITY	DISCOUNT RATE
10	.000
25	.020
100	.025
250	.040
500	.080
1000	.105

11–10. Using the discount table in Problem 11-9, code a routine that calculates discounts based on quantity-sold (QUANT-SOLD) and amount of sale (AMT-SALE). The routine uses QUANT-SOLD to search through the table for low or equal quantity and uses the discount rate to calculate amount of discount as follows:

amount of discount (rounded) = amount of sale × discount rate

(a) Use PERFORM VARYING with a subscript.

(b) Use SEARCH with an index.

11–11. Code the following program that calculates customers' bills based on their electric consumption. Records are in sequence of customer number within Area code.

Col.

1–2	Record code (42)
3–4	Area code
5–8	Customer number
9–28	Name

Col.

29–30	Estimate value
31–35	Previous meter reading
36–40	Present reading
41–80	Unused

There is one record per customer. For each record, calculate kilowatt-hours (KWH) electric consumption:

consumption = present reading − previous reading

EXAMPLES	PRESENT READING	PREVIOUS READING	CONSUMPTION
1.	02050	00800	1,250+
2.	00120	99450	99,330−

In the second example, assume that the meter has "turned over" like a car mileage meter at 99999. The program can correct the consumption by adding 100,000, as

$$-99,330 + 100,000 = 670 \text{ KWH}$$

If the *previous* reading is blank, assume that the customer is new, with a zero reading value. If the *present* reading is blank, the meter was not read for some reason (such as rabid dog); the program is to *estimate* the present reading. The "estimate value" in the record indicates the customers' approximate monthly consumption. The estimate is in hundreds of KWHs, so that a value of 08 means 0800 KWHs; if the customer's previous reading was 03024, then the estimated present reading is 03824. On the print line, show "EST" beside the present reading.

Use the calculated consumption (actual or estimated) to locate the correct rate in the rate table below. You will need a "stopper" of nines at the end of the table for consumptions over 1350. Note that all calculated consumptions are valid.

Using the consumption, locate the rate in the table. Multiply consumption by rate and add the correction factor. Provide test data to check the various features: meter turnover, blank previous reading, blank present reading, and various consumptions. Print total amount billed by Area and final total as well as the complete detail line for each customer.

CONSUMPTION	RATE	CORRECTION FACTOR
Up to 150 KWH	0.000	$ 7.50
151–250	0.050	0.00
251–400	0.044	1.50
401–650	0.040	3.10
651–1000	0.030	9.60
1001–1350	0.024	15.60
over 1350	0.020	21.00

CHAPTER 12

TABLE PROCESSING—II

OBJECTIVE: *To present advanced programming features using tables.*

INTRODUCTION

Chapter 11 introduced tables and sequential table lookup. This chapter introduces more advanced but common techniques involving tables:

- Loading of entries into a table from external storage.
- Sorting of random table entries into ascending sequence.
- Binary search, for efficient searches of large tables.

Also covered are a number of other useful programming techniques.

LOADING TABLES

There are two common ways to provide table entry values. The first and simplest way, as in Chapter 11, is to define and compile table entries into a final machine language program. A second method is to maintain the table entries on an external file, such as punched cards or disk; a program defines a table with no initialized values, and during execution, reads the table entries from the external file into the table area. Both defining values and loading values into a table provide the same effect, but have different advantages:

1. Defining table contents. Simple to program but a program must be recompiled to change, add, or delete a table entry. This approach is useful if table entries seldom change.
2. Loading table contents. More complex to program but versatile because a program does not have to be recompiled to change, add, or delete a table entry, and the table is available to all other programs in the system.

Card and Disk Table Entries

Each table card contains one or more entries, but storing only one entry per card facilitates entry deletion and insertion. Typically, a table card deck immediately precedes the regular input data in this sequence: date card, table cards, data cards (three record types comprising one file). For identification, card formats should contain unique record codes, all in the same positions. Often, the last table card contains a high value such as all 9s in the table entry field.

For table entries stored on a disk file, a program must define a disk table as a unique file, OPEN the file, READ and store each record, and CLOSE the file on end-of-file. Although the table is a separate file, storing of the disk table entries is similar to card processing.

Table Sequence

If table entries are to be in ascending sequence (such as by job number), a program should check the sequence before storing each entry in a table. If the table lookup expects the entries to be sequential, an out-of-sequence entry is a serious error. Some programs, however, accept table entries in random sequence. In this case, there are two possibilities:

1. The most commonly referenced entries are placed at the start of the table so that the processing is efficient. A useful practice to check the activity is to keep a count for each table entry.
2. The program will sort the random entries into ascending sequence.

Table Loading

For a table on cards, a program must ensure that it does not treat the data cards following as table entries. The program can check the record codes or test for a high value in the last table card (assuming such a record will always be present). For disk tables, an attempt to READ the end-of-file causes a program to execute the AT END statement for the disk table file. If a table is sequential, a program should insert a high value following the last stored entry to ensure that table lookup operations have a stopper to indicate that the program has completed the load routine and should now process the regular data records.

Table Overloading

When a program reads and stores table entries, it increments the subscript/index for each entry stored. However, a serious error, known as *table overloading,* can occur: the number of entries may exceed the number of spaces that the program has reserved, and the program attempts to store an entry past the upper boundary of the table. If this error occurs for an index (e.g. OCCURS 100 TIMES and the index is incremented to 101), the program "bombs" automatically. If it occurs for a subscript, the program will continue storing entries in the section of the program following the table with unpredictable results.

To prevent table overloading, a program should define a reserved area large enough to allow for any expected expansion. A program should also count the table entries, and when a specified capacity is reached, print an error message and cancel the job. Perhaps the program could warn when the capacity has been almost reached and print a warning message so that the table can be revised before the need to cancel ever occurs.

Variable Length Tables

If the table is defined extra long, the program will require additional unused storage space. COBOL provides an option in the OCCURS clause for variable length tables and a DEPENDING ON clause to indicate where the table length is stored. Figure 12-1 depicts a variable length table. The OCCURS clause provides for a minimum of 1 entry and a maximum of 51 entries. If the program loads 20 pairs of entries, then the actual table size will be only 20 entries. Under ANS, the minimum is 1 entry, although IBM 370 allows zero entries. Nevertheless, any specified maximum number of entries must be greater than the specified minimum number of entries. The DEPENDING ON clause tells the compiler the location of a variable in Working-Storage containing the actual number of entries, called NO-OF-ENTRIES in Figure 12-1. For each pair of entries stored in the table, the program must add 1 to NO-OF-ENTRIES. Since the compiler generates code to reference NO-OF-ENTRIES during program execution, NO-OF-ENTRIES should not be changed by any other statement.

```
01   JOB-TABLE.
     03   TABLE-ENTRIES      OCCURS 1 TO 51 TIMES
                             DEPENDING ON NO-OF-ENTRIES.
          05   JOBNO-TAB     PIC 99.
          05   RATE-TAB      PIC S999V99 COMP-3.
```

FIGURE 12-1   Variable Length Table.

The general format for the OCCURS with a DEPENDING ON clause is as follows:

```
OCCURS integer-1 TO integer-2 TIMES [DEPENDING ON data-name-1]

    ⎧ ASCENDING  ⎫
[   ⎨           ⎬  KEY IS data-name-2 [data-name-3] ... ] ...
    ⎩ DESCENDING ⎭

    [INDEXED BY index-name-1 [index-name-2] ... ]
```

Summary

Table loading is a useful technique, but requires careful coding:

- Test for a valid record code for a table on cards.
- Check sequence, if necessary.
- Place a test before storing an entry in a table to prevent table overflow.
- Use a variable length table when the defined table length is considerably larger than the actual number of entries.

PROGRAM EXAMPLE

Figure 12-2 is a revision of the program in Figure 11-7 with these differences: The File Section now provides for two types of input records—table cards first, then time cards; JOB-TABLE defines a variable number of entries in the OCCURS and DEPENDING ON clauses instead of having VALUE or REDEFINES clauses.

Two other new features in the program in Figure 12-2 are covered later in this chapter: First, the program does not sequence-check the table entries because, after loading, the routine S000-SORT sorts the entries into ascending sequence. Second, instead of a sequential table lookup, the routine C000-SEARCH performs a binary search. Also, to simplify the program and to highlight the new features, some routines (such as page overflow and total levels) have been eliminated.

```
00001          IDENTIFICATION DIVISION.
00002          PROGRAM-ID. CHAP12A.
00003          REMARKS.  PROGRAM LOADS JOB TABLE, SORTS ENTRIES, &
00004                    PERFORMS BINARY SEARCH.

00006          ENVIRONMENT DIVISION.
00007          CONFIGURATION SECTION.
00008          SPECIAL-NAMES.
00009              C01 IS TOP-PAGE.
00010          INPUT-OUTPUT SECTION.
00011          FILE-CONTROL.
00012              SELECT INPUT-FILE    ASSIGN TO SYS015-UR-2501-S.
00013              SELECT REPORT-FILE   ASSIGN TO SYS014-UR-1403-S.

00015          DATA DIVISION.
00016          FILE SECTION.
00017          FD   INPUT-FILE
00018              LABEL RECORDS ARE OMITTED,
00019              DATA RECORD IS TIME-RECORD, TABLE-RECORD.
00020          01   TIME-RECORD.
00021              05   TIME-CODE-IN    PIC XX.
00022              05   EMPNO-IN        PIC X(5).
00023              05   NAME-IN         PIC X(15).
00024              05   JOB-IN          PIC 99.
00025              05   HOURS-IN        PIC S99V9.
00026              05   FILLER          PIC X(53).
00027          01   TABLE-RECORD.
00028              05   TABLE-CODE-IN   PIC XX.
00029                  88   TABLE-RECORD-CODE      VALUE '01'.
00030              05   JOB-TAB-IN      PIC 99.
00031              05   RATE-TAB-IN     PIC S99V99.
00032              05   FILLER          PIC X(72).

00034          FD   REPORT-FILE
00035              LABEL RECORDS ARE OMITTED
00036              DATA RECORD IS PRINT-RECORD.
00037          01   PRINT-RECORD        PIC X(133).

00039          WORKING-STORAGE SECTION.
00040          01   DISPLAY-ITEMS       DISPLAY.
00041              03   JOB-SAVE        PIC 99.
00042              03   EOF-FLAG        PIC X(3)    VALUE ' '.
00043                  88   END-DATA                VALUE 'END'.
00044              03   TABLE-FLAG      PIC X(4)    VALUE ' '.
00045                  88   TABLE-LOADED            VALUE 'LOAD'.
00046                  88   TABLE-FULL              VALUE 'FULL'.
00047                  88   TABLE-SORTED            VALUE 'END'.
00048              03   SEARCH-FLAG     PIC X(7)    VALUE ' '.
00049                  88   END-SEARCH              VALUE 'FOUND', 'INVALID'.
00050                  88   JOB-FOUND               VALUE 'FOUND'.

00052          01   ARITHMETIC-ITEMS    COMP-3.
00053              03   HOURS           PIC S99V9.
00054              03   RATE            PIC S999V99.
00055              03   WAGE            PIC S9(5)V99.
00056              03   PRINT-CTL       PIC S9          VALUE +1.

00058          01   BINARY-ITEMS        COMP SYNC.
00059              05   NO-OF-ENTRIES   PIC S9(4)   VALUE +1.
00060              05   SUB             PIC S9(4)   VALUE +1.
00061              05   SUBPLUS         PIC S9(4).
00062              05   HI              PIC S9(4).
00063              05   LO              PIC S9(4).
00064              05   MID             PIC S9(4).
00065              05   PREV-MID        PIC S9(4).
```

FIGURE 12-2   Table Loading.

226

```
00067        01   JOB-TABLE.
00068             03  TABLE-ENTRIES      OCCURS 1 TO 51 TIMES
00069                                    DEPENDING ON NO-OF-ENTRIES.
00070                05  JOBNO-TAB        PIC 99.
00071                05  RATE-TAB         PIC S999V99 COMP-3.


00073        01   HEADING-2.
00074             05  FILLER         PIC X(12)    VALUE ' '.
00075             05  FILLER         PIC X(26)    VALUE 'EMPLOYEE    NAME'.
00076             05  FILLER         PIC X(27)    VALUE 'JOB   RATE    HOURS'.
00077             05  FILLER         PIC X(04)    VALUE 'WAGE'.


00079        01   DETAIL-LINE.
00080             05  FILLER         PIC X(14)    VALUE ' '.
00081             05  EMPNO-PR       PIC X(08).
00082             05  NAME-PR        PIC X(17).
00083             05  JOB-PR         PIC X(02).
00084             05  RATE-PR        PIC ZZZ9.99.
00085             05  FILLER         PIC X(03)    VALUE ' '.
00086             05  HOURS-PR       PIC Z9.9-.
00087             05  FILLER         PIC X(04)    VALUE ' '.
00088             05  WAGE-PR        PIC ZZ,ZZ9.99CR.
00089             05  ERR-MESS-PR    PIC X(20)    VALUE ' '.


00092        PROCEDURE DIVISION.
00093        ***  M A I N   L O G I C
00094        A000-MAIN-LOGIC SECTION.
00095             OPEN INPUT INPUT-FILE, OUTPUT REPORT-FILE.
00096             PERFORM H000-HEAD.
00097             READ INPUT-FILE, AT END MOVE 'END' TO EOF-FLAG.
00098             PERFORM L000-LOAD-TABLE UNTIL TABLE-LOADED
00099                 OR   TABLE-FULL OR END-DATA.
00100             PERFORM S000-SORT-TABLE UNTIL TABLE-SORTED.
00101             PERFORM B000-PROC UNTIL END-DATA OR TABLE-FULL.
00102             CLOSE INPUT-FILE, REPORT-FILE.
00103             STOP RUN.
00104        A199-END. EXIT.

00106        ***  E M P L O Y E E   P R O C E S S I N G
00107        B000-PROC SECTION.
00108             MOVE HOURS-IN TO HOURS.
00109             COMPUTE HI = NO-OF-ENTRIES + 1.
00110             MOVE 1    TO LO.
00111             MOVE 0    TO PREV-MID.
00112             MOVE ' ' TO SEARCH-FLAG.
00113             PERFORM C000-SEARCH UNTIL END-SEARCH.
00114             IF JOB-FOUND
00115                 COMPUTE WAGE ROUNDED = HOURS * RATE
00116                 MOVE WAGE TO WAGE-PR
00117                 MOVE HOURS TO HOURS-PR
00118                 MOVE RATE TO RATE-PR.
00119             MOVE JOB-IN    TO JOB-PR.
00120             MOVE NAME-IN TO NAME-PR.
00121             MOVE EMPNO-IN TO EMPNO-PR.
00122             MOVE DETAIL-LINE TO PRINT-RECORD.
00123             WRITE PRINT-RECORD AFTER ADVANCING PRINT-CTL LINES.
00124             MOVE SPACES TO DETAIL-LINE.
00125             MOVE 1 TO PRINT-CTL.
00126             READ INPUT-FILE, AT END MOVE 'END' TO EOF-FLAG.
00127        B999-RETURN. EXIT.
```

FIGURE 12-2   (Cont.)

227

```
00129              ***  T A B L E   S E A R C H
00130              C000-SEARCH SECTION.
00131                  COMPUTE MID = (LO + HI) / 2.
00132                  IF MID = PREV-MID
00133                      MOVE 'JOB NO. NOT IN TABLE' TO ERR-MESS-PR
00134                      MOVE 'INVALID' TO SEARCH-FLAG
00135                      MOVE ZEROS TO HOURS, RATE, WAGE
00136                      GO TO C999-RETURN.
00137                  MOVE MID TO PREV-MID.
00138                  IF JOB-IN < JOBNO-TAB (MID)
00139                      MOVE MID TO HI
00140                  ELSE
00141                  IF JOB-IN > JOBNO-TAB (MID)
00142                      MOVE MID TO LO
00143                  ELSE
00144                      MOVE RATE-TAB (MID) TO RATE.
00145                      MOVE 'FOUND' TO SEARCH-FLAG.
00146              C999-RETURN. EXIT.

00148              ***  P A G E   H E A D I N G
00149              H000-HEAD SECTION.
00150                  MOVE HEADING-2 TO PRINT-RECORD.
00151                  WRITE PRINT-RECORD AFTER ADVANCING TOP-PAGE.
00152                  MOVE 2 TO PRINT-CTL.
00153              H999-RETURN. EXIT.

00155              ***  T A B L E   L O A D I N G
00156              L000-LOAD-TABLE SECTION.
00157                  IF NOT TABLE-RECORD-CODE
00158                      MOVE 'LOAD' TO TABLE-FLAG
00159                      MOVE 99 TO JOBNO-TAB (SUB)
00160                      GO TO L999-RETURN.
00161                  IF SUB > 50
00162                      DISPLAY 'TOO MANY TABLE ENTRIES'
00163                      MOVE 'FULL' TO TABLE-FLAG
00164                      GO TO L999-RETURN.
00165                  MOVE JOB-TAB-IN TO JOBNO-TAB (SUB).
00166                  MOVE RATE-TAB-IN TO RATE-TAB (SUB).
00167                  ADD 1 TO SUB.
00168                  MOVE SUB TO NO-OF-ENTRIES.
00169                  READ INPUT-FILE, AT END MOVE 'END' TO EOF-FLAG.
00170              L999-RETURN. EXIT.

00172              ***  T A B L E   S O R T I N G
00173              S000-SORT-TABLE SECTION.
00174                  MOVE 'END' TO TABLE-FLAG.
00175                  PERFORM S400-SWAP VARYING SUB FROM 1 BY 1
00176                                    UNTIL SUB =  NO-OF-ENTRIES.
00177              S099-RETURN. EXIT.

00179              S400-SWAP SECTION.
00180                  COMPUTE SUBPLUS = SUB + 1.
00181                  IF JOBNO-TAB (SUB) > JOBNO-TAB (SUBPLUS)
00182                      MOVE JOBNO-TAB (SUB) TO JOB-SAVE
00183                      MOVE RATE-TAB (SUB) TO RATE
00184                      MOVE JOBNO-TAB (SUBPLUS) TO JOBNO-TAB (SUB)
00185                      MOVE RATE-TAB (SUBPLUS) TO RATE-TAB  (SUB)
00186                      MOVE JOB-SAVE TO JOBNO-TAB (SUBPLUS)
00187                      MOVE RATE    TO RATE-TAB  (SUBPLUS)
00188                      MOVE ' ' TO TABLE-FLAG.
00189              S499-RETURN. EXIT.
```

FIGURE 12-2   (Cont.)

228

Input Data:

```
01110895
01080925                          Table
01060750                          rate
01050855                          records
01040745
01020615
01010725
01990000
0411111ANDERSON        04105
0411111ANDERSON        01215
0411111ANDERSON        01315
0411111ANDERSON        01105
0411111ANDERSON        04105
0422222BROWN           02400
0422222BROWN           02500
0422233CARPENTER       01999    Employee
0422233CARPENTER       04010̄    time
0422233CARPENTER       02250    records
0422235DIXON           02400
0422240EMMETT          01150
0422240EMMETT          01150
0422240EMMETT          04050
0422301FLANDERS        01255
0422301FLANDERS        01255
0422301FLANDERS        03255
0422301FLANDERS        01050
0422355GAROWSKI        04015
0422355GAROWSKI        04015
0422355GAROWSKI        04015
0422360HENDERSON       02080
0422360HENDERSON       02080
0422360HENDERSON       02080
0422360HENDERSON       02080
0422360HENDERSON       02080
```

Printed Report:

EMPLOYEE	NAME	JOB	RATE	HOURS	WAGE	
11111	ANDERSON	04	7.45	10.5	78.23	
11111	ANDERSON	01	7.25	21.5	155.88	
11111	ANDERSON	01	7.25	31.5	228.38	
11111	ANDERSON	01	7.25	10.5	76.13	
11111	ANDERSON	04	7.45	10.5	78.23	
22222	BROWN	02	6.15	40.0	246.00	
22222	BROWN	02	6.15	50.0	307.50	
22233	CARPENTER	01	7.25	99.9	724.28	
22233	CARPENTER	04	7.45	1.0-	7.45CR	
22233	CARPENTER	02	6.15	25.0	153.75	
22235	DIXON	02	6.15	40.0	246.00	
22240	EMMETT	01	7.25	15.0	108.75	
22240	EMMETT	01	7.25	15.0	108.75	
22240	EMMETT	04	7.45	5.0	37.25	
22301	FLANDERS	01	7.25	25.5	184.88	
22301	FLANDERS	01	7.25	25.5	184.88	
22301	FLANDERS	03				JOB NO. NOT IN TABLE
22301	FLANDERS	01	7.25	5.0	36.25	
22355	GAROWSKI	04	7.45	1.5	11.18	
22355	GAROWSKI	04	7.45	1.5	11.18	
22355	GAROWSKI	04	7.45	1.5	11.18	
22360	HENDERSON	02	6.15	8.0	49.20	
22360	HENDERSON	02	6.15	8.0	49.20	
22360	HENDERSON	02	6.15	8.0	49.20	
22360	HENDERSON	02	6.15	8.0	49.20	
22360	HENDERSON	02	6.15	8.0	49.20	

FIGURE 12-2 (Cont.)

229

SORTING TABLE ENTRIES

Sometimes table entries are in a random sequence that is not suitable for subsequent processing. The program may have loaded the table from some external source, such as cards or disk, in a random sequence, or in a sequence that was suitable for another program. Therefore, a program must sort the table entries into some required sequence. Unlike manufacturer supplied tape and disk storage sort programs, sorting table entries into a predetermined sequence is relatively simple. The technique involves successive comparisons and interchange of entries. For example, the following table lists scores made by candidates on a college entrance test. The maximum score is 150.

ENTRY NUMBER	SCORE
1	120
2	135
3	087
4	106
5	095
6	142
7	116

The basic program steps to sort these scores into ascending sequence are as follows:

1.   Compare entry-1 in the table against entry-2 and exchange them if entry-1 is a higher value.

2.   Compare entry-2 against entry-3 and exchange them if entry-2 is higher.

3.   Continue in this fashion comparing entry-3 to entry-4, entry-4 to entry-5, entry-5 to entry-6, and entry-6 to entry-7.

4.   Repeat the preceding steps until no more exchanges are made.

Let's follow this procedure using the table of scores defined above. Compare entry-1 (score 120) with entry-2 (score 135); since 120 is lower, there is no exchange. Compare entry-2 (135) with entry-3 (087); since 135 is higher, exchange them in the table. Next compare entry-3 (now 135) with entry-4 (106) and exchange; compare entry-4 (now 135) with entry-5 (095) and exchange; compare entry-5 (now 135) with entry-6 (142) and do not exchange; and finally, compare entry-6 (142) with entry-7 (116) and exchange them. After one iteration, the table appears as follows:

ENTRY NUMBER	SCORE
1	120
2	087
3	106
4	095
5	135
6	116
7	142

Repeat the procedure exactly as before comparing entry-1 with entry-2, entry-2 to entry-3, and so forth until a complete pass through the table occurs with no exchanges (you can use a switch to check if an exchange was made). At this point, the table is fully sorted.

Figure 12-3 shows the flowchart for the sort routine and is suitable for a table containing any number of entries (little extra programming effort is required if a table contains functions as well as arguments).

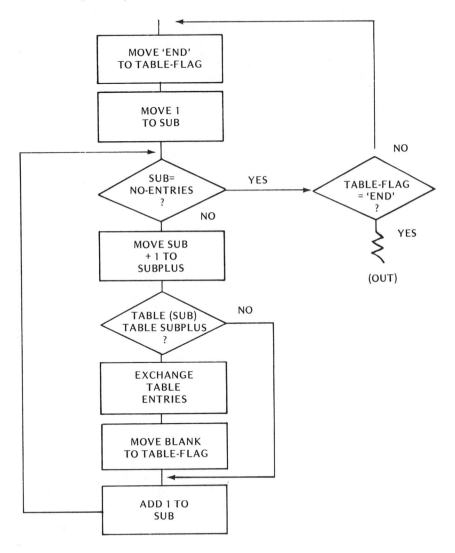

FIGURE 12-3   Flowchart for Sort Routine.

Sort Routine Example

The program in Figure 12-2 sorts a loaded table of job numbers and rates-of-pay into ascending sequence. The Section S000-SORT sets a TABLE-FLAG to 'END' and performs S400-SWAP. If S400-SWAP fails to swap any entries, the entries must all be in sequence, and the sort is completed. If S400-SWAP exchanges any entries, it sets TABLE-FLAG to blank, causing the sort routine to continue. The subscript SUB references the first entry and SUBPLUS references the following entry. For convenience, Figure 12-4 supplies the sort logic. Check the logic with some imaginary table entries, such as 10, 08, 06, 05, 04, 02, 01. Set TABLE-FLAG and increment the subscript just as the program does.

```
          ***   T A B L E   S O R T I N G
          S000-SORT-TABLE SECTION.
               MOVE 'END' TC TABLE-FLAG.
               PERFORM S400-SWAP VARYING SUB FROM 1 BY 1
                                    UNTIL SUB =  NO-OF-ENTRIES.
          S099-RETURN. EXIT.

          S400-SWAP SECTION.
               COMPUTE SUBPLUS = SUB + 1.
               IF JOBNC-TAB (SUB) > JOBNO-TAB (SUBPLUS)
                    MOVE JOBNO-TAB (SUB) TO JOB-SAVE
                    MOVE RATE-TAB   (SUB) TO RATE
                    MOVE JOBNC-TAB (SUBPLUS) TO JCBNC-TAB (SUB)
                    MOVE RATE-TAB  (SUBPLUS) TO RATE-TAB  (SUB)
                    MOVE JOB-SAVE TO JOBNC-TAB (SUBPLUS)
                    MOVE RATE     TO RATE-TAB  (SUBPLUS)
                    MOVE ' ' TO TABLE-FLAG.
          S499-RETURN. EXIT.
```

FIGURE 12-4   SORT Routine.

BINARY SEARCH

If you were to search for numbers in a large telephone directory starting with the first name on page one, you would soon abandon phoning. Instead, you open the book toward the center and flip the pages forward or backward as you close in on the required name. For large tables there is an equivalent programming method called *binary search*.

   If a table contains 100 entries, then a standard table lookup requires an average of 50 compares to find an entry. A binary search can reduce this number considerably. In this technique, the *middle* of a table is tested first to determine in which half is the required entry; the next step checks the midpoint of the half, and so forth, thereby quickly closing in on the required entry. As an illustration, assume a table of 20 job numbers and their associated rates-of-pay:

ENTRY	JOB	RATE	ENTRY	JOB	RATE	ENTRY	JOB	RATE	ENTRY	JOB	RATE
1	01	8.50	6	13	9.25	11	30	9.25	16	56	10.30
2	03	9.25	7	15	9.25	12	32	9.95	17	63	10.20
3	04	9.35	8	16	10.30	13	47	10.30	18	72	9.95
4	06	9.35	9	20	10.30	14	50	8.50	19	74	9.95
5	07	9.25	10	27	10.30	15	52	10.30	20	76	9.35

To locate the position of the middle entry, average the first position (start at zero for the search) and the last position (20):

$$\text{Midpoint} = (0 + 20) \div 2 = 10$$

Therefore, the search begins at the tenth entry, which contains job 27, and comparing the search argument to the value 27 would reveal the following:

- Equal—The required entry has been found.
- Lower—The required entry is in the lower half of the table.
- Higher—The required entry is in the upper half of the table.

If the input record contains job 47, then the first compare of 47 against 27 is high, and you immediately eliminate searching the lower half of the table. You now compute the midpoint of the upper half: $(10 + 20) \div 2 =$ entry 15, which contains job 52. A comparison of job 47 to 52 gives a low condition indicating that the required entry is in the third quarter of the table. The midpoint of the third quarter is $(10 + 15) \div 2 = 25 \div 2 = 12\frac{1}{2}$, rounded to 13. Because the job number of entry 13 is 47, the comparison reveals that the correct entry has been found. Therefore, the rate-of-pay for job 47 is $10.30 and was located with only three compares.

There are two ways to initialize the midpoint calculation:

1. $(0 +$ highest entry$) \div 2$, rounding this and all subsequent calculations.
2. $(1 +$ highest entry $+ 1) \div 2$, with no rounding of this or subsequent calculations. The preceding example could have used $(1 + 21) \div 2$.

Either rule, applied consistently, works for a table with any number of entries. Any deviation, such as by not rounding method 1, or by rounding method 2, will cause the search to miss the first or last entry in a table.

The formula to calculate each midpoint is as follows:

$$\text{MID} = (\text{LO} + \text{HI}) \div 2 \text{ (and round)}$$

where LO is the low entry position and HI is the high entry position. To move up or down a table, place the previously calculated midpoint (MID) in LO or HI. If the comparison of the search argument to the table is low, check lower in the table and place MID in HI. If the comparison is high, place MID in LO. The previous binary search initially calculated MID as $(0 + 20) \div 2 = 10$. The first comparison of job 47 to entry 10 (job 27) was high. Therefore, to check higher in the table, store the contents of MID (10) in LO. The next comparison would be $(10 + 20) \div 2 = 15$.

Missing Entry

One danger in a binary search for a unique entry is that the entry may not be in the table. A conventional table lookup can detect a missing entry by a low comparison, but a binary search does not proceed sequentially through a table. However, there is one device that will work: if two successive calculations result in the same midpoint, then the entry is not in the table. For example, assume the same table of job numbers and rates-of-pay discussed at the beginning of this section and that the input record contains job 12. The calculations and compares are as follows:

STEP	MIDPOINT	COMPARISON SEARCH : TABLE	RESULT
	$(LO + HI) \div 2$		
1	$(\ 0 + 20) \div 2 = 10$	12 : 27	Low
2	$(\ 0 + 10) \div 2 = 5$	12 : 07	High
3	$(\ 5 + 10) \div 2 = 7½$ or 8	12 : 16	Low
4	$(\ 5 +\ \ 8) \div 2 = 6½$ or 7	12 : 15	Low
5	$(\ 5 +\ \ 7) \div 2 = 6$	12 : 13	Low
6	$(\ 5 +\ \ 6) \div 2 = 5½$ or 6	12 : 13	

Midpoint 6 has now been calculated twice in a row and will continue to be calculated unless you provide a test, as shown in the flowchart in Figure 12-5.

Maximum Number of Compares

The following table compares the use of the sequential search with the binary search. A sequential search on the average requires processing half way through the table.

NUMBER OF ENTRIES	MAXIMUM SEQUENTIAL	AVERAGE SEQUENTIAL	MAXIMUM BINARY
20	20	10	5
50	50	25	6
100	100	50	7
400	400	200	9
800	800	400	10
2,000	2,000	1,000	11
10,000	10,000	5,000	14

The figures for maximum binary search are based on the formula

$$2^n > \text{number of table entries}$$

where n is the maximum number of compares required. For example, if there are 50 table entries, then select the smallest n necessary:

$$2^5 = 32 \text{ (too small, because } 32 < 50)$$
$$2^6 = 64 \text{ (correct, because } 64 > 50)$$

As a result, searching a table from 32 to 63 entries in size involves a *maximum* of six compares. But since a binary search generates more machine instructions than a sequential search, use a binary search for tables containing 60 or more entries.

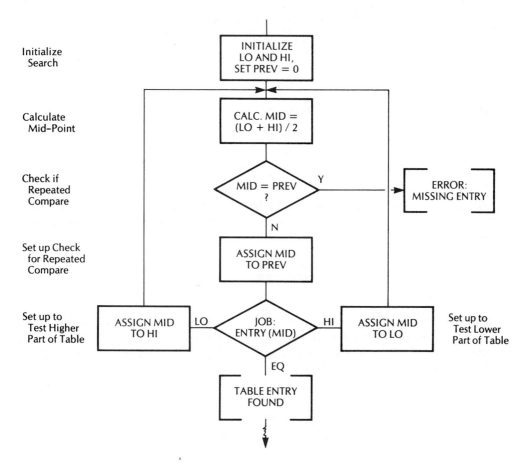

Initialize Search	INITIALIZE LO AND HI, SET PREV = 0
Calculate Mid–Point	CALC. MID = (LO + HI) / 2
Check if Repeated Compare	MID = PREV ? → Y → ERROR: MISSING ENTRY
Set up Check for Repeated Compare	ASSIGN MID TO PREV
Set up to Test Higher Part of Table	ASSIGN MID TO HI — LO — JOB: ENTRY (MID) — HI — ASSIGN MID TO LO — Set up to Test Lower Part of Table
	EQ → TABLE ENTRY FOUND

FIGURE 12-5   Binary Search.

SEARCH ALL

Some COBOL compilers provide a SEARCH ALL statement that automatically performs a binary search. Chapter 11 discussed the use of the SEARCH statement; Figure 12-6 shows the same statement as a binary search with changes underlined.

```
01   STOCK-TAB-RED  REDEFINES STOCK-TAB-VALUES.
     03 STOCK-TAB-OCCUR   OCCURS 6 TIMES
                          ASCENDING KEY IS STOCK-ITEM-TAB
                          INDEXED BY ITEM-NDX.
        05 STOCK-ITEM-TAB PIC X(3)
        05 STOCK-PRICE-TAB PIC S99V99.

     SET ITEM-NDX TO 1.
     SEARCH ALL STOCK-TAB-OCCUR
        AT END PERFORM R000-NOT-IN-TABLE
        WHEN STOCK-IN = STOCK-ITEM-TAB (ITEM-NDX)
             MOVE STOCK-PRICE-TAB (ITEM-NDX) TO STOCK-PRICE.
```

FIGURE 12-6   Use of SEARCH ALL.

The table may be in sequence by more than one control field (key). Each key is a name of a table element that you code in the ASCENDING clause in order of highest to lowest value. The table may even be in descending sequence. The options are as follows:

> ASCENDING KEY IS KEY-1, KEY-2, ...
> DESCENDING KEY IS KEY-1, KEY-2, ...

If there are duplicate keys in the table, it is unpredictable which key SEARCH ALL finds first. Also, if the table is not full, you should fill unused portions with HIGH-VALUES or define the table as variable length. The general format for the SEARCH ALL statement is as follows:

> SEARCH ALL identifier-1 [AT END imperative-statement-1]
>
> WHEN condition-1   { imperative-statement-2 }
>   { NEXT SENTENCE   }

Binary Search Example

The program in Figure 12-2 uses PERFORM to execute a binary search. A condition name, SEARCH-FLAG, controls the search, and the search ends if a job number either is located or is not in the table. Either 'FOUND' or 'INVALID' is moved to SEARCH-FLAG. On return from the routine, the program tests if 'FOUND' to decide if it should MOVE wage, hours, and rate to the print area.

CALCULATION OF DAYS BETWEEN DATES

It is often necessary in business programming to determine how many days have elapsed between two dates. You may need to know the number of days, for example, to calculate interest on loans, to determine if a customer is eligible for a discount for payments made within 30 days, or to determine if customers are delinquent in paying their accounts.

For an interest calculation, a customer may have made one payment on August 12 and the next payment on September 15. You can mentally calculate the number of days between these two dates with little difficulty: 19 days remaining in August plus 15 days expired in September equals 34 days. However, how do you write a program that can calculate the elapsed number of days for any dates of the calendar? One simple way is to determine the day of the year on which each date occurs. August 12 is the 224th day and September 15 is the 258th day. The difference between these two values is $258 - 224 = 34$, which is the same number that was calculated mentally. The next step is to arrange the days of the year into a table. One method organizes a table into 365 entries, with the month and day as the argument and the day of the year as the function:

MON DAY	DAY OF YEAR
01 01	001
01 02	002
01 03	003
.	.
.	.
.	.
12 31	365

This table is unnecessarily long, and unless you use direct table accessing, will take many steps for a table lookup. A much shorter table provides an argument for month only, and a function containing the accumulated days of the year up to that month:

	MONTH	ACCUMULATED DAYS
January	01	000
February	02	031
March	03	059
April	04	090
May	05	120
June	06	151
July	07	181
August	08	212
September	09	243
October	10	273
November	11	304
December	12	334

For this table, you can either omit a month entirely and use direct table accessing, or use table lookup to find a correct month, and then extract the accumulated days. As an illustration, find the day of the year for August 12 and September 15:

- September 15—Accumulated days to September   243
  Add 15 days   15
  Day of the year   258
- August 12—Accumulated days to August   212
  Add 12 days   12
  Day of the year   224
- Difference—Number of days   34

There is a small problem in this method if the days overlap the year-end. For example, assume that you have to calculate the days between December 12 and February 6. The days of the year are as follows:

$$\text{February} \quad 6: \quad 031 + 06 = 037$$
$$\text{December} \quad 12: \quad 334 + 12 = \underline{346}$$
$$\text{Difference} \qquad\qquad\qquad -\underline{\underline{309}}$$

Crossing a year-end requires an adjustment of 365 days. Adding 365 to −309 gives the correct answer, 56. In fact, you have to add 365 for every year that is crossed. Leap years are another problem if you require exact dates. The table does not provide for the additional day of February 29. You can add a day if the days elapsed cross the end of February when there is a leap year, but some additional programming is necessary. A leap year is evenly divisible by 4 (the remainder will be zero). There is one exception: years ending with 00 whose first two digits are not evenly divisible by 4, such as 1700, 1800, and 1900, but not 2000.

DECIMAL ACCUMULATION

When a program accumulates a number of calculated results and rounds each result, a small rounding error may accumulate. If the error is undesirable, you may want to correct it. Consider the following table of sales totals. You have to calculate the percentage of each salesman's sales to the total of all salesmen. The table shows the calculation with straight rounding and with decimal accumulation. (Rounding adds 5 to the first unwanted digit to the right of the decimal point. For negative values, subtract 5.)

(1) SALESMAN	(2) TOTAL SALES ($)	(3) RATIO TO TOTAL	(4) % ROUNDED TO 1 DECIMAL	(5) DECIMAL ACCUMULATION	(6) % USING DEC. ACCUM.
20	137.28	0.048701	4.9%	0.049201	4.9%
23	264.50	0.093834	9.4	0.094035	9.4
24	1,200.73	0.425973	42.6	0.426008	42.6
27	650.33	0.230712	23.1	0.230720	23.0
28	565.95	0.200777	20.1	0.201497	20.1
TOTALS	2,818.79		100.1%		100.0%

Each line in the table represents the sales for one salesman. Column 3 shows a salesman's sales ratio to total sales, calculated to six decimal places. Column 4 gives the result of rounding the ratio and converting to a percent. Because of rounding errors, column 4 does not total exactly 100.0%. But Column 5 shows a technique to ensure that the total equals 100.0%. Instead of adding 0.000500 to each figure, you add it only at the start (0.048701 + 0.000500 = 0.049201). You then print 0.049 as 4.9% and store the three rightmost unwanted decimal places for adding to the next calculation. The procedure is as follows:

1. Initialize the decimal accumulator to 0.000500 (or as many decimal places as necessary).
2. Add the accumulator to the first calculation (0.048701 + 0.000500 = 0.049201). Store 0.049 as the answer and store the rightmost three digits (0.000201) back in the decimal accumulator.
3. Add the decimal accumulator to the second calculation (0.093834 + 0.000201 = 0.094035). Store 0.094 as the answer and store 0.000035 in the decimal accumulator.
4. Continue with the remaining calculations in this way.

By this method, the total will always be 100.0% with two qualifications: First, if there are many divisions, you may generate some imprecision because of the loss of the remainder in each division. The solution is to generate as many decimal places as necessary to ensure 100.0%. Second, a danger is negative values. In this case, you must provide two decimal accumulators—one you initialize with +5 for use with positive values and the other with −5 for negative values. On each calculation you test the sign of the result and add and store the appropriate decimal accumulator.

Cost accounting is another useful application of decimal accumulation. Consider a situation that requires allocating overhead expenses to various departments on a predetermined basis. The total amount allocated to the departments must equal the original expense.

(1) TOTAL OVERHEAD EXPENSE TO BE ALLOCATED	(2) DEPARTMENT	(3) PERCENT TO BE ALLOCATED	(4) CALCULATION (1) X (3)	(5) ALLOCATED AMOUNT, ROUNDED	(6) ALLOCATED AMOUNT USING DEC. ACCUM.
	SUPPLIES	20.3%	$10,000.43975	$10,000.44	$10,000.44
	TRANSPORTATION	16.8	8,276.22600	8,276.23	8,176.23
$49,263.25	PRODUCTION	27.4	13,498.13050	13,498.13	13,498.13
	PACKAGING	9.7	4,778.53525	4,778.54	4,778.53
	DISTRIBUTION	25.8	12,709.91850	12,709.92	12,709.92
		100.0%	$49,263.25000	$49,263.26	$49,263.25

As shown in column 3 of the table, the departments are to carry their share of $49,263.25 overhead expenses by predetermined percents. You calculate the expenses allocated to supplies department by multiplying $49,263.25 by its rate of 20.3%. Since the total of column 3 is 100.0%, the report should distribute the entire expense to all departments. But the use of rounding in column 5 allocates $49,263.26, whereas the use of decimal accumulation in column 6 correctly allocates $49,263.25. Although the difference is trivial, a cost accounting system should allocate the exact amount.

Decimal Accumulation Example

Figure 12-7 illustrates decimal accumulation in COBOL based on the preceding cost allocation example. The routine is intended to process repetitively through each department during program execution. The decimal accumulator, DEC-ACCUM, is initialized to .00500. Assume that the allocation percent for each department is moved successively into ALLOC-PCT; initially, therefore, ALLOC-PCT contains the rate for the first department, supplies, for 20.3% (0.203). The routine multiplies OVERHEAD-EXP (the amount to be allocated) of $49,263.25 by 0.203, giving $10,000.43975 in WORK-FIELD. The program adds the decimal accumulator (.00500) to WORK-FIELD, giving $10,000.44475. WORK-FIELD is moved into ALLOC-AMT, which accepts only two of the five decimal places: $10,000.44. ALLOC-AMT subtracted from WORK-FIELD determines the decimal portion that was truncated by the preceding move statement, .00475, and that value becomes the next

```
WORKING-STORAGE SECTION.
77   DEC-ACCUM        PIC SV99999      COMP-3   VALUE +.00500.
77   ALLOC-PCT        PIC S9V9999      COMP-3.
77   OVERHEAD-EXP     PIC S9(5)V99     COMP-3   VALUE +49263.25.
77   WORK-FIELD       PIC S9(5)V99999  COMP-3.
77   ALLOC-AMT        PIC S9(5)V99     COMP-3.
     ...
PROCEDURE DIVISION.
     ...
     COMPUTE WORK-FIELD =                     WORK-FIELD    ACCUM ALLOC-AMT
          OVERHEAD-EXP * ALLOC-PCT.       10,000.43975  .00500     -
     ADD DEC-ACCUM TO WORK-FIELD.         10,000.44475  .00500     -
     MOVE WORK-FIELD TO ALLOC-AMT.        10,000.44475  .00500 10,000.44
     SUBTRACT ALLOC-AMT FROM WORK-FIELD.      0.00475   .00500 10,000.44
     MOVE WORK-FIELD TO DEC-ACCUM.            0.00475   .00475 10,000.44
```

FIGURE 12-7   Decimal Accumulation.

contents of DEC-ACCUM. The next time through the routine (when ALLOC-PCT presumably would contain the rate for the next department), the program calculates the next allocated amount and rounds using the .00475 as the decimal accumulator, and so forth.

PROBLEMS

12–1. When is it preferable to load table entries from external storage?

12–2. Define a table that is to load from external storage with a variable number of entries, from 1 through 15. The table requires entries for stock numbers and prices, as in Figure 11-5 in the previous chapter.

12–3. Code a routine that reads records containing stock numbers and prices and stores them in the table defined in Problem 12-2. Ensure that the table does not overload. The last stock number in the file is 999.

12–4. Using the stored table and calculated count in Problem 12-3, code a routine that sorts the table entries into sequence by stock item.

12–5. Use the sorted table in Problem 12-4 to perform a binary search routine with an input record that contains a stock number named STOCK-IN. Use QTY-IN in the input record to calculate stock value as follows:

$$\text{stock value} = \text{quantity} \times \text{price}$$

12–6. Combine the previous four questions into one program. You may use the table definition in Figure 11-5 to determine the content of the table records. Provide enough stock input records to test the table thoroughly and be sure to have stock items that are equal to the first and last table entries. Suggestion: to help debug, print the contents of the table after loading and after sorting.

CHAPTER 13

DATA MANIPULATION

OBJECTIVE: To present the advanced COBOL statements for handling character data.

INTRODUCTION

Most programs involve handling the entire contents of distinct data fields, using simple MOVE statements. But there are situations that require handling parts of fields and groups of fields. Therefore, it may be necessary to redefine fields or field groups in different formats or to perform operations upon characters within fields. Usually this type of programming involves data defined as (or defaulted to) DISPLAY: alphabetic (PIC A), alphanumeric (PIC X), and numeric (PIC 9, but not computational).

This chapter introduces a number of new COBOL statements with simple examples; however, not all of the new features are implemented by every COBOL version, and some features are quite complex. Consequently, it may be necessary to reference the appropriate manufacturer's COBOL manual.

QUALIFIED NAMES

In a COBOL program, every statement must reference a unique data item so that the compiler knows which data item to address. It is possible, however, to use one name to define more than one field. For example, two fields may both be defined as CUSTOMER-NO. But a statement such as

MOVE CUSTOMER-NO TO CUST-PR.

does not clearly distinguish which field to move to CUST-PR, and unless you indicate which CUSTOMER-NO to move, the compiler will generate an error message. Therefore, a device called *qualification of names* must be used to reference unique fields.

```
01  CUST-REC-IN.
    03  CUSTOMER-NO        PIC X(5).
    03  CUSTOMER-NAME      PIC X(25).
    03  CUSTOMER-BAL       PIC S9(5)V99.
    03  CREDIT-LIMIT       PIC S9(5)V99.
    03  DATE-LAST-SALE.
        05  LAST-MONTH     PIC XX.
        05  LAST-DAY       PIC XX.
        05  LAST-YEAR      PIC XX.

01  CUST-REC-OUT.
    03  CUSTOMER-NO        PIC X(5).
    03  CUSTOMER-NAME      PIC X(25).
    03  CUSTOMER-BAL       PIC S9(5)V99.
    03  CREDIT-LIMIT       PIC S9(5)V99.
    03  DATE-LAST-SALE.
        05  LAST-MONTH     PIC XX.
        05  LAST-DAY       PIC XX.
        05  LAST-YEAR      PIC XX.
```

FIGURE 13-1   Record Groups with Identical Names.

Consider the definitions in Figure 13-1. Both record names CUST-REC-IN and CUST-REC-OUT are uniquely defined, but contain identical field names. However, qualification of the field names will make the fields unique, for example:

MOVE CUSTOMER-NO IN (or OF) CUST-REC-IN TO CUST-PR.

The compiler can now determine that the CUSTOMER-NO defined in the record group CUST-REC-IN is to be moved. (Either IN or OF may be used in a qualified statement.) A little thought will make it clear that a qualified name must be contained within a record group so that neither level 01 or level 77 can be qualified.

But why code a program with duplicate names? One practical reason arises when such groups are cataloged on disk, so that any program can COPY the record description. This practice saves coding time and ensures that all programs reference data records by the same name, which is a desirable standardization.

Both record groups in Figure 13-1 contain a field called LAST-MONTH defined within DATE-LAST-SALE. Any reference to LAST-MONTH should be to each level in the record group, as follows:

```
MOVE LAST-MONTH OF DATE-LAST-SALE OF CUST-REC-IN TO
     LAST-MONTH OF DATE-LAST-SALE OF CUST-REC-OUT.
```

As can be seen, qualification of names at a low level in a record group can generate some awkward statements. An installation can avoid the need for qualification by cataloging record groups as both input and output so that CUST-REC-IN would contain the names CUST-NO-IN, CUST-NAME-IN, etc., whereas CUST-REC-OUT would contain CUST-NO-OUT, CUST-NAME-OUT, etc. This approach provides the advantages of availability of standard cataloged names and uniqueness of names within a program.

Other rules concerning qualified names include the following:

* Two different Sections may each contain a Paragraph with the same name. But any reference to either Paragraph name must be qualified by the applicable Section name.
* A record group may not contain the same name at two different levels.
* A name that is already unique can be qualified.
* Qualification is not allowed in the REDEFINES clause.
* Subscripted or indexed data items may be qualified in the following manner:

data-name OF data-name-1 (sub).

CORRESPONDING OPERATIONS

Three statements, available on some compilers, that provide for simple processing of data between record groups when data fields in both groups have identical names are MOVE CORRESPONDING, ADD CORRESPONDING, and SUBTRACT CORRESPONDING (or CORR).

MOVE CORRESPONDING

The MOVE CORRESPONDING (or CORR) statement transfers fields from one record group to fields in another record group that have identical names. Although MOVE CORRESPONDING is an ANS standard, it is not available in all COBOL versions. Each matched pair of fields, sender and receiver, must have compatible definitions (nonnumeric or numeric) and similar levels of qualification. FILLER items are ignored, but items in the receiving fields can be edited so that the MOVE CORRESPONDING statement can move items from an input record to an edited print record.

Figure 13-2 illustrates two record groups that contain identical names, although in a different sequence. The MOVE CORRESPONDING statement transfers the contents of STOCK-ITEM, STOCK-MON, STOCK-YR, and STOCK-QTY. Since the statement generates four MOVE statements, the only saving is in coding time.

```
        01    STOCK-RECORD.
              05    STOCK-ITEM        PIC X(5).
              05    STOCK-DESCRIP     PIC X(20).
              05    STOCK-DATE.
                    10   STOCK-MON    PIC XX.
                    10   STOCK-DAY    PIC XX.
                    10   STOCK-YR     PIC XX.
              05    STOCK-QTY         PIC S9(5).

        01    STOCK-STRUCTURE.
              05    STOCK-ITEM        PIC X(5).
              05    STOCK-QTY         PIC S9(5).
              05    STOCK-DATE.
                    10   STOCK-MON    PIC XX.
                    10   STOCK-YR     PIC XX.
              •
              •
              •
        MOVE  CORRESPONDING STOCK-RECORD TO
              STOCK STRUCTURE.
```

FIGURE 13-2   Use of MOVE CORRESPONDING.

One problem: If there are many changes to the record groups, there may be difficulty maintaining the accuracy of the qualified names and the CORRESPONDING statements in all the programs that reference them.

ADD CORRESPONDING and SUBTRACT CORRESPONDING

ADD CORRESPONDING and SUBTRACT CORRESPONDING, which are not available in all COBOL versions, permit adding and subtracting of identically named numeric data fields. There are two options: ROUNDED provides for rounding in the receiving fields, which contain fewer decimal places than the sending fields. ON SIZE ERROR checks for arithmetic overflow after all the arithmetic is completed. Their general formats are as follows:

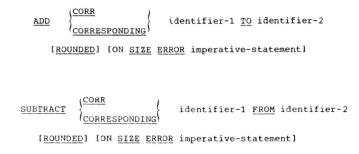

JUSTIFIED RIGHT

The conventional practice in programming languages is to left-justify nonnumeric values and to right-justify numeric values. However, the JUSTIFIED (or JUST) RIGHT clause is used to right-justify nonnumeric values. Therefore, in the following example, ALPHARIGHT would contain ' SAM' instead of 'SAM ':

```
77   ALPHARIGHT       PIC X(5) JUSTIFIED  RIGHT VALUE 'SAM'.
```

The program will attempt to MOVE data to ALPHARIGHT and if the sending field is shorter than five bytes, the MOVE pads blanks on the left, and if the sending field is longer than five bytes, the MOVE truncates on the left.

The next section depicts an example in which an alphanumeric item is REDEFINED on a numeric item, and JUSTIFIED RIGHT right-adjusts the alphanumeric item like a numeric field.

REDEFINES

The REDEFINES clause permits the defining of a field in more than one way. The following example REDEFINES a numeric field ARITH-AMT as an alphanumeric field CHAR-AMT. It is also possible to test the contents of CHAR-AMT for blanks or special characters. Both fields, ARITH-AMT and CHAR-AMT, reference the same storage locations:

```
77   ARITH-AMT        PIC S999V99 VALUE 12.34.
77   CHAR-AMT         REDEFINES ARITH-AMT PIC X(5) JUSTIFIED  RIGHT.
```

A useful example involves percentages. A program may contain a decimal value, such as 0.275, which is to be printed as a percentage, 27.5%. The following example defines a decimal value and REDEFINES it as a percentage:

```
77   DECIMAL-AMT      PIC SV999.
77   PERCENT-AMT      REDEFINES DECIMAL-AMT PIC S99V9.
```

It is also possible to REDEFINE identical fields in record groups. A CORRESPONDING statement MOVEs or ADDs data from one record group to another record group for fields with identical names. You can use redefined names to process the fields individually, without having to qualify the names.

The following rules pertain to REDEFINES:

• REDEFINES cannot be used in the File Section at level 01, but may be used for any other 01 record group, and any group level, elementary level, or independent item. It also cannot be used for level 66 or level 88.

- A REDEFINES item cannot contain a VALUE clause.
- A REDEFINES clause must immediately follow the data name in the redefining item.
- A REDEFINES item must contain the same level number as the item that it defines.
- A REDEFINES item must be coded after the redefined item and must be the first item following that has the same level number.
- A field or record may be redefined more than once.
- It is invalid to REDEFINE an arithmetic (COMP) item as nonarithmetic (DISPLAY) and vice versa because the internal data representations are completely different.

Figure 13-3 illustrates the redefining of an elementary level item.

```
01    CUST-TRAN.
      05    CUST-NO-IN      PIC X(5).
      05    DATE-IN         PIC 9(6).
      05    AMT-PAID-IN     PIC S9(4)V99.
      05    AMT-SOLD-IN     REDEFINES AMT-PAID-IN
                            PIC S9(4)V99.
      05    FILLER          PIC X(12).
```

FIGURE 13-3   The REDEFINES Clause.

RENAMES—LEVEL 66

The RENAMES clause is similar to REDEFINES, but because its use is slightly different, care should be taken to avoid confusing the two clauses. The general format is as follows:

66 data-name-1 RENAMES data-name-2 [THRU data-name-3].

RENAMES has a special level number, 66; contains no PICTURE clause; and appears at the end of the record group that it RENAMES (fully or partially).

```
01   CUST-TRAN.
     05   CUST-NO-IN        PIC X(5).
     05   DATE-IN           PIC 9(6).
     05   AMT-PAID-IN       PIC S9(4)V99.
     05   FILLER            PIC X(12).
66   AMT-SOLD-IN           RENAMES AMT-PAID-IN.
```

FIGURE 13-4   The RENAMES Clause.

Compare the use of REDEFINES in Figure 13-3 with the use of RENAMES in Figure 13-4. They both produce the same result, but RENAMES is valid because the renamed item is to have an identical PICTURE. REDEFINES, however, would permit a different PICTURE definition.

The main advantage of RENAMES is that it allows for the referencing of a group of data items. In Figure 13-5, the renamed group is a 20-byte area and a reference to ITEM-BANDC is to the 20-byte area comprising ITEM-B and ITEM-C.

```
01   RECORD-CODES.
     05   ITEM-A            PIC X(10).
     05   ITEM-B.
          10   ITEM-BA      PIC X(8).
          10   ITEM-BB      PIC X(4).
     05   ITEM-C            PIC X(8).
66   ITEM-BANDC            RENAMES ITEM-B THRU ITEM-C.
```

FIGURE 13-5   Renaming a Group of Data Items.

The following rules pertain to RENAMES:

- RENAMES must be entered on level 66 and must follow the record that it renames.
- A level 66 entry cannot RENAME level 01, 66, 77, or 88 entries.
- Data-name-3 (the THRU item) must follow data-name-2 in a record and cannot be subordinate to data-name-2.
- Data-name-2, data-name-3, or any other subordinate item cannot contain an OCCURS clause.

EXAMINE, INSPECT, AND TRANSFORM

A program should have the ability to analyze the contents of data fields as follows:

1. Check for invalid input data. A numeric data field should contain only digits 0–9 and a sign. (A blank in the units position of a numeric field on IBM 360/370 causes a processing error, although some computers allow blanks and treat them as zeros.) A program could check for invalid characters and optionally replace them with valid characters.
2. Check for unique characters in a field. For example, asterisks that terminate variable length name and address fields.
3. Translate characters into a different code. Data on tape may have been generated on a different computer system from the system that is to process the data; a character translation is therefore required. (For example, IBM 360/370 uses an 8-bit code that is quite different from the 7-bit ASA code used by many other manufacturers.) Also, data may have been entered incorrectly in the same field of every record of a file; therefore, a translate program is required and is more economical than reentering the data.

For this type of processing, there are three similar COBOL statements.

1. EXAMINE—an ANS 68 feature still implemented on many COBOL versions.
2. INSPECT—a more complex statement introduced by ANS 74 and intended to replace EXAMINE.
3. TRANSFORM—an IBM language extension.

EXAMINE

There are several reasons to cover EXAMINE first:

- It is still implemented on many compilers.
- You will probably encounter its use in older programs.
- Being similar to INSPECT but simpler, it is a good introduction.

EXAMINE can count the number of times a specific character occurs in a data field and can replace a specific character with another character. (Be sure that your compiler has EXAMINE before trying to use it.) Format-1 of EXAMINE provides for counting and an optional replacing:

$$\text{EXAMINE data-item TALLYING} \left\{ \begin{array}{l} \text{ALL} \\ \text{UNTIL FIRST} \\ \text{LEADING} \end{array} \right\} \text{literal-1 [REPLACING BY literal-2]}$$

Data-item must be defined as alphanumeric (PICTURE X). The count is made in a special register called TALLY, which is a reserved word that is not defined in the Data Division. TALLY is associated only with EXAMINE and is a reserved word only if EXAMINE exists on the compiler. The three options for TALLYING are as follows:

1.   ALL counts all occurrences of literal-1 in data-item.
2.   UNTIL FIRST starts from the left in data-item and counts the number of characters that precede the first occurrence of literal-1. After execution, TALLY will contain zero only if literal-1 occurs as the first character in data-item.
3.   LEADING starts from the left and counts the number of consecutive occurrences of literal-1 before encountering a different character.

The REPLACING BY option uses literal-2 to replace literal-1 characters that appear in the data-item being processed. There are three features for REPLACING BY:

1.   ALL causes literal-2 to replace all occurrences of literal-1 in the data-item.
2.   UNTIL FIRST replaces all leading (leftmost) nonliteral-1 characters.
3.   LEADING replaces all leading occurrences of literal-1.

The following illustrates all three REPLACING BY features:

```
77  EXFIELD          PIC X(6).
    .
    .                                           BEFORE   AFTER  TALLY
    .
    EXAMINE EXFIELD TALLYING ALL '5'.           342550   342550   2
    EXAMINE EXFIELD TALLYING UNTIL FIRST '5'.   342550   342550   3
    EXAMINE EXFIELD TALLYING UNTIL FIRST ' '    326957   326957   6
    EXAMINE EXFIELD TALLYING LEADING ' '
                    REPLACING BY '0'.              235   000235   3
```

After the EXAMINE, you can test the contents of TALLY, for example, as follows:

IF TALLY = 0 PERFORM . . . .

Format-2 of EXAMINE provides for REPLACING without TALLYING and is more efficient if the count is not required:

EXAMINE data-name REPLACING $\begin{Bmatrix} \text{ALL} \\ \text{FIRST} \\ \text{UNTIL FIRST} \\ \text{LEADING} \end{Bmatrix}$ literal-1 BY literal-2.

The only new feature is the FIRST option that causes the replacement of only the first occurrence of literal-1. Some examples are as follows:

```
                                                 BEFORE      AFTER
EXAMINE EXFIELD REPLACING FIRST '*' BY '$'.      ****50      $***50
EXAMINE EXFIELD REPLACING ALL ' ' BY '/'.        09 05 83    09/05/83
```

The following rules pertain to EXAMINE:

- An examined field must have DISPLAY usage (that is, noncomputational).
- Specified literals must be a single character or a figurative constant (except ALL) and must be consistent with the data-item description: alphabetic, alphanumeric, or numeric. The literal may be alphabetic only if the data-item is PIC A; it may be any character if PIC X; and it may be only numeric if PIC 9. A numeric item may contain invalid blanks, but to replace blanks with numeric zeros, redefining is required as follows:

```
77   AMOUNT-NUM      PIC S999V99.
77   AMOUNT-CHAR     REDEFINES AMOUNT-NUM PIC X(5).
     .
     .
     .
     EXAMINE AMOUNT-CHAR REPLACING ALL ' ' BY '0'.
```

or, using figurative constants:

```
     EXAMINE AMOUNT-CHAR REPLACING ALL SPACES BY ZEROS.
```

- EXAMINE processes from left to right through the data-item, and for numeric data-items, any sign is ignored.
- COBOL automatically defines TALLY as PIC S9(5) COMP and initializes it each time EXAMINE is used.

INSPECT

INSPECT is a feature of ANS 74 COBOL that has not been implemented by all versions. INSPECT is more versatile than EXAMINE, but more complex. INSPECT uses defined counters rather than the TALLY register. Consider a simple EXAMINE and INSPECT that perform the same function:

```
     EXAMINE AMOUNT TALLYING ALL ZEROS.
     INSPECT AMOUNT TALLYING CTR FOR ALL ZEROS.
```

The difference in these two statements is that EXAMINE automatically generates a TALLY register to store the count, whereas for INSPECT you would have to define a counter (called CTR in the example). For EXAMINE, the field being tested must be defined (or redefined) as alphanumeric (PIC X), but INSPECT can process a field as alphanumeric or numeric DISPLAY (PIC 9). In addition, INSPECT can process either a single character or a string of characters in the comparison.

TALLYING Format.   The first format of INSPECT provides for TALLYING with no REPLACING:

Format 1:

$$
\underline{\text{INSPECT}} \text{ identifier-1 } \underline{\text{TALLYING}} \left\{ \text{identifier-2 } \underline{\text{FOR}} \left\{ \begin{array}{l} \left\{\begin{array}{l}\text{ALL} \\ \underline{\text{LEADING}} \\ \text{CHARACTERS}\end{array}\right\} \left\{\begin{array}{l}\text{identifier-3} \\ \text{literal-1}\end{array}\right\} \end{array} \left[\left\{\begin{array}{l}\underline{\text{BEFORE}} \\ \underline{\text{AFTER}}\end{array}\right\} \text{INITIAL} \left\{\begin{array}{l}\text{literal-2} \\ \text{identifier-4}\end{array}\right\} \right] \right\} \cdots \right\} \cdots
$$

In the preceding INSPECT example, the statement adds 1 to CTR for each zero in AMOUNT. CTR is any valid numeric field defined in Working-Storage, as follows:

```
77   CTR        PIC S999 COMP VALUE +0.
```

You have to initialize the counter with MOVE ZEROS each time an INSPECT uses the counter. The use of ALL, LEADING, and CHARACTERS is as follows:

- *ALL.* ALL counts every character in the data item that matches the specified literal, or the string of characters in the data item that matches the literal string. For example:

```
MOVE ZEROS TO CTR.
INSPECT AREA TALLYING CTR FOR ALL 'THE'.
```

   If AREA contains 'THE END OF THE CHAPTER', then CTR will contain the value 2 for the two occurrences of 'THE'.
- *LEADING.* LEADING causes a check of leftmost character(s) in the data item for a match with the literal string. Assume AREA still contains 'THE END OF THE CHAPTER'. The statements

```
MOVE ZEROS TO CTR.
INSPECT AREA TALLYING CTR FOR LEADING 'THE'.
```

   will cause CTR to contain 1.
- *CHARACTERS.* This feature counts the number of characters in the data item and is most commonly used with the BEFORE and AFTER clauses. The following example uses two counters and both BEFORE and AFTER:

```
MOVE ZEROS TO CTRA, CTRB.
INSPECT FIELDA TALLYING
    CTRA FOR CHARACTERS BEFORE '.'
    CTRB FOR CHARACTERS AFTER '.'.
```

If FIELDA contains 1234.567, then after the INSPECT, CTRA will contain 4 (four characters before the decimal point), and CTRB 3. BEFORE and AFTER may be further modified with an INITIAL option that indicates the first occurrence of some character(s). The following tallies the number of characters (if any) before the first asterisk in FIELDB:

```
INSPECT FIELDB TALLYING CTRC FOR CHARACTERS
            BEFORE INITIAL '*'.
```

REPLACING Format.   The second INSPECT format uses the REPLACING clause and has no TALLYING option:

Format 2:
INSPECT identifier-1

$$
\text{REPLACING} \left\{ \begin{array}{l} \text{CHARACTERS BY} \left\{ \begin{array}{l} \text{identifier-6} \\ \text{literal-4} \end{array} \right\} \left[\left\{ \begin{array}{l} \underline{\text{BEFORE}} \\ \underline{\text{AFTER}} \end{array} \right\} \text{INITIAL} \left\{ \begin{array}{l} \text{identifier-7} \\ \text{literal-5} \end{array} \right\} \right] \\ \left\{ \begin{array}{l} \underline{\text{ALL}} \\ \underline{\text{LEADING}} \\ \underline{\text{FIRST}} \end{array} \right\} \left\{ \left\{ \begin{array}{l} \text{identifier-5} \\ \text{literal-3} \end{array} \right\} \underline{\text{BY}} \left\{ \begin{array}{l} \text{identifier-6} \\ \text{literal-4} \end{array} \right\} \left[\left\{ \begin{array}{l} \underline{\text{BEFORE}} \\ \underline{\text{AFTER}} \end{array} \right\} \text{INITIAL} \left\{ \begin{array}{l} \text{identifier-7} \\ \text{literal-5} \end{array} \right\} \right] \right\} \ldots \end{array} \right\} \ldots
$$

As the format indicates, there are many features. Consider some simple examples.

1.   The following statement replaces blanks in a numeric input field with zeros:

```
INSPECT AMT-IN REPLACING ALL SPACES BY ZEROS.
```

2.   The CHARACTERS phrase causes no comparison:

```
INSPECT FIELDA REPLACING CHARACTERS BY '*'.
```

The operation simply replaces every position in FIELDA with asterisks, similar to

```
MOVE ALL '*' TO FIELDA.
```

3.   The following INSPECT checks for the first C in FIELDB:

```
INSPECT FIELDB REPLACING ALL 'A' BY 'B' AFTER INITIAL 'C'.
```

If any As immediately follow the C, they are replaced by Bs. For example:

'CADCDED' becomes 'CBDCDED'
'ADCAACA' becomes 'ADCBBCA'

4. The following checks for leading zeros to the left of the decimal point and replaces the zeros with blanks:

```
INSPECT FIELDC REPLACING ALL ZEROS BY SPACES
              BEFORE INITIAL '.'.
```

'0003.25' becomes '   3.25'
'0000.05' becomes '   .05'.

5. This example changes only the first occurrence of E to A:

```
INSPECT FIELDC REPLACING FIRST 'E' BY 'A'.
```

'SENDER' would become 'SANDER'.

LEADING, FIRST, and INITIAL at first may seem alike, but some study and the use of INSPECT should soon make their distinctions clear.

TALLYING and REPLACING Format.   The third INSPECT format combines TALLYING and REPLACING:

Format 3:

$$\underline{\text{INSPECT}}\ \text{identifier-1}\ \underline{\text{TALLYING}} \left\{ \begin{array}{l} \text{identifier-2 } \underline{\text{FOR}} \left\{ \begin{array}{l} \left\{ \begin{array}{l} \underline{\text{ALL}} \\ \underline{\text{LEADING}} \\ \underline{\text{CHARACTERS}} \end{array} \right\} \left\{ \begin{array}{l} \text{identifier-3} \\ \text{literal-1} \end{array} \right\} \left[\left\{ \begin{array}{l} \underline{\text{BEFORE}} \\ \underline{\text{AFTER}} \end{array} \right\} \text{INITIAL} \left\{ \begin{array}{l} \text{identifier-4} \\ \text{literal-2} \end{array} \right\} \right] \cdots \right\} \\ \underline{\text{CHARACTERS BY}} \left\{ \begin{array}{l} \text{identifier-6} \\ \text{literal-4} \end{array} \right\} \left[\left\{ \begin{array}{l} \underline{\text{BEFORE}} \\ \underline{\text{AFTER}} \end{array} \right\} \text{INITIAL} \left\{ \begin{array}{l} \text{identifier-7} \\ \text{literal-5} \end{array} \right\} \right] \end{array} \right\} \cdots$$

$$\underline{\text{REPLACING}} \left\{ \left\{ \begin{array}{l} \left\{ \begin{array}{l} \underline{\text{ALL}} \\ \underline{\text{LEADING}} \\ \underline{\text{FIRST}} \end{array} \right\} \left\{ \begin{array}{l} \text{identifier-5} \\ \text{literal-3} \end{array} \right\} \underline{\text{BY}} \left\{ \begin{array}{l} \text{identifier-6} \\ \text{literal-4} \end{array} \right\} \left[\left\{ \begin{array}{l} \underline{\text{BEFORE}} \\ \underline{\text{AFTER}} \end{array} \right\} \text{INITIAL} \left\{ \begin{array}{l} \text{identifier-7} \\ \text{literal-5} \end{array} \right\} \right] \right\} \cdots \right\} \cdots$$

During execution, the TALLYING clause executes first, and then the REPLACING clause executes, as if there were two INSPECT statements. The following is a simple example:

```
MOVE ZEROS TO CTRC.
INSPECT FIELDE TALLYING CTRC FOR CHARACTERS
              BEFORE INITIAL '*'
              REPLACING ALL 'CAT' BY 'DOG'.
```

If FIELDE contained 'CATER * PILLAR * CAT', after the INSPECT it would become 'DOGER*PILLAR*DOG', and CTRC would contain 5.
    INSPECT provides a flexibility that is well beyond what most programs require.

TRANSFORM

TRANSFORM is an IBM 360/370 feature directly related to the IBM Assembler instruction Translate (TR). TRANSFORM is more efficient than EXAMINE or INSPECT when performing the same operation, but basically can only do simple replacing. The general format is as follows:

TRANSFORM data-item FROM char-1 TO char-2.

The data-item is a DISPLAY item up to 256 characters long. Char-1 and char-2 can be alphanumeric literals, figurative constants, or identifiers. A figurative constant (e.g. SPACES, ZEROS) is treated as a 1-character literal. TRANSFORM replaces the char-1 characters in data-item with the corresponding character in char-2. The following examples replace blanks in DATE-OUT with slashes, so that 08 09 84 becomes 08/09/84:

```
TRANSFORM  DATE-OUT FROM SPACES TO '/'.
EXAMINE    DATE-OUT REPLACING ALL SPACES BY '/'.
INSPECT    DATE-OUT REPLACING ALL SPACES BY '/'.
```

TRANSFORM permits changing a number of different characters to one character. The following translates the characters plus (+), minus (−), or comma (,) in FIELD1 to an asterisk (*):

```
TRANSFORM FIELD1 FROM '+-,' TO '*'.
```

To accomplish the same result, EXAMINE and INSPECT would require three clauses, as follows:

```
INSPECT FIELD1 REPLACING ALL '+' BY '*'
                         ALL '-' BY '*'
                         ALL ',' BY '*'.
```

Char-2 either must be 1-byte long or must equal the length of char-1. In the following, J (or numeric −1) translates to 1; K (or −2) translates to 2; etc:

```
TRANSFORM AMT-IN FROM 'JKLMNOPQR' TO '123456789'.
```

For the same result, EXAMINE and INSPECT would require considerable coding, as follows:

```
INSPECT AMT-IN REPLACING ALL 'J' BY '1'
                         ALL 'K' BY '2'
                         ALL 'L' BY '3', ETC.
```

STRING AND UNSTRING

Although the STRING and UNSTRING statements are ANS 74 standards, they are not available in all COBOL implementations. These statements are useful in a text-editing application.

STRING

A *string* is a group of characters, and the STRING statement *concatenates* (joins together) two or more data strings into one simple string. The following is a simple STRING format:

> STRING sending-string DELIMITED BY delimiter INTO receiving-string.

The sending-string provides for concatenation of DISPLAY data items, alphanumeric literals, and figurative constants (except ALL). The receiving-string is a DISPLAY data item that receives the concatenated characters from left to right. There are two ways to specify the delimiter: by SIZE and by delimiter values.

SIZE.   SIZE provides for transferring the entire contents of each sending data item. For example:

```
77   FIELDA       PIC X(5)      VALUE 'COBOL'.
77   FIELDB       PIC X(7)      VALUE 'PROGRAM'.
77   FIELDC       PIC X(13).

     STRING FIELDA, SPACE, FIELDB DELIMITED BY SIZE INTO FIELDC.
```

The STRING operation first moves FIELDA, then one blank, and then FIELDB into FIELDC, from left to right. On completion, FIELDC contains 'COBOL PROGRAM'.

Delimiter Values.   Specific delimiter characters terminate transferring if encountered; these include DISPLAY items with characters, alphanumeric literals, and figurative constants (except ALL). For example, SPACES, 'W', or the contents of STOPA will terminate transferring of a specified sending item as follows:

```
77   STOPA        PIC X(2)      VALUE 'PS'.
77   FIELDE       PIC X(5)      VALUE 'HELPS'.
77   FIELDF       PIC X(3)      VALUE 'LOW'.
77   FIELDG       PIC X(8)      VALUE ALL '*'.

     STRING FIELDE, FIELDF DELIMITED BY SPACES, 'W', STOPA INTO FIELDG.
```

STEPS OF STRING OPERATION   FIELDG

1. Prior to the STRING operation, FIELDG contains eight asterisks.   ********
2. STRING first moves the contents of FIELDE ('HEL') and then ter-   HEL *****
   minates because 'PS' is contained in the delimiter STOPA.
3. FIELDF begins in the next position of FIELDG. 'LO' transfers and   HELLO ***
   then the operation terminates because the next character ('W') is
   one of the delimiters.

Termination.   STRING terminates either on transferring the last data item or on filling the receiving field, whichever occurs first. If the receiving field is not filled, as in FIELDG in the example, the remaining positions are unchanged.

Other STRING options are POINTER and ON OVERFLOW. POINTER is used to specify a starting position in the receiving-string. ON OVERFLOW checks if the contents of the specified pointer (perhaps as calculated in the program) is less than one, or greater than the length of the receiving-string. For details, see the COBOL reference manual for your specific compiler version.

UNSTRING

UNSTRING provides the opposite operation to STRING; it separates a longer string into one or more shorter strings. The sending-string is a DISPLAY data item, alphanumeric literal, or figurative constant. The receiving-string is a DISPLAY data item (or items) that receives the characters from left to right. Termination occurs either when the last character is transferred or when the receiving-string is filled. The following are three simple examples:

```
77  FIELDG      PIC X(5)     VALUE 'SPOOL'.
77  FIELDH      PIC X(2)     VALUE SPACES.
77  FIELDJ      PIC X(3)     VALUE SPACES.
77  FIELDK      PIC X(8)     VALUE 'A*BC*DEF'.
    UNSTRING 'COB' INTO FIELDG.          FIELDG = 'COBOL'
    UNSTRING 'COBOL' INTO FIELDH, FIELDJ.  FIELDH = 'CO' FIELDJ = 'BOL'.
    UNSTRING FIELDK DELIMITED BY '*'
        INTO FIELDH, FIELDJ.          FIELDH = 'A ' FIELDJ = 'BC'.
```

Other UNSTRING options include COUNT, POINTER, TALLYING, and ON OVERFLOW, which are covered in detail in the appropriate COBOL reference manual.

PROBLEMS

13–1. Discuss the advantages and disadvantages of using qualified names.

13–2. The following defines a record group:

```
01   ACCOUNT-RECORD.
     03   ACCOUNT-NO      PIC X(5).
     03   AMT-RECEIVABLE  PIC S9(5)V99.
     03   FILLER          PIC X(3).
```

Recode the record group for the following requirements:

(a) Define an item AMT-PAYABLE that REDEFINES AMT-RECEIVABLE.

(b) Define an item AMT-PAYABLE that RENAMES AMT-RECEIVABLE.

13–3. Use EXAMINE for the following, based on the contents of AMT-FIELD. Determine the result in AMT-FIELD and in the TALLY register. Questions are unrelated.

```
77   AMT-FIELD          PIC X(8)    VALUE '00012300'.
```

(a) Tally all zeros and replace with asterisks.

(b) Tally leading zeros and replace with asterisks.

(c) Tally up to the first zero and replace it with an asterisk.

(d) Replace the first occurrence of 1 with 2.

13–4. Use INSPECT for the following, based on the contents of AMOUNT. Determine the result in AMOUNT and define a TALLY counter and show its results.

```
77   AMOUNT             PIC 9(5)99   VALUE 00012.50.
```

(a) Tally all zeros in AMOUNT.

(b) Tally all leading zeros in AMOUNT.

(c) Tally the number of zeros before the decimal point.

(d) Replace leading zeros with blanks.

(e) Replace the first occurrence of 3 with 6.

(f) Replace all zeros with blanks.

(g) Tally all zeros and replace with asterisks.

13–5. Code a TRANSFORM statement to convert all commas, slashes, and decimal points to blanks in the following field:

```
77   FIELD              PIC X(25).
```

13–6. Use the following defined declaratives to answer the following questions:

```
77   FIELDA              PIC X(4)      VALUE 'CCMP'.
77   FIELDB              PIC X(6)      VALUE 'SYSTEM'.
77   FIELDC              PIC X(4)      VALUE 'UTER'.
77   FIELDX              PIC X(20)     VALUE SPACES.
```

(a) Code a STRING statement to form the value 'COMPUTER SYSTEM' in FIELDX using the contents of FIELDA, FIELDB, and FIELDC.

(b) Use STRING to form a value as in (a), but delimit each move by 'T'. Show the result in FIELDX.

(c) Assume that FIELDX contains the value 'COMPUTER SYSTEM' (left-adjusted in the field). UNSTRING the contents into the other three fields so that FIELDC contains 'COMP', FIELDA contains 'UTER', and FIELDB contains 'SYSTEM'.

PART V
FILE ORGANIZATION METHODS

CHAPTER 14

TAPE AND DISK SEQUENTIAL FILES

OBJECTIVE: *To introduce the concepts and uses of magnetic tape and disk storage.*

INTRODUCTION

A file, or data set, is a collection of related records. Most data processing applications require data files of such a volume that they cannot be kept in the computer's main storage. Historically, the device for maintaining these files has been the punched card. Punched cards, however, have some disadvantages:

- They are easily damaged, lost, or placed in the wrong sequence.
- They require considerable space for storing.
- They can be punched only once.
- They are limited to 80 or 96 characters of data.
- Input/output is slow.

Magnetic tape and disk, as external (or secondary) storage, overcome these drawbacks and are relatively inexpensive. Tape and disk provide mass external storage with extremely fast input/output, allow records of almost any length, and may be reused many times.

MAGNETIC TAPE

The magnetic tape that is used in a computer system is similar to magnetic tape that is used in a home music system because both can be recorded and erased. In this way, a tape can be used and reused, making it an economical storage medium. Data records on tape are usually stored sequentially, and a program that processes these records starts with the first record and reads or writes each record consecutively. Although tape processing is extremely fast, it is an inefficient method when accessing a specific record in a file.

The major users of tape are installations such as department stores and utility companies that require a great quantity of sequential processing and need to access many records when updating a file. Many installations use a mixture of magnetic tape and disk; magnetic tape is used as a backup to store the contents of the disk master files onto tape at the end of each workday. Therefore, backup tape copies are always available if it is necessary to rerun a job because of errors or damage.

Tape Characteristics

Magnetic tape consists of a thin metallic oxide coating on flexible plastic, with a width of ½-inch, although ¾-inch and 1-inch tape are also used. The length of a reel

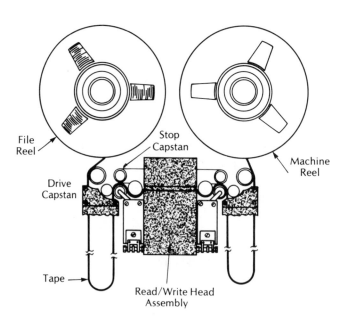

FIGURE 14-1   Magnetic Tape Drive.

of tape ranges from 200 feet to the common 2400 feet, with some as long as 3600 feet. Data are recorded as magnetic spots (bits) on the oxide side of the tape. Tape density is measured by the number of stored characters, or bytes, per inch (BPI), such as 800, 1600, or 6250 BPI. Therefore, a 2400-foot reel with a recording density of 1600 characters per inch would contain 46 million characters, which is equal to over a half-million 80-column punched cards. Tape read/write speeds vary from 36 to 200 inches per second.

Tape Format

A reflective strip, called a *load point marker,* that indicates where a system will begin reading or writing data is located about 15 feet from the beginning of a tape reel. Another reflective strip, called an *end-of-tape marker,* is located about 14 feet from the end of a reel and warns the system that the end of the reel is near and to conclude writing data. The load point marker and the end-of-tape marker are both placed physically on the tape on the side opposite the oxide.

Following the load point marker at the beginning of the tape is a *header label,* which is a record that describes a file. This record contains the name of the file (for example, CUSTOMER ACCOUNTS), the date the file was created, and the date the file will become obsolete and can be reused. The data file follows the header label with records stored as a *block,* with one or more records to a block. Records (and blocks) may be fixed length, such as 500 characters for each record, or variable length, with each record a different length. A file may be contained on one reel, or on many reels. The last record on a tape is called a *trailer label,* which is similar to the header label, but also contains the number of blocks written on the reel of tape. Unlike the load point marker and the end-of-tape marker, the header and trailer labels are actual *records* on tape, rather than physical strips. The system automatically handles the load point marker, header label, trailer label, and end-of-tape marker.

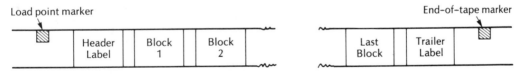

FIGURE 14-2   Magnetic Tape Format.

Blocked and Unblocked Records

Each block of data on tape is separated by a blank space ½ to ¾ inch long called an *interblock gap,* or *IBG.* Its purpose is to define the start and end of each block and to provide space for the tape to stop and restart. Records that are stored one to a block are called *unblocked.* An IBG follows each block and is shown in Figure 14-3A. To conserve tape storage and to speed input/output, you may specify a *blocking factor,* such as three records per block (see Figure 14-3B); the system writes an entire block of three records from main storage onto tape, and when reading, reads the entire block from tape into storage. All programs that reference this file must specify the same record and block length.

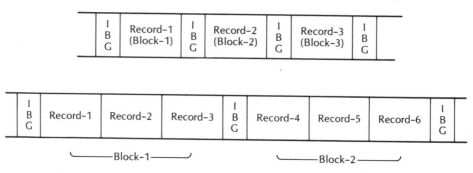

FIGURE 14-3   Tape Blocking

Tape Processing

Reading and writing magnetic tape is much like processing punched cards because the computer system handles most of the complexities. When a tape block writes from main storage, the computer automatically erases any previous data on tape.

Assuming that data records are already on magnetic tape, Figure 14-4 illustrates a typical tape file update. The customer sale and payment transactions are applied against the customer master record, with both transactions and master records in customer sequence. The system consists of four tape drives with one input tape as the old customer master and another input tape as the transaction file. A program reads all the transactions that match a master record and updates each customer's balance with sales and payments by writing each new updated master record on an output tape drive. For each master record that has no transactions, the program simply copies the unchanged master record onto the output file. The input files are only read, and not changed (this feature is useful if the program must be rerun). Another output tape drive may be used to produce a tape containing information to print a detailed report if the run is in balance and valid. The program may also print any warning messages or required control totals on the printer. Both the old customer master and the transaction file may require more than one reel. If a system has only four drives (as in Figure 14-4), after a reel is completely read, the operator has to cause the drive to rewind the reel. It is then replaced with the next reel for the file. Otherwise, additional tape drives must be used.

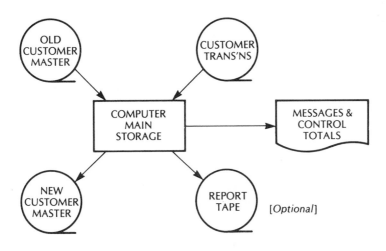

FIGURE 14-4   Tape File Updating.

PROGRAM EXAMPLE—CREATING A TAPE FILE

The program shown in Figure 14-5 creates a file of records on tape by reading card records and writing data onto tape, three records per block. Although the program appears to simply read one card and write one tape record, internally code is generated to move each output record into a buffer area that is large enough for a three-record block. After three output records have been moved successively into the buffer, the program writes the entire block of three records onto tape. In effect, the program reads three records and then writes one block, until all the input has been read. The last block may validly contain one, two, or three records. The blocking is automatically handled by compiler generated code.

There are several new features in this program. The SELECT statement indicates

ASSIGN TO SYS026-UT-3420-S-TAPEOUT.

SYS026 is the symbolic file name under DOS IBM (or whatever number is usually assigned by the installation). UT is the utility class for sequential (S) tape processing, and 3420 is an IBM tape drive model.   Following this is an external file name (TAPEOUT) used in job control entries, three to seven characters long. If present, the name must be the same as the one the job control entry used to create the file. Under OS, the statement could appear as:

ASSIGN TO UT-3420-S-TAPEOUT or ASSIGN TO UT-S-TAPEOUT.

This device number is optional for OS because at execute time the Data Definition

```
      IDENTIFICATION DIVISION.
      PROGRAM-ID. CHAP14A.
      *           CREATES A TAPE FILE FROM CARD RECORDS.

      ENVIRONMENT DIVISION.
      INPUT-OUTPUT SECTION.
      FILE-CONTROL.
          SELECT CARD-PAYT-FILE ASSIGN TO SYS015-UR-2501-S.
          SELECT TAPE-PAYT-FILE ASSIGN TO SYS026-UT-3420-S-TAPEPAY.

      DATA DIVISION.
      FILE SECTION.
      FD  CARD-PAYT-FILE
          LABEL RECORDS ARE OMITTED
          DATA RECORD IS PAY-REC-IN.
      01  PAY-REC-IN.
          03  CODE-IN          PIC X.
          03  FILLER           PIC X(4).
          03  CUST-IN          PIC X(7).
          03  PAYT-IN          PIC S9(4)V99.
          03  DATE-IN          PIC S9(6).
          03  FILLER           PIC X(56).


      FD  TAPE-PAYT-FILE
          LABEL RECORDS ARE STANDARD
          RECORD CONTAINS 20 CHARACTERS
          BLOCK  CONTAINS 10 RECORDS
          DATA RECORD IS PAY-REC-OUT.
      01  PAY-REC-OUT.
          03  CODE-OUT         PIC X.
          03  CUST-OUT         PIC X(7).
          03  PAYT-OUT         PIC S9(5)V99 COMP-3.
          03  DATE-OUT         PIC S9(6).
          03  FILLER           PIC X(2).

      WORKING-STORAGE SECTION.
      77  EOF-FLAG             PIC X(3)    VALUE ' '.
          88  END-FILE                     VALUE 'EOF'.

      PROCEDURE DIVISION.
      A000-MAIN SECTION.
          OPEN INPUT CARD-PAYT-FILE
               OUTPUT TAPE-PAYT-FILE.
          MOVE SPACES TO PAY-REC-OUT.
          READ CARD-PAYT-FILE
              AT END MOVE 'EOF' TO EOF-FLAG.
          PERFORM B000-PROC UNTIL END-FILE.
          CLOSE CARD-PAYT-FILE, FILEIN.
          STOP RUN.
      A999-END. EXIT.

      B000-PROC SECTION.
          MOVE CUST-IN TO CUST-OUT.
          MOVE CODE-IN TO CODE-OUT.
          MOVE PAYT-IN TO PAYT-OUT.
          MOVE DATE-IN TO DATE-OUT.
          WRITE PAY-REC-OUT.
          READ CARD-PAYT-FILE
              AT END MOVE 'EOF' TO EOF-FLAG.
      B999-RETURN. EXIT.
```

FIGURE 14-5   Creating a Tape File.

268

(DD) entry designates the device to be used. Under CDC this entry would be as follows:

ASSIGN TO TAPE01.

The FD statement in Figure 14-5 contains the following new entries:

- LABEL RECORDS ARE STANDARD. A standard descriptive label is to precede the file on tape. The input/output system stores information about the file in this area (such as the date when the file becomes obsolete and may be erased).
- RECORD CONTAINS 20 CHARACTERS. The length of each output record is 20 characters. Although the input record is 80 characters, tape and disk output records may be almost any length (the minimum length varies by computer system). A shorter record length permits a larger amount of records to be stored on a tape. Under IBM DOS, IBM OS, CDC, and many other compilers, this entry is only descriptive because the compiler calculates the record length from the data record definition.
  Note that both PAY-REC-OUT and the RECORD CONTAINS entry contain 20 characters; every program that subsequently reads this file must define the file with this record and block size.
- BLOCK CONTAINS 10 RECORDS. The program defines a buffer area large enough for ten records. It requires ten WRITE statements to fill the buffer, and when full, the program physically writes the block onto tape. Since an interblock gap precedes and follows each tape block, blocking of records in this way reduces the amount of unused tape space. The BLOCK CONTAINS entry is required if there is more than one record per block. Under IBM OS and some other systems, a common practice is to code

BLOCK CONTAINS 0 RECORDS

and to specify the blocking value in a job control entry.

The tape record and fields follow the FD statement and are described in a similar way to card and printer files. Although records are blocked, PAY-REC-OUT defines only one record. The program creates the record in PAY-REC-OUT and on a WRITE statement, the system delivers the record to a buffer large enough for three records. Tape and disk records can contain fields defined as COMP or COMP-3. On the 360/370, it is common practice to store arithmetic data on tape or disk in packed format (two digits per byte, plus a half-byte for the sign) as follows:

03   PAYT-OUT   PIC S9(5)V99 COMP-3.

In this case, the field length is four bytes, as nn/nn/nn/ns, where n is any digit and s is sign. If the field is binary, then the correct format is COMP, but SYNC should not be used (because it may cause erroneous alignment).

The OPEN statement creates the tape header label according to job control entries. The WRITE handles blocking of output records, and the CLOSE writes an appropriate end-of-file marker and trailer label. As a result, coding in the Procedure Division for tape and sequential disk is similar to coding for card and printer. OPEN and CLOSE can also handle more than one reel for a file *(multireel file)*. It is also possible to have more than one file on one tape reel *(multifile reel)*, and for this, DOS and OS require no special coding because they can automatically locate the specified file (however, some COBOL versions require a special I-O-CONTROL paragraph in the Environment Division). The system automatically rewinds tape reels when they are closed, but for a multifile reel, you may want to continue processing subsequent files. Therefore, to prevent rewinding, use the NO REWIND option:

CLOSE filename NO REWIND.

And to prevent the file from being reopened during program execution, use the LOCK option:

CLOSE filename LOCK.

DISK STORAGE

Devices that can access any record on a file directly are called *direct access storage devices,* or *DASD* (the ANS term is *mass storage*). These include magnetic disk storage (the most common), drum storage, and diskette storage. Each magnetic disk storage device uses a removable *pack* that contains a number of thin circular plates. Both sides of each plate (except the outer top and bottom) are coated with a ferrous oxide material to permit recording. Each plate, or disk, is stacked one on top of the other and contains circular *tracks* on which data records are stored as magnetized bits (Figure 14-6).

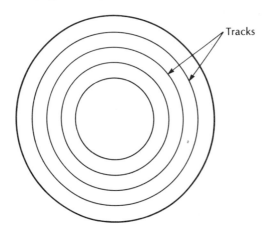

FIGURE 14-6   Disk Surface and Tracks.

The disks are constantly rotating on a vertical shaft. The disk device has a set of access arms that move read/write heads from track to track to read data records from the disk track into main storage, or to write records from main storage onto the disk track. Because disk packs are removable, another file may be placed on the disk drive for processing.

Magnetic disk storage is characterized by its versatility because it can be used to process records both sequentially and randomly (directly). Therefore, programs can randomly update master files on disk with unsorted transactions. Such processing is feasible where the files are not extremely large and there is not a large volume of transactions to process.

Disk Format

The amount of data that a disk device can store varies considerably by model, ranging from small disks with 1 million characters to large disks with 300 million characters or more. Some disk models use fixed-length *sectors* on each track to store one or more records. The system addresses a record by disk number, track number, and sector number. Other disk models do not use sectors, can store records almost any length with one or more records on a track, and address the records by disk surface number and track number. All records may be unblocked or blocked, and fixed or variable in length.

Like magnetic tape, a disk file contains header and trailer labels, and gaps between each block of data. A data file may be so large that it requires space on more than one disk pack, or so small that a disk pack may contain more than one file. Disk storage begins with the top outermost track (track-0) and then continues consecutively down track by track through to the bottom outermost track. It then continues

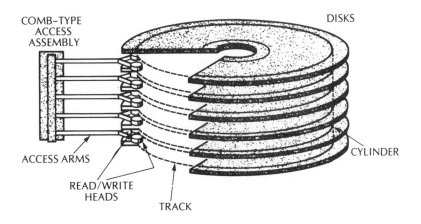

FIGURE 14-7   Disk Read/write Mechanism.

with the next inner set of tracks (track-1), starting with the top track through to the bottom track. On IBM systems, the vertical set of tracks is called a *cylinder*. Thus, if there are 20 surfaces on a disk, then there are 20 tracks called track-0, each on a different surface. The outer set of 20 tracks is called cylinder-0, and the next inner vertical set of tracks is cylinder-1, the next is cylinder-2, and so on. If the device contains 200 sets of tracks, then there are 200 cylinders numbered 0 through 199, each with 20 tracks.

PROGRAM EXAMPLE—CREATING A DISK FILE

The program in Figure 14-8 creates a sequential file of records on disk using as input the tape file created in Figure 14-5. The program reads each tape record (which are three per block) and writes six records per block onto disk. Once again, the program as coded appears to read and write one record at a time, but remember that the blocking is performed by generated code. To the programmer, sequential programming of disk and tape is similar to card processing.

The SELECT statement indicates SYS030-UT-3340-S-DISKPAY. SYS030 is the symbolic file name (or the number usually assigned by an installation). UT is the utility class for sequential processing on an IBM 3340 disk device. DISKPAY is a name (from 3 to 7 characters) by which job control may recognize the file. The entries shown are for an IBM DOS COBOL version and may vary considerably under other systems. Two optional entries in the SELECT statement for sequential disk are ORGANIZATION and ACCESS MODE, as follows:

```
SELECT ...
       ORGANIZATION IS SEQUENTIAL
       ACCESS MODE  IS SEQUENTIAL
```

However, most programmers omit these entries and allow the compiler to default to sequential processing. The ASSIGN clauses for other COBOL versions are as follows:

```
IBM OS:    ASSIGN TO UT-3340-S-DISKPAY.      (disk device, 3340, is optional)
CDC-6000: ASSIGN TO DISK01.
```

The WRITE statement contains an INVALID KEY clause to indicate an attempt to write beyond the area (extent) allocated for the output file. You may read this clause as "If the attempt to write is invalid . . . ." For sequential writing, the ANS specifications no longer require this clause, but it is still used by many COBOL versions. Sequential reading of a disk file requires the usual AT END clause. Other disk organization methods (Indexed Sequential, Virtual Storage, Direct, and Relative) require the use of INVALID KEY for nonsequential reading and writing. The precise meaning of INVALID KEY varies according to its use.

```
IDENTIFICATION DIVISION.
PROGRAM-ID. CHAP14B.
*          CREATES A DISK FILE FROM A TAPE INPUT FILE.

ENVIRONMENT DIVISION.
INPUT-OUTPUT SECTION.
FILE-CONTROL.
     SELECT TAPE-PAYT-IN.  ASSIGN TO SYS026-UT-3420-S-TAPEPAY.
     SELECT DISK-PAYT-OUT. ASSIGN TO SYS030-UT-3340-S-DISKPAY.

DATA DIVISION.
FILE SECTION.
FD   TAPE-PAYT-IN
     LABEL RECORDS ARE STANDARD
     RECORD CONTAINS 20 CHARACTERS
     BLOCK  CONTAINS 10 RECORDS
     DATA RECORD IS PAY-REC-IN.
01   PAY-REC-IN          PIC X(20).

FD   DISK-PAYT-OUT
     LABEL RECORDS ARE STANDARD
     RECORD CONTAINS 20 CHARACTERS
     BLOCK  CONTAINS 16 RECORDS
     DATA RECORD IS PAY-REC-OUT.
01   PAY-REC-OUT         PIC X(20).

WORKING-STORAGE SECTION.
77   EOF-FLAG            PIC X(3)    VALUE ' '.
     88  END-FILE                    VALUE 'EOF'.

PROCEDURE DIVISION.
A000-MAIN SECTION.
     OPEN INPUT TAPE-PAYT-IN
          OUTPUT DISK-PAYT-OUT.
     READ TAPE-PAYT-IN
          AT END MOVE 'EOF' TO EOF-FLAG.
     PERFORM B000-PROC UNTIL END-FILE.
     CLOSE TAPE-PAYT-IN, DISK-PAYT-OUT.
     STOP RUN.
A999-END. EXIT.

B000-PROC SECTION.
     MOVE PAY-REC-IN TO PAY-REC-OUT.
     WRITE PAY-REC-OUT
          INVALID KEY DISPLAY PAY-REC-OUT, 'INVALID WRITE'.
     READ TAPE-PAYT-IN
          AT END MOVE 'EOF' TO EOF-FLAG.
B999-RETURN.  EXIT.
```

FIGURE 14-8 Creating a Sequential Disk File.

VARIABLE LENGTH RECORDS

Variable Length Record Format

When record formats provide for fields or groups of fields that may or may not be present, it may be economical to define the records as *variable length* in order to compress the file size. There are two common approaches to variable length records:

1. *Variable length fields.* For customer name and address fields that vary considerably in length, a program may store only significant characters and not store trailing blanks. One approach is to follow each variable field with a special delimiter character, such as an asterisk, so that to find the end of the field, the program could scan for the delimiter using the EXAMINE or INSPECT statements, which are covered in Chapter 13.
2. *Variable number of fields.* Records may contain a variable number of fields. For example, a telephone company may store a variable number of long-distance call charges for customers' bills, or in the example that follows, each record contains sales amounts for a variable period of one to twelve months.

Coding Variable Length Records

Coding for variable length records requires only a familiarity with subscripts. As an example, assume product sales records that accumulate sales for a twelve-month period. Each record contains fields for product number, description, sales amount, and a field (NO-MOS-IN) for the number of months' sales. For example, if NO-MOS-IN contains 02, then the record contains sales amounts for January and February. By the end of the year, the record contains a maximum of twelve months' sales. In Figure 14-9, the FD statement specifies the following:

*   RECORDING MODE indicates V for variable. Since the compiler can determine that the record is variable length, the statement is optional, but useful for documentation.
*   RECORD CONTAINS provides the minimum number of characters (one month's sales) and the maximum number of characters (twelve months' sales).
*   BLOCK CONTAINS provides an arbitrary block size. The system will store as many records as possible into this length. Consequently, blocks and records are variable length. Under IBM OS, you could code BLOCK CONTAINS min TO max RECORDS, or BLOCK CONTAINS 0 RECORDS (with the value in a job control entry).

```
FD   MONTHS-SALES-FILE
     LABEL RECORDS ARE STANDARD
     RECORDING MODE IS V
     RECORD CONTAINS 31 TO 75 CHARACTERS
     BLOCK CONTAINS 292 CHARACTERS
     DATA RECORD IS SALES-RECORD-IN.
01   SALES-RECORD-IN.
     05   PRODUCT-IN       PIC X(5).
     05   DESCRIP-IN       PIC X(20).
     05   NO-MOS-IN        PIC S99        COMP-3.
     05   SALES-IN         OCCURS 1 TO 12 TIMES
                           DEPENDING ON NO-MOS-IN
                           PIC S9(5)V99 COMP-3.
     .
     .
     .
     MOVE NO-MOS-IN TO SUB-2.
     PERFORM M200-ADD VARYING SUB-1 FROM 1 BY 1
                   UNTIL SUB-1 > SUB-2.
     .
     .
     .
 M200-ADD SECTION.
     ADD SALES-IN (SUB-1) TO TOTAL-SALES.
 M299-RETURN. EXIT.
```

FIGURE 14-9   Variable Length Records.

The input record in Figure 14-9 defines NO-MOS-IN *before* the variable sales data SALES-IN and also references it in the DEPENDING ON clause. It is the programmer's responsibility when creating the file to store the correct count in NO-MOS-IN. The program uses a subscript to reference SALES-IN. The partial code in the figure adds the contents of the months' sales field to a sales accumulator, TOTAL-SALES. The PERFORM statement executes a variable number of times, depending on the value in NO-MOS-IN.

Use of Variable Length Records

Variable length records, when used appropriately, can provide more efficient use of tape and disk storage. But beware of trivial applications, because the system generates overhead that may defeat any expected savings. On IBM 360/370, the system inserts a 4-byte record length in front of each record, and a 4-byte block length in front of each block. Therefore, the actual stored block, if as in the example all records were maximum length (twelve months), would be as follows:

Block length for one block	4
Record length for four records	16
Four records (4 × 75)	300
	320 bytes

Under OS, you code the DCB parameters to include the maximum lengths: LRECL=77, and BLKSIZE=312.

PROBLEMS

14-1. What are the major uses of magnetic tape?

14-2. Distinguish between a record and a block.

14-3. What indicates the beginning and the end of a block of data on tape?

14-4. Code a program to create a tape file. Customer input records are on cards, with the following fields:

Col.		Col.		
1–3	Branch number	35–40	Current amount due	(xxxx.xx)
4–8	Customer number	41–46	31–60 days due	(xxxx.xx)
9–28	Customer name	47–52	61–90 days due	(xxxx.xx)
31–34	Credit limit (no cents)	53–58	Over 90 days due	(xxxx.xx)

Amount fields are for balances owing, aged by month. Store arithmetic fields on the tape record in computational format (COMP-3 if IBM). Ensure that records are in ascending sequence by customer number. Accumulate and print total amounts owing.

14-5. Code a program to print the contents of the tape file created in Problem 14-4. Format the print area for clarity, allowing for decimal points and negative current amount owing (caused by overpayments). Show with asterisks any customer whose total amount owing (current, 31, 61, plus over 90) exceeds the credit limit.

14-6. What advantage does disk storage have compared with magnetic tape?

14-7. What is a "cylinder"?

14-8. Determine the method of disk storage in your system.

    (a) If the disk devices store records by track and cylinder as do IBM devices, determine the number of bytes that one track and one cylinder can contain.

(b) If the devices store data by sectors, determine the amount of storage in one sector and the entire disk.

14–9. Revise problem 14-4 so that the output is on disk.

14–10. Code a program to age customer balances. Disk records are those created by the previous problem, in sequence of customer number.

At the end of each month, the program has to "age" each customer's balances. (Subsequently during the month, another program updates the balances by adding sales to current due and deducting payments from the oldest balance(s)—see problem 15-7.) For each customer, age balances as follows:

- Add 61–90 to over 90.
- Move 31–60 to 61–90.

Move current due only if positive to 31–60, and clear current due. Negative balances are not aged. Accordingly, the current due field will now contain either zero or negative balances. For example:

	CURRENT DUE	31–60	61–90	OVER 90
Before aging:	$50	$75	$45	$20
After aging:	0	50	75	65

Write a new aged master file. Suggestion: to check the contents of output records, also DISPLAY each record's contents.

14–11. What is the advantage of using variable length records?

CHAPTER 15

FILE MERGING AND UPDATING

OBJECTIVE: To cover the requirements for merging and updating sequential disk files.

INTRODUCTION

Much data processing activity is involved with processing two or more input files. Some programs *merge* data from separate files into a single file, and others *update* master files with transaction records. This chapter covers file processing and terminology in general, and the particular programming requirements to merge and to update disk files.

DATA PROCESSING SYSTEMS

There are three basic phases in a typical business computer system, as shown in Figure 15-1. The example illustrates a *batch system* in which the source documents are gathered in a batch, keyed, and then entered into the computer system for processing. The three phases are as follows:

1. File creation
2. File updating
3. File reporting

A computer program usually prints information pertaining to the work that has been accomplished, which can be considered as a form of "audit trail."

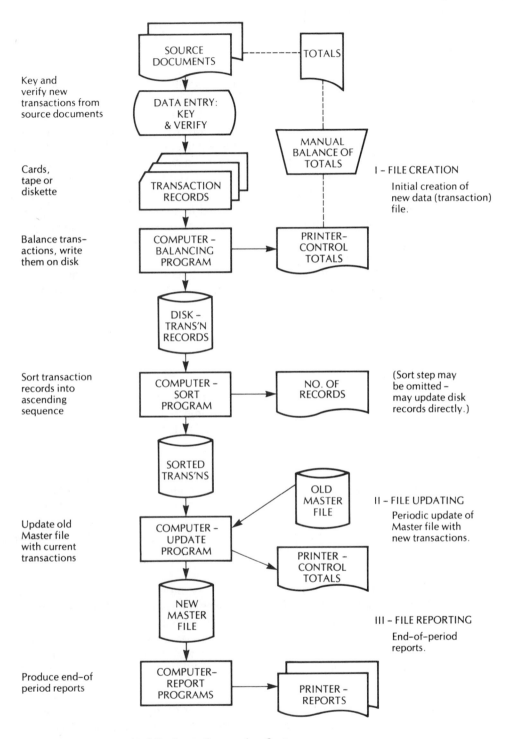

Key and
verify new
transactions from
source documents

Cards,
tape or
diskette

Balance trans-
actions, write
them on disk

Sort transaction
records into
ascending
sequence

Update old
Master file
with current
transactions

Produce end-of
period reports

SOURCE
DOCUMENTS

TOTALS

DATA ENTRY:
KEY
& VERIFY

MANUAL
BALANCE OF
TOTALS

I – FILE CREATION

Initial creation of
new data (transaction)
file.

TRANSACTION
RECORDS

COMPUTER –
BALANCING
PROGRAM

PRINTER-
CONTROL
TOTALS

DISK –
TRANS'N
RECORDS

COMPUTER –
SORT
PROGRAM

NO. OF
RECORDS

(Sort step may
be omitted –
may update disk
records directly.)

SORTED
TRANS'NS

OLD
MASTER
FILE

COMPUTER –
UPDATE
PROGRAM

II – FILE UPDATING

Periodic update of
Master file with
new transactions.

PRINTER –
CONTROL
TOTALS

NEW
MASTER
FILE

III – FILE REPORTING

End-of-period
reports.

COMPUTER-
REPORT
PROGRAMS

PRINTER –
REPORTS

FIGURE 15-1   Typical Business Processing System.

279

File Creation

The first phase, the file creation run, requires input data from any source in an acceptable format for subsequent updating of the master file. As an example, assume that transaction records are unsorted payments made by customers and are to be used to update customer master records. Before updating the master file, the file creation program must ensure that the total of payments is in balance. Control clerks should already have counted the total number of payments and added the total dollar value of payments from the source documents. The file creation program adds the total payments, counts the number of records, and prints these at the end of the run. The Control clerks then check that the printed totals agree with the totals from the source documents to ensure that the records were keyed correctly. They also check for missing records by using the printed list of transaction records, since the file is still in the same sequence as the source documents. Once the transaction file is found to be correct, the records are sorted into ascending sequence by customer (this step is necessary for card and tape master files and optional for disk files because many disk systems apply transactions directly to the master file).

File Updating

The second phase, the file update run, applies one or more transaction files against a master file. As in the file creation example, assume that the transactions are customer payment records. The update method varies by system and devices; however, most file updates follow a common pattern:

1. Each master record contains a unique control field (customer account number) with only one master record for each account number, and with customer records stored in ascending sequence. (The customer numbers are not necessarily consecutive.)
2. There may be any number of transactions (payments) for a master (customer) record, or none.

Tape Files.   A typical tape-oriented system has three or more tape drives that are used for either input or output. The master tape file is loaded on one tape drive, and the transactions, in the same sequence, are loaded on another tape drive. The program writes a new updated master tape file on a third drive. (You temporarily preserve rather than erase the old master file so that there is a backup master file in case the job must be rerun because of error or breakdowns.)

Disk Files.   A disk system may have any number of disk drives. A disk file update can be performed similar to a tape file update, or by random or direct processing with transactions in any sequence, and disk master records updated *in place*—the program locates the master record for the transaction and rewrites the new changed record directly over the original master disk record. Random processing must be done carefully because there is no automatic backup if the job must be rerun.

A major problem in a file update is the existence of a transaction for which there is no corresponding master record. The program logic can be quite complex, and a programmer must adopt some rational strategy.

File Reporting

The third phase, file reporting, is a large part of the programming effort. Reports may be based on transaction files, master files, or both. A system may produce a summarized report file on tape or disk as a by-product of some other processing, and consequently the report file may be selectively used to produce various reports.

MULTIPLE INPUT DEVICES AND FILES

Most computer systems today use disk or tape storage with the capability of processing data with multiple inputs. This capability simplifies the system but complicates programming, but fortunately, there is a standard approach for processing more than one input called the *balance line method*. In this method, the first record of each file is read to determine which file has the lowest control field (some call this the *low key*). The program then processes the file or files with the low control by either *file merging* or *file updating*. Typically, a merge combines several transaction files into one file, whereas an update applies transaction records against a master file.

File Merging

The flowchart in Figure 15-2 merges three transaction input files (customer sales, payments, and adjustments) into one output file. The files are all in ascending sequence by customer, with any number of transactions for each customer. Any file can contain the lowest control field at any time. After reading the first record of each file (at BEGIN), the merge program performs the following steps:

1. Selects the lowest customer number from among the three files and stores the number in a field called LOWCTL.
2. Checks if LOWCTL contains the highest possible value. This check is an end-of-job test, explained in steps 4 and 6.
3. Checks the sales file, the payment file, and the adjustment file and processes the file whose customer number equals LOWCTL (it may be one, two, or all three files). If a file's customer number is equal to LOWCTL, its record is written

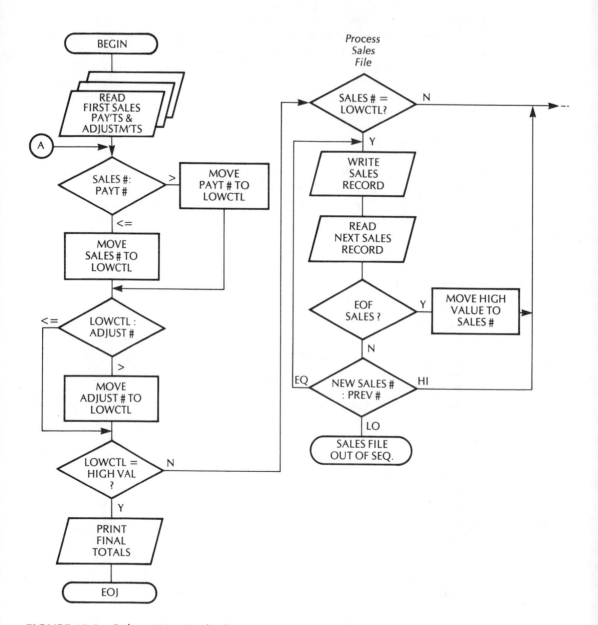

FIGURE 15-2 Balance Line Method—Merging Three Input Files.

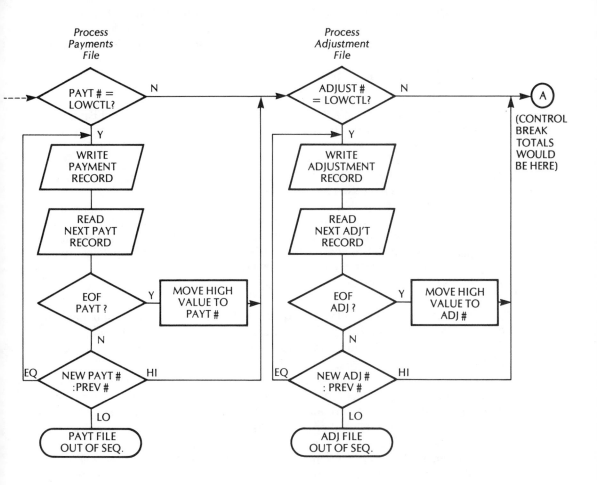

on tape or disk, and the next input record for that file is read and checked for sequence. Each file when read is sequenced against itself as follows:

- LOW Out-of-sequence customer—error (not shown in detail in Figure 15-2).

- EQUAL Same customer number—write the record.

- HIGH Branch to process the next file.

4. Assigns the system's highest value into its customer number field if a read operation encounters an end-of-file. This is to prevent the program from attempting to read another record for that file. But the program must continue processing the other files not at their end-of-file.

5. After reading and writing all the records for a customer, returns to step 1 to determine which file now has the lowest customer number.

6. For each input file that reaches an end-of-file, stores the high value in its customer number. Once all files reach end-of-file, each file will contain the high value, and the comparison for the lowest customer number in step 1 results in storing this highest value in LOWCTL. At this point, step 2 determines that all files have been read and processed.

7. Prints final totals and terminates the run.

The balance line method works equally well for more than three input files. For each additional file, simply insert another test to find the low control word and one more vertical column to process the file. The input files may be on any combination of devices, such as card reader, tape, or disk.

The flowchart in Figure 15-2 is conventional and illustrates the typical approach to solving a merge problem in any language. Figure 15-3 shows the code for merging two input files into one output file using the flowchart as a guide, with some adaptations for structured programming conventions. The two input disk files, PAYT-FILE-IN and SALE-FILE-IN, merge into one output file, TRAN-FILE-OUT. The program moves HIGH-VALUES into the control field of the input files when they reach their end. Either file may run out first, and when both contain HIGH-VALUES, the program terminates.

File Updating

Quite often, one file is a master file and the others are transactions. A program has to *update* the master file balances with the current transaction amounts. The solution is similar to that for merging files, but with several important differences. The logic requires that there be only one record for each master, but none or any number for the transactions. Also, the lowest control word must be that of the master file.

The flowchart in Figure 15-4 updates an inventory master file with two transaction files: stock receipt records and stock issues. Restrictions regarding this inventory file update are as follows:

1. There is only one master file record for each stock item;
2. There may be none or any number of receipts and issues for each stock item;
3. Each file is in stock item sequence.

```
00002          IDENTIFICATION DIVISION.
00003          PROGRAM-ID. CHAP15A.
00004      *             MERGES PAYMENT & SALES FILE INTO ONE TRANSACTION FILE.
00005
00006          ENVIRONMENT DIVISION.
00007          INPUT-OUTPUT SECTION.
00008          FILE-CONTROL.
00009              SELECT PAYT-FILE-IN,   ASSIGN TO SYS007-UT-3340-S-CUSTPAY.
00010              SELECT SALE-FILE-IN,   ASSIGN TO SYS008-UT-3340-S-CUSTSAL.
00011              SELECT TRAN-FILE-OUT,  ASSIGN TO SYS009-UT-3340-S-CUSTRAN.
00012
00013          DATA DIVISION.
00014          FILE SECTION.
00015          FD  PAYT-FILE-IN,
00016              LABEL RECORDS ARE STANDARD
00017              RECORD CONTAINS 20 CHARACTERS
00018              BLOCK  CONTAINS 10 RECORDS
00019              DATA RECORD IS PAYT-REC-IN.
00020          01  PAYT-REC-IN.
00021              05   PAY-CODE-IN         PIC X.
00022              05   PAYT-CTL-IN         PIC X(07).
00023              05   FILLER              PIC X(12).
00024
00025          FD  SALE-FILE-IN,
00026              LABEL RECORDS ARE STANDARD
00027              RECORD CONTAINS 20 CHARACTERS
00028              BLOCK  CONTAINS 10 RECORDS
00029              DATA RECORD IS SALE-REC-IN.
00030          01  SALE-REC-IN.
00031              05   SALE-CODE-IN        PIC X.
00032              05   SALE-CTL-IN         PIC X(07).
00033              05   FILLER              PIC X(12).
00034
00035          FD  TRAN-FILE-OUT,
00036              LABEL RECORDS ARE STANDARD
00037              RECORD CONTAINS 20 CHARACTERS
00038              BLOCK  CONTAINS 10 RECORDS
00039              DATA RECORD IS TRAN-REC-OUT.
00040          01  TRAN-REC-OUT.
00041              05   FILLER              PIC X(20).
00042
00043          WORKING-STORAGE SECTION.
00044          77  LOW-CTL-KEY              PIC X(7)     VALUE LOW-VALUES.
00045              88   PROCESSING-COMPLETE              VALUE HIGH-VALUES.
```

FIGURE 15-3   File Merge Program.

```
00047              PROCEDURE DIVISION.
00048              A000-MAIN-LOGIC SECTION.
00049                  OPEN   INPUT PAYT-FILE-IN
00050                              SALE-FILE-IN
00051                       OUTPUT TRAN-FILE-OUT.
00052                  READ PAYT-FILE-IN
00053                       AT END MOVE HIGH-VALUES TO PAYT-CTL-IN.
00054                  READ SALE-FILE-IN
00055                       AT END MOVE HIGH-VALUES TO SALE-CTL-IN.
00056                  IF PAYT-CTL-IN NOT > SALE-CTL-IN
00057                       MOVE PAYT-CTL-IN TO LOW-CTL-KEY
00058                  ELSE
00059                       MOVE SALE-CTL-IN TO LOW-CTL-KEY.
00060                  PERFORM B000-PROCESS UNTIL PROCESSING-COMPLETE.
00061                  DISPLAY 'END OF MERGE'.
00062                  CLOSE PAYT-FILE-IN
00063                        SALE-FILE-IN
00064                        TRAN-FILE-OUT.
00065                  STOP RUN.
00066              A999-END. EXIT.

00068              B000-PROCESS SECTION.
00069                  IF PAYT-CTL-IN = LOW-CTL-KEY
00070                       PERFORM C000-PAYT UNTIL PAYT-CTL-IN NOT = LOW-CTL-KEY
00071                  ELSE
00072                       PERFORM D000-SALE UNTIL SALE-CTL-IN NOT = LOW-CTL-KEY.
00073                  IF PAYT-CTL-IN NOT > SALE-CTL-IN
00074                       MOVE PAYT-CTL-IN TO LOW-CTL-KEY
00075                  ELSE
00076                       MOVE SALE-CTL-IN TO LOW-CTL-KEY.
00077              B999-RETURN. EXIT.

00079              C000-PAYT SECTION.
00080                  MOVE PAYT-REC-IN TO TRAN-REC-OUT.
00081                  WRITE TRAN-REC-OUT   INVALID KEY DISPLAY 'INVALID WRITE'.
00082                  READ PAYT-FILE-IN
00083                       AT END MOVE HIGH-VALUES TO PAYT-CTL-IN.
00084              C999-RETURN. EXIT.

00086              D000-SALE SECTION.
00087                  MOVE SALE-REC-IN TO TRAN-REC-OUT.
00088                  WRITE TRAN-REC-OUT   INVALID KEY DISPLAY 'INVALID WRITE'.
00089                  READ SALE-FILE-IN
00090                       AT END MOVE HIGH-VALUES TO SALE-CTL-IN.
00091              D999-RETURN. EXIT.
```

FIGURE 15-3 (Cont.)

The update program performs the following steps:

1. Reads the first record for each input file.
2. Determines which file has the lowest stock number and stores the number in LOWCTL, as in the merge. The master file must contain every valid stock

number; the master, therefore, must be equal to or lower than receipts or issues stock numbers.

3. Tests contents of LOWCTL for the high value, as in the merge flowchart. At this point, LOWCTL contains the lowest stock number (the master's).

4. Branches to the next column to process the master file, stores the fields of the master record, and sets up the output record for the new master file.

5. Reads the next master record and if it is at end-of-file, stores the high value into the input master stock number, therefore, preventing the program from attempting to read more master records. If not at end-of-file, compares the new master just read with the previous master stock number. It must be *higher;* low and equal conditions are errors.

6. Branches to the next column to process the receipts file and compares receipts stock numbers with LOWCTL, the current lowest stock number. The receipts should not be low; if high, there are no receipts for this stock number, and branches to process issues (in the next column).

7. If a receipts stock number equals LOWCTL, adds the receipt quantity to the stored master quantity and to total receipts; reads the next receipt record, and if it is at end-of-file, stores the high value into the input receipt stock number.

8. If not at end-of-file, compares the new receipt stock number just read with the previous stock number (low comparison is an out-of-sequence error). Equal comparison is for the same stock number, branches back to process the record (step 7), and to read the next receipt. If high comparison, record is for a higher stock number, branches to the next column to process the issues file.

9. Processing of issues is similar to that for receipts; at end-of-file, stores the high value into the input issues stock number.

10. After processing all issues for the stock item, branches to the next column to check the sequence of the output and to write the new updated inventory master record (this procedure could also perform a control break and print totals on branch or region number).

11. Returns to the beginning (step 2) to test and process new records.

The flowchart in Figure 15-4 is conventional and illustrates the typical approach to solving an update program in any language. Figure 15-5 shows the coding for a program that updates a master file with one transaction file, adapted for structured programming conventions. There is one master record for each customer and any amount of transaction records per customer. The program matches the transactions to the masters and adds the transaction amount to each customer's balance. Note that the input/output record amount fields are defined as computational so that the program can perform arithmetic directly on the fields. The only complication in the program is handling transactions for which no master record exists. For these the program bypasses the unmatched transactions and prints a warning message. Either file may run out first, and the logic handles both cases. If the Master File runs out first, the remaining mismatched transactions print as error messages.

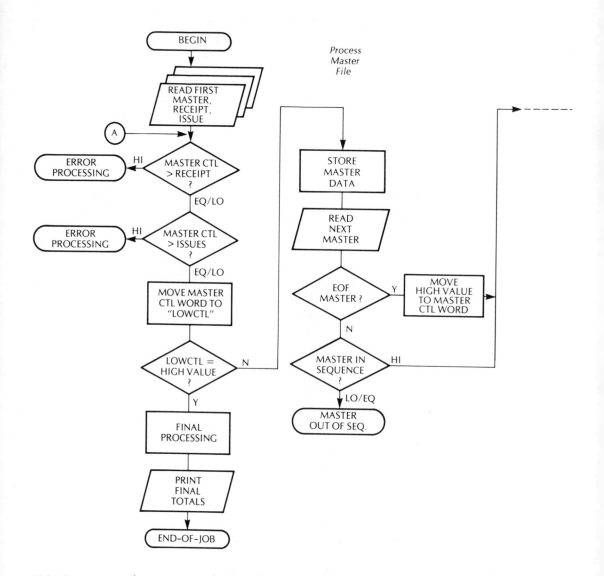

FIGURE 15-4   Balance Line Method—File Updating.

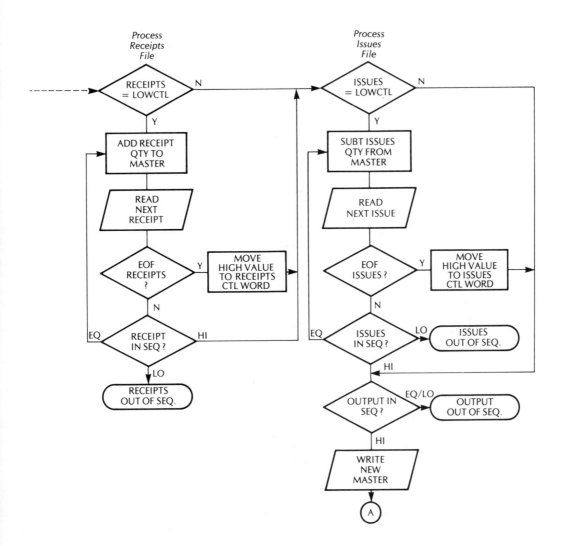

289

```
00002            IDENTIFICATION DIVISION.
00003            PROGRAM-ID. CHAP15B.
00004       *         SEQUENTIALLY UPDATES A DISK MASTER FILE
00005       *         WITH TRANSACTION RECORDS.

00007            ENVIRONMENT DIVISION.
00008            INPUT-OUTPUT SECTION.
00009            FILE-CONTROL.
00010                SELECT MAST-FILE-IN   ASSIGN TO SYS008-UT-3340-S-CUSTMAS.
00011                SELECT TRAN-FILE-IN   ASSIGN TO SYS009-UT-3340-S-CUSTRAN.
00012                SELECT MAST-FILE-OUT  ASSIGN TO SYS010-UT-3340-S-CUSTMAS.
00013
00014            DATA DIVISION.
00015            FILE SECTION.
00016            FD  MAST-FILE-IN
00017                LABEL RECORDS ARE STANDARD
00018                RECORD CONTAINS 40 CHARACTERS
00019                BLOCK CONTAINS 5 RECORDS
00020                DATA RECORD IS MAST-REC-IN.
00021            01  MAST-REC-IN.
00022                05   MAST-CTL-IN    PIC X(07).
00023                05   FILLER         PIC X(22).
00024                05   MAST-AMT-IN    PIC S9(5)V99      COMP-3.
00025                05   FILLER         PIC X(7).

00027            FD  TRAN-FILE-IN
00028                LABEL RECORDS ARE STANDARD
00029                RECORD CONTAINS 20 CHARACTERS
00030                BLOCK  CONTAINS 16 RECORDS
00031                DATA RECORD IS TRAN-REC-IN.
00032            01  TRAN-REC-IN.
00033                05   CODE-IN        PIC X.
00034                05   TRAN-CTL-IN    PIC X(7).
00035                05   TRAN-AMT-IN    PIC S9(5)V99      COMP-3.
00036                05   FILLER         PIC X(8).

00038            FD  MAST-FILE-OUT
00039                LABEL RECORDS ARE STANDARD
00040                RECORD CONTAINS 40 CHARACTERS
00041                BLOCK CONTAINS  5 RECORDS
00042                DATA RECORD IS MAST-REC-OUT.
00043            01  MAST-REC-OUT.
00044                05   MAST-CTL-OUT   PIC X(7).
00045                05   FILLER         PIC X(22).
00046                05   MAST-AMT-OUT   PIC S9(5)V99      COMP-3.
00047                05   FILLER         PIC X(7).

00049            WORKING-STORAGE SECTION.
00050            77  LOW-CTL-KEY         PIC X(7)     VALUE LOW-VALUES.
00051                88  PROCESSING-COMPLETE          VALUE HIGH-VALUES.
00052            77  MAST-BALANCE        PIC S9(5)V99     COMP-3  VALUE ZEROS.
```

FIGURE 15-5   File Update Program.

290

```
00054          PROCEDURE DIVISION.
00055          A000-MAIN-LOGIC SECTION.
00056              OPEN INPUT MAST-FILE-IN
00057                        TRAN-FILE-IN
00058              OUTPUT MAST-FILE-OUT.
00059          READ MAST-FILE-IN
00060              AT END MOVE HIGH-VALUES TO MAST-CTL-IN.
00061          READ TRAN-FILE-IN
00062              AT END MOVE HIGH-VALUES TO TRAN-CTL-IN.
00063          PERFORM C000-SELECT.
00064          PERFORM B000-PROCESS UNTIL PROCESSING-COMPLETE.
00065          DISPLAY 'END OF UPDATE'.
00066          CLOSE MAST-FILE-IN
00067                TRAN-FILE-IN
00068                MAST-FILE-OUT.
00069          STOP RUN.
00070          A999-END. EXIT.

00072          B000-PROCESS SECTION.
00073              PERFORM D000-MAST.
00074              IF TRAN-CTL-IN = LOW-CTL-KEY
00075                  PERFORM E000-TRAN
00076                      UNTIL TRAN-CTL-IN NOT = LOW-CTL-KEY.
00077          MOVE MAST-BALANCE TO MAST-AMT-OUT.
00078          WRITE MAST-REC-OUT
00079              INVALID KEY DISPLAY MAST-CTL-OUT, 'INVALID WRITE'.
00080          PERFORM C000-SELECT.
00081          B999-RETURN. EXIT.

00083          C000-SELECT SECTION.
00084              IF TRAN-CTL-IN < MAST-CTL-IN
00085                  PERFORM F000-UNMATCHED
00086                      UNTIL TRAN-CTL-IN NOT < MAST-CTL-IN.
00087          MOVE MAST-CTL-IN TO LOW-CTL-KEY.
00088          C999-RETURN. EXIT.

00090          D000-MAST SECTION.
00091              MOVE MAST-AMT-IN TO MAST-BALANCE.
00092              MOVE MAST-REC-IN TO MAST-REC-OUT.
00093              READ MAST-FILE-IN
00094                  AT END MOVE HIGH-VALUES TO MAST-CTL-IN.
00095          D999-RETURN. EXIT.

00097          E000-TRAN SECTION.
00098              ADD TRAN-AMT-IN TO MAST-BALANCE.
00099              READ TRAN-FILE-IN
00100                  AT END MOVE HIGH-VALUES TO TRAN-CTL-IN.
00101          E999-RETURN. EXIT.

00103          F000-UNMATCHED SECTION.
00104              DISPLAY TRAN-CTL-IN, ' UNMATCHED TRANSACTION'.
00105              READ TRAN-FILE-IN
00106                  AT END MOVE HIGH-VALUES TO TRAN-CTL-IN.
00107          F999-RETURN. EXIT.
```

Mismatched Transactions.   It is common for a program to encounter transactions for which there are no master records. This is caused by the following:

1.   The transaction contains an incorrect control field, such as stock number;
2.   The master record has been deleted because it is obsolete;
3.   The transaction is for a new stock item, but the master record has not yet been entered.

Some systems reject a mismatched transaction and print an error message, whereas other systems accept the transaction and use its control field(s) (such as stock number) to set up a temporary *dummy* master record. The dummy master record is written as a new updated master, but contains a special code to indicate that it is a dummy. A subsequent program may write over the dummy with the correct data record or delete the dummy if necessary.

PROBLEMS

15–1. What are the basic phases in a typical batch processing system?

15–2. What is the standard method for processing more than one input file in a program?

15–3. In what way can updating a disk master file differ from updating a tape master file?

15–4. Draw the flowchart to merge four disk files into one. The four files contain customer transactions for week 1, week 2, week 3, and week 4. The control field is customer number. For each customer, merge the transactions for week 1 ahead of week 2, week 2 ahead of week 3, etc.

15–5. Code the program for the preceding problem. Record format is:

Col.

1–2   Record code
3–7   Customer number
8–13   Date
14–19 Amount of transaction ($\pm$)
20–25 Unused

Each file contains transactions with code 15 for payments and 16 for sales. Assume any suitable blocking factor.

15–6. In what particular way does a file update differ from a file merge?

15–7. Code the program that updates customers' aged balances with sales and payments. The customer master file is the one created in problem 14-9 and aged in 14-10. Input is in sequence of customer number.

The program applies sales and payments to the master file. The transaction file contains any number of (or no) transactions per customer. The format is:

Col.

1	Transaction code
2–4	Branch number
5–9	Customer number
10–15	Transaction date
16–21	Source document code
22–27	Amount of transaction ($\pm$)

Transaction codes are 'S' for sales and 'P' for payments. On the master, only the current balance may be negative because of overpayments. Transaction amounts may be negative because of correcting entries and NSF checks. For sales, add sales amounts to the master current due. If a payment is negative, subtract it from current due. If the payment is positive, subtract from the oldest balance first. For example:

	CURRENT DUE	31–60	61–90	OVER 90
Before payment:	$25	$30	$25	0
After payment of $50:	25	5	0	0

Normally, such a program would write a new updated customer master file. For this program, print the updated balances and detail for each customer, including total owing by customer. "Flag" any customer whose total owing exceeds credit limit. Print final totals of all customer balances.

CHAPTER 16

INDEXED SEQUENTIAL FILE ORGANIZATION

OBJECTIVE: To present the Indexed Sequential Access Method and its programming requirements.

INTRODUCTION

For many applications, sequential processing involving reading each record in a file successively is adequate; however, there are many applications where random (or direct) accessing of records is more efficient: for example, when there are few records in a file to be updated, or when transactions are in an unsorted sequence. Also, an on-line system may require that remote terminals have direct and immediate access to any record in a file.

There are four primary methods that permit random accessing. One of these methods, Indexed Sequential Access Method (ISAM), is introduced in this chapter, and the following two chapters introduce the other three methods: Virtual Storage Access Method (VSAM), Relative files, and Direct files.

There is a distinct difference between updating a sequential file and updating a random file. The sequential processing system rewrites an entire file, and although this feature involves more disk space and more I/O operations, it does leave the original file as a convenient backup file in case the job must be rerun. The random processing system updates a file directly in place, thereby providing no automatic backup. Consequently, backups must be created periodically by copying the file onto tape or into another disk area.

The Indexed Sequential file organization provides the benefits of both sequential and random processing, and therefore has been one of the most popular file organization methods used by business. Incredibly, until the ANS 74 COBOL version, there was no Indexed Sequential ANS standard, although there were specifications for the less popular Direct file organization. As a result, manufacturers produced their own Indexed Sequential versions, with their own features. The belated ANS 74 standard has yet to be universally adopted and implemented.

The flexibility of the Indexed Sequential Access Method is realized at a cost of both storage space and accessing time. First, the system requires various levels of *indexes* to locate records randomly. Second, because the system does not rewrite the entire file when updating records, it stores new records in special reserved *overflow* areas. But in spite of these shortcomings, its flexibility has made it extremely popular.

INDEXED SEQUENTIAL CHARACTERISTICS

Indexed files are unique because records are stored sequentially (at least initially) and can be accessed sequentially or randomly. The features that provide this flexibility are indexes to locate a correct cylinder and track, and keys to locate a record on a track. This chapter uses the abbreviation ISAM for Indexed Sequential Access Method.

Keys

ISAM writes each record with a *key* preceding each block. The key is a record control field, such as employee number or inventory stock number. The records are arranged in order of key to permit sequential processing, but a READ operation reads the data block, not the key, into main storage. For *unblocked records,* the key is usually embedded within the data record because most programs need the key for processing (such as printing the employee number). For *blocked records,* the key preceding the block is the key number of the last record in the block, as shown in Figure 16-1. Each blocked record must contain an embedded key because the READ operation must be able to locate the specific record within the block.

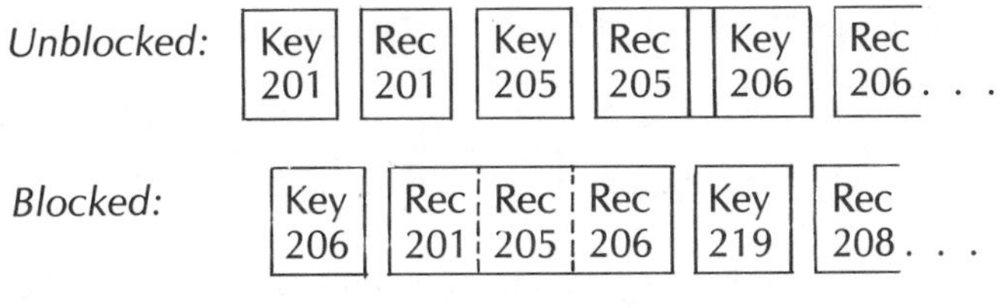

FIGURE 16-1   Keys for Blocked and Unblocked Records.

Indexes

ISAM stores three *indexes* on a disk to facilitate the locating of records directly: *track index, cylinder index,* and optionally, *master index.*

1.   *Track Index.* When ISAM creates a file, it stores a track index in track-0 of each cylinder that the file uses. The track index contains the highest key number for each track on the cylinder. For example, if a DASD has ten tracks per cylinder, then there are ten key entries for each track index, in ascending sequence.
2.   *Cylinder Index.* When ISAM creates a file, it stores a cylinder index on a separate cylinder. The cylinder index contains the highest key number for each cylinder. For example, assume a program has as its key a stock number stored in a declarative called STOCK. The program uses this key to locate a specific inventory stock number on an ISAM file.
3.   *Master Index.* The optional master index is used if the cylinder index exceeds four cylinders and facilitates locating the appropriate cylinder index.

PROCESSING AN INDEXED FILE

Consider a small indexed file that uses tracks 01, 02, and 03 of cylinder 05. There are five prime data records on tracks 01 and 02, and four on track 03. Track 01, for example, contains records with keys 205, 206, 208, 210, and 213.

track

01	205	206	208	210	213
02	214	219	220	222	225
03	226	227	230	236	unused

Prime data records on cylinder 05

Track 00 of cylinder 05 contains the track index for the cylinder, with an entry for each track indicating the high key for each track. The first track index entry, for example, specifies that 213 is the highest key on cylinder 05, track 01:

	Key	cyl/tr	Key	cyl/tr	Key	cyl/tr
Track index	213	0501	225	0502	236	0503

The cylinder index contains an entry for each cylinder that contains prime data, indicating the high key for each cylinder. The first (and, in this case, only) cylinder index entry specifies that 236 is the highest key on cylinder 05 (the track number is not important here):

$$\text{key} \quad \text{cyl}$$

Cylinder index | 236   0500 |

If a program needs to randomly locate a record with key 227, the READ statement directs the system to perform the following:

1. Check the cylinder index (assuming no master index) comparing key 227 against the first entry. Since 227 is lower than high key 236 in the entry, the required record should be on cylinder 05.

2. Access the track index in cylinder 05, track 00, comparing key 227 successively against each entry: 213 (low), 225 (low), and 236 (high). According to the entry for 236, the required record should be on cylinder 05, track 03.

3. Check the keys on track 03; find key 227 and deliver the record to the program's input area. If the key (and the record) does not exist, an INVALID KEY error occurs.

As can be seen, locating a record involves a number of additional processing steps, although little extra programming effort is required. Even more steps are involved if a new record is stored in an *overflow area*.

Overflow Areas

When a program first creates a file, ISAM stores the records sequentially in the prime data area. But subsequently, it may be necessary to insert new records into the file. Unlike tape and sequential disk, ISAM does not need to rewrite the entire file to insert records. Instead, ISAM stores new records in an *overflow area* and maintains links to point to these areas. For example, if a record with key 209 is to be added to the file in the preceding example, the system "bumps" key 213 into an overflow area, moves 210 into its place, and inserts 209 in the place vacated by 210. The track index is changed to high key 210, with a pointer now to key 213 in the overflow area.

Because there is a limit to the number of records that an overflow area can store, a special program can be used periodically to rewrite (reorganize) a file into sequence. (This simply involves reading the records sequentially and writing them into another disk area, dropping deleted records.)

There are two types of overflow areas:

1. *Cylinder overflow areas* reserve tracks on a cylinder for all the overflow data that is stored on the specific cylinder. Each cylinder has its own overflow track area. The advantage of cylinder overflow is that less seek time is required because there is no access motion to find records on a different cylinder. The

disadvantage is that too many overflow records may be on one cylinder, with very few overflow records on other cylinders.

2.   *Independent overflow areas* reserve a number of separate cylinders for overflow records, and all cylinders in a file use this area for storing overflow records. The advantage of independent overflow is that the distribution of overflow records does not matter. The disadvantage is in the additional access time necessary to seek the overflow area.

Many systems adopt both types: the cylinder overflow area for initial overflows, and the independent overflow area in case the cylinder overflow area itself overflows.

Deleting Records

Some systems, such as IBM OS, reserve the first byte of each record in an indexed file to indicate that the record is to be deleted. For this purpose, a user delete program simply inserts HIGH-VALUES into the first position. The system physically deletes the record only when reorganizing the file or when "bumping" a record into an overflow area. Many other computer systems have also adopted the practice of storing HIGH-VALUES in the first byte of obsolete records. They can physically delete such records when reorganizing the file: copy the file into another disk area, bypassing records tagged as deleted.

PROGRAMMING AN ISAM FILE

Since ISAM entirely handles indexes and overflow areas, little added programming is involved in the use of indexed files. However, some processing modes involve special requirements in the Environment and Data Divisions, and in the use of READ and WRITE. They are as follows:

1.   Creating an indexed file.
2.   Sequential reading of an indexed file.
3.   Random reading and updating of an indexed file.
4.   Adding records to an indexed file.

The programming differences between modes are usually minor, but critical. For example, the SELECT statement for sequential processing specifies ACCESS IS SEQUENTIAL, whereas for random processing it is ACCESS IS RANDOM.

Creating an Indexed File

Creating an indexed file involves writing a special program. Input data must be in ascending sequence by a predetermined control field (key), and all keys must be unique. The program in Figure 16-2 creates a customer master file from cards using DOS FCOBOL. (Other versions will have unique differences.) The SELECT statement for CUST-FILE-IS contains in part DA-3340-I-CUSFILE. One new feature is the use of I for indexed instead of S for sequential organization. But although the file is *organized* as indexed, the program is to *process* the file sequentially, as indicated by the clause ACCESS IS SEQUENTIAL. Under IBM OS, the ASSIGN clause would be ASSIGN TO DA-I-ddname. Another SELECT clause, RECORD KEY IS CUST-NO-OUT, tells the system the location of the key. The key must be contained in the record definition in the File Section (and not in Working-Storage), and in this case it is in the output record because the program writes records (check CUST-REC-OUT for the field name CUST-NO-OUT in Figure 16-2). The system ensures that records are in ascending sequence by key and copies the key number into a key field preceding each record (if unblocked) or each block (if blocked) on the disk file.

For the IBM DOS system, there are some optional entries under an I-O-CONTROL statement:

- APPLY WRITE-VERIFY ON CUST-FILE-IS directs the system to check the validity of the written records by rereading them.
- APPLY CYL-OVERFLOW OF 2 TRACKS ON CUST-FILE-IS directs the system to reserve two tracks per cylinder for overflow records. If you omit this option, the system assumes 20 percent of the tracks for overflow. Under OS, you can stipulate an independent overflow area by a DD job control entry.

The WRITE statement provides for an INVALID KEY clause in case an output record contains a duplicate or out-of-sequence key.

Sequential Reading of an Indexed File

Reading an indexed file sequentially involves few changes from reading a file organized as sequential. The ASSIGN statement under IBM requires an I for indexed instead of an S for sequential file. The other statements are similar to the statements in Figure 16-2:

```
ACCESS IS SEQUENTIAL
RECORD KEY IS key
```

Because the program is to process sequentially, the READ statement specifies an AT END clause rather than an INVALID KEY. Note also that the program in Figure 16-2 defines the delete code.

It is also possible to begin reading a record other than the first record. For this, the SELECT statement would require an additional entry:

```
NOMINAL KEY IS name
```

```
IDENTIFICATION DIVISION.
PROGRAM-ID. CHAP16A.
*      CREATES AN INDEXED SEQUENTIAL FILE.

ENVIRONMENT DIVISION.
INPUT-OUTPUT SECTION.
FILE-CONTROL.
    SELECT CUST-FILE-IN
        ASSIGN TO SYS015-UR-2501-S.
    SELECT CUST-FILE-IS
        ASSIGN TO SYS026-DA-3340-I-CUSFILE
        ACCESS IS SEQUENTIAL
        RECORD KEY IS CUST-NO-OUT.
I-O-CONTROL.
    APPLY WRITE-VERIFY ON CUST-FILE-IS.
    APPLY CYL-OVERFLOW OF 2 TRACKS ON CUST-FILE-IS.

DATA DIVISION.
FILE SECTION.
FD  CUST-FILE-IN
    LABEL RECORDS ARE OMITTED
    DATA RECORD IS CUST-REC-IN.
01  CUST-REC-IN.
    05  CODE-IN          PIC XX.
    05  CUST-NO-IN       PIC 9(7).
    05  CUST-NAME-IN     PIC X(22).
    05  BALANCE-IN       PIC S9999V99.
    05  CREDIT-LIM-IN    PIC S9999.
    05  FILLER           PIC X(39).

FD  CUST-FILE-IS
    LABEL RECORDS ARE STANDARD
    RECORD CONTAINS 40 CHARACTERS
    BLOCK CONTAINS 10 RECORDS
    DATA RECORD IS CUST-REC-OUT.
01  CUST-REC-OUT.
    05  DELETE-CODE-OUT PIC X.
    05  CUST-NO-OUT      PIC 9(7).
    05  CUST-NAME-OUT    PIC X(22).
    05  BALANCE-OUT      PIC S9(5)V99 COMP-3.
    05  CREDIT-LIM-OUT   PIC S9(5)     COMP-3.
    05  FILLER           PIC X(3).

WORKING-STORAGE SECTION.
77  EOF-FLAG          PIC X(3)       VALUE ' '.
    88  END-FILE                     VALUE 'EOF'.
```

```
PROCEDURE DIVISION.
A000-MAIN SECTION.
    OPEN INPUT CUST-FILE-IN
         OUTPUT CUST-FILE-IS.
    MOVE SPACES TO CUST-REC-OUT.
    MOVE LOW-VALUES TO DELETE-CODE-OUT.
    READ CUST-FILE-IN
        AT END MOVE 'EOF' TO EOF-FLAG.
    PERFORM B000-PROC UNTIL END-FILE.
    CLOSE CUST-FILE-IN, CUST-FILE-IS.
    STOP RUN.
A999-END. EXIT.

B000-PROC SECTION.
    MOVE CUST-NO-IN       TO CUST-NO-OUT.
    MOVE CUST-NAME-IN     TO CUST-NAME-OUT.
    MOVE BALANCE-IN       TO BALANCE-OUT.
    MOVE CREDIT-LIM-IN TO CREDIT-LIM-OUT.
    WRITE CUST-REC-OUT
        INVALID KEY DISPLAY CUST-NO-IN, ' INVALID'.
    READ CUST-FILE-IN
        AT END MOVE 'EOF' TO EOF-FLAG.
B999-RETURN. EXIT.
```

FIGURE 16-2   Creating an Indexed Sequential File.

NOMINAL KEY is an item defined in Working-Storage. The program would move the starting key number to the nominal key and issue a START statement, as follows:

```
                    NOMINAL KEY IS START-ADDR.
                      •
                      •
        77  START-ADDR        PIC X(4).
                      •
                      •
                      •
                    OPEN INPUT FILE-IS ...
                    MOVE '1234' TO START-ADDR.
                    START FILE-IS, INVALID KEY ...
```

Prior to the first READ, the program initializes the file to begin with key '1234'. INVALID KEY arises if the nominal key does not exist on the file.

Random Reading and Updating of an Indexed File

The main purpose of organizing an Indexed Sequential file is to be able to access records randomly. For this, there are a number of special coding entries; the SELECT clause should include the following:

```
        ASSIGN TO ...
        ACCESS IS RANDOM
        NOMINAL KEY IS (KEY NUMBER IN WORKING-STORAGE)
        RECORD  KEY IS (KEY FIELD  IN RECORD)
        RESERVE NO ALTERNATE AREAS
```

Updating a record involves reading the record (READ), changing its contents, and writing the record back in the same disk location (REWRITE). Consequently, the file is both input and output, and the OPEN statement specifies it as I-O:

```
        OPEN I-O CUST-FILE-IS . . .
```

Reading.   To access a particular record, a program must first move its key into the NOMINAL KEY field. The READ does not use an AT END clause because it is seeking a record randomly and is not supposed to encounter the end-of-file condition. The INVALID KEY clause, however, is required to handle the possibility that the key does not exist on the file.

Updating.   Once a record has been successfully retrieved, a program can change its contents. The REWRITE statement assumes the same RECORD KEY and NOMINAL KEY—changing them between the READ and REWRITE would cause an INVALID KEY condition. The REWRITE statement, like WRITE, specifies the record name.

Buffers.   A program requires at least one buffer area in main storage for storing the data block being read or written. For sequential processing, extra buffer areas enable a program to read ahead and to overlap reading, processing, and writing. For random processing, there is no advantage in requesting additional buffer areas. The IBM 370 system assumes two buffers if there is no specification; however, you can designate only one buffer with a SELECT clause:

DOS :   RESERVE NO ALTERNATE AREAS
OS :   RESERVE 0 AREAS
ANS :   RESERVE 1 AREA

In this way, IBM compilers will generate one buffer but no additional ones. The ANS standard is to designate the actual number of buffers.

PROGRAM EXAMPLE

The program in Figure 16-3 reads a sequential transaction file TRAN-FILE-IN containing customer transactions, and updates an Indexed Sequential file CUST-FILE-IS randomly. The key is customer number, which the program moves from the input record to the nominal key, IS-KEY. Since the cylinder index is on disk, each access of a record could involve an access of the cylinder index and then another access motion to the cylinder containing the track index for the required key. But you can eliminate the access to the cylinder index by directing the program to read it into main storage at the beginning of execution. The statement that does this is under I-O-CONTROL:

APPLY CORE-INDEX TO INDEX-AREA ON CUST-FILE-IS.

IBM DOS requires you to calculate the size of the index area in the program as follows:

$$\text{size} = (\text{number of entries} + 3) \times (\text{key length} + 6)$$

The "number of entries" is the number of cylinders that the file requires for prime data, one index entry for each cylinder.* For Figure 16-3, if the number of cylinders were seven, then the calculation would be $(7 + 3) \times (7 + 6) = 130$. In the APPLY statement, CORE-INDEX is a COBOL word, but INDEX-AREA may be any valid nonreserved name, as indicated in the entry in Working-Storage as PIC X(130). This area is reserved for the ISAM system and you should not use it for any other purpose.

---

*For an explanation of IBM space requirements of records by track and cylinder, see the highly recommended manual, *Introduction to IBM Direct-Access Storage Devices and Access Methods*, Student Text GC20-1649, IBM Corporation, Poughkeepsie, N.Y. (updated regularly).

IBM OS performs its own calculation of the cylinder index in main storage, and its APPLY statement is as follows:

APPLY CORE-INDEX ON CUST-FILE IS.

```
        IDENTIFICATION DIVISION.
        PROGRAM-ID. CHAP168.
        *          UPDATES INDEX SEQUENTIAL FILE WITH TRANSACTIONS.

        ENVIRONMENT DIVISION.
        INPUT-OUTPUT SECTION.
        FILE-CONTROL.
            SELECT TRAN-FILE-IN
                ASSIGN TO SYS009-UT-3340-S-CUSTRAN.
            SELECT CUST-FILE-IS
                ASSIGN TO SYS026-DA-3340-I-CUSFILE
                ACCESS IS RANDOM
                NOMINAL KEY IS IS-KEY
                RECORD KEY IS CUST-NO-IS
                RESERVE NO ALTERNATE AREA.
        I-O-CONTROL.
            APPLY WRITE-VERIFY ON CUST-FILE-IS.
            APPLY CORE-INDEX TO INDEX-AREA ON CUST-FILE-IS.

        DATA DIVISION.
        FILE SECTION.
        FD  TRAN-FILE-IN
            LABEL RECORDS ARE STANDARD
            RECORD CONTAINS 20 CHARACTERS
            BLOCK  CONTAINS 16 RECORDS
            DATA RECORD IS TRAN-REC-IN.
        01  TRAN-REC-IN.
            05  CODE-IN          PIC X.
            05  CUST-NO-IN       PIC 9(7).
            05  TRAN-AMT-IN      PIC S9(5)V99 COMP-3.
            05  FILLER           PIC X(8).

        FD  CUST-FILE-IS
            LABEL RECORDS ARE STANDARD
            RECORD CONTAINS 40 CHARACTERS
            BLOCK  CONTAINS 10 RECORDS
            DATA RECORD IS ISEQ-RECORD.
        01  ISEQ-RECORD.
            05  DELETE-CODE-IS  PIC X.
            05  CUST-NO-IS      PIC 9(7).
            05  CUST-NAME-IS    PIC X(22).
            05  BALANCE-IS      PIC S9(5)V99 COMP-3.
            05  FILLER          PIC X(6).

        WORKING-STORAGE SECTION.
        77  IS-KEY              PIC 9(7).
        77  EOF-FLAG            PIC X(3)    VALUE ' '.
            88  END-FILE                    VALUE 'EOF'.
        77  INV-KEY-FLAG        PIC X(7)    VALUE ' '.
            88  VALID-KEY                   VALUE 'VALID'.
        77  INDEX-AREA          PIC X(130).
```

FIGURE 16-3   Random Updating of an Indexed Sequential File.

```
        PROCEDURE DIVISION.
        A000-MAIN SECTION.
            OPEN INPUT TRAN-FILE-IN
                 I-O   CUST-FILE-IS.
            READ TRAN-FILE-IN
                AT END MOVE 'EOF' TO EOF-FLAG.
            PERFORM B000-PROC UNTIL END-FILE.
            CLOSE TRAN-FILE-IN
                  CUST-FILE-IS.
            STOP RUN.
        A999-END. EXIT.

        B000-PROC SECTION.
            MOVE 'VALID' TO INV-KEY-FLAG.
            MOVE CUST-NO-IN TO IS-KEY.
            READ CUST-FILE-IS
                INVALID KEY MOVE 'INVALID' TO INV-KEY-FLAG
                    DISPLAY CUST-NO-IN, ' INVALID CUST NO.'.
            IF VALID-KEY PERFORM C000-REWRITE.
            READ TRAN-FILE-IN
                AT END MOVE 'EOF' TO EOF-FLAG.
        B999-RETURN.  EXIT.

        C000-REWRITE SECTION.
            ADD TRAN-AMT-IN TO BALANCE-IS.
            REWRITE ISEQ-RECORD   INVALID KEY
                DISPLAY CUST-NO-IN, ' INVALID REWRITE'.
        C999-RETURN. EXIT.
```

FIGURE 16-3   (Cont.)

Adding Records to an Indexed File

The addition of new records to an indexed file will displace records into the overflow area (unless the new records have high keys that all add to the end of the file). The program must specify ACCESS IS RANDOM, open the file as I-O, and use WRITE (rather than REWRITE). WRITE requires an INVALID KEY clause in case the key already exists on the file. The SELECT statement would contain the following:

ACCESS IS RANDOM
NOMINAL KEY IS . . .
RECORD KEY IS . . .
TRACK AREA IS n CHARACTERS

TRACK AREA is an optional clause that improves efficiency. The system can read an entire disk track into main storage, perform the "bumping" of inserted records, and write the track back onto disk, thereby reducing considerable disk I/O. The calculation for TRACK AREA is as follows:

$$\text{size} = 24 + \text{number of blocks} (40 + \text{key length} + \text{block size})$$

Technically, you need to provide for only two blocks, although the more blocks, the more efficient is the processing. If there are 20 bytes per record and 16 records per block, then the block size is 320. A calculation for the minimum size is as follows:

$$24 + 2 (40 + 7 + 320) = 24 + 2 (367) = 758 \text{ bytes}$$

PROBLEMS

16–1. What is the main processing difference between a disk file organized as sequential and a disk file organized as indexed sequential?

16–2. The following block of five records shows the key values only. What is the key that the system stores for the entire block?

/ 842 / 844 / 852 / 853 / 857 /

16–3. Where are the following stored, and what is their purpose?
(a) track index,
(b) cylinder index,
(c) master index.

16–4. Given the following prime data on cylinder 08, show the contents of the track index and the cylinder index:

TRACK	KEYS OF STORED RECORDS				
01	520	543	544	560	565
02	567	568	572	574	578
03	580	584	585	-	-

16–5. Using the stored keys in Problem 16-4, determine the effect on the stored records, the track index, and the cylinder index by adding
(a) first, a record with key 532;
(b) second, a record with key 579.

16–6. Code a program to create an indexed sequential file. Use the same record formats and requirements as in Problem 14-4 in Chapter 14.

16–7. Update the indexed file in Problem 16-6 with sales records as in Problem 15-7. In this case, however, perform *random updating*.

16–8. Code a program to print the contents of the updated file in Problem 16-7 as in Problem 14-5.

CHAPTER 17

VIRTUAL STORAGE ACCESS METHOD—VSAM

OBJECTIVE: To present the Virtual Storage Access Method and its programming requirements.

INTRODUCTION

Virtual Storage Access Method (VSAM) is a file organization method for users of IBM DOS/VS and OS/VS and corresponds to the current ANS standard for indexed files. VSAM facilitates both sequential and random processing and is more efficient and simpler to understand than the Indexed Sequential Access Method (ISAM). Fortunately, the coding for both methods is similar.

There are three types of VSAM data sets:

1. *Key-sequenced data sets,* in which records are in ascending sequence by key (such as employee or part number). This is the most commonly used type.
2. *Entry-sequenced data sets,* in which records are in sequence by the order that the records were entered.
3. *Relative record data sets,* in which records are in sequence by relative record number.

STORAGE OF RECORDS—CONTROL INTERVAL

Regardless of the type of file, VSAM stores records in groups (one or more) in *control intervals.* The user may select the control interval size, or VSAM will optimize the size based on record length and the type of disk device to be used. The maximum control interval size is 32,768 bytes. A convenient size would be the length of one track, although VSAM is not dependent on the disk storage device used. At the end of each control interval is control information that describes the data records, as shown in Figure 17-1.

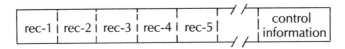

FIGURE 17-1   VSAM Control Interval.

VSAM addresses a data record by its displacement in bytes from the beginning of the data set, called the *relative byte address (RBA)*. Thus, the first record in a data set is at RBA zero, and if the record is 200 bytes long, the second record is at RBA 200.

KEY-SEQUENCED DATA SETS

A control interval contains one or more data records. (Technically, an extremely large record could spread across more than one control interval, a *spanned record*.) A specified number of control intervals comprises a control area. Figure 17-2 depicts a simplified overview of a Key-Sequenced data set organization.

A *sequence set* contains an entry for each control interval in a control area. Entries in the sequence set consist of the highest key in each control interval with the address of the control interval. For example, assume the first control area consists of three control intervals containing records with keys as shown:

Keys of records
in control intervals

| 6, 9, 18, 22 | 25, 26, 30, 32 | 35, 37, 38, 40 |

Index set:

Sequence set:

Data set:

| control interval | control interval | control interval | control interval | control interval | control interval |

FIGURE 17-2   Key-sequenced Organization.

The high key for each control interval is 22, 32, and 40; therefore, VSAM stores these keys in the sequence set for the control area (one entry for each control interval with a key and an address for each control interval). At a higher level, the *index set* (various levels depending on the file size) contains the high keys and addresses of records at the sequence set level.

Free Space

When creating a Key-Sequenced data set, you can tell VSAM to allocate free space in two ways:

1.   Leave space at the end of each control interval.
2.   Leave some control intervals vacant.

If a program deletes or shortens a record, VSAM reclaims the space by shifting to the left all following records in the control interval. However, if a program adds or lengthens a record, VSAM inserts the record in its correct space and moves to the right all following records in the control interval. VSAM updates RBAs and indexes accordingly.

Control Interval Splits

What would happen if a control interval did not contain enough free space for an inserted record? Assume the following four control intervals in a control area:

A program needs to insert a new record with key 233, but because there is insufficient space in the control interval, VSAM causes a *control interval split:*

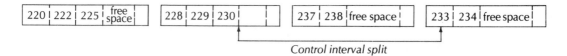

Control interval split

VSAM removes about half the records to a vacant control interval in the same control area. Although the records are now no longer precisely in key order, the updated sequence set index will control the sequence for retrieval.

What if no vacant control interval were in the control area? VSAM would cause a *control area split* using free space outside the control area. However, such a split seldom occurs because a VSAM file is somewhat self-organizing and does not require reorganization as often as an ISAM file.

CREATING A KEY-SEQUENCED DATA SET

The coding to create a VSAM data set is similar to the coding required to create an ISAM file. IBM requirements, other than for ASSIGN, are according to ANS standards. The program in Figure 17-3 creates a Key-Sequenced data set with the following SELECT entries for the VSAM output data set:

- ASSIGN. This entry, which must be first, does not indicate any specific file organization (as S or I). Under OS/VS, the clause would be ASSIGN TO system-name (device number is optional).
- ACCESS IS SEQUENTIAL. The program is to write the data set in sequence.
- ORGANIZATION IS INDEXED. The entry INDEXED coupled with the ASSIGN clause causes the compiler to determine that the organization is to be VSAM.
- RECORD KEY IS CUST-NO-OUT. This entry defines the control word key in the output record, and VSAM uses this key for storing and locating the record. The key is defined as alphanumeric (PIC X) or unsigned numeric (PIC 9).

In the Procedure Division, the INVALID KEY clause in the WRITE is invoked if records are not in ascending sequence.

SEQUENTIAL READING OF A KEY-SEQUENCED DATA SET

The SELECT statements for the sequential reading of a Key-Sequenced data set are identical to the statements for the creation of a Key-Sequenced data set, except for RECORD KEY, which is omitted. Also, the READ statement requires the usual AT END clause for the end-of-file condition.

Beginning at a particular key involves the START statement, as follows:

$$\text{START filename KEY} \begin{Bmatrix} < \\ = \\ > \end{Bmatrix} \text{identifier INVALID KEY} \ldots$$

VSAM positions a file at the first record that has a key that corresponds to the coding. For example, if the specified identifier contains the value 01234, then the possibilities are as follows:

KEY < identifier	Position at the first key that is lower than 01234
KEY = identifier	Position at the first key that equals 01234
KEY > identifier	Position at the first key that is higher than 01234

START merely positions at a record; a READ statement is required to read a record.

```
IDENTIFICATION DIVISION.
PROGRAM-ID. CHAP17A.
*          CREATE A VSAM DATA SET.

ENVIRONMENT DIVISION.
INPUT-OUTPUT SECTION.
FILE-CONTROL.
    SELECT CUST-FILE-IN
        ASSIGN TO SYS015-UR-2501-S.
    SELECT CUST-FILE-VS
        ASSIGN TO SYS026-DA-3340-PARFILE
        ACCESS IS SEQUENTIAL
        ORGANIZATION IS INDEXED
        RECORD KEY IS CUST-NO-OUT.

DATA DIVISION.
FILE SECTION.
FD CUST-FILE-IN
    LABEL RECORDS ARE OMITTED
    DATA RECORD IS CUST-REC-IN.
01 CUST-REC-IN.
    05 CODE-IN         PIC XX.
    05 CUST-NO-IN      PIC X(7).
    05 CUST-NAME-IN    PIC X(22).
    05 BALANCE-IN      PIC S9999V99.
    05 CREDIT-LIM-IN   PIC S9999.
    05 FILLER          PIC X(39).

FD CUST-FILE-VS
    LABEL RECORDS ARE STANDARD
    RECORD CONTAINS 40 CHARACTERS
    BLOCK  CONTAINS 10 RECORDS
    DATA RECORD IS CUST-REC-OUT.
01 CUST-REC-OUT.
    05 DELETE-CODE-OUT PIC X.
    05 CUST-NO-OUT     PIC X(7).
    05 CUST-NAME-OUT   PIC X(22).
    05 BALANCE-OUT     PIC S9(5)V99 COMP-3.
    05 CREDIT-LIM-OUT  PIC S9(5)    COMP-3.
    05 FILLER          PIC X(3).

WORKING-STORAGE SECTION.
77 EOF-FLAG        PIC X(3)     VALUE ' '.
88 END-FILE                     VALUE 'EOF'.


PROCEDURE DIVISION.
A000-MAIN SECTION.
    OPEN INPUT CUST-FILE-IN
         OUTPUT CUST-FILE-VS.
    MOVE SPACES TO CUST-REC-OUT.
    MOVE LOW-VALUES TO DELETE-CODE-OUT.
    READ CUST-FILE-IN
        AT END MOVE 'EOF' TO EOF-FLAG.
    PERFORM B000-PROC UNTIL END-FILE.
    CLOSE CUST-FILE-IN, CUST-FILE-VS.
    STOP RUN.
A999-END. EXIT.

B000-PROC SECTION.
    MOVE CUST-NO-IN      TO CUST-NO-OUT.
    MOVE CUST-NAME-IN    TO CUST-NAME-OUT.
    MOVE BALANCE-IN      TO BALANCE-OUT.
    MOVE CREDIT-LIM-IN   TO CREDIT-LIM-OUT.
    WRITE CUST-REC-OUT
        INVALID KEY DISPLAY CUST-NO-IN, ' INVALID'.
    READ CUST-FILE-IN
        AT END MOVE 'EOF' TO EOF-FLAG.
B999-RETURN. EXIT.
```

FIGURE 17-3 Creating Key-sequenced Data Set.

RANDOM READING OF A KEY-SEQUENCED DATA SET

The coding for the random reading of a Key-Sequenced data set is identical to the random reading of an ISAM file. The SELECT clause requires ACCESS IS RANDOM and a RECORD KEY clause. The program moves the required key to RECORD KEY and uses READ with INVALID KEY (in case the key does not exist).

SEQUENTIAL UPDATING OF A KEY-SEQUENCED DATA SET

To sequentially update a Key-Sequenced data set, the SELECT statement requires ACCESS IS SEQUENTIAL. You OPEN the file as I-O and use READ with an AT END clause. The only difference from ISAM is the use of REWRITE:

REWRITE recordname [FROM record] [INVALID KEY . . .]

The INVALID KEY occurs if the program has failed to read a record previously.
        You can delete a record by first reading it and then deleting it, as follows:

DELETE filename RECORD [INVALID KEY . . .]

VSAM physically deletes a record from a file, but to delete, the file must have been opened as I-O. Note the use of the reserved word RECORD for this statement.

RANDOM UPDATING OF A KEY-SEQUENCED DATA SET

Random updating of a Key-Sequenced data set is similar to sequential updating except the SELECT statement requires ACCESS IS RANDOM, as illustrated in Figure 17-4. You open the file as I-O and use READ with an INVALID KEY clause. Updating of an old record involves changing the record as required (but not the key), and using REWRITE with an INVALID KEY clause (in case the record key does not exist). Although the program in Figure 17-4 does not write new records, it could by moving the key value to RECORD KEY, and using WRITE with INVALID KEY (in case the record already exists). The program could also delete a record using the DELETE statement.
        If you need to combine sequential reading with random reading, code ACCESS IS DYNAMIC. Random reading uses READ, REWRITE, WRITE, and DELETE, and sequential reading uses the READ NEXT statement to read the "next" record, as follows:

READ filename NEXT INTO record AT END . . .

```
IDENTIFICATION DIVISION.
PROGRAM-ID. CHAP17B.
*        UPDATES VSAM DATA SET .

ENVIRONMENT DIVISION.
INPUT-OUTPUT SECTION.
FILE-CONTROL.
    SELECT TRAN-FILE-IN
        ASSIGN TO SYS009-UT-3340-S-CUSTRAN.
    SELECT CUST-FILE-VS
        ASSIGN TO SYS026-DA-3340-PARFILE
        ACCESS IS RANDOM
        ORGANIZATION IS INDEXED
        RECORD KEY IS CUST-NO-VS.

DATA DIVISION.
FILE SECTION.
FD  TRAN-FILE-IN
    LABEL RECORDS ARE STANDARD
    RECORD CONTAINS 20 CHARACTERS
    BLOCK CONTAINS 16 RECORDS
    DATA RECORD IS TRAN-REC-IN.
01  TRAN-REC-IN.
    05  CODE-IN        PIC X.
    05  CUST-NO-IN     PIC X(7).
    05  TRAN-AMT-IN    PIC S9(5)V99 COMP-3.
    05  FILLER         PIC X(8).

FD  CUST-FILE-VS
    LABEL RECORDS ARE STANDARD
    DATA RECORD IS VSAM-RECORD.
01  VSAM-RECORD.
    05  DELETE-CODE-VS  PIC X.
    05  CUST-NO-VS      PIC X(7).
    05  CUST-NAME-VS    PIC X(22).
    05  BALANCE-VS      PIC S9(5)V99 COMP-3.
    05  FILLER          PIC X(6).

WORKING-STORAGE SECTION.
77  EOF-FLAG       PIC X(3)    VALUE ' '.
    88  END-FILE               VALUE 'EOF'.
77  INV-KEY-FLAG   PIC X(7)    VALUE ' '.
    88  VALID-KEY              VALUE 'VALID'.
```

```
PROCEDURE DIVISION.
A000-MAIN SECTION.
    OPEN INPUT TRAN-FILE-IN.
    OPEN I-O  CUST-FILE-VS.
    READ TRAN-FILE-IN, AT END MOVE 'EOF' TO EOF-FLAG.
    PERFORM B000-PROC UNTIL END-FILE.
    CLOSE TRAN-FILE-IN, CUST-FILE-VS.
    STOP RUN.
A999-END. EXIT.

B000-PROC SECTION.
    MOVE CUST-NO-IN TO CUST-NO-VS.
    MOVE 'VALID' TO INV-KEY-FLAG.
    READ CUST-FILE-VS
        INVALID KEY MOVE 'INVALID' TO INV-KEY-FLAG
            DISPLAY CUST-NO-IN, INVALID CUST NO.'.
    IF VALID-KEY PERFORM C000-REWRITE.
    READ TRAN-FILE-IN, AT END MOVE 'EOF' TO EOF-FLAG.
B999-RETURN.  EXIT.

C000-REWRITE SECTION.
    ADD TRAN-AMT-IN TO BALANCE-VS.
    REWRITE VSAM-RECORD  INVALID KEY
            DISPLAY CUST-NO-IN, ' INVALID REWRITE'.
C999-RETURN. EXIT.
```

FIGURE 17-4 Random Updating of a Key-sequenced Data Set.

ENTRY-SEQUENCED AND RELATIVE RECORD DATA SETS

Entry-sequenced and Relative record data sets have fewer applications than Key-sequenced data sets. Therefore, check the *IBM DASD Student Text* and your compiler's COBOL reference manual for details. The following list compares the three VSAM types:

FEATURE	KEY-SEQUENCED	ENTRY-SEQUENCED	RELATIVE RECORD
Record Sequence	In sequence by key.	In sequence in which entered.	In sequence by relative record number.
Record Length	Fixed or variable.	Fixed or variable.	Fixed length only.
Access of Records	By key through index or RBA.	By RBA.	By relative record number.
Change of Address	Can change record's RBA.	Cannot change record's RBA.	Cannot change relative record number.
New Records	Distributed free space for new records.	Space at end of data set for new records.	Empty slots in data set for new records.
Recovery of Space	Reclaims space if record deleted.	Does not delete, but can overwrite a new record over an old record.	Can reuse deleted space.

Coding for Entry-sequenced Data Sets

For Entry-Sequenced data sets, the SELECT clause involves the following formats:

• ASSIGN TO sysname-AS-name.

The AS indicates an Entry-Sequenced data set for both DOS and OS, and name relates to the job control filename. ASSIGN must be the first entry following SELECT.

• ORGANIZATION IS SEQUENTIAL. The file is always sequentially organized.
• ACCESS IS SEQUENTIAL. The file is always sequentially updated.

PROBLEMS

17–1. What is a control interval?

17–2. VSAM is required to insert a new record, key 532, but there is insufficient space in the following control interval:

/ 527 / 529 / 558 / 562 /

How does VSAM handle this situation?

17–3. What does VSAM do if there is no vacant control interval in a control area?

17–4. Create a Key-Sequenced data set using the same record format and requirements as the tape file in Problem 14-4.

17–5. Randomly update the VSAM data set created in Problem 17-4 using the sales records in Problem 15–7.

17–6. Print the contents of the VSAM data set in Problem 17-5. Allow for editing of decimal point and possible negative amount owed. Print a total for the customer amount owed field.

CHAPTER 18

RELATIVE AND DIRECT FILES

OBJECTIVE: To present Relative and Direct file organization methods and their programming requirements.

INTRODUCTION

Although Sequential and Indexed files are the most common disk file organization methods, Relative and Direct files are sometimes used. Relative files are also known as *Relative record* organization, and Direct files are also known as Relative track organization. This text uses the simpler and less confusing names Relative and Direct. Although IBM OS supports Relative files, DOS and DOS/VS do not. For information on Relative and Direct files not covered in this chapter, use the COBOL reference manual for your installation.

RELATIVE FILES

Characteristics

Although Relative file organization is an ANS standard, for IBM, only OS supports it. The records in a Relative file are fixed length and unblocked. Assume a file containing twelve records with keys 1, 2, 3, 5, 6, 8, 9, 10, 11, 12, 14, and 17. The Relative system stores the records consecutively as 1, 2, 3, then a dummy record for the missing 4, then 5, 6, a dummy for 7, etc. In all, there are

17 record spaces, although only 12 are occupied. (IBM Relative files begin with zero and leave a space for a dummy record 0.) You can access the relative file either sequentially or randomly. The system can easily locate the relative position of records because they are fixed length and there are a fixed number of records per sector or track. Thus, if an input key is 8, the system can directly access the position of the eighth record with one read operation. As long as keys are reasonably consecutive, it is possible to create a Relative file. If the keys begin at a number such as 1001, you need only subtract 1000 from them before storing the records in the file. Thus, key 1001 is stored as record 1, key 1002 as record 2, and so forth.

Potentially, Relative files are efficient because records are in sequence, access is fast, and there is no overflow problem. They are used in specialized situations, such as a file of sales records by months or by years, or records by states (where Alabama is record 01 and Wyoming is 50).

Many coding systems, when first designed, start out consecutively, but because of additions and deletions to the codes, gaps soon occur. Also, the code may contain digit positions with particular meaning, such as department or part number, causing large gaps between numbers.

Creating a Relative File

A Relative file must be created sequentially. For dummy records, IBM COBOL sets the first byte to HIGH-VALUES. Figure 18-1 shows the code for creation of a simple Relative file; it uses the key from the input record for the NOMINAL KEY; presumably the keys begin near to 001 and are consecutive. The program could even generate the key value by initializing it to 001 and incrementing it for each output record. The KEY must be defined in Working-Storage and its format under IBM OS is PIC S9(8) COMP. In the SELECT statement, NOMINAL KEY indicates the key for the stored records (the ANS standard is RELATIVE KEY). Omission of NOMINAL KEY causes the Relative file system to supply the key numbers as 0 through *n*. The following are ASSIGN clause entries for two COBOL versions:

1. IBM OS. This version uses the letter R in the organization field to indicate a Relative file and DA to signify Direct Access.

    ASSIGN TO DA-3340-R-name.   *(the device number is optional)*

2. CDC-6000. This version uses the suffix -A to indicate a Relative file, and it follows the implementor name:

    ASSIGN TO name-A
    ORGANIZATION IS RELATIVE
    RELATIVE KEY IS key . . .

```
           IDENTIFICATION DIVISION.
           PROGRAM-ID. CHAP18A.
     *          PROGRAM CREATES A DISK FILE ORGANIZED AS RELATIVE.


           ENVIRONMENT DIVISION.
           INPUT-OUTPUT SECTION.
           FILE-CONTROL.
               SELECT PART-FILE-IN
                   ASSIGN TO UR-2540R-S-SYSIN.
               SELECT RELTVE-PART-FILE
                   ASSIGN TO DA-3340-R-PARFILE
                   ACCESS IS SEQUENTIAL
                   NOMINAL KEY IS PART-KEY.


           DATA DIVISION.
           FILE SECTION.
           FD  PART-FILE-IN
               LABEL RECORDS ARE OMITTED
               DATA RECORD IS PART-REC-IN.
           01  PART-REC-IN.
               03  PART-NO-IN       PIC 9(6).
               03  PART-DESCR-IN    PIC X(20).
               03  PART-COST-IN     PIC S999V99.
               03  FILLER           PIC X(49).

           FD  RELTVE-PART-FILE
               LABEL RECORDS ARE STANDARD
               RECORDING MODE IS F
               DATA RECORD IS PART-REC-OUT.
           01  PART-REC-OUT.
               03  STATUS-CODE-OUT PIC X.
               03  PART-NO-OUT     PIC 9(6).
               03  PART-DESCR-OUT  PIC X(20).
               03  PART-COST-OUT    PIC S999V99 COMP-3.

           WORKING-STORAGE SECTION.
           77  PART-KEY            PIC S9(8)   COMP.
           77  EOF-FLAG            PIC X(3)    VALUE ' '.
               88  END-FILE                    VALUE 'EOF'.

           PROCEDURE DIVISION.
           A000-MAIN SECTION.
               OPEN INPUT PART-FILE-IN
                   OUTPUT RELTVE-PART-FILE.
               MOVE LOW-VALUES TO STATUS-CODE-OUT.
               READ PART-FILE-IN
                   AT END MOVE 'EOF' TO EOF-FLAG.
               PERFORM B000-PROC UNTIL END-FILE.
               CLOSE PART-FILE-IN, RELTVE-PART-FILE.
               STOP RUN.
           A999-END. EXIT.


           B000-PROC SECTION.
               MOVE PART-COST-IN TO PART-COST-OUT.
               MOVE PART-NO-IN TO PART-NO-OUT, PART-KEY.
               WRITE PART-REC-OUT
                   INVALID KEY DISPLAY PART-NO-IN, 'INVALID KEY'.
               READ PART-FILE-IN
                   AT END MOVE 'EOF' TO EOF-FLAG.
           B999-RETURN. EXIT.
```

FIGURE 18-1   Creating a Relative File.

Sequential Reading of a Relative File

To sequentially read a Relative file, specify ASSIGN TO DA-R (according to the compiler version) and ACCESS IS SEQUENTIAL. Because the system reads dummy records, you should code a test to bypass them. The READ statement requires an AT END clause.

Random Reading of a Relative File

To randomly read a Relative file, use ACCESS IS RANDOM and a NOMINAL KEY clause. The program moves the key of the wanted record to the nominal key. The READ statement requires an INVALID KEY clause in case the nominal key addresses an area outside the file limit. You should also test for dummy records.

Random Updating of a Relative File

Random updating of a Relative file is similar to random reading of a Relative file. OPEN the file as I-O. After reading a relative record by means of the nominal key, you update the contents of the record. You then REWRITE the record using an INVALID KEY clause in case the program has inadvertently changed the nominal key value. To delete a record, use the ANS standard DELETE statement, or if under IBM, REWRITE the record with HIGH-VALUES in the first byte, therefore making it a dummy record.

DIRECT FILES

Characteristics

Direct file organization, also known as *relative track* organization, is not an ANS standard (check for its implementation in the reference manual for your compiler). A Direct file stores records according to key. Typically, a program performs a computation on the key to determine the sector or relative track that contains a record using a *randomizing formula* (which is explained in the *IBM DASD Student Text*).

One important characteristic of a Direct file is that the range of possible key values is greater than the available record spaces on the disk file. Thus, a file could contain keys with values ranging from 01000 to 25000 (24,000 possible keys), although the file contains only 5,000 records. Therefore, the randomizing formula would *compress* the possible disk space (24,000) to an area closer to the actual (5,000). A common rule of thumb is to select a file space so that the records occupy 80 percent of the allocated space (a *packing factor* of 80 percent). In this case, 5,000 ÷ .80 = 6,250; consequently, the disk space reserved for the file needs to be only large enough for 6,250 records, and the randomizing formula has to slot all 5,000 records randomly into this space. For example, a file of nine records is to be stored randomly in a disk area large enough for 12 records. The system can store three records per track; so four tracks are reserved: cylinder 08, tracks 00, 01, 02, and 03. The randomizing formula selected divides the key by the number of tracks, so the *remainder* can contain only the value 00, 01, 02, and 03. The remainder stipulates the track address of each record as follows:

KEY	TRACK (KEY ÷ 4, REMAINDER)
122	02
208	00
269	01
324	00
359	03
366	02
441	01
523	03
622	02

The records are now distributed across the tracks quite evenly, as follows:

TRACK	KEYS
00	208, 324
01	269, 441
02	122, 366, 622 (full)
03	359, 523

The file creation program would insert each record into these tracks, and any other program that references the file must use the same formula. You may have already suspected a potential problem in this method. What if there were another record to add with key 374? It generates a remainder of 02, but track 02 is already full. The result is a *synonym:* there is no space for the record. Technically, any key that generates an identical address is a synonym, such as keys 122, 366, and 622 (which all generate 02). The Direct organization system will have to insert the record for key 374 into an overflow area.

To minimize synonyms, there are two options:

1. Increase the allocated disk space (for example, use a 70 or 60 percent packing factor). The cost, of course, is more unused disk space.
2. Change the randomizing formula. There is no rule that dictates a precise formula; you may have to use a trial-and-error approach.

Randomizing Formula. The randomizing formula should have two characteristics:

1. Every possible key must generate an address within the allocated disk area.
2. It should distribute records evenly throughout the disk area with a minimum of synonyms.

To minimize synonyms, the division/remainder method usually divides the key by the largest *prime number* not greater than the number of tracks allocated for the file. (A prime number is evenly divisible only by 1 and by itself, such as 2, 3, 5, 7, 11, 13, and 17.) Therefore, if a file requires 500 tracks, then the number to divide into each key would be prime number 499.

The randomizing formula generates a relative track address. Assume that a disk device has 20 tracks per cylinder. Consequently, relative track 02 is on cylinder 00, track 02, and relative track 22 is on cylinder 01, track 02, and so on. The program provides the relative track, and the system converts it to the actual cylinder/track.

Unique Features of Direct Files. The following features make Direct files unique:

- A randomizing formula distributes the records fairly evenly across the disk area.
- Records are not in sequence, a problem if you want to process the file sequentially.
- The formula can generate synonyms, which the system stores in overflow areas—a potential cause of inefficient direct accessing.

ASSIGN Clause. As usual, the ASSIGN clause in the SELECT statement varies by compiler version. IBM DOS makes the ASSIGN clause particularly complicated; the organization field has four options:

1. D—relative track addressing
2. W—relative track addressing using the REWRITE statement
3. A—actual track addressing
4. U—actual track addressing using the REWRITE statement

An example of relative track addressing is as follows:

ASSIGN TO SYS024-DA-3340-D-MASTDIR.

For IBM OS, the organization field has two options, D for Direct organization and W for Direct using the REWRITE statement. An example using D is as follows:

ASSIGN TO DA-3340-D-MASTDIR.

And for CDC-6000, the ORGANIZATION clause defines the file method as follows:

ASSIGN TO name
ORGANIZATION IS DIRECT.

Creating a Direct File

The program in Figure 18-2 creates a Direct file from input records that are in any sequence. The ASSIGN clause specifies DA-3340-D, with D for Direct file. The entry ACTUAL KEY IS PART-KEY-AREA is the name of the area in Working-Storage that contains the calculated relative track and the key:

```
01    PART-KEY-AREA.
      03   KEY-REL-TRACK  ...        RELATIVE TRACK
      03   KEY-PART-NO    ...        KEY
```

The TRACK-LIMIT entry specifies the number of tracks for the file. Note in the Procedure Division that the DIVIDE uses a REMAINDER clause for storing the calculated relative track. Since the number of tracks is 500, the randomizing formula divides by prime number 499. Field definitions are COMP, the most efficient format. On the WRITE, the INVALID KEY clause checks for a calculated relative track outside of the allocated disk area.

Random Updating of a Direct File

For random updating of a Direct file, the SELECT clause and fields for ACTUAL KEY and quotient/remainder are similar to the Direct file creation example, but the TRACK-LIMIT entry is omitted. The Direct file is opened as I-O, and the program must perform the same calculation as in Figure 18-2 to access the required record directly. It READs with an INVALID KEY clause, changes the retrieved record, WRITEs with an INVALID KEY clause, and then restores the updated record to disk.

```
IDENTIFICATION DIVISION.
PROGRAM-ID. CHAP18B.
*   PROGRAM CREATES A DISK FILE ORGANIZED AS DIRECT.

ENVIRONMENT DIVISION.
INPUT-OUTPUT SECTION.
FILE-CONTROL.
    SELECT PART-FILE-IN
        ASSIGN TO SYS015-UR-2501-S.
    SELECT DIRECT-PART-FILE
        ASSIGN TO SYS026-DA-3340-D-PARFILE
        ACCESS IS RANDOM
        ACTUAL KEY IS PART-KEY-AREA.

DATA DIVISION.
FILE SECTION.
FD  PART-FILE-IN
    LABEL RECORDS ARE OMITTED
    DATA RECORD IS PART-REC-IN.
01  PART-REC-IN.
    03  PART-CODE-IN     PIC X(2).
    03  PART-NO-IN       PIC 9(6).
    03  PART-DESCR-IN    PIC X(20).
    03  PART-COST-IN     PIC S999V99.
    03  FILLER           PIC X(47).

FD  DIRECT-PART-FILE
    LABEL RECORDS ARE STANDARD
    RECORDING MODE IS F
    DATA RECORD IS PART-REC-OUT.
01  PART-REC-OUT.
    03  STATUS-CODE-OUT  PIC X.
    03  PART-NO-OUT      PIC 9(6).
    03  PART-DESCR-OUT   PIC X(20).
    03  PART-COST-OUT    PIC S999V99 COMP-3.

WORKING-STORAGE SECTION.
77  EOF-FLAG             PIC X(3)    VALUE ' '.
    88  END-OF-FILE                  VALUE 'EOF'.
01  BINARY-ITEMS                     COMP SYNC.
    03  DIVID-FIELD      PIC S9(5).
    03  QUOT-FIELD       PIC S9(5).
01  PART-KEY-AREA.
    03  KEY-REL-TRACK    PIC S9(5)   COMP SYNC.
    03  KEY-PART-NO      PIC 9(6)    DISPLAY.
```

```
PROCEDURE DIVISION.
    OPEN INPUT PART-FILE-IN, OUTPUT DIRECT-PART-FILE.
    READ PART-FILE-IN, AT END MOVE 'EOF' TO EOF-FLAG.
    PERFORM C000-CREATE UNTIL END-OF-FILE.
    CLOSE PART-FILE-IN, DIRECT-PART-FILE.
    STOP RUN.

C000-CREATE SECTION.
    MOVE LOW-VALUES TO STATUS-CODE-OUT.
    MOVE PART-DESCR-IN  TO PART-DESCR-OUT.
    MOVE PART-COST-IN   TO PART-COST-OUT.
    MOVE PART-NO-IN     TO PART-NO-OUT
                          KEY-PART-NO
                          DIVID-FIELD.
    DIVIDE DIVID-FIELD BY 499 GIVING QUOT-FIELD
                          REMAINDER KEY-REL-TRACK.
    WRITE PART-REC-OUT
        INVALID KEY DISPLAY PART-NO-IN, 'INVALID KEY'.
    READ PART-FILE-IN, AT END MOVE 'EOF' TO EOF-FLAG.
C999-RETURN. EXIT.
```

FIGURE 18-2   Creating a Direct File.

SUMMARY OF DISK FILE ORGANIZATIONS

The selection of file organization may at first seem bewildering. The first choice, however, should be sequential. If there is no reason for random processing, sequential organization will use the least disk space and program overhead. If there is a need for both random processing and sequential processing, the first choice is Indexed or VSAM. Indexed requires more disk space than sequential but facilitates random processing. (It may still be more efficient to sort transactions before updating, especially if they are to update more than 15 percent of the indexed file.) If fast access is required, especially for an on-line system, the choice should be Direct file processing, but keep in mind its problem areas: extra disk space, a randomizing formula, and synonyms.

PROBLEMS

18–1. Under what circumstances would you consider using Relative file organization?

18–2. A file is to be converted to Relative file organization, and the record keys are 3, 4, 5, 7, 9, 13, 14, 15, and 18. What will be the total number of record spaces, and what will be dummy records?

18–3. Create a Relative file from the following input data for an employee file. Test the program using records starting with employee 0001 through 0020.

COL.

1–4	Employee number
5–24	Employee name
25–26	Department code
27	Job category code
28–29	Education code
30–35	Date of birth
36–41	Date hired
42	Marital status code
43	Male/female code

18–4. Write program to read the file created in Problem 18-3. Print the contents of each record.

18–5. Under what circumstances would you consider using Direct file organization?

18–6. Assume that a file of 6,000 records is to be stored as a Direct file. The range of keys for the file is 23000 through 64999 (42,000 possible keys). How much disk space in terms of number of records should be reserved for the file?

18–7. Refer to the Direct file example in this chapter that stored records on tracks 0 through 3. Calculate the track addresses for the following keys and determine if there is any space left on the track: 160, 561, 231, 222.

18–8. What are two ways to reduce the number of synonyms in a Direct file?

18–9. The division/remainder randomizing formula uses a prime number to divide into the key. What prime number would you use if a file of 5,000 records is to be stored on 200 tracks? What is the value that results from dividing the prime number into the key?

18–10. Revise Problem 18-3 to create a Direct file. Assume that there are ten tracks available for storing the file randomly.

CHAPTER 19

COBOL SORT

OBJECTIVE: To present the COBOL SORT feature used for the sorting of external records.

INTRODUCTION

The *sorting* of data—arranging data into some predetermined ascending or descending sequence—is a large part of data processing. There are two distinct types of sorts:

1. *Internal sort.* An example is the program in Chapter 12 that sorted table entries into ascending sequence by job number. The internal sort is always coded by installation programmers.
2. *External sort.* This sort is complicated and is supplied by the manufacturer. The external sort is generalized to accept various numbers of records, record lengths, and sort fields (keys). It typically alters the sort logic based on these variables, the amount of available main storage, and the available tape drives or disk work areas.

You can invoke the external sort either by a job control statement that executes a utility sort between programs or by a COBOL SORT statement that executes a utility sort during execution of a program. The COBOL SORT statement and its use is the topic of this chapter.

A word of caution: The COBOL external sort program is relatively inefficient, and consequently it is usually better to use a standard utility sort program for large files.

325

SORT CHARACTERISTICS

A sort can be in either ascending or descending sequence. Typical fields to be sorted into ascending sequence are account number and customer name, and for a descending sequence, employee salary and regional sales. A sort can order records by more than one key (control field); for example, a *major* (or primary) key could be branch office in ascending sequence, and a *minor* (or secondary) key could be weekly sales volume in descending sequence. The precise sort (or *collating*) sequence depends on a computer's binary representation of characters:

Honeywell 6000	0–9, blank, A–Z
IBM 360/370	blank, A–Z, 0–9
PDP-11	blank, 0–9, A–Z

The OBJECT-COMPUTER paragraph indicates the collating sequence, although it is obvious that no compiler could possibly generate the collating sequence for all computer systems. ANS-74 provides for a COLLATING SEQUENCE phrase in the SORT to handle this problem, but it may not be available in all compilers.

A sort operation involves the following three files:

1. An *input file* that contains the original unsorted data on an input device (card reader, tape, disk).
2. A *sort file* (tape or disk) that is used as a temporary work area for sorting the input records.
3. An *output file* that stores the sorted records on tape or disk (the output could be a printed file, or may even specify the same file as the input, so that the sorted records overwrite the original file).

The input file must contain valid data, but both the sort file and the output file could be vacant or contain obsolete, unwanted data.

SORT REQUIREMENTS FOR USING AND GIVING

The coding to request a COBOL sort is relatively simple. The following specifications are required:

- Environment Division: SELECT statements for the input, sort, and output files.
- Data Division: a SD statement to define the sort file, with specifications similar to the regular FD.

- Procedure Division: a SORT statement coded at a logical place in the program where sorting is required.

Let's examine each of these requirements.

SELECT

The SELECT statement for the sort file designates the tape or disk file that the sort is to use as a temporary work area and is coded like other SELECT statements (but check your compiler version for unique features, such as specifying more than one tape drive):

SELECT sort-file, ASSIGN TO . . .

DOS ASSIGN.   The following provides for sorting a sequential file (S) on an IBM 3340 disk device under DOS:

ASSIGN TO SYS001-UT-3340-S-SORTWK1.

DOS uses SYS001 for the system name. The name SORTWK1 is required if the sort file processes standard tape or disk labels. A sort program using tape with standard labels and four IBM 3420 tape drives would contain the following statement:

ASSIGN TO 4 SYS001-UT-3420-S-SORTWK1.

OS ASSIGN.   An OS ASSIGN statement for a sort using IBM 3420 tape drives would be as follows:

ASSIGN TO UT-3420-S-name.

Under OS, the ASSIGN clause may be used to describe the sort work files, but since the system receives this information at execution by job control entries, the SELECT and ASSIGN are only for documentation.

CDC ASSIGN.   An ASSIGN clause for the CDC 6000 series to sort using tape would be as follows:

ASSIGN TO TAPE02.

SD

The SD statement describes the sort file and its data record format as follows:

```
SD  sort-file
        DATA RECORD IS record-name.
01  record-name.
        .
        .
        .
```

DATA RECORD contains the keys (or control fields) that the SORT stipulates. Some COBOL versions may require LABEL RECORDS ARE STANDARD.

SORT

The SORT statement provides the names of the key fields to be sorted and the names of the input and output files. The SORT format is as follows:

$$\text{SORT} \quad \text{sort-file}$$
$$\text{ON} \begin{Bmatrix} \text{ASCENDING} \\ \text{DESCENDING} \end{Bmatrix} \text{KEY} \quad \text{key-1,} \left[\begin{Bmatrix} \text{ASCENDING} \\ \text{DESCENDING} \end{Bmatrix} \text{KEY} \quad \text{key-2} \right] \dots$$
$$\text{USING} \quad \text{input-file}$$
$$\text{GIVING} \quad \text{output-file}$$

The SORT verb designates the name of the sort file to be sorted (the SD entry). USING names the input file containing the records to be sorted, and GIVING names the final sorted file. Both USING and GIVING automatically OPEN, READ, WRITE, and CLOSE a file and may specify the same file. The ON ASCENDING (or DESCENDING) KEY lists the key field or fields from left to right in descending order of significance (major to minor). The key fields, defined in the sort file record, must be fixed length, cannot contain an OCCURS clause, and must be in the same position in every record. The maximum number of keys varies by compiler version (IBM allows 12). The statement

ON ASCENDING KEY DEPARTMENT, EMPLOYEE-NO

sorts employee numbers within departments in ascending sequence, whereas

ON ASCENDING KEY DEPARTMENT
DESCENDING KEY SALARY

sorts salaries in descending sequence within departments in ascending sequence.

A program can sort a file, and then use the same sorted file as input for further processing, as shown in the skeleton program in Figure 19-1. Or, a program can process a file, write new updated records, and then sort the file; the next phase of the program, or another program, could then process the sorted file.

The program in Figure 19-1 first sorts the input file. Note that the SORT automatically OPENs, READs, SORTs, WRITEs, and CLOSEs the files. On completion of the sort operation, the program OPENs the output file and READs and prints the sorted records.

SORT REQUIREMENTS FOR INPUT AND OUTPUT PROCEDURES

Sometimes it is necessary to process a file during the sort operation. For example, a program may have to bypass certain departments or employee numbers, or reformat input records. (Actually, a program could perform such processing before the sort; for example, the program in Figure 19-1 could initially read the file and rewrite the selected records.) The general format is as follows:

```
SORT  sort-file
          ASCENDING (or DESCENDING) KEY IS . . .
          INPUT PROCEDURE IS section-name-1
          OUTPUT PROCEDURE IS section-name-2
```

The INPUT PROCEDURE replaces the USING clause, and the OUTPUT PROCEDURE replaces GIVING. Both enable a program to perform special processing during a sort. The valid combinations are as follows:

USING GIVING	No special handling of either input or output.
INPUT PROCEDURE GIVING	Special handling during reading of the input file.
USING OUTPUT PROCEDURE	Special handling of the output file.
INPUT PROCEDURE OUTPUT PROCEDURE	Special handling of both input and output files.

Input Procedure

The Input Procedure specifies a Section of code in the Procedure Division that only the SORT performs. It must provide the OPEN and READ statements, as shown in Figure 19-2. Instead of WRITE, however, RELEASE is used to write a record onto the sort file; the program bypasses departments 24 and 32, and RELEASEs (writes) all other departments. Otherwise, the program is similar to the program in Figure 19-1.

```
IDENTIFICATION DIVISION.
PROGRAM-ID. CHAP19A.

ENVIRONMENT DIVISION.
INPUT-OUTPUT SECTION.
FILE-CONTROL.
    SELECT EMPL-INP, ASSIGN TO SYS002-UT-3350-S.
    SELECT EMPL-SRT, ASSIGN TO SYS001-UT-3350-S-SORTWK1.
    SELECT EMPL-OUT, ASSIGN TO SYS003-UT-3350-S.

DATA DIVISION.
FILE SECTION.
FD  EMPL-INP
    LABEL RECORDS ARE STANDARD
    DATA RECORD IS EMPL-REC-IN.
01  EMPL-REC-IN.
    03  DEPT-IN         PIC X(2).
    03  EMPLOY-IN       PIC X(5).
    03  SALARY-IN       PIC S9(5)V99.
    03  FILLER          PIC X(22).

SD  EMPL-SRT
    LABEL RECORDS ARE STANDARD
    DATA RECORD IS SORT-WORK.
01  SORT-WORK.
    03  DEPT-WK         PIC X(2).
    03  EMPLOY-WK       PIC X(5).
    03  SALARY-WK       PIC S9(5)V99.
    03  FILLER          PIC X(22).

FD  EMPL-OUT
    LABEL RECORDS ARE STANDARD
    DATA RECORD IS EMPL-REC-OUT.
01  EMPL-REC-OUT.
    03  DEPT-OUT        PIC X(2).
    03  EMPLOY-OUT      PIC X(5).
    03  SALARY-OUT      PIC S9(5)V99.
    03  FILLER          PIC X(22).

WORKING-STORAGE SECTION.
77  TOTAL-SALARY        PIC S9(7)V99 VALUE ZERO.
77  EOF-FLAG            PIC X(3)     VALUE SPACES.
    88  END-FILE                     VALUE 'EOF'.
01  EMPL-REC-WS         PIC X(36).

PROCEDURE DIVISION.
    SORT EMPL-SRT
        ASCENDING   KEY IS DEPT-WK
        DESCENDING KEY IS SALARY-WK
        USING  EMPL-INP
        GIVING EMPL-OUT.
    OPEN INPUT EMPL-OUT.
    READ EMPL-OUT
        AT END MOVE 'EOF' TO EOF-FLAG.
    PERFORM B000-PROC UNTIL END-FILE.
    CLOSE EMPL-OUT.
    STOP RUN.

B000-PROC SECTION.
    MOVE EMPL-REC-OUT TO EMPL-REC-WS.
    DISPLAY EMPL-REC-WS.
    READ EMPL-OUT
        AT END MOVE 'EOF' TO EOF-FLAG.
B999-RETURN. EXIT.
```

FIGURE 19-1 Use of SORT USING and GIVING.

```
            PROCEDURE DIVISION.
                SORT EMPL-SRT
                    ASCENDING  KEY IS DEPT-WK
                    DESCENDING KEY IS SALARY-WK
                    INPUT PROCEDURE IS C000-CHECK
                    GIVING EMPL-OUT.
                MOVE SPACES TO EOF-FLAG.
                OPEN INPUT EMPL-OUT.
                READ EMPL-OUT
                    AT END MOVE 'EOF' TO EOF-FLAG.
                PERFORM B000-PROC UNTIL END-FILE.
                CLOSE EMPL-OUT.
                STOP RUN.

            B000-PROC SECTION.
                MOVE EMPL-REC-OUT TO EMPL-REC-WS.
                DISPLAY EMPL-REC-WS.
                READ EMPL-OUT
                    AT END MOVE 'EOF' TO EOF-FLAG.
            B999-RETURN. EXIT.

            C000-CHECK SECTION.
                OPEN INPUT EMPL-INP.
                READ EMPL-INP
                    AT END MOVE 'EOF' TO EOF-FLAG.
                PERFORM C200-SELECT UNTIL END-FILE.
                CLOSE EMPL-INP.
            C199-RETURN. EXIT.

            C200-SELECT SECTION.
                IF DEPT-IN NOT = '00024' OR '00032'
                    MOVE EMPL-REC-IN TO SORT-WORK
                    RELEASE SORT-WORK.
                READ EMPL-INP
                    AT END MOVE 'EOF' TO EOF-FLAG.
            C299-RETURN. EXIT.
```

FIGURE 19-2   Use of SORT Input Procedure.

Output Procedure

The Output Procedure also specifies a Section of code in the Procedure Division that only the SORT performs. In Figure 19-3, the Output Procedure is D000-WRITE. The Section first opens the sorted output file, uses RETURN to read the sort file (the coding is similar to that for READ), formats the print area, and writes each record on the printer. In this case, EMPL-OUT is a printer file. The CLOSE statement in the Output Procedure causes the Procedure to terminate and to return to the statement following the SORT.

```
PROCEDURE DIVISION.
    SORT EMPL-SRT
        ASCENDING  KEY IS DEPT-WK
        DESCENDING KEY IS SALARY-WK
        USING  EMPL-INP
        OUTPUT PROCEDURE IS D000-WRITE.
    STOP RUN.

D000-WRITE SECTION.
    OPEN OUTPUT EMPL-OUT.
    RETURN EMPL-SRT
        AT END MOVE 'EOF' TO EOF-FLAG.
    PERFORM D200-OLT UNTIL END-FILE.
    MOVE TOTAL-SALARY TO SALARY-OUT.
    WRITE EMPL-REC-OUT AFTER ADVANCING 2 LINES.
    CLOSE EMPL-OUT.
D199-RETURN. EXIT.

D200-OUT SECTION.
    ADD SALARY-WK  TO TOTAL-SALARY.
    MOVE DEPT-WK   TO DEPT-OUT.
    MOVE EMPLOY-WK TO EMPLOY-OUT.
    MOVE SALARY-WK TO SALARY-OUT.
    WRITE EMPL-REC-OUT AFTER ADVANCING 1 LINES.
    MOVE SPACES TO EMPL-REC-OUT.
    RETURN EMPL-SRT
        AT END MOVE 'EOF' TO EOF-FLAG.
D299-RETURN. EXIT.
```

FIGURE 19-3   Use of SORT Output Procedure.

SORT REGISTERS

IBM provides four sort registers (not ANS) to facilitate the SORT operation. They are reserved words that may be referenced, but not defined, and are as follows:

1.   SORT-CORE-SIZE. The more main storage available, the more efficient is the sort operation. The following provides for 64,000 storage locations:

MOVE +64000 TO SORT-CORE-SIZE.

2.   SORT-FILE-SIZE. You can provide an estimate of the number of records to be sorted that will generate an optimum sort algorithm. A common practice is to estimate about 15–25 percent more than necessary. For example, if a file contains 10,000 records, the estimate is 12,000 records:

MOVE +12000 TO SORT-FILE-SIZE.

3.   SORT-MODE-SIZE. If records are variable length, this register provides the most common record length, if any.

4.   SORT-RETURN. This register indicates the success or failure of a sort. For a successful sort, the register will contain 0, and for a failure, it will contain 16.

SUMMARY

Sorting is a major operation in a data processing installation. Most sorting should be done using standard utility sort programs, but there are times when a COBOL SORT may be useful. The USING/GIVING options should enable you to handle most conventional applications.

PROBLEMS

19–1. Under what circumstances is the COBOL SORT preferable to a standard utility sort?

19–2. A sort file named SORT-WK-FILE contains the following fields to be sorted:

NAME	CONTROL LEVEL	SEQUENCE
DATE-IN	major	descending
ORDER-NO-IN	intermediate	ascending
ITEM-NO-IN	minor	ascending

The input file is ORDER-FILE-IN and the output file is ORDER-FILE-OUT. Provide the SORT statement.

19–3. Revise the SORT statement in Problem 19-2 to bypass all orders that contain an order number greater than 6000. The bypass routine is called P25-BYPASS.

PART VI
MISCELLANEOUS TOPICS

CHAPTER 20

REPORT WRITER

OBJECTIVE: To present the Report Writer feature and to enable the reader to use the Report Writer to produce reports.

INTRODUCTION

The printing of reports is a large part of the programmer's task. Much of the coding involves defining print lines, moving data to print fields, and using control break logic. To replace much of this time-consuming detail, COBOL provides a Report Writer feature that is remarkably simple to use.

PROGRAM EXAMPLE

Figure 20-1 illustrates a program that uses the Report Writer feature to print product sales records and total sales. The Identification, Environment, and Data Divisions are coded as in previous example programs in this text. The program contains a number of new features.

FD Entry

The FD for the print file contains a REPORT IS entry that tells the compiler to use the Report Writer feature:

```
FD   PRINT-FILE
     LABEL RECORDS ARE OMITTED
     REPORT IS SALES-REPORT.
```

```
00001          IDENTIFICATION DIVISION.
00002          PROGRAM-ID. CHAP20A.
00003          REMARKS.  USE OF REPORT WRITER TO PRODUCE FINAL TOTAL ONLY.

00005          ENVIRONMENT DIVISION.
00006          INPUT-OUTPUT SECTION.
00007          FILE-CONTROL.
00008              SELECT SALES-FILE, ASSIGN TO SYS015-UR-2501-S.
00009              SELECT PRINT-FILE, ASSIGN TO SYS014-UR-1403-S.

00011          DATA DIVISION.
00012          FILE SECTION.
00013          FD  SALES-FILE
00014              LABEL RECORDS ARE OMITTED
00015              DATA RECORD IS SALES-RECORD.
00016          01  SALES-RECORD.
00017              03  FILLER        PIC X(4).
00018              03  DEPT-IN       PIC X(3).
00019              03  PROD-IN       PIC X(4).
00020              03  DESCRIP-IN    PIC X(20).
00021              03  QTY-IN        PIC S999.
00022              03  SALES-IN      PIC S9(5)V99.
00023              03  FILLER        PIC X(39).

00025          FD  PRINT-FILE
00026              LABEL RECORDS ARE OMITTED
00027              REPORT IS SALES-REPORT.

00029          WORKING-STORAGE SECTION.
00030          77  END-FILE-FLAG      PIC X(3)     VALUE ' '.
00031              88  END-FILE                    VALUE 'END'.

00033          REPORT SECTION.
00034          RD  SALES-REPORT
00035              CONTROL FINAL
00036              PAGE LIMIT 25 LINES
00037              HEADING 1
00038              FIRST DETAIL 3.
00039
00040          01  HEADING-LINE
00041              TYPE PAGE HEADING
00042              LINE 1.
00043              03  COLUMN 26     PIC X(10)    VALUE 'DPT    PROD'.
00044              03  COLUMN 39     PIC X(11)    VALUE 'DESCRIPTION'.
00045              03  COLUMN 61     PIC X(16)    VALUE 'QTY       SALES($)'.
00046
00047          01  SALES-LINE
00048              TYPE DETAIL
00049              LINE PLUS 1.
00050              03  COLUMN 26     PIC X(3)     SOURCE DEPT-IN.
00051              03  COLUMN 32     PIC X(4)     SOURCE PROD-IN.
00052              03  COLUMN 39     PIC X(20)    SOURCE DESCRIP-IN.
00053              03  COLUMN 61     PIC ZZ9-     SOURCE QTY-IN.
00054              03  COLUMN 68     PIC ZZ,ZZ9.99CR SOURCE SALES-IN.
00055
00056          01  TOTAL-LINE
00057              TYPE CONTROL, FOOTING FINAL
00058              LINE PLUS 2.
00059              03  COLUMN 35     PIC X(19)    VALUE '*** TOTAL SALES ***'.
00060              03  COLUMN 65     PIC Z,ZZZ,ZZ9.99CR  SUM SALES-IN.
```

FIGURE 20-1   Report Writer—Final Total Only.

338

```
00062          PROCEDURE DIVISION.
00063              OPEN INPUT SALES-FILE
00064                  OUTPUT PRINT-FILE.
00065              INITIATE SALES-REPORT.
00066              READ SALES-FILE
00067                  AT END MOVE 'END' TO END-FILE-FLAG.
00068              PERFORM 800C-SALES UNTIL END-FILE.
00069              TERMINATE SALES-REPORT.
00070              CLOSE SALES-FILE, PRINT-FILE.
00071              STOP RUN.

00073          800C-SALES SECTION.
00074              GENERATE SALES-LINE.
00075              READ SALES-FILE
00076                  AT END MOVE 'END' TO END-FILE-FLAG.
00077          8999-RETURN. EXIT.
```

Input data:

Code	Dpt	Prod		Qty	Amount
05	025	2430	TURNTABLES	0010	024300
05	025	2430	TURNTABLES	0030	064535
05	025	2430	TURNTABLES	0010	011900
05	025	2628	RECEIVERS	0010	022600
05	025	2628	RECEIVERS	0020	014050
05	025	2628	RECEIVERS	0010	068050
05	040	0320	PROCESSORS	0010	216400
05	040	0440	DISK STORAGE	0040	184750
05	040	0440	DISK STORAGE	0060	324290
05	040	1623	TERMINALS	0150	662735
05	040	1623	TERMINALS	0030	122530
05	125	0347	RECORDS	0200	008560
05	125	0392	CASSETTE TAPE	0120	004912
05	125	0395	8-TRACK TAPE	0070	002520

Printed report:

DPT	PROD	DESCRIPTION	QTY	SALES($)
025	2430	TURNTABLES	1	243.00
025	2430	TURNTABLES	3	645.35
025	2430	TURNTABLES	1	119.00
025	2628	RECEIVERS	1	226.00
025	2628	RECEIVERS	2	140.50
025	2628	RECEIVERS	1	680.50
040	0320	PROCESSORS	1	2,164.00
040	0440	DISK STORAGE	4	1,847.50
040	0440	DISK STORAGE	6	3,242.90
040	1623	TERMINALS	15	6,627.35
040	1623	TERMINALS	3	1,225.30
125	0347	RECORDS	20	85.60
125	0392	CASSETTE TAPE	12	49.12
125	0395	8-TRACK TAPE	7	25.20
		*** TOTAL SALES ***		17,321.32

FIGURE 20-1   (cont.)   Program Output.

339

Unlike in a conventional program, SALES-REPORT is defined in a later REPORT SECTION, rather than immediately following the FD entries.

Report Section

Following the Working-Storage Section is a new REPORT SECTION containing all the entries that describe the printed output.

RD SALES-REPORT.   This entry provides the *report description* for the report that the FD statement specified earlier.

CONTROL FINAL.   This entry tells the compiler that control totals are to occur for final totals only.

PAGE LIMIT 25 LINES.   This entry indicates that the number of lines per page is 25 and to overflow to a new page when this limit is exceeded.

HEADING 1.   This entry indicates that the first (and in this case only) heading line is to print on line 1 of each page.

FIRST DETAIL 3.   This entry indicates that the first detail line (the detail information from input records) of each page is to print on line 3.

Report Group Descriptions.   The following are the three report group description entries. Each group—heading, detail, and total—begins with a level 01 entry and has a unique description:

1.   HEADING-LINE. The first group (any descriptive name) contains the following:
     - TYPE PAGE HEADING indicates that the line is to be a page heading at the top of each page.
     - LINE 1 indicates printing on the first line of the page.
     - The 03 entries (any number 02 through 49) specify the starting position, the PICTURE, and the value of each heading field. It is not necessary to define FILLER entries for blank areas in the print records.

     In this example, the name HEADING-LINE is only for documentation. It is not referenced in the program, and the report group description entry could be coded without a name, as follows:

              01 TYPE PAGE HEADING

2.   SALES-LINE. The second group (any descriptive name) contains the following:

- TYPE DETAIL indicates that this group describes each detail line that the program is to print.

- LINE PLUS 1 indicates single spacing between each detail line. LINE PLUS 2 would indicate double-spacing between each detail line.

- The 03 entries specify the starting position of the PICTURE for each detail field. The SOURCE clauses indicate the data fields from the input record or from Working-Storage that the Report Writer is to insert. The first SOURCE entry, for example, indicates that DEPT-IN from the input record is to print as a three-character field beginning in column 26. PICTURE definitions are exactly like those in the previous programs of this text.

- The name SALES-LINE is required because it is referenced by Section B000-SALES in the Procedure Division.

3.   TOTAL-LINE. The third group (any descriptive name, or none) contains the following:

- TYPE CONTROL, FOOTING FINAL. TYPE CONTROL defines a line used for a control total, and FOOTING FINAL indicates that this is a final total.

- LINE PLUS 2 tells the compiler to space two lines before printing the final total line.

- The two 03 entries provide for the print fields. The amount field is to print a final total of sales by adding the SALES-IN field from every input record and printing a final total.

Because the program does not reference TOTAL-LINE by name, another valid group description would be:

```
01 TYPE CONTROL, FOOTING FINAL
```

Procedure Division

The Procedure Division is particularly easy to code with the usual OPEN, READ, CLOSE, and STOP RUN statements. But in place of the usual WRITE and MOVE statements, there are three new statements:

1.   INITIATE SALES-REPORT references the defined RD entry and initializes the registers that the Report Writer uses: LINE-COUNTER (to count the number of lines printed and spaced), PAGE-COUNTER (to count the number of pages printed), and SUM counters.

2.   GENERATE SALES-LINE indicates the point at which the program is to print each detail line. The first time GENERATE executes, it prints the first headings.

3.   TERMINATE SALES-REPORT prints a final total prior to closing the files and stopping the run.

The programming approach to the Report Writer is similar to conventional COBOL coding, and as can be seen, the Report Writer feature is simple, clear, and considerably reduces the coding. It allows the usual calculations and table searches in the Procedure Division and prints the results from Working-Storage using SOURCE clauses.

REPORT DESCRIPTION (RD) ENTRY

The Report Section contains a report description (RD) entry for each report that a program is to print. But there is usually only one report and consequently only one RD entry. The RD entry defines the unique name of the report (SALES-REPORT in Figure 20-1). The three entries following the report-name are optional:

> RD report-name
>   CONTROL clause (or CONTROLS)
>   PAGE LIMIT clause
>   CODE clause

CONTROL Clause

The CONTROL clause specifies the field(s) to be used for control breaks. There are three options:

1.   CONTROL FINAL
2.   CONTROL field(s)
3.   CONTROL FINAL, field(s)

- Option 1 tells a program to print final totals only at the end of a run, as in Figure 20-1.
- Option 2 checks the contents of a specified control field when reading an input record. Any change of the control field causes the automatic printing of accumulated totals for the control group. For multiple control fields, the coding sequence is major, intermediate, and minor.
- Option 3 prints control fields by group and final totals at the end of a report. The fields are in descending sequence of importance: final, major, intermediate, and minor. For example, if a program were to break control on stock number (minor), branch office number (intermediate), and final, the CONTROL entry would be

CONTROL FINAL, BRANCH-IN, STOCK-IN

PAGE LIMIT Clause

The PAGE LIMIT clause describes the format of a page. The options are as follows:

PAGE LIMIT max LINES	Maximum number of lines per page.
HEADING integer-1	First line of the heading group.
FIRST DETAIL integer-2	First line on a page of a detail group.
LAST DETAIL integer-3	Last line on a page of a detail group.
FOOTING integer-4	A line for printing a total.

The entries are all optional, and any one option can be used above. The FOOTING entry is useful if a final total is to always print on a specific line. Integer-4 should be within the range of max lines so that if the maximum number of lines is 55, then no line can specify a larger value. Also, integer-4 must be greater than integer-3, which must be greater than integer-2, which must be greater than integer-1.

CODE Clause

The CODE clause is useful when a program produces more than one report because it inserts a code in the first position of each line to distinguish one report from another.

REPORT GROUP DESCRIPTION ENTRIES

Each report group must have a description beginning with a level 01 entry with the following format:

```
01  [group-name]
    TYPE clause
    [LINE NUMBER clause]
    [NEXT GROUP clause]
```

The group-name must be defined only if a statement in the Procedure Division references it, but the examples in this chapter always define a group-name for consistency and clarity.

TYPE Clause

The TYPE clause defines the particular type of report group. A group may consist of one or more related lines. The TYPEs are as follows:

```
REPORT HEADING (or RH)
PAGE HEADING (or PH)
DETAIL (or DE)
CONTROL HEADING (or CH) { identifier-n
                        { FINAL
CONTROL FOOTING (or CF) { identifier-n
                        { FINAL
REPORT FOOTING (or RF)
PAGE FOOTING (or PF)
```

- REPORT HEADING indicates a report group that is to print only once at the start of execution. The entry also handles special detailed information that is to be printed on the first page of a report, for example, a company name or an explanation of codes that the report prints.
- PAGE HEADING specifies a report group that is to print page heading line(s) at the top of each page.
- DETAIL defines each detail line—in effect, each input record. The GENERATE statement in the Procedure Division produces the report group for each input record. The group must have a unique level 01 group-name.
- CONTROL HEADING and CONTROL FOOTING indicate control breaks. HEADING indicates a report group that prints at the start of a control break. For example, you may need to print a department name on a separate line before printing the detail information for the department. FOOTING, which is more commonly used, indicates a report group that prints at the end of a control break, typically a simple control break such as department total. Both HEADING and FOOTING require an entry to designate the type of total. For example:

CONTROL FOOTING FINAL	Total only at the end of the report.
CONTROL FOOTING DEPT-IN	Total on change of department number (assume that DEPT-IN is defined in the input record).

- REPORT FOOTING indicates a report group that prints only at the end of a report. The previous example printed a single line for sales total.
- PAGE FOOTING indicates a report group that prints at the bottom of each page. Some reports require totals or page numbers at the bottom of each page.

The TYPE entries are coded in the following sequence:

```
REPORT HEADING
PAGE HEADING
CONTROL HEADING
DETAIL
CONTROL FOOTING
PAGE FOOTING
REPORT FOOTING
```

LINE Clause

The LINE clause indicates the actual or relative line number where the report group is to print. For example:

- LINE 10 indicates that the group is to print on line 10 of each page.
- LINE PLUS 2 indicates spacing two lines past the last line printed.
- LINE NEXT PAGE indicates printing on the page that follows (this clause has restricted use).

NEXT GROUP Clause

The NEXT GROUP clause spaces the report group that *follows* the report group being defined. A typical use is the spacing after a minor or major total line. The options are identical to the LINE NUMBER clause options. NEXT GROUP, however, cannot be coded for PAGE HEADING, PAGE FOOTING, or REPORT FOOTING.

REPORT GROUPS

The program in Figure 20-1 was intentionally simple in order to illustrate the basic features of the Report Writer. Each group—heading, detail, and final total—required only one line. But, often, a group will require more than one line (for example, a heading). To indicate two or more lines, define each line at a specific level number and the fields within each line at a higher level number. The level numbers can be between 02 and 49. Figure 20-2 uses 03 for the line number and 05 for the field definitions. The first heading line prints on line 1 of each page, and the second heading line prints on line 3. Therefore, the first detail line must print on a line higher than 3.

```
01   HEADING-LINE
        TYPE PAGE HEADING.
        03   LINE 1.
              05   COLUMN 22   PIC X(8)     SOURCE CURRENT-DATE.
              05   COLUMN 41   PIC X(12)    VALUE 'SALES REPORT'.
        03   LINE 3.
              05   COLUMN 26   PIC X(10)    VALUE 'DPT    PROD'.
              05   COLUMN 39   PIC X(11)    VALUE 'DESCRIPTION'.
              05   COLUMN 61   PIC X(16)    VALUE 'QTY     SALES($)'.
```

FIGURE 20-2   Defining Two Heading Lines.

CONTROL BREAKS

A program may need to take control break totals on specified input fields. For example, input records could be in sequence by department (major) and product (minor), with totals required for department, product, and final total. The RD statement would contain the following entry:

CONTROL FINAL, DEPT-IN, PROD-IN

The control fields are coded from the highest level (final) to the lowest level (minor).

The Report Writer uses a CONTROL line for each total level. Figure 20-3 shows the coding for three total lines. A change of value in the input field PROD-IN causes a control break and prints the total sales for the preceding group of equal product numbers. In the figure, each total line has its own accumulator for sales amount:

TOTAL LINE	ACCUMULATOR	ADDED FROM (SUM)
PROD-LINE	PROD-TOTAL	SALES-IN
DEPT-LINE	DEPT-TOTAL	PROD-TOTAL
FINAL-LINE	(no name)	DEPT-TOTAL

PROD-LINE defines a level 03 entry called PROD-TOTAL that contains the clause SUM SALES-IN. For equal product numbers, the program accumulates total SALES-IN in PROD-TOTAL, but for a change of product number, it prints PROD-TOTAL, adds PROD-TOTAL to DEPT-TOTAL (see DEPT-LINE), and clears PROD-TOTAL. The accumulator for DEPT-LINE is DEPT-TOTAL. For a change of department number, the program initiates a product control break (prints product, adds to department, and clears product), prints DEPT-TOTAL, adds DEPT-TOTAL to FINAL-TOTAL, and clears DEPT-TOTAL. For end-of-file, the program forces an automatic control break on both product and department and then prints FINAL-TOTAL.

```
01   PROD-LINE
     TYPE CONTROL FOOTING PROD-IN
     LINE PLUS 1 NEXT GROUP PLUS 1.
     03   PROD-TOTAL
          COLUMN 65          PIC Z,ZZZ,ZZ9.99CR  SUM SALES-IN.
     03   COLUMN 79          PIC X         VALUE '*'.

01   DEPT-LINE
     TYPE CONTROL FOOTING DEPT-IN
     LINE PLUS 2 NEXT GROUP PLUS 1.
     03   DEPT-TOTAL
          COLUMN 65          PIC Z,ZZZ,ZZ9.99CR   SUM PROD-TOTAL.
     03   COLUMN 79          PIC XX        VALUE '**'.

01   FINAL-LINE
     TYPE CONTROL FOOTING FINAL
     LINE PLUS 2.
     03   COLUMN 35          PIC X(19)    VALUE '*** TOTAL SALES ***'.
     03   COLUMN 65          PIC Z,ZZZ,ZZ9.99CR   SUM DEPT-TOTAL.
```

FIGURE 20-3   Defining Total Level Lines.

PROGRAM EXAMPLE

Figure 20-4 illustrates a program that is similar to the program in Figure 20-3. It prints two heading lines and breaks control on product and department as before. But it also has some new features:

- The page number is printed at the bottom of each page (a useful practice if pages are to be bound horizontally at the top). The Report Writer stores the page count in a register called PAGE-COUNTER, which is available for printing.
- The NEXT GROUP clause forces spacing after total lines.
- The GROUP INDICATE clause prints the department and product numbers only at the beginning of the group and at the top of each page. The GROUP INDICATE clause appears only on a detail line.

The Report Section contains one page heading type, one detail type, three control types, and one page footing type. The program spaces after total lines. Both PROD-LINE and DEPT-LINE use NEXT GROUP PLUS 1 to cause one space after the group, but the group consists of these two CONTROL types and FINAL-LINE. Therefore, there are two possibilities:

1.   If the control break is PROD-IN only, the program prints PROD-LINE, and because the program is at the end of the group, spaces one more line (NEXT GROUP). The detail line that follows also spaces, leaving a blank line between the product total and the following detail line.

```
00001        IDENTIFICATION DIVISION.
00002        PROGRAM-ID. CHAP20A.
00003        REMARKS.  USE OF REPORT WRITER.

00005        ENVIRONMENT DIVISION.
00006        INPUT-OUTPUT SECTION.
00007        FILE-CONTROL.
00008            SELECT SALES-FILE, ASSIGN TO SYS015-UR-2501-S.
00009            SELECT PRINT-FILE, ASSIGN TO SYS014-UR-1403-S.

00011        DATA DIVISION.
00012        FILE SECTION.
00013        FD  SALES-FILE
00014            LABEL RECORDS ARE OMITTED
00015            DATA RECORD IS SALES-RECORD.
00016        01  SALES-RECORD.
00017            03  FILLER          PIC X(4).
00018            03  DEPT-IN         PIC X(3).
00019            03  PROD-IN         PIC X(4).
00020            03  DESCRIP-IN      PIC X(20).
00021            03  QTY-IN          PIC S999.
00022            03  SALES-IN        PIC S9(5)V99.
00023            03  FILLER          PIC X(39).

00025        FD  PRINT-FILE
00026            LABEL RECORDS ARE OMITTED
00027            REPORT IS SALES-REPORT.

00029        WORKING-STORAGE SECTION.
00030        77  END-FILE-FLAG       PIC X(3)      VALUE ' '.
00031            88  END-FILE                      VALUE 'END'.

00033        REPORT SECTION.
00034        RD  SALES-REPORT
00035            CONTROL FINAL, DEPT-IN, PROD-IN
00036            PAGE LIMIT 58 LINES
00037            HEADING 1
00038            FIRST DETAIL 5
00039            LAST  DETAIL 50.
00040
00041        01  HEADING-LINE
00042            TYPE PAGE HEADING.
00043            03  LINE 1.
00044                05  COLUMN 22   PIC X(8)      SOURCE CURRENT-DATE.
00045                05  COLUMN 41   PIC X(12)     VALUE 'SALES REPORT'.
00046            03  LINE 3.
00047                05  COLUMN 26   PIC X(10)     VALUE 'DPT    PRCD'.
00048                05  COLUMN 39   PIC X(11)     VALUE 'DESCRIPTION'.
00049                05  COLUMN 61   PIC X(16)     VALUE 'QTY     SALES($)'.
```

FIGURE 20-4   Use of Report Writer for Control Breaks.

348

```
000051      01  SALES-LINE
000052          TYPE DETAIL
000053          LINE PLUS 1.
000054          03  COLUMN 26        PIC X(3)     SOURCE DEPT-IN
000055                                            GROUP INDICATE.
000056          03  COLUMN 32        PIC X(4)     SOURCE PROD-IN
000057                                            GROUP INDICATE.
000058          03  COLUMN 39        PIC X(20)    SOURCE DESCRIP-IN.
000059          03  COLUMN 61        PIC ZZ9-     SOURCE QTY-IN.
000060          03  COLUMN 68        PIC ZZ,ZZ9.99CR SOURCE SALES-IN.
000061
000062      01  PROD-LINE
000063          TYPE CONTROL FOOTING PROD-IN
000064          LINE PLUS 1 NEXT GROUP PLUS 1.
000065          03  PROD-TOTAL
000066              COLUMN 65        PIC Z,ZZZ,ZZ9.99CR SUM SALES-IN.
000067          03  COLUMN 79        PIC X        VALUE '*'.
000068
000069      01  DEPT-LINE
000070          TYPE CONTROL FOOTING DEPT-IN
000071          LINE PLUS 2 NEXT GROUP PLUS 1.
000072          03  DEPT-TOTAL
000073              COLUMN 65        PIC Z,ZZZ,ZZ9.99CR  SUM PROD-TOTAL.
000074          03  COLUMN 79        PIC XX       VALUE '**'.
000075
000076      01  FINAL-LINE
000077          TYPE CONTROL, FOOTING FINAL
000078          LINE PLUS 2.
000079          03  COLUMN 35        PIC X(19)    VALUE '*** TOTAL SALES ***'.
000080          03  COLUMN 65        PIC Z,ZZZ,ZZ9.99CR  SUM DEPT-TOTAL.
000081
000082      01  TYPE PAGE FOOTING
000083          LINE 57.
000084          03  COLUMN 45        PIC X(4)     VALUE 'PAGE'.
000085          03  COLUMN 50        PIC ZZ9      SOURCE PAGE-COUNTER.

000087      PROCEDURE DIVISION.
000088          OPEN INPUT SALES-FILE
000089              OUTPUT PRINT-FILE.
000090          INITIATE SALES-REPORT.
000091          READ SALES-FILE
000092              AT END MOVE 'END' TO END-FILE-FLAG.
000093          PERFORM B000-SALES UNTIL END-FILE.
000094          TERMINATE SALES-REPORT.
000095          CLOSE SALES-FILE, PRINT-FILE.
000096          STOP RUN.

000098      B000-SALES SECTION.
000099          GENERATE SALES-LINE.
000100          READ SALES-FILE
000101              AT END MOVE 'END' TO END-FILE-FLAG.
000102      B999-RETURN. EXIT.
```

FIGURE 20-4   (cont.) Report Output.

349

```
19/06/85                SALES REPORT

     DPT    PROC    DESCRIPTION           QTY       SALES($)

     025    2430    TURNTABLES             1         243.00
                    TURNTABLES             3         645.35
                    TURNTABLES             1         119.00
                                                   1,007.35   *

     025    2628    RECEIVERS              1         226.00
                    RECEIVERS              2         140.50
                    RECEIVERS              1         680.50
                                                   1,047.00   *

                                                   2,054.35   **

     040    0320    PROCESSORS             1       2,164.00
                                                   2,164.00   *

     040    0440    DISK STORAGE           4       1,847.50
                    DISK STORAGE           6       3,242.90
                                                   5,090.40   *

     040    1623    TERMINALS             15       6,627.35
                    TERMINALS              3       1,225.30
                                                   7,852.65   *

                                                  15,107.05   **

     125    0347    RECORDS               20          85.60
                                                      85.60   *

     125    0392    CASSETTE TAPE         12          49.12
                                                      49.12   *

     125    0395    8-TRACK TAPE           7          25.20
                                                      25.20   *

                                                     159.92   **

            ***  TOTAL SALES  ***                 17,321.32
```

FIGURE 20-4   (cont.) Report Output.

2.   If the control break is DEPT-IN, the program breaks control automatically on both product and department. It first prints PROD-LINE, but is not yet at the end of the group because DEPT-LINE is to print next. In PROD-LINE, the NEXT GROUP clause has no effect (because DEPT-LINE is part of the same CONTROL group). Consequently, the DEPT-LINE entry contains LINE PLUS 2 to force a double-space after PROD-LINE. For the same reason, FINAL-LINE also contains LINE PLUS 2.

The only difference between this example program and the program in Figure 20-3 is the REPORT SECTION. All other Data Division and Procedure Division statements are identical.

Note: For the current date, the program in Figure 20-4 must exit to the Supervisor which extracts the date and returns to the program. This step is required every time a page heading executes as SOURCE CURRENT-DATE. A more efficient method would be to extract the date only once during execution. To do this, the program would define a date field in Working-Storage and assign the date during initialization (before or after the OPEN statement). If the Working-Storage date field were called DATE-WS, then the PAGE HEADING entry would be SOURCE DATE-WS, and the initialization statement in the Procedure Division would be

MOVE CURRENT-DATE TO DATE-WS.

SUMMARY

The Report Writer feature facilitates coding programs that produce reports. The program examples in this chapter illustrated most of its features and coding requirements. For other specialized features, see your manufacturer's COBOL reference manual.

PROBLEMS

20–1. Cash payment records have the following definition:

```
01   PAYT-RECORD.
     03   FILLER             PIC  X(4).
     03   CUST-NO-IN         PIC  X(5).
     03   RECEIPT-NC-IN      PIC  X(5).
     03   DATE-IN            PIC  X(6).
     03   AMT-IN             PIC  S9(5)V99.
     03   FILLER             PIC  X(53).
```

Use the Report Writer feature to list all payment records and to print the total amount of all payments. Provide a simple one-line heading.

20–2. Revise the program in Problem 20-1 according to the following. The first field is now called REGION-NO-IN. The heading now contains two lines, as follows:

PAYMENT REPORT mm/dd/yy
REGION CUSTOMER DATE AMOUNT PAID RECEIPT NO.

The file is in sequence by region number (major) and customer number (minor). Total payments are required for customer, region, and final. Space a line after each total. Optionally use GROUP INDICATE for suppressing the printing of region number and customer number.

CHAPTER 21

SUBPROGRAMS

OBJECTIVE: To cover the linkage and execution of separately compiled main and subprograms.

INTRODUCTION

A common practice is to link together separately compiled programs: One program, the *calling program*, calls another program, the *subprogram*. Both programs compile independently, but both programs execute together to produce a required result.

Why link a program with one or more subprograms?

- Subprograms have been previously written and tested and are therefore easily compiled and cataloged.
- Subprograms can be used by any program in a system.
- Subprograms facilitate team projects by dividing a program into smaller programs.
- Subprograms can be written in another language and used by a program of another language. For example, it may be desirable to use an Assembler language routine to handle data communications. Therefore, a main COBOL program can use the Assembler subprogram for the specialized processing of data communications.

When designing subprogram logic, you have only two new areas to consider, both fortunately quite simple in COBOL:

1. The linkage between the calling program and the called subprogram.
2. The provision for handling data that both programs must use in common.

PROGRAM LINKAGE

The calling program requires only the CALL statement to link to the subprogram. Its general format is as follows:

CALL 'entry-name' [USING data-name-1, . . .]

CALL directs an exit from a main program to a called subprogram. The entry-name is usually the name of the subprogram (its PROGRAM-ID name), but may also be the name of some entry point within the Procedure Division of the subprogram.

The entry point of the called subprogram depends on whether the CALL specifies the PROGRAM-ID or some other entry. If the PROGRAM-ID is specified, the subprogram begins execution at the start of its Procedure Division. If some other entry is specified, a special ENTRY statement is required within the Procedure Division before the called procedure name to indicate the entry point.

The statement in the subprogram that returns to the calling program is as follows:

para-name.   EXIT PROGRAM.

The return point is the statement that immediately follows the invoking CALL statement. EXIT PROGRAM must be the only statement in its paragraph. A subprogram may CALL another subprogram, but it must not attempt to CALL the calling program. IBM supports another statement, GOBACK, which may be used in place of EXIT PROGRAM. GOBACK does not require a paragraph-name. It is recommended, however, to use the ANS standard of EXIT PROGRAM as much as possible to keep programs universal.

COMMON DATA

Typically, the calling program delivers some data names to the subprogram. The subprogram uses these data names and data of its own to produce information for the main program. For example, assume that a main program is to deliver product cost and quantity sold. The subprogram is to multiply the cost by the quantity and store the result in a value sold field. Figure 21-1 shows the skeleton coding. In the main program, the CALL USING statement delivers the names PROD-COST, QTY-SOLD, and VALUE-SOLD to the subprogram, CALCPROG. In the subprogram, a USING clause in the PROCEDURE DIVISION statement also specifies three names: PROD-COST, QTY-SOLD, and VALUE-CALC. The last name cited is intentionally different from the last name in the CALL statement for illustrative purposes. The following rules pertain to these defined names (also called *arguments* or *parameters*):

1. The two USING statements must contain the same number of names. The names need not be identical.

2. The first name in the called PROCEDURE must match the first name in the CALL USING statement; the second name must match the second, and so on.

Calling program:	PROD-COST,	QTY-SOLD,	VALUE-SOLD.
	↓	↓	↓
Subprogram:	PROD-COST,	QTY-SOLD,	VALUE-CALC.

3. The subprogram contains a Linkage Section (coded after Working-Storage, if any) where it defines all names that the USING specifies. Matched names must be defined identically. Thus, the first name of the USING statement for both the main program and the subprogram is defined as follows:

    PIC S9(3)V99 COMP-3.

    Although the arguments must be identically defined, they may have different names. The Linkage Section contains names only with level 77 or 01 (although the 01 group could contain, for example, 03, 05, etc.). You may find that using identical names results in a clearer program.

4. The main program must define the original names. The subprogram references these names, but they are defined in the Linkage Section because they do not actually exist in the subprogram. The subprogram uses the *addresses* of the names to locate and reference their contents. For example, when the subprogram in Figure 21-1 computes VALUE-SOLD, it stores the result in the Working-Storage Section of the *main* program. Accordingly, the subprogram does not have to return the computed value to the main program.

An efficient way to pass arguments between programs is to use one or more level 01 entries. For example, you could pass an entire level 01 data group of 10 or 12 arguments by specifying only one level 01 name—one address. The subprogram may actually reference only some of the arguments, but since they exist only in the main program, there is no additional space required in the subprogram.

ENTRY POINTS

When a main program needs to enter a subprogram at a point other than the beginning of the Procedure Division, the ENTRY statement is required, and although not an ANS standard, is available on some compilers. The format of the ENTRY statement for IBM DOS and OS is as follows:

    ENTRY name [USING data-name-1, . . .]

```
MAIN (CALLING) PROGRAM:

DATA DIVISION.
  ...
WORKING-STORAGE SECTION.
77   PROD-COST           PIC S9(3)V99   COMP-3.
77   QTY-SOLD            PIC S9(4)      COMP-3.
77   VALUE-SOLD          PIC S9(7)V99   COMP-3.

PROCEDURE DIVISION.
     .
     .
     .
     CALL 'CALCPROG' USING PROD-COST, QTY-SOLD, VALUE-SOLD.
     .               \
     .                \
     .                 \
                        \
                         \
                          |
                          |
CALLED SUBPROGRAM:        |
                          |
IDENTIFICATION /DIVISION.
PROGRAM-ID. CALCPROG.

ENVIRONMENT DIVISION.
  ...

DATA DIVISION.
  ...

WORKING-STORAGE SECTION.
  ...

LINKAGE SECTION.
77   PROD-COST           PIC S9(3)V99   COMP-3.
77   QTY-SOLD            PIC S9(4)      COMP-3.
77   VALUE-CALC          PIC S9(7)V99   COMP-3.

PROCEDURE DIVISION USING
             PROD-COST, QTY-SOLD, VALUE-CALC.
A000-MAIN SECTION.
     COMPUTE VALUE-CALC ROUNDED = PROD-COST * QTY-SOLD.
A999-RETURN. EXIT PROGRAM.
```

FIGURE 21-1   Linkage Between Main Program and Subprogram.

Figure 21-2 shows the skeleton code for a main program that calls a subprogram at two points within its Procedure Division. Note that each called routine has its own EXIT PROGRAM statement.

```
MAIN (CALLING) PROGRAM:

     CALL 'PENS-RTN' USING ...

     CALL 'TAX-RTN' USING ...


CALLED SUBPROGRAM:

PROCEDURE DIVISION.
   ...

     ENTRY 'PENS-RTN' USING ...
P000-PENSION.
   ...
P999-RTN. EXIT PROGRAM.


     ENTRY 'TAX-RTN' USING ...
S000-PENSION.
   ...
S999-RTN. EXIT PROGRAM.
```

FIGURE 21-2   Entry Points to Subprogram.

PROGRAM EXAMPLE

Figure 21-3 shows a program example consisting of a main program and one subprogram. The main program delivers the addresses of hours worked and job code to the subprogram. The subprogram performs a table lookup on job code, locates rate-of-pay in the table, and calculates wage (hours times rate). Note that the Working-Storage Section contains the table because it is unique to the subprogram and not common to the main program.

```
00001            IDENTIFICATION DIVISION.
00002            PROGRAM-ID. CHAP21.
00003            ENVIRONMENT DIVISION.
00004            INPUT-OUTPUT SECTION.
00005            FILE-CONTROL.
00006                SELECT TIME-FILE.    ASSIGN TO SYS015-UR-2501-S.
00007                SELECT REPORT-FILE. ASSIGN TO SYS014-UR-1403-S.

00009            DATA DIVISION.
00010            FILE SECTION.
00011            FD  TIME-FILE
00012                LABEL RECORDS ARE OMITTED.
00013            01  TIME-RECORD.
00014                05  CODE-IN          PIC XX.
00015                05  EMPNO-IN         PIC X(5).
00016                05  NAME-IN          PIC X(15).
00017                05  JOB-IN           PIC 99.
00018                05  HOURS-IN         PIC S99V9.
00019                05  FILLER           PIC X(53).
00020            FD  REPORT-FILE
00021                LABEL RECORDS ARE OMITTED.
00022            01  PRINT-RECORD.
00023                05  FILLER           PIC X(14).
00024                05  EMPNO-PR         PIC X(08).
00025                05  NAME-PR          PIC X(17).
00026                05  JOB-PR           PIC X(02).
00027                05  RATE-PR          PIC ZZZ9.99.
00028                05  FILLER           PIC X(03).
00029                05  HOURS-PR         PIC Z9.9-.
00030                05  FILLER           PIC X(04).
00031                05  WAGE-PR          PIC ZZ,ZZ9.99CR.
00032                05  FILLER           PIC X(62).

00034            WORKING-STORAGE SECTION.
00035            77  EOF-FLAG             PIC X(3)     VALUE ' '.
00036                88  END-FILE                     VALUE 'EOF'.
00037            01  COMMON-DATA.
00038                03  JOBNO           PIC 99.
00039                03  HOURS           PIC S99V9    COMP-3.
00040                03  RATE            PIC S999V99  COMP-3.
00041                03  WAGE            PIC S9(5)V99 COMP-3.

00043            PROCEDURE DIVISION.
00044                OPEN INPUT TIME-FILE, OUTPUT REPORT-FILE.
00045                READ TIME-FILE, AT END MOVE 'EOF' TO EOF-FLAG.
00046                PERFORM B000-PROC UNTIL END-FILE.
00047                CLOSE TIME-FILE, REPORT-FILE.
00048                STOP RUN.

00050            B000-PROC SECTION.
00051                MOVE SPACES TO PRINT-RECORD.
00052                MOVE HOURS-IN TO HOURS.
00053                MOVE JOB-IN TO JOBNO, JOB-PR.
00054                CALL 'SUBR21' USING COMMON-DATA.
00055                MOVE WAGE TO WAGE-PR.
00056                MOVE HOURS TO HOURS-PR.
00057                MOVE RATE TO RATE-PR.
00058                MOVE NAME-IN TO NAME-PR.
00059                MOVE EMPNO-IN TO EMPNO-PR.
00060                WRITE PRINT-RECORD AFTER ADVANCING 1 LINES.
00061                READ TIME-FILE, AT END MOVE 'EOF' TO EOF-FLAG.
00062            B999-RETURN. EXIT.
```

FIGURE 21-3 Main Program and Subprogram.

357

```
00001          IDENTIFICATION DIVISION.
00002          PROGRAM-ID. SUBR21.
00003          ENVIRONMENT DIVISION.
00004          DATA DIVISION.
00005          WORKING-STORAGE SECTION.
00006          77  SEARCH-FLAG          PIC X(3)      VALUE ' '.
00007              88  END-SEARCH                     VALUE 'END'.
00008          01  JOB-TABLE.
00009              05  FILLER           PIC X(6)      VALUE '010725'.
00010              05  FILLER           PIC X(6)      VALUE '020615'.
00011              05  FILLER           PIC X(6)      VALUE '040745'.
00012              05  FILLER           PIC X(6)      VALUE '050855'.
00013              05  FILLER           PIC X(6)      VALUE '060750'.
00014              05  FILLER           PIC X(6)      VALUE '080925'.
00015              05  FILLER           PIC X(6)      VALUE '100895'.
00016              05  FILLER           PIC X(6)      VALUE '990000'.
00017          01  JOB-TABLE-DEF        REDEFINES JOB-TABLE.
00018              03  TABLE-ENTRIES    OCCURS 8 TIMES INDEXED BY NDX.
00019                  05  JOBNO-TAB    PIC 99.
00020                  05  RATE-TAB     PIC 99V99.

00022          LINKAGE SECTION.
00023          01  COMMON-DATA.
00024              03  JOBNO            PIC 99.
00025              03  HOURS            PIC S99V9    COMP-3.
00026              03  RATE             PIC S999V99  COMP-3.
00027              03  WAGE             PIC S9(5)V99 COMP-3.
00028
00029          PROCEDURE DIVISION USING COMMON-DATA.
00030          A000-MAIN SECTION.
00031              MOVE SPACES TO SEARCH-FLAG.
00032              PERFORM C000-SEARCH VARYING NDX FROM 1 BY 1
00033                      UNTIL END-SEARCH.
00034          A999-RTN. EXIT PROGRAM.
00035
00036          ***  T A B L E   S E A R C H   &   C A L C   W A G E
00037          C000-SEARCH SECTION.
00038              IF JOBNO  = JOBNO-TAB (NDX)
00039                  MOVE 'END' TO SEARCH-FLAG
00040                  MOVE RATE-TAB (NDX) TO RATE
00041                  COMPUTE WAGE ROUNDED = HOURS * RATE
00042              ELSE IF JOBNO  < JOBNO-TAB (NDX)
00043                  MOVE 'END' TO SEARCH-FLAG
00044                  MOVE ZEROS TO HOURS, RATE, WAGE.
00045          C999-RETURN. EXIT.
```

FIGURE 21-3   (cont.)

LINKAGE EDITOR

To execute a program, it must first be compiled and then *link-edited* by the Linkage Editor program. The compile step involves translating the COBOL source program into machine language object code. At that point, the program may not yet be executed. The link-edit step performs two main functions:

1. The Linkage Editor program includes all necessary input/output modules. These are precompiled routines required for input/output and cataloged in the system library.
2. The Linkage Editor program links together separately compiled programs (as in Figure 21-3) and accounts for the addresses of all data that the programs reference in common. For a COBOL program, the Linkage Editor is concerned with the CALL USING in the calling program, and the Linkage Section and the USING in the called program.

The Linkage Editor stores the compiled, link-edited object program in the system library where it may be executed once and then erased by the next link-edited program, or it may be cataloged permanently in the library for regular execution.

Figure 21-4 shows the *map* that the Linkage Editor produced for Figure 21-3.

The program actually consists of a number of CSECT entries (Control Sections) that the Editor has linked together. Note, for example, that the first CSECT is called CHAP21 and is the name of the calling program. Following this are some CSECT modules for input/output that the Editor included. The CSECT called SUBR21 is the name of the subprogram. The map shows the addresses where each CSECT loads, a feature that can be useful for tracing bugs through storage dumps.

The Chapter on Job Control covers the job control requirements for compiling, link-editing, and executing subprograms.

PHASE	XFR-AD	LOCORE	HICORE	DSK-AD	ESD TYPE	LABEL	LOADED	REL-FR
PHASE***	080078	080078	0811F3	03D 00 03	CSECT	CHAP21	080078	080078
					CSECT	IJCFZII3	080E28	080E28
					CSECT	IJDFAPIZ	080F80	080F80
					* ENTRY	IJDFAZIZ	080F80	
					CSECT	ILBDMNS0	081CA8	081CA8
					CSECT	ILBDTC20	081100	081100
					CSECT	SUBR21	080808	080808
UNRESOLVED EXTERNAL REFERENCES					WXTRN	ILBDTC00		
					WXTRN	ILBDTCC1		
					WXTRN	ILBDDBGC		not errors
					WXTRN	ILBDDBG7		
					WXTRN	ILBDDBG8		
					WXTRN	ILBDTC3C		

FIGURE 21-4   Link-edit Map.

Special Features

Defining Files.   You may code READ and WRITE only in the program or subprogram that defines its FD. To WRITE in more than one subprogram, you could pass a print record as a parameter to a common print subprogram.

Use of SORT.   An IBM DOS SORT statement is coded in the *last* subprogram. An ENTRY job statement is required to notify the Linkage Editor where execution is to begin.

Lower Level Subprogram.   A subprogram may CALL a lower level subprogram, and may pass parameters from its Working-Storage and Linkage Sections.

Assembler Linkage.   COBOL can CALL an IBM Assembler subprogram. For a statement such as CALL 'ASSRPROG' USING COST, SALES the COBOL program automatically establishes an address constant for each parameter, DC A(COST) and DC A(SALES), and loads the address of the *first* constant, A(COST), in register 1. The Assembler subprogram should contain standard linkage (SAVE, etc.) and can load base addresses for COST and SALES with an instruction such as LM 6,7,0(0,1) that loads register 6 with the address of COST and 7 with the address of SALES. The subprogram can reference COST and SALES by DSECTs or explicit base/displacement addressing. Return from the subprogram is by means of the standard RETURN macro.

PROBLEMS

21–1. For what reasons would it be desirable to link a program with subprograms?

21–2. Refer to Figure 21-1. Comment on the effect of the changes to the coding in the following unrelated questions:

    (a) The CALL statement references 'CALCSUB' instead of 'CALCPROG'.

    (b) The subprogram's Linkage Section defines PROD-COST without a COMP-3 clause.

    (c) The subprogram's Linkage Section and USING clause specify the name QTY-ISSUED instead of QTY-SOLD.

    (d) The subprogram's USING clause reverses the sequence of PROD-COST and QTY-SOLD.

    (e) The subprogram's Linkage Section reverses the sequence of PROD-COST and QTY-SOLD.

    (f) The subprogram defines PROD-COST in Working-Storage rather than in the Linkage Section.

    (g) The subprogram contains STOP RUN instead of EXIT PROGRAM.

    (h) The subprogram contains GOBACK instead of EXIT PROGRAM.

21–3. Recode a recent program, splitting it into a main program and one (or more) subprograms. Check that on execution it produces the same results as the original program.

CHAPTER 22

DEBUGGING

OBJECTIVE: *To present debugging techniques.*

INTRODUCTION

Earlier chapters provided simple debugging methods for common program errors. Some errors however, are more difficult to diagnose, and for these, COBOL compilers furnish advanced debugging techniques that include traces of program execution, disclosure of invalid statements, and dumps of main storage. Although this chapter concentrates on IBM DOS and OS debugging, other COBOL versions use similar techniques.

IBM 360/370 DEBUGGING AIDS

The statements EXHIBIT and TRACE are the two chief IBM debugging aids. EXHIBIT displays the contents of variables during program execution, and TRACE shows the steps that the program has executed.

EXHIBIT

The EXHIBIT statement uses the standard SYSOUT file, which it automatically opens and closes. EXHIBIT may be placed anywhere in the Procedure Division where you want to see the contents of a specified item. A typical use of EXHIBIT is when a program calculates incorrectly, and you need to analyze the contents of various fields before and after the calculation. The three formats of EXHIBIT are as follows:

1.   EXHIBIT NAMED item-1, item-2, . . ., item-n.
2.   EXHIBIT CHANGED NAME item-1, item-2, . . ., item-n.
3.   EXHIBIT CHANGED item-1, item-2, . . ., item-n.

The items printed may be literals or defined identifiers, but not indexes. Format 1 is for the simple printing of named items. An example is as follows:

EXHIBIT NAMED 'TAX ROUTINE', NET-PAY, RATE.

On execution of this statement, the program prints

TAX ROUTINE NET-PAY = xxxxx.xx RATE = xx.xx

Format 2 is for printing the contents of items only if they have changed since the last time the EXHIBIT executed. This statement always executes the first time that it is encountered. The advantage of this format is that it reduces the printout if there are many repetitions of the EXHIBIT statement. Format 3 also prints only changed items, but does not print the name of the identifier. An obvious use for this format is when the EXHIBIT prints only one specified item.

TRACE

The TRACE statement is useful when a program produces unexpected results and you are unable to determine the flow of program execution. There are two TRACE statements:

1.   READY TRACE
2.   RESET TRACE

The READY TRACE statement activates the TRACE from the point where it is executed. It prints all Procedure names (Paragraph and Section names) that are executed. (Some COBOL versions print the line number instead of the name.) The TRACE continues until the program encounters either a RESET TRACE statement or a termination of program execution. A program may contain many READY TRACE and RESET TRACE statements.

TRACE and EXHIBIT used together should locate most serious bugs.

ON

Another IBM debugging aid is the ON statement, which is useful if a file contains many records. Its format is as follows:

ON integer-1 [AND EVERY integer-2] [UNTIL integer-3] statement . . .

For example, the following will EXHIBIT fields starting with the one hundredth record and every tenth record thereafter:

ON 100 AND EVERY 10 EXHIBIT NAMED NET-PAY, TAX-RATE.

Another IBM debugging aid, the DEBUG card, is explained in the *IBM DOS and OS COBOL Programmer's Guide*. If after using TRACE, EXHIBIT, and ON, you are still unable to locate the cause of an error, try a dump of main storage, which is explained in a later section of this chapter.

CDC DEBUGGING AIDS

CDC COBOL debugging aids are useful for debugging during the program testing stage, but should be removed once the program becomes operational.

For tracing, the CDC COBOL control card allows for a parameter list of options, as follows:

COBOL(parameter-list) or COBOL,parameter-list.

The parameter entry DB1 directs the compiler to generate code for the trace. You must also provide ENTER statements in the Procedure Division to turn on or to turn off the trace:

ENTER 'D.ONTR'   Starts the trace from this point and prints an output line naming each paragraph entered.

ENTER 'D.OFFTR'   Turns off the trace.

ENTER 'D.CLOTR'   Closes the trace output file when it is no longer required.

The system writes trace messages onto a file called COBTRFL that you can copy to OUTPUT or to another file for printing with COPYSBF.

ANS DEBUGGING STANDARD

The ANS debugging standard is the USE FOR DEBUGGING statement, and to make it effective, you code a DEBUGGING MODE entry in the SOURCE-COMPUTER paragraph:

```
CONFIGURATION SECTION.
SOURCE-COMPUTER. computer-name DEBUGGING MODE.
```

This clause causes the compilation of all USE FOR DEBUGGING statements and all statements with D in column 7 of the COBOL source program. The first entry in the Procedure Division is DECLARATIVES, which specifies one or more USE FOR DEBUGGING sections as follows:

```
PROCEDURE DIVISION.
DECLARATIVES.
section-name SECTION.      ⎫
   USE FOR DEBUGGING ON    ⎬   USE FOR DEBUGGING Section
   statements.             ⎭
END DECLARATIVES.
```

You may code a D in column 7 of any statement in the Procedure Division that the Debugging Section is to monitor. The USE FOR DEBUGGING statement options include the following:

$$
\text{USE FOR DEBUGGING ON} \begin{cases} \text{ALL identifier} \\ \text{ALL PROCEDURES} \\ \text{procedure-name} \\ \text{file-name} \end{cases}
$$

The Debugging Section is invoked based on the following:

- ALL identifier. For every reference of identifier during program execution.
- ALL PROCEDURES. For every execution of Procedures (Paragraphs and Sections) in the program.
- procedure-name. For every reference of the specified procedure-name.
- file-name. After every OPEN, CLOSE, READ (except if AT END or INVALID KEY conditions), or DELETE that references file-name.

When a program executes a Debugging Section, it fills information into a special register (actually a record) called DEBUG-ITEM to explain the reason for invoking the Debugging Section.

STATEMENT OPTION

Some processing errors cause a program to terminate execution. A typical example is an attempt to perform arithmetic on a field that does not contain valid arithmetic data. The program terminates with an error message (usually obscure), and you may have trouble determining which statement actually caused the error. A COBOL feature that can be inserted prior to recompiling the program will supply the error statement number, depending on compiler version:

1. DOS Statement. For IBM DOS, the CBL card forces an error statement number to print. This statement begins in column 2 and is inserted directly after the EXEC statement as follows:

```
// EXEC FCOBOL
CBL STATE
```

2. OS Statement. For IBM OS, the PARM (parameter) entry on the EXEC statement forces an error statement number to print as Follows:

```
//STEP1 EXEC COBUCLG,PARM=(STATE)
```

For OS, you must also supply a DD job control statement after the source program to force the debugging statement to print:

```
//GO.SYSDBOUT DD SYSOUT=A
```

This option generates considerable additional machine code and should be deleted once the program is working properly. Figure 22-1 shows a program that has terminated because of an execution error. The printed message indicates that statement number 88 caused the error:

```
ADD PAYT-IN TO CUST-TOTAL.
```

Both DOS and OS indicate the cause of a program termination by an error message:

```
DOS:  INTERRUPT CODE 7
OS:  COMPLETION CODE SYSTEM = 0C7
```

In both cases, the 7 indicates a *data exception* that the system generates when a program attempts arithmetic on an invalid field (Appendix C contains a complete list of error codes with explanations).

In the COBOL statement in Figure 22-1 that caused the termination, either PAYT-IN or CUST-TOTAL could be invalid. PAYT-IN is an input field; it could be blank, which is an error on the 360/370 and is easy to check and correct. Also, CUST-TOTAL is an accumulator, but it does not contain a VALUE clause to initialize it to zero. This common error causes "garbage" to remain in a field after compilation. In this case, defining CUST-TOTAL with VALUE ZEROS will cause the program to execute correctly.

STORAGE DUMPS

During program execution, a serious error can occur, and you may need to see the actual contents of storage locations, especially Working-Storage accumulators. To do this, you force a storage dump to print (for IBM systems) with the following job control entries:

```
DOS:    // OPTION DUMP (or // OPTION PARTDUMP if partitioned)
OS:     //GO.SYSUDUMP DD SYSOUT=A (included after the source program)
```

You may have trouble locating Working-Storage in a dump. Consequently, you should insert a literal at the beginning of Working-Storage that is easy to find on the printout, such as the following:

```
WORKING-STORAGE SECTION.
77 FILLER    PIC X(28)   VALUE 'BEGINNING OF WORKING-STORAGE'.
```

You could also place descriptive literals in different parts of Working-Storage to indicate alphanumeric items, arithmetic items, and tables. But remember that all level-77 items must precede all other items. Also, the following generates a compiler error:

```
01 ARITHMETIC-ITEMS   COMP-3.
   03 FILLER    PIC X(28)   VALUE 'BEGINNING OF ARITHMETIC DATA'.
```

Why? PIC X cannot be defined as COMP-3 (or COMP).

Hexadecimal Representation

The IBM 360/370 uses an 8-bit code to represent data in one storage location (byte) that allows up to 256 different characters in one byte, or two digits of decimal data in one byte. Figure 22-2 shows related decimal, binary, and hexadecimal values from 0 through 15. Hexadecimal, or base 16, has 16 digits numbered 0 through F. As can be seen in the figure, one hex digit represents four bits, and as a result, two hex digits can represent the contents of any byte.

```
   CBL STATE
   00001              IDENTIFICATION DIVISION.
   00002              PROGRAM-ID. CHAP 22.
   00003              REMARKS.   ONE-LEVEL CONTROL BREAK ON CUSTOMER NUMBER.

   00005              ENVIRONMENT DIVISION.
   00006              CONFIGURATION SECTION.
   00007              SPECIAL-NAMES.
   00008                  C01 IS TOP-PAGE.
   00009              INPUT-OUTPUT SECTION.
   00010              FILE-CONTROL.
   00011                  SELECT  PAYT-FILE, ASSIGN TO SYS015-UR-2501-S.
   00012                  SELECT  PRINT-FILE, ASSIGN TO SYS014-UR-1403-S.

   00014              DATA DIVISION.
   00015              FILE SECTION.
   00016              FD   PAYT-FILE
   00017                  LABEL RECORDS ARE OMITTED
   00018                  DATA RECORD IS   PAYT-RECORD.
   00019              01   PAYT-RECORD.
   00020                  03   FILLER          PIC X(5).
   00021                  03   CUST-IN         PIC X(5).
   00022                  03   NAME-IN         PIC X(20).
   00023                  03   PAYT-IN         PIC S9(4)V99.
   00024                  03   DATE-IN         PIC 9(6).
   00025                  03   FILLER          PIC X(38).

   00027              FD   PRINT-FILE
   00028                  LABEL RECORDS ARE OMITTED
   00029                  DATA RECORD IS PRINT-RECORD.
   00030              01   PRINT-RECORD        PIC X(133).

   00032              WORKING-STORAGE SECTION.
   00033              77   FILLER              PIC X(15)   VALUE 'WORKING-STORAGE'.
   00034              01   ALPHANUMERIC-ITEMS  DISPLAY.
   00035                  03   END-FILE-FLAG   PIC X(3)    VALUE ' '.
   00036                       88   END-FILE               VALUE 'END'.
   00037                  03   PREV-CUST       PIC X(5)    VALUE LOW-VALUES.

   00039              01   ARITHMETIC-ITEMS    COMP-3.
   00040                  03   CUST-TOTAL      PIC S9(5)V99.
   00041                  03   FINAL-TOTAL     PIC S9(7)V99  VALUE +0.
   00042                  03   LINE-COUNT      PIC S999      VALUE +0.
   00043                       88   END-PAGE                 VALUE +25 THRU +999.
   00044                  03   PAGE-COUNT      PIC S999      VALUE +1.
   00045                  03   SPACE-CTL       PIC S9        VALUE +2.

   00047              01   HEADING-LINE.
   00048                  03   FILLER          PIC X(20)     VALUE ' '.
   00049                  03   FILLER          PIC X(07)     VALUE 'CUSTR'.
   00050                  03   FILLER          PIC X(23)     VALUE 'NAME'.
   00051                  03   FILLER          PIC X(13)     VALUE 'PAYMENT'.
   00052                  03   FILLER          PIC X(14)     VALUE 'DATE    PAGE',
   00053                  03   PAGE-HD-PR      PIC ZZ9.

   00055              01   CUST-PAYT-LINE.
   00056                  03   FILLER          PIC X(20)     VALUE ' '.
   00057                  03   CUST-PR         PIC X(7).
   00058                  03   NAME-PR         PIC X(21).
   00059                  03   PAYT-PR         PIC ZZ,ZZ9.99CR.
   00060                  03   FILLER          PIC X(2)      VALUE ' '.
   00061                  03   DATE-PR         PIC 99B99B99.

   00063              01   TOTAL-PAYT-LINE.
   00064                  03   FILLER          PIC X(46)     VALUE ' '.
   00065                  03   CUST-TOT-PR     PIC ZZZZ,ZZ9.99CR.
   00066                  03   ASTERISK-PR     PIC X(2)      VALUE '*'.
```

FIGURE 22-1   Program Execution Error.

```
00069              PROCEDURE DIVISION.
00070          *** M A I N   L O G I C
00071              A000-MAIN SECTION.
00072                  OPEN INPUT PAYT-FILE, OUTPUT PRINT-FILE.
00073                  PERFORM H000-HEAD.
00074                  READ PAYT-FILE, AT END MOVE 'END' TO END-FILE-FLAG.
00075                  MOVE CUST-IN TO PREV-CUST.
00076                  PERFORM B000-PROC-CUST UNTIL END-FILE.
00077                  PERFORM F000-FINAL.
00078                  CLOSE PAYT-FILE, PRINT-FILE.
00079                  STOP RUN.
00080              A199-END. EXIT.

00083          *** C U S T O M E R   P R O C E S S I N G
00084              B000-PROC-CUST SECTION.
00085                  IF CUST-IN > PREV-CUST PERFORM C000-HIGH-CUST.
00086                  IF END-PAGE PERFORM H000-HEAD.
00087                  MOVE PAYT-IN TO PAYT-PR.
00088                  ADD PAYT-IN TO CUST-TOTAL.
00089                  MOVE CUST-IN TO PREV-CUST.
00090                  MOVE DATE-IN TO DATE-PR.
00091                  MOVE CUST-IN TO CUST-PR.
00092                  MOVE NAME-IN TO NAME-PR.
00093                  WRITE PRINT-RECORD FROM CUST-PAYT-LINE AFTER ADVANCING
00094                      SPACE-CTL LINES.
00095                  MOVE SPACES TO CUST-PAYT-LINE.
00096                  ADD SPACE-CTL TO LINE-COUNT.
00097                  MOVE 1 TO SPACE-CTL.
00098                  READ PAYT-FILE, AT END MOVE 'END' TO END-FILE-FLAG.
00099              B999-RETURN. EXIT.

00101          *** C U S T O M E R   T O T A L S
00102              C000-HIGH-CUST SECTION.
00103                  MOVE CUST-TOTAL TO CUST-TOT-PR.
00104                  MOVE TOTAL-PAYT-LINE TO PRINT-RECORD.
00105                  WRITE PRINT-RECORD AFTER ADVANCING 1 LINES.
00106                  ADD CUST-TOTAL TO FINAL-TOTAL.
00107                  MOVE ZEROS TO CUST-TOTAL.
00108                  ADD 2 TO LINE-COUNT.
00109                  MOVE 2 TO SPACE-CTL.
00110              C999-RETURN. EXIT.

00112          *** F I N A L   T O T A L S
00113              F000-FINAL SECTION.
00114                  PERFORM C000-HIGH-CUST.
00115                  MOVE FINAL-TOTAL TO CUST-TOT-PR.
00116                  MOVE '**' TO ASTERISK-PR.
00117                  WRITE PRINT-RECORD FROM TOTAL-PAYT-LINE
00118                      AFTER ADVANCING 2 LINES.
00119              F999-RETURN. EXIT.

00121          *** P A G E   H E A D I N G
00122              H000-HEAD SECTION.
00123                  MOVE PAGE-COUNT TO PAGE-HD-PR.
00124                  WRITE PRINT-RECORD FROM HEADING-LINE
00125                      AFTER ADVANCING TOP-PAGE.
00126                  MOVE 3 TO LINE-COUNT.
00127                  MOVE 2 TO SPACE-CTL.
00128                  ADD 1 TO PAGE-COUNT.
00129              H999-RETURN. EXIT.
```

FIGURE 22-1   (cont.)

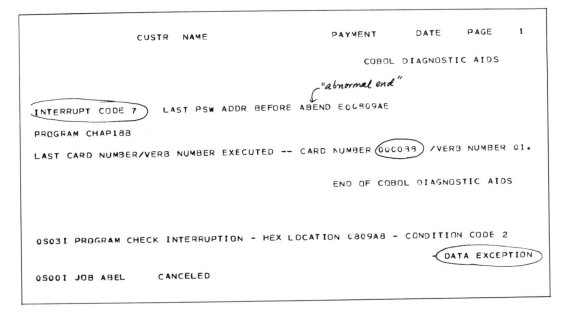

CUSTR   NAME   PAYMENT   DATE   PAGE   1

COBOL DIAGNOSTIC AIDS

"abnormal end"

INTERRUPT CODE 7   LAST PSW ADDR BEFORE ABEND E0C809AE

PROGRAM CHAP18B

LAST CARD NUMBER/VERB NUMBER EXECUTED -- CARD NUMBER 00C039 /VERB NUMBER 01.

END OF COBOL DIAGNOSTIC AIDS

0S03I PROGRAM CHECK INTERRUPTION - HEX LOCATION C809A8 - CONDITION CODE 2
DATA EXCEPTION

0S00I JOB ABEL   CANCELED

FIGURE 22-1   (cont.)

DECIMAL	BINARY	HEXADECIMAL	DECIMAL	BINARY	HEXADECIMAL
0	0000	0	8	1000	8
1	0001	1	9	1001	9
2	0010	2	10	1010	A
3	0011	3	11	1011	B
4	0100	4	12	1100	C
5	0101	5	13	1101	D
6	0110	6	14	1110	E
7	0111	7	15	1111	F

FIGURE 22-2   Decimal, Binary, and Hexadecimal Representation.

On the IBM 360/370, the standard plus sign is a hexadecimal 'C' and sometimes 'F', with the minus sign as 'D' (these can also be expressed for convenience as X'C', X'F', and X'D'. A Working-Storage item defined as

77 AMOUNT PIC S9(5)V99 COMP-3 VALUE 1.25.

appears in main storage as four bytes (packed):

/00/00/12/5C/

The IBM 360/370 represents character data as one character per byte, as follows:

CHARACTER	HEX REPRESENTATION
A–I	C1–C9
J–R	D1–D9
S–Z	E2–E9
0–9	F0–F9

A blank (or space) character appears in storage as X'40'. Assume an alphanumeric item defined in Working-Storage as follows:

77 MONTH   PIC X(7)   VALUE 'JUNE 17'.

It would appear in a dump of main storage as seven bytes:

/D1/E4/D5/C5/40/F1/F7/

Binary data defined as COMP SYNC is fixed in length, depending on the definition as follows:

DEFINITION	BYTES	NAME
PIC S9(1) - S9(4)	2	halfword
PIC S9(5) - S9(9)	4	fullword
PIC S9(10) - S9(18)	8	2 fullwords

A binary field is a string of data bits, with the leftmost bit the sign (0 = plus and 1 = minus). A binary item defined in Working-Storage as

77 SUBSCR   PIC S9(4)   COMP SYNC   VALUE 5.

would appear in a storage dump as two bytes:

/00/05/   (actually bits 00000000 00000101)

Input Records.   Assume an input record defined as the following:

```
                                                    BYTES:
01  CUST-RECORD.
    05  ACCOUNT-IN        PIC X(3).                   3
    05  NAME-IN           PIC X(10).                 10
    05  BALANCE-IN        PIC S9(5)V99.               7
    05  FILLER            PIC X(60).                 60
                                                     ──
                                                     80
```

The character contents of this input record could appear in main storage as follows:

characters: | 2 | 4 | 5 | A | | S | M | I | T | H | | | | 0 | 0 | 1 | 3 | 5 | 2 | 5 | // | |
hex: | F2 | F4 | F5 | C1 | 40 | E2 | D4 | C9 | E3 | C8 | 40 | 40 | 40 | F0 | F0 | F1 | F3 | F5 | F2 | F5 | 40 . . . | . . .40 |

Note that both numbers and letters are represented as characters, with two hex digits per byte. The program could move the contents of BALANCE-IN to a COMP-3 field in Working-Storage as follows:

```
77  BALANCE-AMT          PIC S9(5)V99  COMP-3.
    .
    .
    .
    MOVE BALANCE-IN TO BALANCE-AMT.
```

Therefore, the contents of BALANCE-IN would be packed into BALANCE-AMT as follows:

/00/13/52/5F/

The plus sign is an F at this point, although any arithmetic operation on BALANCE-AMT will change the sign to the standard plus sign C (if still positive).

Alignment.   The compiler aligns binary values to begin on halfword or fullword boundaries, depending on their length. A *halfword boundary* is at a storage location evenly divisible by 2, and a *fullword boundary* is at a storage location evenly divisible by 4. The compiler also aligns level 01 entries to begin on a *doubleword boundary*—a location evenly divisible by 8. The purpose of alignment is to make computer execution more efficient, but it can cause unused bytes between some storage areas called *slack bytes* whose content is unpredictable; however, because a program never references these bytes, any "garbage" that they may contain does not affect the program.

Dump Example

The program in Figure 22-1 was coded to generate a storage dump. Figure 22-3 illustrates only the first page of this dump and contains the relevant section of Working-Storage. Under OS the contents of *register saveareas* (not shown in Figure 22-3) would precede the dump along with the contents of the registers at the time of the dump. These registers are computer hardware features that the IBM 360/370 uses for addressing and binary arithmetic. They are not the same as COBOL registers such as the TALLY register, which is an unfortunate term. The contents of the floating-point and general purpose registers are usually not of interest to the COBOL programmer.

A dump of main storage is organized into three areas:

1.   Left—the hexadecimal address of the first (leftmost) byte that is printed on a line.
2.   Middle—eight groups of eight hex digits (4 bytes). Blank columns separate each group to facilitate readability. Each line depicts 64 hex digits, or 32 characters.
3.   Right—an alphanumeric representation of storage contents, one character per byte. The system prints all characters, but because some byte contents are nonprintable, the dump shows these as a period (.). This area is useful in helping to locate recognizable parts of a program.

You can locate Working-Storage in Figure 22-3 by scanning the alphanumeric right side for the value WORKING-STORAGE that the program has defined at the start of Working-Storage. It is on the twelfth line of the dump and overlaps onto the line following at 80180. The next program entry is a level 01, which the compiler begins at an address evenly divisible by eight, 80188. There is one unused slack byte at 80187. Since the leftmost byte on this line is 80180, you can count each pair of hex digits as one byte, and each group of eight hex digits as four bytes. Accordingly, the address of the leftmost byte of each group on the line is as follows:

80180, 80184, 80188, 8018C, 80190, 80194, 80198, 8019C

Starting at 80188 are two DISPLAY items defined in the program: END-FILE-FLAG (three bytes of blanks, or X'40's), and PREV-CUST (five bytes containing X'F0F0F1F2F3', or character value 00123). The next group of data items is also defined as level 01, which the compiler begins at an address evenly divisible by eight, 80190. This address references the first arithmetic data item, CUST-TOTAL, which is a seven-digit (four-byte) field containing X'00000000', and since it contains no rightmost sign, it is an invalid arithmetic field. (CUST-TOTAL has no VALUE

```
080000  D7C8C1E2 C55C5C5C 071D2000 0008C9AE   00080BB6 00080078 00080078 00080720   PHASE***........  ................
080020  000804C0 8008087A 0008098A 000808A4   0008092A 00080954 00016258 000802C0   ................  ................
080040  50080BEC 00080178 00080350 00080438   00008E0B CEED0760 40200000 00000000   &..........&....  .......- .......
080060  42400000 00000000 4222581B 4E81B4E8   41200000 00000000 05F00700 900EF00A   . ..........+..Y  .........C.....0.
080080  47F0F082 00080078 00080C78 0008FFFF   00016258 000163BE 80000015 80000015   .00.............  ................
0800A0  0008FFFF 800814E8 0A16180C C0000000   182F07F1 C0080078 D7C8C1E2 C55C5C5C   .......Y........  ...1....PHASE***
0800C0  00000000 00000000 00000000 00000000   C0000000 CC000000 00080178 00080350   ................  ...............&
0800E0  000803A8 00080BB6 C0080078 00080078   00080720 000804C0 00000000 58C0F0C6   ................  ..............0F
080100  58E0C000 58D0F0CA 9500E000 4770F0A2   9610D048 92FFE000 47F0F0AC 98CEF03A   ......0.......C.  ..........00....0.
080120  90ECD00C 185D989F F0BA9110 D0480719   07FF0700 00080BB6 00080078 00080078   ........C.......  ................
080140  00080720 000804C0 000807F2 00080B9C   C3D6C2C6 F2F4F0F0 C3C8C1D7 F1F8C240   ...........2....  COBF2400CHAP18B
080160  00000000 F0F961F0 F361F7F9 F2F14BF0   F54BF4F7 302005EF E6D6D9D2 C9D5C760   ....09/03/7921.0  5.47....WORKING-
080180  E2E3D6D9 C1C7C540 404040F0 F0F1F2F3   00000000 00000000 0C003C00 2C2C0C00   STORAGE     00123  ................
0801A0  40404040 40404040 40404040 40404040   40404040 C3E4E2E3 D9404040 C1D4C540                   CUSTR    NAME
0801C0  40404040 40404040 40404040 40404040   4040D7C1 E8D4C5D5 E3404040 404040C4                 PAYMENT        D
0801E0  C1E3C540 404040D7 C1C7C540 404040F1   40404040 40404040 40404040 40404040   ATE      PAGE        1
080200  40404040 --SAME--
080220  404040F1 F0F04BF0 F0404040 40404040   40404040 40404040 40404040 40404040      100.00
080240  40404040 --SAME--
080260  40404040 40400000 00008000 0000010F   0008025C 40000000 00080D90 00000000         ..........  ...* ..........
080280  00008000 0C00010F 000802A0 000802A8   00080D50 C2C40202 C2080350 00080888   ................  ....&.D......&....
0802A0  020802F8 20000050 4120E000 47000000   000002D0 00000000 00080EE8 00000000   ...8...&........  ..............Y....
0802C0  00008000 0C00010E 000802E8 000802FC   00080EA8 08B48BF1 01080439 00000000   ............Y...0  .........1........
0802E0  07004120 E000000C 010803A9 20000084   00080308 0000000C 40404040 40F0F0F1   ................  ........       001
080300  F2F3C1C4 C1D440E2 D4C9E3C8 40404040   40404040 4040F0F0 F1F2F3F5 F0F5F1F4   23ADAM SMITH            0012350514
080320  F8F04040 40404040 40404040 40404040   40404040 40404040 40404040 40404040   80
080340  40404040 40404040 07004120 E0000000   40404040 40F0F0F1 F2F3C1C4 C1D440E2          ........            00123ADAM S
080360  D4C9E3C8 40404040 40404040 4040F0F1   F0F0F0F0 F0F5F1F2 F8F04040 40404040   MITH            01  0000051280
080380  40404040 --SAME--
0803A0  000803C0 00000000 F1404040 40404040   40404040 40404040 40404040 C3E4E2E3   ........1                    CUST
0803C0  D94040D5 C1D4C540 40404040 40404040   40404040 40404040 4040D7C1 E8D4C5D5   R   NAME                   PAYMEN
0803E0  E3404040 404040C4 C1E3C540 404040D7   C1C7C540 404040F1 40404040 40404040   T       DATE      P  AGE      1
080400  40404040 --SAME--
080420  40404040 40404040 40404040 40F03088   182F5810 20184180 329858F0 101045E0                0..  ...........0....
```

080190; 80178; END-FILE-FLAG; PREV-CUST; CUST-TOTAL; FINAL-TOTAL; LINE-COUNT; PAGE-COUNT; SPACE-CTL

FIGURE 22-3 Storage Dump.

clause in its definition; the contents of an undefined field is unpredictable.) The next fields in storage are as follows:

LOCATION	NAME	BYTES	CONTENTS
80194	FINAL-TOTAL	5	000000000C
80199	LINE-COUNT	2	003C
8019B	PAGE-COUNT	2	002C
8019D	SPACE-CTL	1	2C

The rightmost hex digit of each field is X'C', the standard plus sign. All other digits are valid 0–9 numeric digits.

For your own program, you should be able to locate the input and output areas and their associated buffers. If there are two buffers for each file, then assuming the program has read records, each buffer should contain a different record, with one of these records in the input area for the FD.

PROBLEMS

22–1. What debugging statements would cause the contents of AMTA, AMTB, and AMTC to print: (a) each time the statement executes? (b) each time the statement executes and the contents have changed?

22–2. What debugging statement prints the names of each Paragraph and Section that is encountered?

22–3. How do you force a program to print the number of a statement that has caused an execution error?

22–4. How do you force a dump of storage on a serious execution error?

22–5. Determine the hexadecimal contents of the following items:

```
FIELDA    PIC X(8)   VALUE 'COMPUTER'.
FIELDB    PIC 9(4)   VALUE 2468.
FIELDC    PIC S9(3)V99   VALUE 123.45 COMP-3.
```

22–6. Assume a storage dump that shows the hexadecimal contents of a portion of Working-Storage as follows:

```
F0F1F2F300001C00253C
```

The address of the leftmost byte (F0) is hex 40000. The first field is four bytes, the second is three bytes, and the third is three bytes. What are the hex addresses of the leftmost bytes of the second and third fields?

CHAPTER 23

THE COPY STATEMENT

OBJECTIVE: To cover the basic requirements to include cataloged COBOL code into a program.

INTRODUCTION

In most installations, the same block of coding appears in many programs. For example, a number of programs may have to process the data defined in an Employee's Earnings file, and all require the same record definition. The record can be coded once and cataloged in the system library. (The steps to catalog, although not difficult, vary considerably by operating system. See the systems programmer or the appropriate manual for your installation.) The COBOL COPY statement provides for included cataloged code into a program.

EXAMPLE USE OF COPY

The following defines an Employee Earnings record that is cataloged in the system library under the name EMP-EARN-YD:

```
01  EMPLOYEE-RECORD.
    03  EMPLOYEE-NO      PIC X(5).
    03  EMPLOYEE-NAME    PIC X(25).
    03  REGULAR-PAY      PIC S9(5)V99  COMP-3.
    03  PAY-TO-DATE      PIC S9(5)V99  COMP-3.
```

Any COBOL program may now include this record definition by means of a COPY statement, as in the following record (01) level:

```
DATA DIVISION.
FILE SECTION.
FD   EMPL-FILE
     LABEL RECORDS ARE STANDARD
     ...
01   EMPLOYEE-RECORD COPY EMP-EARN-YD.
```

Under IBM DOS, you must also include an entry CBL LIB, to tell the compiler that the program is to reference the system library.

During compilation, the COPY statement causes the COBOL compiler to access the cataloged code under the name EMP-EARNINGS from the library. The compiler then includes the complete library entry at the point of the COPY statement. The result would be:

```
DATA DIVISION.
FILE SECTION.
FD   EMPL-FILE
     LABEL RECORDS ARE STANDARD
     ...
01   EMPLOYEE-RECORD.
     03   EMPLOYEE-NO      PIC X(5).
     03   EMPLOYEE-NAME    PIC X(25).
     03   REGULAR-PAY      PIC S9(5)V99  COMP-3.
     03   PAY-TO-DATE      PIC S9(5)V99  COMP-3.
```

Advantages

The advantages of copying cataloged code are:

- It reduces the amount of repetitious coding.
- It promotes standardization in the installation.
- It reduces programming errors.
- It reduces program revisions. If the record definition changes, it is necessary only to change the cataloged record (although you may still have to recompile the programs that use it).

COPY Features

The cataloged code may not contain a COPY statement. The general format of the COPY statement is:

```
+---------------------------------------------------------------------+
|                            Format                                   |
+---------------------------------------------------------------------+
|                                                                     |
|   COPY library-name                                                 |
|                                         (word-2      )              |
|       [REPLACING   word-1   BY   {literal-1    }              |
|                                         (identifier-1)              |
|                                                                     |
|                                   (word-4      )                    |
|           [word-3   BY   {literal-2    }      ]...].         |
|                                   (identifier-2)                    |
|                                                                     |
+---------------------------------------------------------------------+
```

The REPLACING option enables you to change data names copied from the cataloged entry. Replacing, however, does not change names in the cataloged library entry itself. IBM COBOL also has a SUPPRESS option that causes the compiler to suppress printing the copy code. This feature is useful if the content is confidential or extremely long.

File Section entries are the most commonly cataloged. You may also COPY library entries into such areas as the following:

Configuration Section:
      SOURCE-COMPUTER.   COPY name.
      SPECIAL-NAMES.   COPY name.

Input-Output Section:
      FILE-CONTROL.   COPY name.
      I-O-CONTROL.   COPY name.

File Section.
      FD file-name   COPY name.
      SD sort-file-name   COPY name.

Report Section:
      RD report-name   COPY name.

Working-Storage Section:
      01 data-name   COPY name.

Procedure Division:
      Section-name SECTION.   COPY name.
      Paragraph-name.   COPY name.

If the COPY statement appears in a record (01) level, the copied code replaces the level 01 name.

CHAPTER 24

JOB CONTROL

OBJECTIVE: *To present the basic job control statements for IBM DOS and OS COBOL.*

INTRODUCTION

The user of a computer system submits requests for specific processing through a system of statements called *job control language (JCL)*. The job control statements primarily involve the functions of program compilation and execution. Each manufacturer provides a job control language unique to its own computer system, and although all the languages are similar conceptually, the specific commands vary considerably. This chapter only provides the basic job control requirements for IBM DOS and OS systems, but even these may vary slightly among installations, and according to a particular job. Accordingly, this chapter is intended only as a guide; for additional information, see your manufacturer's Programmer's Guide and job control manuals.

DOS JOB CONTROL

The three main DOS job statements—JOB, OPTION, and EXEC—all begin with a pair of slashes (//) in columns 1 and 2, followed by at least one blank.

JOB Statement

The first entry of the job statement specifies the name of the job:

// JOB jobname

The jobname is 1–8 characters long; the first character must be a letter.

OPTION Statement

The user indicates various options that a job is to perform with the OPTION statement. Some common COBOL options are as follows:

// OPTION LINK,SYM,ERRS,XREF,LISTX,PARTDUMP

LINK	Indicates that the compiled program is to be link-edited (see EXEC LNKEDT); suppress with NOLINK.
SYM	Prints a map of the Data Division and other miscellaneous information (suppress with NOSYM).
ERRS	Lists COBOL compiler diagnostics.
XREF	Prints a cross-reference of the symbolic names used in the program (or NOXREF).
LISTX	Prints the Assembler code that the Compiler has generated from the COBOL source program.
PARTDUMP	Prints a hexadecimal dump of the program's partition on an abnormal program termination (DUMP on some systems).

These options may appear in any sequence. If omitted, an option will *default* to a particular value, depending on the installation (one typical default would be NOLISTX).

EXEC Statement

The EXEC statement causes the system to load a specified program or procedure into main storage for execution. The following statement causes the DOS FCOBOL compiler to begin execution:

// EXEC FCOBOL

To execute a program that has just been compiled and link-edited, omit the operand, as follows:

// EXEC

If there is no operand, the system loads into main storage the last link-edited program in the job stream and begins execution.

Example.   The following is a simple job stream that compiles a COBOL program with no execution. This is a useful procedure for a first compilation when there is a strong possibility of serious errors:

// JOB jobname	Job statement.
// EXEC FCOBOL	Execute the COBOL compiler.
(COBOL source program)	
/*	End of the COBOL source program.
/&	End of job.

Other DOS JCL Statements

Some additional job control statements are /*, ACTION, and ASSGN.

/* Statement.   A slash/asterisk (/*) in columns 1 and 2 tells the operating system that this point is the end-of-file of either a COBOL source program or a data file.

/& Statement.   A slash/ampersand (/&) in columns 1 and 2 tells the operating system that this point is the end of the job. A job may contain a number of /* entries, but only one /&, at the end.

ACTION Statement.   ACTION denotes a Linkage Editor control statement. A common entry is

ACTION MAP

This entry prints a map of a link-edited program (suppress with NOMAP). The map is useful as an indication of the relative storage addresses of subprograms. It also prints error messages if the Linkage Editor is unable to locate a subprogram or an input/output module that is supposed to be cataloged in the system library. Since the map's generation involves additional computer time, only use the MAP option when a link-edit map is required.

ASSGN Statement. The ASSGN statement relates the system number in the SELECT statement to a particular system device. Note that the entry is spelled ASSGN, whereas the SELECT statement is spelled ASSIGN. In the DOS example 1 that follows, the SELECT statements could be as follows:

```
SELECT rdrfile ASSIGN TO SYS015-UR-2501-S.
SELECT printer ASSIGN TO SYS014-UR-1403-S.
```

In the job control for the program, ASSGN statements (watch the spelling) will relate SYS015 to the system input device, SYSIN, and will relate SYS014 to the system listing device, SYSLST, as follows:

```
// ASSGN SYS015,SYSIN
// ASSGN SYS014,SYSLST
```

The values SYS015 and SYS014 could be any other numbers acceptable to the operating system, as long as the SELECT and ASSGN entries match by SYSnnn.

DOS JCL Examples

The following are three DOS JCL job stream examples:

1. Card input and printer output.
2. A main program with one subprogram.
3. Card input and disk output.

DOS Example 1: JCL for Card Input and Printer Output. This example shows the typical job control for a program that reads input records (via SYS015) and prints output records (via SYS014).

```
// JOB jobname
// OPTION LINK,NOSYM,ERRS,XREF,PARTDUMP
     ACTION NOMAP                  Delete link-edit map.
// EXEC FCOBOL                     Begin execution of COBOL compiler.
  (COBOL source program)
/*                                 End of compilation.
// ASSGN SYS015,SYSIN              Assign SYS015 as input device.
// ASSGN SYS014,SYSLST             Assign SYS014 as printer device.
// EXEC LNKTST                     Suppress link-edit/execute if there is a
                                     serious compile error.
// EXEC LNKEDT                     Perform link-edit: include input/output
                                     modules.
// EXEC                            Load compiled/linked program into
                                     main storage; begin its execution.
```

```
    (input data)
/*                              End of input data.
/&                              End of job, return control to Supervisor.
```

DOS Example 2: JCL for a Main Program with One Subprogram. This example shows the job control for compilation, link-editing, and execution of a main program and one subprogram.

```
// JOB jobname
// OPTION LINK, etc.            Specify options.
   ACTION MAP                   Generate a link-edit map.
// EXEC FCOBOL                  Compile the main program.
   (main COBOL program)
/*                              End of main program.
// EXEC FCOBOL                  Compile subprogram.
   (COBOL subprogram)
/*                              End of subprogram.
// ASSGN SYS015,SYSIN
// ASSGN SYS014,SYSLST
// EXEC LNKTST
// EXEC LNKEDT                  Link-edit main program and subpro-
                                   gram and include input/output
                                   modules.

// EXEC

   (input data)
/*                              End of input data.
/&                              End of job.
```

DOS Example 3: JCL for Card Input and Disk Output. This example shows the job control for a program that reads card input records and writes disk output records.

```
// JOB jobname
// OPTION LINK, etc.            Specify options.
   ACTION NOMAP
// EXEC FCOBOL
   (COBOL source program)
/*                              End of compilation.
// ASSGN SYS015,SYSIN
// ASSGN SYS020,X'nnn'          Assign SYS020 to a physical disk ad-
                                   dress (a hexadecimal value, installa-
                                   tion-dependent).
```

// DLBL filename,'file-id',dates,codes

file-name: name of the disk file in the
SELECT statement.
'file-id': 1–44 characters within apostrophes, such as 'CUSTOMER-FILE'.
date, one of two formats:
dddd = retention period in days,
yy/ddd = date of retention.
codes: type of file (e.g., SD is sequential
disk, ISC is Indexed Sequential, DA
is direct access).

// EXTENT symbolic-unit,serial-no,type,
sequence-no,relative-track,no-of-tracks

symbolic-unit = SYSnnn, in this case,
SYS020.
serial-no: the volume serial number for
the disk volume.
type: the type of disk extent (usually 1).
sequence-no: the sequence number for
the extent if the file is on more than
one disk area. Usually omitted.
relative-track: the sequential track
number, relative to zero, where the
extent begins.
no-of-tracks: tracks allocated for this
extent (or file, if on one extent).

// EXEC LNKTST
// EXEC LNKEDT
// EXEC
(input data)
/*   End of input data.
/&   End of job.

If a program uses nonsequential disk files, a LBLTYP entry is required before the
LNKEDT. For example, if there are two nonsequential files, the entry is

// LBLTYP NSD(2)

Magnetic tape requires a // LBLTYP TAPE entry and a // TLBL entry for each tape file.

OS JOB CONTROL

The three main OS job control statements—JOB, EXEC, and DD—all begin with a
pair of slashes (//) in columns one and two, but unlike DOS job control, they are not
followed by a space.

JOB Statement

The first entry of the OS JCL, the JOB statement, specifies the name of the job and provides optional accounting information. Its general format is as follows:

//jobname JOB options

The jobname begins in column 3 starting with a letter and followed by up to 7 alphanumeric characters. The options include account number, user name, job priority, job class, and message class. A simple example is as follows:

//PROG34 JOB (4275,25),'DEPRECIATION',CLASS=A

The items in parentheses are accounting information according to an installation's standards. 'DEPRECIATION' is an optional descriptive name that provides additional identification. CLASS=A indicates a priority class according to an installation's standards.

EXEC Statement

The EXEC statement executes a specified program or procedure and provides separate EXEC entries for compile, link-edit, and execution. For example, the following entries are only for a compile:

//stepname EXEC PGM=COBOL   *(PGM means program)*

The stepname is 1–8 alphanumeric characters; the first character must be a letter. To reduce coding and errors, many OS installations use cataloged procedures in which commonly used job control is already cataloged. Therefore, to compile, link-edit (load), and execute (go) under a cataloged procedure, the following format is used:

//stepname EXEC COBUCLG
or //stepname EXEC PROC=COBUCLG   *(PROC means procedure)*

COBUCLG is IBM COBOL version 2, and COBACLG is IBM COBOL version 4. In either version, CLG indicates the following:

- C = Compile.
- L = Link-edit the compiled program.
- G = Go, or execute the link-edited program.

For compile with no execute, simply use COBUC (or COBAC).

PARM and Debugging Options. The EXEC COBUCLG (or COBACLG) statement may contain PARM (parameter) entries, as follows:

```
//stepname EXEC COBUCLG,PARM=(XREF,STATE)
```

XREF prints a cross-reference table of data names (or use NOXREF). STATE prints the number of any statement that causes an abnormal termination. This option is expensive in program size, and should be used only for program testing. Also, a SYSDBOUT entry is required to direct the debugging message onto the system printer. For a dump of main storage, use the SYSUDUMP entry. Both entries precede other //GO entries:

```
//GO.SYSDBOUT DD SYSOUT=A
//GO.SYSUDUMP DD SYSOUT=A
```

Other PARM options include DMAP (Data Map) and PMAP (Procedure Map); these are equivalent to DOS. SYM and LISTX respectively. See the *OS COBOL Programmer's Guide* for other PARM entries.

DD Statement

The DD (or Data Definition) statement describes the data sets (files) that a job uses. The format is as follows:

```
//ddname DD operands
```

The ddname relates to the system-name in the ASSIGN clause of the SELECT statement as follows:

	system-name
Program:	SELECT PRINT-FILE ASSIGN TO UR-1403-S-SYSOUT.
Job control:	//GO.SYSOUT DD SYSOUT=A
	ddname

The GO entry in job control indicates an execute step. Technically, the ddname and the system-name need not be SYSOUT as long as the two match. The operand SYSOUT=A is necessary to assign the data set to the printer. System-name is limited to 8 characters, the first of which must be a letter.

A card file may be identified as follows:

Program:	SELECT INPUT-FILE ASSIGN TO UR-2501R-S-SYSIN.
Job control:	//GO.SYSIN DD *

The asterisk in the operand of the DD entry indicates that input data for this file immediately follows in the job stream.

OS JCL Examples

The following are three OS JCL job stream examples:

1.   Card input and printer output.
2.   A main program with one subprogram.
3.   Card input and disk output.

Assume that the ASSIGN clauses of the SELECT statements specify the system-names SYSIN and SYSOUT (although they could be descriptive names such as FILEIN and PRINTER).

OS Example 1:   JCL for Card Input and Printer Output. This example shows the job control for a cataloged procedure that compiles, link-edits, and executes a program with a card input and a printed output.

```
// jobname JOB [optional entries]
// stepname EXEC COBUCLG
// SYSIN   DD   *
```
The * indicates that the source program immediately follows in the job stream.

```
    (COBOL source program)
/*
// GO.SYSOUT DD SYSOUT=A,DCB=
    (FBSM,LRECL=133,BLKSIZE=665)
    (some installations use just DD
    SYSOUT=A)
```
Indicates end of the compile.
SYSOUT specifies the system printer for the program.
FBSM indicates fixed length, blocked records (assuming that the system temporarily writes output on disk prior to printing).
LRECL=133 indicates the logical record length of records.
BLKSIZE=665 indicates blocking five records on disk.

```
// GO.SYSIN   DD   *
```
Data Definition for card reader. The * indicates that input data immediately follows in the job stream.

```
/*
```
End of input data.
```
//
```
End of job.

OS Example 2: JCL for a Main Program and One Subprogram. This example shows the job control for compilation, link-editing, and execution of a main program and one subprogram and the use of the STATE option and the SYSDBOUT entry for debugging.

```
// PROLINK JOB [optional entries]
// STEP1     EXEC COBUC,PARM=          Compile main program.
             (STATE)
// SYSIN     DD  *
             (main program)
/*
// STEP2     EXEC COBUCLG,PARM=        Compile, link, and execute.
             (STATE)
// SYSIN     DD  *
             (subprogram)
/*
// GO.SYSDBOUT DD SYSOUT=A             Define debugging output.
// GO.SYSOUT     DD SYSOUT=A,DCB       Printer data set.
                 =(dcb entries)
// GO.SYSIN      DD  *                 Input data set.
             (input data)
/*                                     End of input data.
//                                     End of job.
```

A compilation may involve more than one subprogram. The EXEC COBUC statement applies to all compiles except the last compile, which uses EXEC COBUCLG to link-edit and execute the set of subprograms.

OS Example 3: JCL for Card Input and Disk Output. This example shows the job control for a program that reads card input records and writes disk output records. Assume that the disk file is named DISKOUT.

```
// CARDISK  JOB [optional entries]
// STEP1    EXEC COBUCLG
// SYSIN     DD  *
             (COBOL source program)
/*
// GO.DISKOUT DD DSN=dsname,        DSN=dsname supplies the data set
//               UNIT=3370,            name used by the system to cat-
//               DISP=(NEW,CATLG),     alog the disk file.
//               SPACE=(TRK,(no. of UNIT identifies the particular disk de-
                 tracks),RLSE),        vice, in this case an IBM 3370.
```

```
//                    DCB=(RECFM=FB,
                          LRECL=mm,
                          BLKSIZE=nnn,
                          BUFNO=p)
```
(The preceding five entries can all be
coded on one or two lines.)

DISP   indicates disposition: this is a new
        file and is to be cataloged.
SPACE defines the number of disk tracks
        (TRK) that the data set will re-
        quire (CYL would indicate the
        number of cylinders). RLSE per-
        mits unused tracks to be released
        to the system.
DCB   (Data Control Block) specifies the
        conventional entries: FB indicates
        fixed, blocked; LRECL provides
        the logical length of each record;
        BLKSIZE is the length of each
        block (a multiple of record size);
        and BUFNO indicates the number
        of buffers.

```
// GO.SYSIN DD    *
/*
//
```
End of input data.
End of job.

APPENDIX A

KEYPUNCH PROCEDURE

This Appendix illustrates the punching of COBOL cards on an IBM 029 keypunch machine. Figure A-1 shows the IBM 029 keyboard. The important keys are as follows:

- FEED—feeds a card from the read hopper into the punch area.
- REG—moves or "registers" a card into the punch station, ready for punching.
- SKIP—if there is a drum card initialized for automatic processing, advances the card to the next field according to the drum card format.
- DUP—duplicates information from the card immediately preceding (at the read station) into a card at the punch station. This feature is useful for correcting cards.
- REL—releases or ejects the card.

Punched cards can be keypunched manually or keypunched automatically by using a program drum card.

MANUAL OPERATION

The following procedure is for the manual keying of punched cards and is recommended only if there is a small number of cards to be punched.

1. Insert a few blank cards in the input hopper with cards face forward and 9-edge down.

2. Turn on the power switch which is under the keyboard on the right front face of the cabinet.

3. Set all six switches, which are above the keyboard as shown in Figure A-1, to off (down) except PRINT, which prints the punched characters at the top of each card.

4. Turn off the program control lever, which is used for drum cards, by pressing it to the right. The lever is below the small window that indicates the card column being punched.

5. Press the FEED and REG keys to feed and register the first card.

6. Begin punching the card by entering the data from the program coding sheet position-for-position:

   • To space one card column, press the space bar at the bottom of the keyboard.

   • The keyboard is normally in alphabetic mode, as indicated by the characters printed on the lower part of each key: characters A through Z (all letters are capitals).

   • For the characters 0 through 9 and the special characters shown on the upper part of the keys, press the numeric key to put the keyboard into numeric mode while punching.

   • To backspace, press the backspace key.

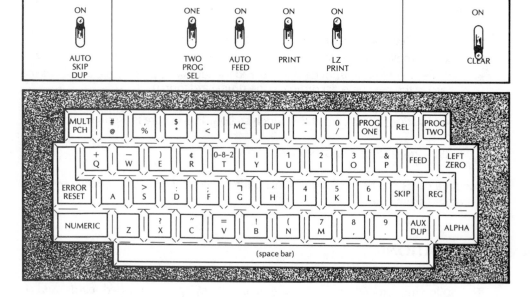

FIGURE A-1   IBM 029 Keyboard.

7. When you have completed punching a card, press the REL key, the FEED key, and then the REG key. The punched card is now at the read station, and a new blank card is ready for punching at the punch station.

8. To duplicate all or part of the card, place the previously punched card in the read station and a blank card in the punch station. Press the DUP key for all positions to be duplicated.

9. To clear all cards from the read and punch stations, flip up the CLEAR switch (it should spring back down).

10. If you have a large number of cards to punch, you can automatically feed cards by turning on the AUTO FEED switch. Press the FEED key twice to feed the first and second card into the punch station. When you release a punched card, another card is automatically fed into the punch station.

AUTOMATIC OPERATION—DRUM CARD

The drum card facilitates the keypunching of a large amount of cards. The following is a typical COBOL drum card format that you can copy or modify for your own purposes:

COLUMN	PUNCH	PURPOSE
1	− (minus)	Skip column 1.
2–7	&&&&&&	Skip columns 2–7 following.
8–11	1AAA	Set Area-A to alphabetic punch mode.
12–15	1AAA	Start of Area-B.
16–19	1AAA	Start of first indentation.
20–31	1 (followed by As)	Start of second indentation.
32–43	1 (followed by As)	Start of PIC clause.
44–72	1 (followed by As)	Start of VALUE clause.
73–80	− (followed by &s)	Skip to the end of the card.

Columns 8, 12, 16, 20, 32, and 44 all contain tab stops to separate punched fields. The card fits onto a drum that inserts onto a spindle that is inside the window that displays the column being punched. Be sure that the program control lever is turned off. It is best to have an experienced keypunch operator provide instruction in placing the program card on the drum and inserting it onto the spindle.

The procedure for operating the drum card is as follows:

1. Turn on the program control level (turn to the left), set the PROG SEL switch to ONE, and then turn on AUTO FEED and PRINT. All other switches should be off.

2. Depress the FEED key twice; the first card should advance directly to column 8. (If not, check the lever and switch settings. If these are correct, check if the drum card is correctly punched and properly inserted onto the drum.)

3. Either key in a value at column 8 or depress the SKIP key to advance to column 12. The drum card is designed to advance to columns 16, 20, 32, and 44 successively.

4. If you need to enter a character in column 7 (such as an asterisk or a hyphen), switch off the program control lever. Backspace from column 8 to column 7 and enter the required character.

5. Press the REL key to eject the card and feed another card automatically.

6. When you have finished, clean up your coding sheets and damaged cards, and because the next person to use the keypunch machine may not need the drum card, turn off the program control lever to disconnect the drum card.

APPENDIX B
LIST OF IBM ANS COBOL RESERVED WORDS

No word in the following list should appear as a programmer-defined name. The keys that appear before some of the words, and their meanings, are:

(xn)   before a word means that the word is an IBM extension to American National Standard COBOL.

(xac)   before a word means that the word is an IBM extension to both American National Standard COBOL and CODASYL COBOL.

(ca)   before a word means that the word is a CODASYL COBOL reserved word not incorporated in American National Standard COBOL or in IBM American National Standard COBOL.

(sp)   before a word means that the word is an IBM function-name established in support of the SPECIAL-NAMES function.

(spn)   before a word means that the word is used by an IBM American National Standard COBOL compiler, but not this compiler.

(asn)   before a word means that the word is defined by American National Standard COBOL, but is not used by this compiler.

	ACCEPT		BLANK	(xn)	COMP-3	(sp)	C05
	ACCESS		BLOCK	(xn)	COMP-4	(sp)	C06
	ACTUAL	(ca)	BOTTOM		COMPUTATIONAL	(sp)	C07
	ADD		BY	(xn)	COMPUTATIONAL-1	(sp)	C08
(arn)	ADDRESS			(xn)	COMPUTATIONAL-2	(sp)	C09
	ADVANCING			(xn)	COMPUTATIONAL-3	(sp)	C10
	AFTER	(xn)	CALL	(xn)	COMPUTATIONAL-4	(sp)	C11
	ALL	(xn)	CANCEL		COMPUTE	(sp)	C12
	ALPHABETIC	(xac)	CBL		CONFIGURATION		
(ca)	ALPHANUMERIC	(xn)	CD	(sp)	CONSOLE		DATA
(ca)	ALPHANUMERIC-EDITED		CF		CONTAINS	(xn)	DATE
	ALTER		CH		CONTROL		DATE-COMPILED
	ALTERNATE	(xac)	CHANGED		CONTROLS		DATE-WRITTEN
	AND	(xn)	CHARACTER		COPY	(xn)	DAY
(xn)	APPLY		CHARACTERS	(xac)	CORE-INDEX	(xac)	DAY-OF-WEEK
	ARE	(asn)	CLOCK-UNITS		CORR		DE
	AREA		CLOSE		CORRESPONDING	(xac)	DEBUG
	AREAS	(asn)	COBOL	(xn)	COUNT	(ca)	DEBUG-CONTENTS
	ASCENDING		CODE	(sp)	CSP	(ca)	DEBUG-ITEM
	ASSIGN		COLUMN		CURRENCY	(ca)	DEBUG-LINE
	AT	(spn)	COM-REG	(xac)	CURRENT-DATE	(ca)	DEBUG-NAME
	AUTHOR		COMMA	(spn)	CYL-INDEX	(ca)	DEBUG-SUB-1
		(xn)	COMMUNICATION	(spn)	CYL-OVERFLOW	(ca)	DEBUG-SUB-2
			COMP	(sp)	C01	(ca)	DEBUG-SUB-3
(xac)	BASIS	(xn)	COMP-1	(sp)	C02	(ca)	DEBUGGING
	BEFORE	(xn)	COMP-2	(sp)	C03		
	BEGINNING			(sp)	C04		

393

DECIMAL-POINT
DECLARATIVES
| (za) DELETE
(za) DELIMITED
(za) DELIMITER
DEPENDING
(za) DEPTH
DESCENDING
(za) DESTINATION
DETAIL
(ca) DISABLE
(zac) DISP
DISPLAY
(zac) DISPLAY-ST
(ca) DISPLAY-n
DIVIDE
DIVISION
DOWN
| (ca) DUPLICATES
| (za) DYNAMIC

(za) ECI
(zac) EJECT
ELSE
(za) EMI
(ca) ENABLE
END
END-OF-PAGE
(za) ENDING
ENTER
(zac) ENTRY
ENVIRONMENT
(za) EOP
EQUAL
(ca) EQUALS
ERROR
(za) ESI
EVERY
EXAMINE
(ca) EXCEEDS
| (za) EXCEPTION
(zac) EXHIBIT
EXIT
| (za) EXTEND
(spn) EXTENDED-SEARCH

FD
FILE
FILE-CONTROL
FILE-LIMIT
FILE-LIMITS
FILLER
FINAL
FIRST
FOOTING
FOR
FROM

GENERATE
GIVING
GO
(zac) GOBACK
GREATER
GROUP

HEADING
HIGH-VALUE
HIGH-VALUES
(ca) HOLD

I-O
I-O-CONTROL
(zac) ID
IDENTIFICATION
IF
IN
INDEX
(ca) INDEX-n
INDEXED
INDICATE
(ca) INITIAL
| (ca) INITIALIZE
INITIATE
INPUT

INPUT-OUTPUT
(zac) INSERT
(ca) INSPECT
INSTALLATION
INTO
INVALID
IS

JUST
JUSTIFIED

| KEY

LABEL
(zac) LABEL-RETURN
LAST
LEADING
(zac) LEAVE
LEFT
(za) LENGTH
LESS
(ca) LIBRARY
LIMIT
LIMITS
(ca) LINAGE
(ca) LINAGE-COUNTER
LINE
LINE-COUNTER
LINES
(za) LINKAGE
LOCK
LOW-VALUE
LOW-VALUES
|
(spn) MASTER-INDEX
MEMORY
(za) MERGE
(za) MESSAGE
MODE
MODULES
(zac) MORE-LABELS
MOVE
MULTIPLE
MULTIPLY

(zac) NAMED
NEGATIVE
NEXT
NO
(zac) NOMINAL
NOT
NOTE
(spn) NSTD-REELS
NUMBER
NUMERIC
(ca) NUMERIC-EDITED

OBJECT-COMPUTER
(ca) OBJECT-PROGRAM
OCCURS
OF
— OFF
OMITTED
ON
OPEN
OPTIONAL
OR
| (za) ORGANIZATION
(zac) OTHERWISE
OUTPUT
— (za) OVERFLOW

PAGE
PAGE-COUNTER
| (zac) PASSWORD
PERFORM
PF
PH
PIC
PICTURE
PLUS
(za) POINTER
POSITION
(zac) POSITIONING
POSITIVE
— (zac) PRINT-SWITCH

__ (cn)	PRINTING			SOURCE
	PROCEDURE			SOURCE-COMPUTER
(cn)	PROCEDURES			SPACE
	PROCEED			SPACES
(cn)	PROCESS			SPECIAL-NAMES
	PROCESSING			STANDARD
(za)	PROGRAM		| (xa)	START
	PROGRAM-ID			STATUS
				STOP
(za)	QUEUE		(za)	STRING
	QUOTE		(xa)	SUB-QUEUE-1
	QUOTES		(xa)	SUB-QUEUE-2
			(xa)	SUB-QUEUE-3
__	RANDOM			SUBTRACT
	RD			SUM
	READ		(cn)	SUPERVISOR
(zac)	READY		(za)	SUPPRESS
(za)	RECEIVE		(cn)	SUSPEND
	RECORD		(za)	SYMBOLIC
(zac)	RECORD-OVERFLOW			SYNC
(za)	RECORDING			SYNCHRONIZED
	RECORDS		(sp)	SYSIN
	REDEFINES		(spn)	SYSIPT
	REEL		(spn)	SYSLST
(cn)	REFERENCES		(sp)	SYSOUT
| (cn)	RELATIVE		(spn)	SYSPCH
	RELEASE		(sp)	SYSPUNCH
(zac)	RELOAD		(sp)	S01
	REMAINDER		(sp)	S02
	REMARKS			
| (cn)	REMOVAL		| (cn)	TABLE
	RENAMES			TALLY
(zac)	REORG-CRITERIA			TALLYING
	REPLACING			TAPE
	REPORT		(cn)	TERMINAL
	REPORTING			TERMINATE
	REPORTS		(za)	TEXT
(zac)	REREAD			THAN
	RERUN		(zac)	THEN
	RESERVE			THROUGH
	RESET			THRU
	RETURN		(za)	TIME
(zac)	RETURN-CODE		(zac)	TIME-OF-DAY
	REVERSED			TIMES
	REWIND			TO
| (za)	REWRITE		| (cn)	TOP
	RF		(zac)	TOTALED
	RH		(zac)	TOTALING
	RIGHT		(zac)	TRACE
	ROUNDED		(zac)	TRACK
	RUN		(zac)	TRACK-AREA
			(zac)	TRACK-LIMIT
(cn)	SA		(zac)	TRACKS
	SAME		(za)	TRAILING
	SD		(zac)	TRANSFORM
	SEARCH			TYPE
	SECTION			
	SECURITY		(cn)	UNEQUAL
	SEEK			UNIT
(za)	SEGMENT		(za)	UNSTRING
	SEGMENT-LIMIT			UNTIL
__	SELECT			UP
(za)	SEND		__	UPON
	SENTENCE		(spn)	UPSI-0
(za)	SEPARATE		(spn)	UPSI-1
	SEQUENTIAL		(spn)	UPSI-2
(zac)	SERVICE		(spn)	UPSI-3
	SET		(spn)	UPSI-4
	SIGN		(spn)	UPSI-5
	SIZE		(spn)	UPSI-6
(zac)	SKIP1		(spn)	UPSI-7
(zac)	SKIP2			USAGE
(zac)	SKIP3			USE
	SORT			USING
(zac)	SORT-CORE-SIZE			
(zac)	SORT-FILE-SIZE			VALUE
(cn)	SORT-MERGE			VALUES
(zac)	SORT-MESSAGE			VARYING
(zac)	SORT-MODE-SIZE			
| (spn)	SORT-OPTION			WHEN
(zac)	SORT-RETURN		| (zac)	WHEN-COMPILED
				WITH
				WORDS
				WORKING-STORAGE
				WRITE
			(zac)	WRITE-ONLY
			(spn)	WRITE-VERIFY
				ZERO
				ZEROES
				ZEROS

APPENDIX C

IBM 360/370 PROGRAM CHECKS

A clean program compilation is no insurance of a clean program execution. A bug or invalid data may cause a program to attempt an operation that the CPU cannot execute. For such an error, the program is terminated and the Supervisor prints the error diagnostic. IBM OS systems print only a code as a clue to the precise error, as

COMPLETION CODE SYSTEM = 0Cn

where n is the error termination code. The following is a list of these program checks or error codes for IBM 360 and 370 computers using DOS and OS.

1. Operation Exception—an attempt to execute an invalid machine operation.
2. Privileged-operation Exception—an attempt to execute a "privileged instruction" that only the Supervisor is permitted to execute.
3. Execute Exception—an error concerned with the EX machine code that should never occur in a COBOL program.
4. Protection Exception—an attempt to move data into the protected Supervisor area or into a partition for another program.
5. Addressing Exception—an attempt to reference an address outside of available storage.
6. Specification Exception—a machine instruction that violates a rule of its use, such as incorrect boundary alignment.

7. Data Exception—an attempt to perform decimal arithmetic on a field containing invalid data (valid data is 0–9 and sign). The most common cause of this error is failure to initialize an accumulator to zero. Another cause is an incorrect subscript value that references an arithmetic field outside of a table.

8. Fixed-point-overflow Exception—a calculated binary value is too large to be contained in a register.

9. Fixed-point-divide Exception—an attempt to divide a binary field (COMP) by zero.

A. Decimal-overflow Exception—an arithmetic (COMP-3) value is too large. Normally, the COBOL compiler generates machine code that truncates this value on the left, so that although there is an actual error, no error message is generated.

B. Decimal-divide Exception—an attempt to divide a decimal value (COMP-3) by zero.

C through F. These are various floating-point (COMP-1 and COMP-2) errors that presumably your program will never incur.

The COBOL compiler generates code that protects the data as much as possible. Error codes 1, 2, 4, 5, and 6 usually occur in advanced programs that use subscripts for table processing; an invalid subscript attempts to move or add data to an area outside of the referenced table, causing unpredictable results.

INDEX